AUREL STEIN

Kensington and Chelsea: A Social and Architectural History

AUREL STEIN

Pioneer of the Silk Road

———————◆———————

ANNABEL WALKER

JOHN MURRAY
Albemarle Street, London

© Annabel Walker 1995

First published in 1995
by John Murray (Publishers) Ltd.,
50 Albemarle Street, London W1X 4BD

A catalogue record for this book is available from the British Library

ISBN 0–7195–5751 8

Typeset in 12 on 14pt Monotype Garamond by Servis Filmsetting Ltd, Manchester

Printed and bound in Great Britain by The University Press, Cambridge

For John, with love

Contents

Illustrations

ACKNOWLEDGEMENTS

The author and publishers would like to thank the following for permission to reproduce illustrations: Plates 1, 2, 3, 6, and 29, The Department of Western Manuscripts, Bodleian Library, Oxford; 4, Hungarian Academy of Sciences, Budapest; and 5, The Syndics of Cambridge University Library. Other illustrations are taken from C.P. Skrinc's *Chinese Central Asia*, 1926 (7); Stein's *Ruins of Desert Cathay*, 1912 (9–15 and 17–25); Filippo de Filippi's *Himàlaia Caracorùm*, 1924 (16); E.F. Neve's *Beyond the Pir Panjal*, 1912 (26); and Stein's *Archaeological Reconnaissances in Northwest India and Southeast Iran*, 1937 (28). The front jacket illustrations all come from Stein's *Ruins of Desert Cathay*; the back jacket illustration is reproduced courtesy of the Department of Western Manuscripts, Bodleian Library, Oxford.

Acknowledgements

THIS BOOK COULD not have been attempted without the help of many people. Some I name below. Others must remain anonymous, partly because it would be difficult to list all the friends and acquaintances who have generously shown an interest in my work and discussed its problems; and partly because people whose names I never knew, in Sinkiang, Pakistan, India and Hungary, all added to my impressions of their countries and helped me remember them in the sterile surroundings of a London study. To my Tibetan friends in India I owe a particular debt, since it was through living with them that I was introduced to the East.

Thanks to the Stein Trustees, I have been able to quote extensively from Stein's papers, which are scattered among a variety of institutions. The majority lie in 450 boxes in the Bodleian Library in Oxford, and I am grateful to Colin Harris, whose supervision of Room 132 helped to make the many days I spent there profitable and pleasant; also to Dr B. C. Barker-Benfield for leading me through the Bodleian's Allen Papers. Professor Roderick Whitfield and Professor David Bivar (now retired) of London University's School of Oriental and African Studies (SOAS) both enlightened me on many points, and Dr Frances Wood, head of the Chinese Section of the British Library, has been a valued and ever-helpful source of information.

At the British Museum the Keeper of the Department of Oriental

Antiquities, Robert Knox, Dr Anne Farrer, Assistant Keeper, Helen Wang of the Department of Coins and Medals, and Dr Wladimir Zwalf (now retired) supplied useful information, and the archivist, Janet Wallace, introduced me to the interesting collection of papers concerning Stein's abortive fourth expedition to Chinese Turkestan.

In Hungary, support for my project from Professor Géza Bethlenfalvy of the Kőrösi Csoma Society, Dr János Kubassek, Director of the Hungarian Geographical Museum, and Dr Maria Ferenczy, Chief Curator of the Ferenc Hopp Museum of Eastern Asiatic Arts, made my stay in Budapest worthwhile and enjoyable. I much regret being unable to see the Stein papers which exist in the archives of the Hungarian Academy of Sciences, but hope that the Academy will soon feel able to make them accessible, as they were when Jeanette Mirsky wrote the first biography of Stein, nearly twenty years ago (see Bibliography). Miss Mirsky's book consequently proved useful on Stein's early years which are covered by the Budapest papers.

I should point out that none of the above-mentioned scholars is responsible in any way for the views expressed in this book.

Invaluable help came from Kati Evans, Christine Crowley, Tiggy Sharland, Miklós Lojkó and Bálint Bethlenfalvy, as translators; and from Mukhtar Ahmed in Srinagar, who traced the story of the Bali family. Suzy Price of the BBC World Service visited the Christian cemetery in Kabul on my behalf; Clare and Richard Staughton, Maggie Roe and Al Laius also acted as eyes and ears in places I could not reach. I have benefited, too, from the interest and experience of my editor, Gail Pirkis, and from the generosity of Kath and Peter Hopkirk, who have been a source of constant encouragement and information.

I am grateful to Edward Faridany and Caroline Davidson for originally suggesting this book; to Sir Isaiah Berlin, Sylvia Matheson Schofield and Hugh Richardson for their recollections of Stein; to Jeanne Stein's family, His Excellency Géza Fehérvári, Sir Mark Heath and Sir Harold Bailey for the information they provided.

Thanks are due to the archivists and/or librarians of the India Office Library; Corpus Christi College, Oxford; the Royal Geographical Society; the British Academy; SOAS; the Royal Asiatic Society; the London Library; the Royal Commonwealth Society (whose library is now part of Cambridge University Library); Oxford University Press; and Warren Murton, Stein's solicitors.

My research could not have been carried out in Budapest without the hospitality of Éva Bruck, whose generosity was a marvellous introduction to Hungary. Nor, in England, could I have worked comfortably in Oxford without the knowledge that the Armstrong-Littlewood household would always make me feel welcome. I should also like to thank my parents, for occupying their small grand-daughter so splendidly at critical times during the completion of this book in Devon, and for providing holidays for my faithful dog, Sam, who has kept me company throughout the writing of this biography.

Most of all, I thank my husband John for his tireless support and encouragement, without which I would never have reached the point of writing acknowledgements. He has endured manfully the troughs of the writing process, for which this tribute is inadequate thanks.

Note on Place Names

THE FACT THAT places in Chinese Turkestan often have more than one name – whether Turki, Chinese, Mongolian or historic – can lead to confusion. In general I have given names in a form recognizable to anyone who reads Stein's books. The modern pinyin form of romanization for Chinese place names is given below. Similarly, I have given the names of historical characters as Stein spelt them, with the pinyin in brackets immediately after their first appearance only. In the case of individuals whom Stein knew, I have left his spellings unchanged but have converted into English the appendages which he used to denote their status: thus Pan-darin becomes Governor Pan, and Chiang-ssu-yeh becomes Secretary Chiang.

I have also dispensed with diacritical marks, except in the case of European names, on the grounds that they will be unfamiliar and unhelpful to the general reader.

Despite the fact that Iran was known as Persia for most of the period covered by this book, I have called the country Iran throughout, since this name has ethnic significance and was thus used often by Stein.

The spelling of Hungarian names may seem inconsistent but, again, in general reproduces the forms used by Stein, French or English partial translations of names being common in his day among Hungarians outside their own country.

Stein's usage	Pinyin
Kansu	Gansu
Karakhoja	Gaochang
Kashgar	Kashi
Khara-khoto	Etzina
Khotan	Hetian
Nanking	Nanjing
Niya	Minfeng xian
Peking	Beijing
Sinkiang	Xinjiang
Su-chou	Jiuquan
Tashkurgan	Taxkorgan
Tun-huang	Dunhuang
Turfan	Tulufan
Urumchi	Ulumuqi

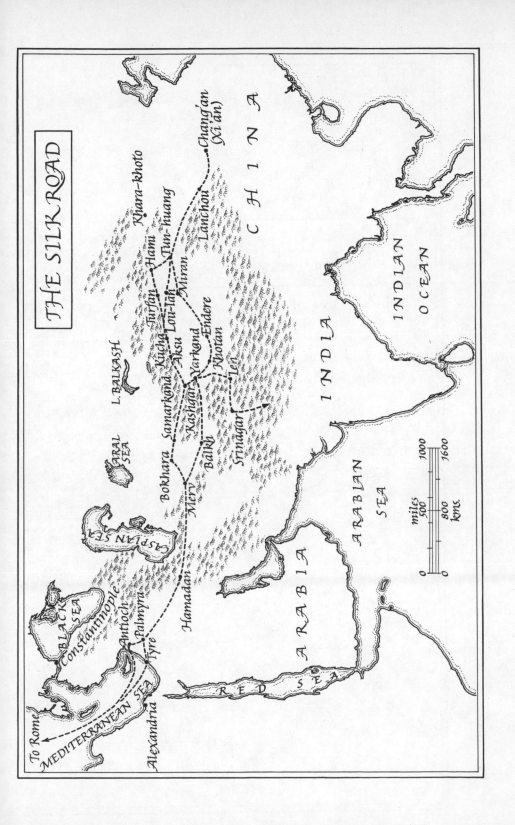

THE SILK ROAD

To Rome
MEDITERRANEAN SEA
Alexandria
Tyre
Antioch
Palmyra
Constantinople
BLACK SEA
CASPIAN SEA
ARAL SEA
L. BALKASH
Hamadan
Merv
Balkh
Bokhara
Samarkand
Kashgar
Yarkand
Srinagar
Leh
Khotan
Endere
Kucha
Aksu
Lou-lan
Miran
Turfan
Hami
Khara-khoto
Tun-huang
Lanchou
Chang'an (Xi'an)
CHINA
INDIA
ARABIA
RED SEA
ARABIAN SEA
INDIAN OCEAN

miles
500   1000
0
kms.
800   1600
0

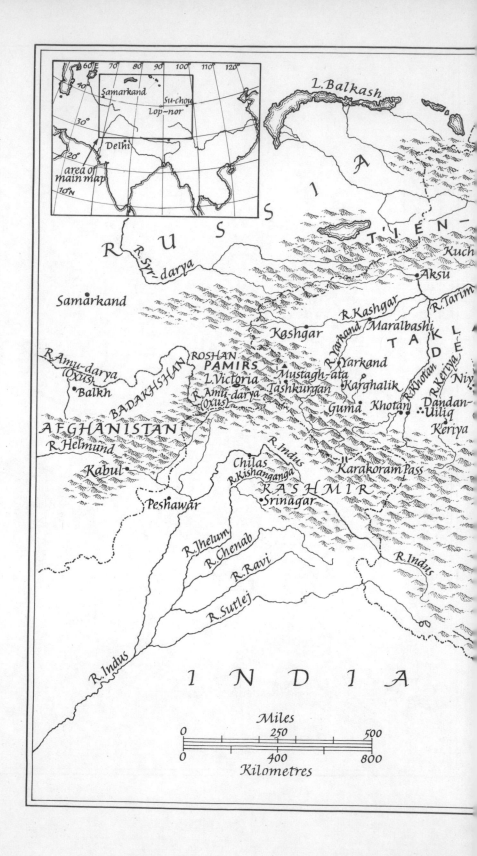

Samarkand
Su-chou
Lop-nor
Delhi
area of
main map

L.Balkash

R U S S I A

T'IEN-

Kucha
Aksu

R.Syr-darya

Samarkand

R.Kashgar
R.Tarim

Kashgar
R.Yarkand
Maralbashi
TAKL

R.Amu-darya
(Oxus)

ROSHAN
PAMIRS

Mustagh-ata
Yarkand
DE

L.Victoria
Karghalik
R.Keriya

Balkh

BADAKHSHAN
R.Amu-darya
(Oxus)
Tashkurgan

R.Khotan
Niy

Gumá
Khotan
Dandan-
Uiliq

AFGHANISTAN

Keriya

R.Helmund

R.Indus
Karakoram Pass

Kabul

Chilas
R.Kishanganga

KASHMIR

Peshawar
Srinagar

R.Jhelum
R.Chenab

R.Indus

R.Ravi

R.Sutlej

R.Indus

I N D I A

Miles
0   250   500

0   400   800
Kilometres

MONGOLIA

Urumchi

·Bezeklik
Turfan· ·:Astana
·:Karakhoja   ·Hami

HAN

ara-shahr·
·Korla   LOP

GOBI
DESERT

Khara-khoto

R.Etsin-gol

MAKAN
RT

·Lou-lan·
Lop-nor DESERT
·:Miran
·Charkhlik

·Tun-huang   ·Su-chou

Kan-chou

R.Charchan   NAN-SHAN

·Charchan

andere

N-LUN RANGE   C H I N A

Su-lo-ho R.

T I B E T

PART of SINKIANG,
THE TAKLAMAKAN, LOP
and GOBI DESERTS
as mapped by STEIN and ASSISTANTS

Salt-encrusted lake basins

·: Archaeological sites

Note: modern boundaries of Northern India/
Pakistan are not shown. The boundaries
are as in 1916

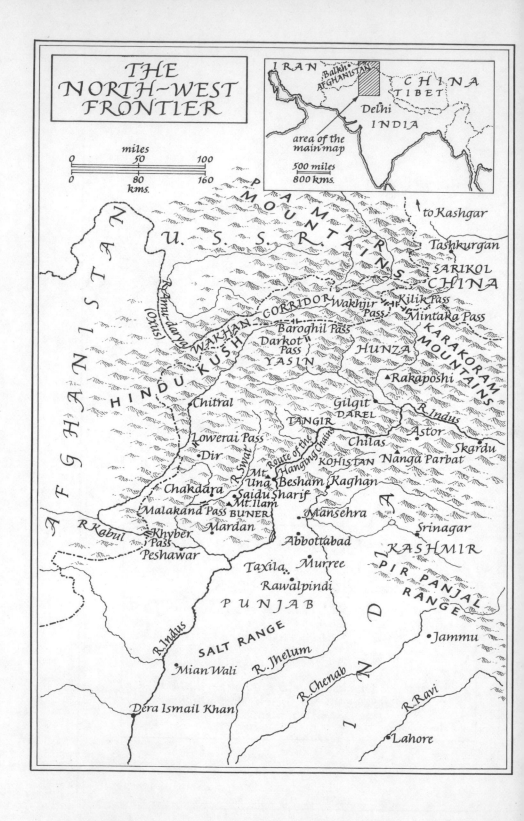

THE
NORTH-WEST
FRONTIER

miles
50   100
0
0   80   160
kms.

IRAN   Balkh   CHINA
AFGHANISTAN   TIBET

Delhi
INDIA

area of the
main map

500 miles
800 kms.

P A M I R   M O U N T A I N S

U. S. S. R.

to Kashgar

Tashkurgan

SARIKOL
CHINA

Kilik Pass

R. Amu-darya (Oxus)

WAKHAN CORRIDOR   Wakhjir
Pass

Mintaka Pass

Baroghil Pass
Darkot
Pass

YASIN

HUNZA

KARAKORAM
MOUNTAINS

H I N D U   K U S H

Rakaposhi

Chitral

Gilgit
DAREL

R. Indus

TANGIR

Astor

A F G H A N I S T A N

Lowerai Pass

Dir

Chilas

Skardu

R. Swat

Route of the
Hanging Chains

KOHISTAN

Nanga Parbat

Mt.
Una
Besham

Kaghan

Chakdara

Saidu Sharif

Malakand Pass

Mt. Ilam

BUNER

Mansehra

Srinagar

R. Kabul

Khyber
Pass

Mardan

KASHMIR

Peshawar

Abbottabad

PIR PANJAL

Taxila

Murree

RANGE

Rawalpindi

P U N J A B

I N D I A

Jammu

SALT RANGE

Mian Wali

R. Jhelum

R. Chenab

R. Ravi

Dera Ismail Khan

R. Indus

Lahore

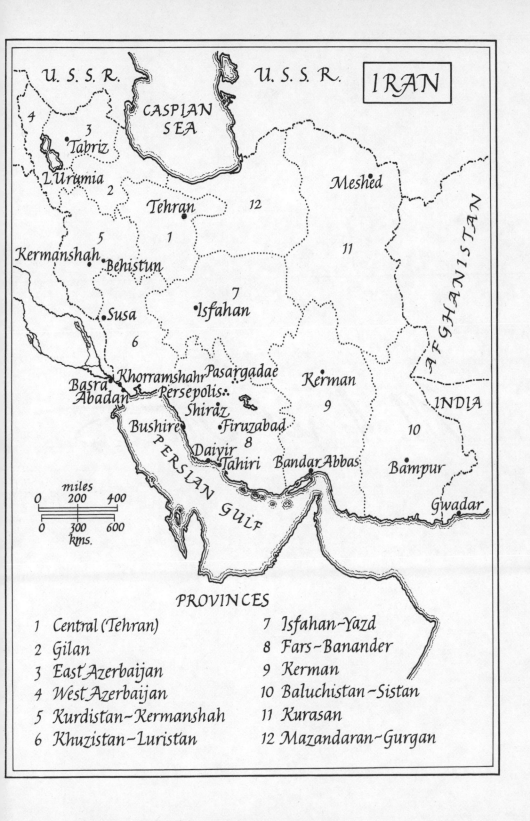

IRAN

U.S.S.R.
U.S.S.R.
CASPIAN SEA
AFGHANISTAN
INDIA
PERSIAN GULF

4
3 •Tabriz
L. Urumia
2
5
Kermanshah •Behistun
•Susa
6
Tehran
12
Meshed
11
7
•Isfahan
1
Khorramshahr Pasargadae
Basra Persepolis:•
Abadan
Shiraz
Bushire•
Daiyir •Firuzabad
•Tahiri
Kerman
9
8
Bandar Abbas
Bampur
10
Gwadar

miles
0   200   400
0   300   600
kms.

PROVINCES

1 Central (Tehran)
2 Gilan
3 East Azerbaijan
4 West Azerbaijan
5 Kurdistan–Kermanshah
6 Khuzistan–Luristan
7 Isfahan–Yazd
8 Fars–Banander
9 Kerman
10 Baluchistan–Sistan
11 Kurasan
12 Mazandaran–Gurgan

M. Aurel Stein

Prologue

———————◆———————

ON A DRY, dusty morning in late October 1943, a procession moved slowly along the road leading from the diplomatic quarter of Kabul to the Christian cemetery, on the eastern outskirts of the city. The route had been specially watered for the distinguished company, among whom were representatives of the King of Afghanistan and his Foreign Minister, the British, American and Iraqi Ministers, the Iranian Ambassador and the Soviet Chargé d'Affaires. In the distance the pale mountains lent their presence to a ceremony that was Afghanistan's belated tribute to a man whose greatest wish she had denied for forty years. Sir Aurel Stein, archaeologist, explorer and scholar, had finally reached the country five weeks before his eighty-first birthday and several decades after first applying for permission to visit its ancient sites. The lure of this forbidden region had only grown with the passing years. So perhaps it was achievement enough to have arrived, and to die, a week later, in its lap.

The resistance to his proposals which Stein encountered in Afghanistan was unusual. During his long career, he developed an almost infallible technique for overcoming opposition. Confronted by his relentless determination and dogged persistence, most people simply gave in. Without such tenacity, he would never have been able to embark on the expeditions to Central Asia which established his reputation as an archaeologist and explorer, and brought the long-lost culture of the Silk Road, the ancient overland trading route between China and the West, back to life.

'The Greatest Explorer of Our Time' was how one newspaper described Stein shortly before his death, in 1942. 'Let us first pay homage', exhorted another, 'to the intrepidity, tenacity and enthusiasm which have carried him through such enormous journeys in [the] face of continual hardship, acute discomfort, and frequent danger. If it were only for his record as a traveller and his services to geographical science Sir Aurel's name would stand high in the history of exploration.'

Stein caught the public imagination with his expeditions north across the mountains from his base in Kashmir to the desert wastes of Chinese Turkestan (known today as the Autonomous Region of Xinjiang). The press cast his journeys in a heroic mould. He was a lone figure, travelling without European companions through treacherous terrain, risking his life in order to liberate the riches of a forgotten civilization from burial beneath the sands and reveal them to the eagerly waiting West.

And riches they certainly were. The arid desert yielded paintings, manuscripts, fragments of silk, figured textiles and carpets, architectural carved wood, sculpture, coins and household objects, some of them two thousand years old and all preserved to a remarkable degree by the dryness of that desolate area. The colours of the pigments were still bright, food left in tombs remained intact, sacred Buddhist texts lay safely rolled where they had been stored centuries before. In the course of three expeditions to Chinese Turkestan, and in the face of competition from other archaeologists from France, Germany, Russia, America and Japan, Stein uncovered a civilization long assumed destroyed by the combined forces of nature and the sword of Islam.

What the sands of the Chinese desert did to that civilization for a thousand years, the Chinese themselves would gladly have done to Stein's activities and reputation. Having ignored his expeditions during the dying days of the Manchu Empire and the chaos that followed, they came to regret their insouciance. By the time they were able to ban him from the country, antiquities by the ton had crossed their borders. The West hailed Stein as the first and greatest of Silk Road archaeologists, but China's reaction to his successes cast them in a rather different light. Of all the 'foreign devils' who had ransacked her historic sites, she unequivocally branded Stein the most pernicious.

Stein received such criticism stoically. He never changed his view as to the wisdom of removing objects from vulnerable sites and preserving them in the museums of the West. On the rare occasions when he was utterly thwarted, he simply turned his attention to another project. Acquaintances admired, but were somewhat baffled by, the inner strength and self-sufficiency which enabled him to work tirelessly, travel over huge distances, live sometimes for years at a time with no close companion other than his dog, and return home to nothing more elaborate than a modest mountain camp.

This modesty, which characterized his habits while alive, seems to have transferred itself to his reputation since death. For decades, hardly anything from the huge collection of his finds at the British Museum has been on permanent display. Despite the romantic popular image of the Silk Road, there is little in that magnificent institution to explain how archaeologists unearthed the history behind the image, less than a hundred years ago.

In part this may be explained by the shift in interest away from an area which once held the attention of empires. When Stein arrived in India, in 1887, Russia and Britain were obsessively involved in their 'Great Game' of espionage on the Asian extremities of their territories. His expeditions to Chinese Turkestan attracted the attention of many followers of the flag; many people had either lived in India or had connections there, and they had an informed interest in Central Asian matters. But Stein lived a long life and, by the time he died in 1943, much had happened to divert the public eye. Battlegrounds had shifted to Europe, there was now a major power on the far side of the Atlantic and old empires were shrinking. Four years later, the British left India, and Asia began to recede from their memory.

Deference to Chinese feelings may also have affected Stein's posthumous reputation. Neglect of controversial Silk Road archaeology has perhaps been considered a price worth paying for the sake of good relations and access to other fields of interest in the Far East. Unlike the Elgin Marbles, the figurines, wall-paintings and wooden tablets from the Taklamakan Desert have mostly remained in the basements of the British Museum. No public debate has raged over their ownership, or the question of whether they would have survived equally well in their original locations. Had China been less isolated from the West, her opinion might have been more widely disseminated. And had that happened, Stein would undoubtedly be a better-known figure than he is today. Controversy would have done him more justice than the meagre display which has been his only public memorial in this country for so long.

The cycles of history may once more be turning in Stein's favour, however. Central Asia, remote though it has seemed to the West in terms of geography and traditions, is poised on the edge of political events that could merit larger headlines than those written by the old imperialists of Calcutta, London and St Petersburg. Perhaps the history of the Silk Road, and the remote and spectacular region it traverses, will then receive the attention it deserves, the museum collections will come out of hiding and the spotlight will focus on the man who brought that history to life, and who first dreamt of the East while a schoolboy in nineteenth-century Budapest.

I

A Singular Inheritance

BUDAPEST IN THE 1860s was a city in waiting; even its name lay in the future. The towns of Buda and Pest faced each other across the half-mile stretch of the Danube, linked by a bridge but separated by cultural and historic differences of the kind the Austrian Empire had exploited throughout Hungary for two centuries. Nationalist sentiment, however, had become a powerful unifying influence and the imperial grasp was beginning to weaken. In 1867, the coronation of Emperor Franz Josef as King of Hungary gave the country separate recognition and inaugurated a period of expansion and vigour that was to make Budapest the fastest-growing city in Europe. From the obscurity of nineteenth-century provincial middle Europe, it rapidly evolved into a cosmopolitan capital, and in the vanguard of its development came the most dynamic group among its people, the Jewish community.

The Stein family belonged to that community and Aurél was a small child when the historic Compromise of 1867 came into effect. Besides granting Hungary independence from Austria in internal affairs, this agreement also gave her Jewish population full political and civil rights. In the case of the youngest Stein, that aspect of its terms was irrelevant, since he had already been baptized. Aurél was born five years before the Compromise, on 26 November 1862 and, like his brother before him, had been made a member of the Lutheran Church.

The baptism in itself was not an unusual event, for a large number of Hungarian Jews had followed the same path. Indeed many had embraced conversion more completely by changing their names to the Magyar equivalent. That the Stein parents did not consider this necessary was perhaps a reflection of their sense of security and standing in a city that was to earn renown for its social integration over the next quarter-century.

The unifying factor behind this integration was nationalism. Not since the early sixteenth century had Hungary been free of foreign rule: Turkish occupation had been followed by absorption into the Habsburg Empire and relegation to provincial status. By the time many other parts of Europe were erupting in the social upheaval of 1848, Hungary's radicals had also precipitated a revolution, and among their supporters were many Jews. Like their Magyar comrades, they felt oppressed by the Habsburgs and, in addition, were discriminated against by ethnic Germans. Though they could not claim the same ethnic motives for wanting a Magyar state, they embraced the cause with enthusiasm. Increasing numbers of them spoke the newly revitalized Magyar language and took Magyar names, abandoning their own inheritance of German names and language. Some also embraced Christianity (though not the Catholicism of the Habsburgs), so that their assimilation was rapid. By the end of the nineteenth century they had contributed to the transformation of Budapest from a mainly German-speaking to an overwhelmingly Magyar city.

Aurél's father, Nathan, was one of those who supported the revolution – though he changed neither his name nor his religion, and was probably of too early a generation to know Magyar well. Born in the early years of the century, he came from the north of the country, now part of Slovakia. Little is known of his background, but the Hirschler family into which he married was prosperous. His father-in-law, Mark Hirschler, was in commerce in Pozsony – at that time part of greater Hungary but now known as Bratislava, the capital of Slovakia – and wealthy enough to have his son Ignaz educated in Vienna and Paris. Hirschler's daughter Anna was probably born in 1817 and married Nathan Stein twenty-two years later.

Anna's new husband was destined to be an unsuccessful businessman. At one time he seems to have been a wholesale corn merchant, but is said to have been bankrupt at the time of Aurél's birth. His wife's family wealth sustained him, however: the Hirschler net was finely meshed, and he seems to have been in no danger of falling through. He and his family divided their time between Budapest and Vienna, leading the relatively sophisticated, urban life of the Hungarian bourgeoisie – which in any case was Jewish to a large extent, there being little historical precedent for such a class in a country whose population traditionally had divided into aristocrats and peasants. They also enjoyed, vicariously, the stimulation of Budapest's intellectual circles through Anna's brother, Ignaz; and it was this gleam of light from beyond the close confines of home life that was to play such a large part in forming the mind of the young Aurél.

Uncle Ignaz Hirschler was clever, cultivated and well-connected. Born in 1823, he had studied and travelled in western Europe and returned home to become a pioneer in eye surgery. He operated on famous people and fraternized with them at the Academy of Sciences, the learned society founded by one of Hungary's greatest heroes, Count István Széchenyi. Ignaz was a leading proponent of Jewish assimilation into national life – though he wrote always in German and never used the Magyar form of his name – and his own Jewish origins were no barrier in the liberal atmosphere of the times. Indeed, the academy would have been a lesser place without its many Jewish members.

Ignaz was Anna Hirschler Stein's adored younger brother, the prodigy of the family in whose success they could all take pride and through whom they could enjoy the sense of being involved in great affairs. It was natural to consult him whenever important family matters were under consideration or problems needed solving. And Nathan's ineptitude for business only made a necessity of this natural inclination.

Anna and Nathan had two children early in their marriage, Theresa, born in 1841, and Ernst, born in 1843; and these two were young adults aged, respectively, 21 and 19 by the time Aurél arrived. Nathan would refer fondly to the youngest member of the family as 'my Benjamin'; but the boy was christened Marc Aurél after the Roman emperor, Marcus Aurelius, the French version of whose name was fashionable at the time. Mark was a name common to both families; but perhaps Ignaz influenced the decision to give the child an unequivocally classical version. Like many middle-class assimilated Jews, he had an unshakeable faith in the ideals of the Enlightenment and to someone steeped in such a culture, the meditations of Marcus Aurelius (who died near Budapest) were a fine example.

Aurél (pronounced 'Owrel' by both Magyar and German speakers) was born in a Hirschler-owned apartment in Tüköry utca, a small street in central Pest near the Danube.[1] It was a respectable area in which none of the houses was very old. The medieval city of Pest had been pulled down at the turn of the nineteenth century and in the years following Aurél's birth a new, orderly metropolis rose swiftly, with boulevards and avenues and geometrically planned blocks, and a great thoroughfare that formed an arc, from one bridge at the northern end of Pest to another on the southern side, in conscious imitation of Vienna's Ringstrasse.

In 1862, much of this development lay in the future but Pest was, nevertheless, the more dynamic of the two cities lying on either side of the Danube. Buda, standing on its hill 300 feet above the river, was the seat of Hungary's medieval kings and its old buildings housed a traditional, conservative population. At the foot of the hill, equally conservative and mostly German-speaking artisan communities inhabited the Water Town and Óbuda districts. It was across the water, in the progressive, modern city of Pest, that commerce, the arts and Magyar assertiveness throve. And this was where the city's Jewish citizens lived.

Aurél's early years there were happy. He had a cheerful, spirited mother and an affectionate, doting father, and other family members lived nearby. In later years, when he was alone and far from Hungary, he would remember the atmosphere of his home with an almost maudlin nostalgia which was intensified, perhaps, by the unusual nature of his relationship with his parents.

When he was born his father's business interests had collapsed and his brother Ernst was already old enough to be a father himself. Ernst was soon earning his own living and it was he and Uncle Ignaz who organized, funded and oversaw Aurél's education. Nathan and Anna, in their mid-fifties and mid-forties respectively at the time of their youngest child's birth, assumed a role akin to that of grandparents. They lavished affection on Aurél, taught him pretty manners, and wrote him encouraging and news-filled letters when he was away from home. Nathan, in particular, followed his academic progress with uncritical devotion. Ernst, so much older than his young brother and already feeling the weight of responsibility for his improvident parents, witnessed this devotion with a stoicism which only occasionally weakened enough to allow jealousy to surface.

As the elder brother, Ernst had a view of his father's impecuniosity which Aurél did not. The baby of the family was well looked after, his education was arranged and his parents played a wholly benign part in his life. While Ernst, too, had had a decent education, he could not afford to enjoy an irresponsible youth, or to indulge his love of literature. The prospect of providing for his parents lay before him and his duty was to find himself a secure position which would provide the necessary funds.

Though he was too dutiful to express much resentment of the future which family circumstances dictated for him, there is often an undertone of repression and dissatisfaction in his letters to his uncle, who stood as a constant suggestion of what might have been. Through Ignaz he shared a little of the concerns and interests of Budapest's intellectual élite. To him he could confide his opinion of Aurél's progress and, occasionally, his exasperation with an amiable, unrealistic father and the favouritism he showed his 'Benjamin'.

During the first few years of Ernst's working life, while he was a clerk in Vienna, his uncle would take him to concerts and accompany the family on holidays in the Alps. Ignaz saw, perhaps, that his intense young nephew's obsession with literature and philosophy was threatening to impede his progress in a career, for he advised Ernst to restrict his cultural interests to his private life, and to look for a position in banking. But Ernst disliked the Viennese business world. In 1879 or 1880 he moved to the small town of Jaworzno in Galicia, a province of the Austro-Hungarian Empire in what is now Poland, to become company secretary to a coal-mining business.

Whatever compensations he may have expected from settling in this eastern outpost of the empire, they did not materialize. Amid a Polish-speaking population and in a business which provided no outlet for his real interests, he felt like an exile, despite the responsibility and better pay of his new work. A flood of letters to his uncle replaced the cultural life he saw himself as having sacrificed for the sake of his family. Ignaz consoled him with a continuing epistolary debate on the ideas of writers and philosophers as diverse as Laurence Sterne and Schopenhauer, with books and periodicals sent from Budapest and with the thought that he could now provide for his younger brother.

Ernst was already supporting himself and his parents, and from a purely financial viewpoint might have considered this enough. But by now he had come to see in Aurél much more than simply another financial responsibility. He was already taking a didactic role in his upbringing, plotting a course such as he might have wished for himself, transferring his ambitions to Aurél. He was a strict guardian – his daughter, many years later, described him as 'a staunch Calvinist'[2] – but he never lost his pupil's loyalty.

The brothers' relationship was, inevitably, dictated by their difference in age. Their parents schooled them well in the manners and mores of family life and they remained faithful to their training all their lives; but they seldom communicated as equals. Ernst belonged to a different generation, and his letters to his brother were by turns anxious, admonitory and encouraging. Aurél's were full of reports on work, expressions of gratitude and affection and, later, reassuring explanations for the paternal figure who fretted over health, climate, work, mountain walking and many other aspects of his brother's life of which he had no experience and which he could no longer control. Female influence in Aurél's life was confined to that of his mother, whom he adored. His sister had left home to marry, probably when he was still an infant, and was to die young, in 1882.

Aurél's education began at an elementary school and continued at the gymnasium in Pest run by the Catholic Piarist order. The standard of schools in the capital was good and the Piarists had a reputation for their patriotic approach. Several national heroes, including the poet Mihály Vörösmarty and the great reformer Count István Széchenyi, had been educated there. And, since the Piarists were less dogmatic than the other leading teaching order, the Benedictines, there were many Jewish children in their classes.

Besides Magyar language and literature, Aurél learnt Latin, Greek, mathematics, and Hungarian and classical history. The teachers were highly qualified and no doubt communicated their enthusiasm for nationalism to their pupils. Certainly Aurél took to marking in his schoolboy diaries the Sixth of October, the anniversary of the execution of the heroes of 1848–9, with suitably patriotic comments. After two years at the gymnasium, however, his uncle and brother decided to send him away from home, to the Lutheran Kreuzschule in Dresden.

Ernst had inherited from Ignaz a belief in German Enlightenment values of rationality and self-improvement. Together the two men decided that it was essential for Aurél to study at a good school in a small town where he would benefit from that tradition and learn to speak and write first-rate German. Though their letters over the next few years suggest that they were rarely satisfied with the standard he reached, Aurél was to continue to use German throughout his life, in letters to his family as well as to German-speaking colleagues.

Contrary to the wishes of his guardians, however, it was the Magyar language that held his affections. During his first few years in India, he often used it to jot down notes in his pocket diaries. He delighted in speaking it whenever opportunity arose, linking it sentimentally with his old, emotional attachment to his home. Perhaps he continued to think in Magyar, even during the long periods when he was using either English or a variety of native Asian languages; for a Hungarian, meeting him in 1928 in Kashmir, wrote later that he used it as though he spoke it every day.[3]

In 1873, however, aged 10, Aurél was dispatched to Dresden, beyond the northern border of the Austro-Hungarian Empire. His first, eager letters to his father in faulty German circulated among interested members of the family in Budapest and Vienna, and Ernst waited impatiently for signs of progress that never came soon enough for his satisfaction. Ignaz was a gentler commentator, touched by the uncanny maturity of the letters and concerned that the boy was almost too diligent.

The reason for Aurél's diligence, however, lay in more than a mere sense of duty. For in Dresden one of his teachers, a Dr Hausmann, gave him a copy of *The Campaigns of Alexander* by Arrian; and from the moment that the child began to read of the great Macedonian conqueror and his exploits in the East, he was gripped by a fascination that lasted all his life and inspired many of his happiest excursions into the mountains and deserts of Asia.

A fascination for travels in far-off places seems to have been an inherited characteristic in the Stein family. One forebear in the late eighteenth century ran away from home and reached Holland before being traced, and another went to Italy to fight for Garibaldi. Several more were armchair voyagers, passing their spare time immersed in travellers' tales. Perhaps it was this influence that prompted Nathan to take up the study of Semitic languages in his youth, though he abandoned it because of the amount of memorizing required.

Aurél showed similar tastes. But it was not simply the scale of Alexander's achievements that captivated him. He was intrigued by the idea of Greek culture being transported so far into the heart of Asia. Alexander's soldiers had endured appalling conditions to follow their king through deep snow into unknown, wild and mountainous country north of the Hindu Kush (known to them as the Indian Caucasus); and many had settled in the cities he founded or conquered along the way. What had happened to those men who never returned from Bactria and Sogdiana (northern Afghanistan and Russian Turkestan)? Had they been absorbed into the local populations, or had they perpetuated the Greek ways in which they had been raised, to pass them down to succeeding generations? Were there remnants still of their civilization, lying lost in the distant mountains and plains of Central Asia? These were questions which Aurél began to ask while still a schoolboy poring over his Latin and Greek histories, and he was to go on asking them throughout his life.

Perhaps, too, his enthusiasm for Alexander the Great helped to occupy thoughts which would otherwise have turned to family, and the distance that separated him from his beloved parents. During his four years in Dresden he learnt habits of self-reliance that were to sustain him throughout life; and he remained loyal to the Kreuzschule. But he was an affectionate child as well as a dutiful one, and he missed the loving home in which he had been raised. Fortunately, Ignaz recognized the signs of loneliness. As a result of his prompting, Ernst arranged for Aurél to return to Budapest in 1877 and attend its Lutheran gymnasium.

He was often alone here, too – with no siblings of his own age or, it seems, close friends – but probably not lonely. The historical sense already developing in him found plenty of interest in his surroundings, and he would spend hours rambling round the old streets and castle walls on the historic hill of Buda, contemplating its associations with Hungary's past.[4] In later life he was to remember being enthralled, too, by his father's story of the Roman remains he had stumbled across in the countryside, probably while serving in the revolutionary army in 1848–9. This appetite for topographical history found satisfaction also in the rural surroundings of the northern estate owned by Nathan's brother, Mark, where Aurél sometimes passed part of the summer holiday.

At home in Pest, his uncle Ignaz encouraged the studious side of the boy's character. A few minutes' walk from the family apartment in Tüköry utca stood the handsome new building of the Academy of Sciences, completed in neo-Renaissance style in 1864, where Ignaz met his learned friends and where there was a magnificent library. To this he introduced his bookish nephew and Aurél soon became a regular visitor, absorbing its atmosphere and reading its scholarly volumes. Years later, he wrote that it was with this 'noble abode of learning' that he associated 'many of the happiest recollections of my early youth'.[5]

It was here, in the academy's library, that Aurél was able to indulge his nascent interest in philology and Sanskrit (though not in the Semitic tongues which would have gratified his father). The study of languages other than Latin and Greek, and in particular those of the Orient, was a young science at this period. But it was already a popular one, and Hungarians had particular reasons for their interest in the subject. The origins of their own race and language were the subject of much discussion and dispute, which the patriotic temper of the times only intensified.

Earlier in the century, a young Hungarian named Sándor Kőrösi Csoma had set out for the East in search of Magyar roots. Though he had been diverted from his purpose and had died an obscure death in the foothills of the Himalayas, his journey had assumed great symbolic importance for a nation emerging from centuries of submission to foreign rule. The Magyars had come to the Danube basin from somewhere east of the Ural Mountains more than nine centuries before, bringing with them a language that bore no relation to those of neighbouring countries, and which now played a vital part in the revival of national feeling. Csoma's quest for the ancient homeland of the Magyars would have been familiar to the young teenager who pored over the volumes of the academy library. How direct an influence it had on him is debatable, for his later interest in the origins of Magyar seems to have been polite rather than real, albeit well-informed. But the facts of Csoma's life touched his imagination.

———◆◀———

Kőrösi Csoma was born in 1784 into an ancient family which had long been settled in Transylvania (now part of Romania). Having benefited from what was then the fledgling study of oriental languages in Germany, he set out on foot from Hungary in 1820 with the single aim of identifying the Asian origins of Magyar. After a journey lasting more than two years, across regions seldom seen by Europeans, he reached the harsh, remote mountains of Ladakh, on the western fringes of Tibet; and there he met William Moorcroft, an official of the East India Company.

Moorcroft was himself an adventurous traveller who had recently been, with two companions, the first Englishman ever to see Leh, the capital of Ladakh. He recruited Csoma, on behalf of his own employers, to begin work on a study of the Tibetan language. After several years' labour in conditions of extreme isolation and privation, during which British officials in India failed to provide the consistent support which would have eased his situation, Csoma travelled to Calcutta to work on a Tibetan grammar. When he set out again, in 1842, it was in the hope of reaching the well-nigh inaccessible capital of Tibet, Lhasa, where he believed he would find documents relevant to his original mission. He had travelled only as far as Darjeeling when malarial fever struck, and he died there shortly afterwards.

To a boy already fascinated by Alexander the Great's conquests in Central Asia, the romance and mystery of Csoma's life could only have enhanced the appeal of the East. Aurél wrote much later that, sitting in his Kashmir mountain camp and looking down at the Sind valley, he often thought of the lonely Hungarian wanderer passing that way on his journey to Ladakh. Csoma had obeyed the instincts of his obsession and gone to the East where, already, Aurél sensed there was so much to be discovered. But there were other Hungarian sources of inspiration, too, for his interests, all ripples from the wave of academic interest in oriental studies that had recently spread rapidly across Europe.

It was among the gentlemen of the East India Company, naturally enough, that orientalism began as a dilettante interest. But the creative force that transformed it into an altogether more rigorous academic study came from Sir William Jones (1746–94). Jones was one of the earliest proponents of what later became known as philology, the comparative study of languages, through his interest in Latin, Greek, Persian and, after his appointment as a judge in the Supreme Court of Bengal, Sanskrit. He was the first to recognize the similarities between Sanskrit and the so-called classical languages, and he managed to complete translations of several important Sanskrit texts before his early death.

Gradually, oriental literature became available in the West. Scholars began to study it at universities such as that in Göttingen where Kőrösi Csoma started learning Persian, Turkish and Arabic in 1815. The first translations of India's early Aryan texts introduced a new source of ideas and images to European culture, so that when Sanskrit literature reached Hungary, it inspired poets and writers there as it had in Germany (where Goethe and Herder, among others, came under its influence). The Hungarian poet János Arany (1817–82), whose works Aurél was later to take with him on his expeditions, based some of his poems on Sanskrit stories and made his own translation, from the German, of part of Kalidasa's play, *Sakuntala*.

In 1873, at the time that Aurél was sent away to Dresden, a new chair was founded at the university in Budapest for Indo-European comparative linguistics, with the study of Sanskrit as one of its aims. Aurél Mayr, who ran the new department, had been a student in Berlin, Tübingen and Vienna, and inaugurated the translation of texts from their original languages directly into Magyar.

By the late nineteenth century, therefore, oriental studies and Indology held an important place in the work of many European universities. Every two or three years an International Congress of Orientalists took place in a European city, and the reports of its sessions grew increasingly weighty. The Academy of Sciences in Budapest followed all the latest academic and intellectual developments, so that Aurél, already imbued with the classical historians' intriguing reports of Asia, had ready access to a good deal of new material rather different from the resources usually available to schoolboys.

His were precocious interests, prompting an early beginning to mature habits of study. To a boy who had always been familiar, through his uncle, with high intellectual standards, perhaps this did not seem unusual. He had been encouraged to be studious, and there were plenty of examples among his uncle's friends of what might be achieved, so it is not surprising that he soon developed an ambition to become an academic. This was certainly in line with the expectations of his unofficial guardians; though there were times when both Ignaz and Ernst doubted his ability to live up to their standards.

The letters that passed between Aurél's uncle and brother show that they maintained a close watch on their charge.⁶ Indeed, at times it seems almost as though some experiment in education and upbringing was being conducted, with Aurél, in effect the only child of elderly, trusting parents, an ideal and willing guinea-pig. He seems to have had nothing but grateful memories of the concern shown him by Ernst and Ignaz. And certainly, the breadth of knowledge he gained from his schooling was impressive. But one cannot help wondering at his forbearance when one reads some of the remarks in these letters – though, of course, they were not intended for his eyes. Perhaps the attitude of his guardians would have been different had a female member of the family been more involved in Aurél's upbringing. But his mother, though apparently a lively character, seems to have been content to leave her younger son's future in the hands of her brother and elder son.

So the two men were free to pursue their chosen course, and they waged sporadic war on what they considered to be Aurél's faults. They grumbled repeatedly to each other about his inadequate grasp of German, fearing that his interest in other, classical languages was preventing him from refining it to the degree necessary for an academic career. His knowledge of Italian and English also came under fire. And when Aurél inherited some money from his paternal uncle Mark (who died in 1885), they worried that the interest he received from it, the equivalent of about £1,760 now, would weaken his resolve or find its way, through Aurél's generosity, into the hands of his spendthrift father (which it did).

Sometimes they complained that he was a slow developer, at other times that his success was bringing him more praise than was good for him. On one occasion they agreed that he had an attractive manner, on another that his self-confidence was off-putting. They fretted that he was too bookish, then that he was not taking his studies seriously. Once, in 1882 (when Aurél was nearly 20), Ernst asked his uncle for an assessment of his brother's character, and Ignaz's reply gives an indication of the Germanic rigour with which they approached their self-imposed task.

Aurél, he said, had become rather boring. Frequent repetition and hesitation over the most appropriate form of words made his conversation dull. Facial grimaces, the lowering of eyelids and ticking of the upper lip gave him the appearance of haughtiness – though Ignaz conceded that they might simply be indications of shyness. He also asked too many questions; but it should be possible to cure him of that.

Ignaz advised a strict regime to 'harden' the young student: a cold wash in the morning, rough towelling, exercises for fifteen minutes, all to take place before six o'clock in the morning during winter. He should walk for at least one hour a day (but not against the wind), always keep his mouth closed while outside during cold weather and be in bed by nine. Food should be nourishing, and taken with a little wine or beer. Daily half-hour readings aloud would improve intonation and breathing; but he should never read in bed. Ernst was grateful for the advice. But he puzzled over the difference between his and his uncle's dissatisfaction with Aurél's demeanour, and the apparent favour with which the young man was greeted by strangers. He found his brother so boring, he wrote to Ignaz, that he could hardly bear to listen to him.

At the same time as they were subjecting Aurél to this unsparing examination, however, Ignaz and Ernst were also reading Sanskrit texts in translation in order to follow his studies, and contriving how best to gain grants on his behalf so that he could travel to whichever university provided the best instruction. Occasionally they admitted to each other that Aurél was really showing a good deal of promise. In 1881 Ernst, sitting at his writing desk in the cheerless atmosphere of his lonely home, added a simple statement to a letter to his uncle: life without Aurél, he wrote, would be impossible.

———————————◄———————————

In 1879, before he was yet 17, Aurél matriculated from the Lutheran gymnasium in Pest and began his undergraduate studies in Sanskrit and philology in Vienna, moving to Leipzig after two terms in order to hear the lectures of J.G. Bühler (1837–98). Georg Bühler was an authority on Indian palaeography and a rarity among orientalists in having lived and worked in the East. While most of his colleagues knew India only through her literature, he had been a professor of oriental languages in Bombay. He had also travelled on the subcontinent in the course of compiling a catalogue of privately owned Sanskrit manuscripts for the Indian government, which had lately grown to appreciate the need for a systematic record of India's cultural history.

Perhaps it was here in Leipzig, during the single term in which Aurél was able to study under Bühler before the latter left to become professor of Indian philology and antiquities at the university in Vienna, that the idea of working in India first began to germinate in the young student's mind. While Ignaz and Ernst fretted over Aurél's academic prospects in Europe, their protégé was slowly forming the idea for a future which would take him farther, in distance and achievement, than any of them could have envisaged.

Once Bühler had left Leipzig, Aurél moved again, this time to Tübingen to hear the lectures of Rudolf von Roth, professor of Indo-European languages and the history of religions, and co-author of a Sanskrit-German dictionary completed in 1875. There was no better place to study the Vedic period – the first millennium of Aryan occupation in India during which the beautiful hymns collectively known as the Rig-Veda were written – for Roth was the acknowledged authority. On his death in 1895 an obituarist wrote that his work had formed 'the foundation on which nearly all subsequent researches on the language, institutions, religion and mythology of the Veda are based'.[7] Under the influence of this learned man – whose photograph Aurél kept all his life, and on the back of which he wrote *Mein theuerer Meister*, my dear master – Aurél buried himself in his studies, allowing his family to take him on occasional Alpine holidays only with reluctance.

Uncle Ignaz, meanwhile, continued to use his influence in Budapest to maintain Aurél's grant, first extracted from the Hungarian Minister of Cultural Affairs in 1880. Ágoston Trefort had been Minister since 1872 and became president of the Academy of Sciences in 1881. He and Ignaz were old acquaintances and at first he made the grant with enthusiasm. But he had many calls on his resources and many projects to fund, including the reform of secondary schools and the building of a new university of technology. By the time he died in 1888, he had exceeded his budget. Ignaz's letters, referring to occasions on which he pressed Trefort for the money, suggest that Aurél was lucky to receive anything after the first couple of years for what was, after all, a rather low priority.

At his uncle's suggestion, Aurél wrote a scholarly essay entitled 'Old Persian Religious Literature' to bolster his claims to state support, which Ignaz then helped place in a well-regarded Budapest periodical, *Szemle*, in 1885. Thanks to Ignaz's persistence, he had funds enough not only to complete his studies at Tübingen, where he was awarded his doctoral degree in 1883, but also to venture farther afield when he decided to follow the example of his teachers and go to England.

For an orientalist, England was the next-best place to the East. Or rather, it was a better place altogether, for it was possible to study original texts there without having to endure the infamous climate of the Indian subcontinent. Many German orientalists, including Bühler and Roth, had made the pilgrimage to the Bodleian Library in Oxford and the archives of East India House. One, Max Müller, had edited the Rig-Veda for the East India Company and had become a pioneer of comparative philology at Oxford.

Aurél had been studying the English language (at the expense of his German, his brother and uncle noted) and had probably already mentioned to his family the idea of going to India. To his father Nathan it seemed a splendid ambition. Not only did the East appeal to his romantic imagination, but it seemed fitting that his talented son should have ambitions beyond the confines of Europe. Perhaps his enthusiasm for the suggestion precipitated Aurél into a course of action which had been, until then, only one of several possibilities. For in a letter to his brother written after Nathan's death, Aurél refers to his move to India as having been undertaken at their father's 'urgent wishes'.

At the time of his departure for England in 1884, however, both Ignaz and Ernst still hoped and expected that Aurél would find a position in a German-speaking university. Indeed Ernst preferred the prospect of his brother being safely settled within the Hungarian border. But academic opportunities for a philologist and Sanskritist in Hungary were rare and Aurél had found none, either there or elsewhere. His experience in England was to point persuasively towards the future his father desired.

The period Aurél spent in England amounted in total to no more than a couple of years – interrupted by a year in Hungary, 1885–6 – during which he studied oriental collections in Oxford, London and Cambridge. He wrote two more papers: one entitled 'Hindu Kush and Pamir in Ancient Iranian Geography' for the 1886 International Congress of Orientalists at Vienna, the other the result of his study of numismatics, 'Zoroastrian Deities on Indo-Scythian Coins' (published in the *Oriental and Babylonian Record*, 1887). More important than these early attempts at academic respectability, however, was the development of his feeling of affinity with Britain and things British. Often in later years he was to refer to this affinity, claiming that he was drawn to the country and its ways while still a boy. Such sentiments were an important factor, not only at the outset of his career but in many subsequent decisions, both professional and personal.

Perhaps his affection was nurtured by the help he received there from a number of much older men, all eminent in their chosen fields. He had become accustomed to look to such men for advice and support while he was growing up among his uncle's friends in Budapest. And here in England, again, Ignaz's influence was at work. Soon after his arrival in London, armed with an introduction, Aurél made his way to Nevern Square in Earls Court (known at the time as Asia Minor because of its popularity with those returning from the East), to the house of a distinguished Hungarian *émigré* named Dr Theodore Duka.

It was a fortuitous and significant meeting. Duka was a veteran of the 1848–9 revolution in Hungary who had served as aide-de-camp to General Aurél Görgey, leader of the army after Hungary's declaration of independence. He had been forced into exile after the Austrians crushed the uprising, studied medicine in England and served as a military surgeon in India for twenty years before retiring on a pension. While in the East, he had begun to collect information on Kőrösi Csoma and was now busy with a biography of the lone Hungarian wanderer.[8] This work, together with his patriotism, his interest in oriental languages and his experience of India, would have been enough to attract Aurél without the additional fact that he showed a paternal interest in the young student and welcomed him into his home and family.

On his frequent visits there, Aurél was shown photographs of Simla and told tales of colonial life. It was the first time he had come into close contact with anyone who had lived in India, and the impressions he gained all contributed to the picture that was gradually developing in his mind. He wrote optimistic letters home on the subject of rewarding salaries and prospects, which infuriated his brother. 'I can't see why he can't be content in a minor but safe position', Ernst wrote petulantly to Ignaz, 'instead of having this urge for a grand position in India. He has a sudden, childish enthusiasm for earning money and the idea that he can share my care of our parents instead of endeavouring to stand on his own feet in a suitable job.'[9]

Ernst, the older brother, defining himself in terms of his responsibilities towards the other members of his family, had cause for concern. Aurél was now 22 years old, on his own in a country beyond the German and Austro-Hungarian empires, susceptible to the influence of unknown people who were by no means sure to recommend a course which would meet with Ernst's approval. Ernst had been angry a couple of years earlier when Aurél had seemed unambitious; now things seemed to be happening too fast for him to keep up.

In fact, Aurél's expectations at first remained unfulfilled. The exciting new prospects which he had visualized failed to appear and an academic career of any kind remained depressingly unattainable. He studied the coin collections at the Ashmolean Museum in Oxford and the British Museum, the oriental manuscripts in the possession of the India Office (inherited from the old East India Company) and those at the Bodleian Library in Oxford. Then he returned home in 1885 to undergo a year's military service at the Ludovica Academy in Budapest, living with his parents in the apartment to which they had moved in Akadémia utca, a stone's throw from their old home.

Again Ignaz found himself lobbying on his nephew's behalf in the offices of the Ministry of Cultural Affairs and enlisting the help of Hungarian friends such as Ignaz Goldziher, the eminent Islamicist, and Ármin Vámbéry, the prominent traveller and orientalist. His patience began to wear thin with his ambitious but raw young nephew. Ernst, by contrast, showed some sympathy for his frustrated brother. The new note of compassion in his letters at this time may have had something to do with the change in his own life for, on 5 June 1886, in Krakow, he married Henriette Rosalie Hein of Vienna. He was 43, she 32. He had felt unable to consider marriage until Trefort's government grants took care of his brother's studies and allowed him some freedom from financial responsibilities.

The time was fast approaching when Aurél's position, too, would change dramatically. He spent his period of military service at the Ludovica Academy learning surveying and mapmaking, skills to which he was probably attracted through his interest in topography. Attendance at the academy was considered a relatively civilized way for educated young civilians to undergo compulsory military training, from which they emerged with officer status.

The students learned their craft in the wooded Buda hills, where wealthy Pest families had their summer houses. It was a rather different environment from that in which Aurél later put his surveying to the test, in the mountains of Asia. But it was a lesson well learnt. In subsequent dealings with cautious Indian authorities, his surveying skills may well have been the deciding factor in winning permission and funding for his expeditions. In return, he used his Ludovica training to spectacular effect, mapping vast areas known to cartographers until then only as blank spaces.

At the conclusion of his studies at the Ludovica, Aurél returned to England in 1886 with more money from a harassed Trefort in his bank account. His address book from the years he spent there show that he lived nowhere for very long – in London's Euston Square on first arrival in December 1884; in Oxford lodgings for a few months of the following year; at a house in Belsize Park Gardens, North London, during June 1885 before leaving for his year at the Ludovica. On his return in 1886, he stayed for almost a year in Belsize Park again, during which time he seems to have consulted Persian manuscripts at Trinity College, Cambridge.

The impermanence of his living arrangements was balanced by the steady influence of the senior figures whose company and assistance he sought. One of these was the Librarian of the India Office Library, Dr Reinhold Rost (1822–96), another German-born orientalist whose position included advising the Secretary of State for India on philological matters. Rost read many languages and had acquired such a knowledge of archaeology, ethnology and history over his years of study that he had become an authority of international stature. Aurél also met Sir Monier Monier-Williams (1819–99), who had begun his career teaching Sanskrit at the East India Company's school, Haileybury, and had gone on to be Boden Professor of Sanskrit at Oxford, where he was overseeing the creation of the Indian Institute (now part of the Bodleian Library).

It was after a lecture at the Royal Asiatic Society in 1887, however, that Aurél first encountered Sir Henry Rawlinson (1810–95) and, probably through him, Sir Henry Yule (1820–89), two highly influential figures in Anglo-Indian affairs whose interest in his career was to prove decisive. Both men were on the India Council, the body, composed mainly of former members of the Indian Civil Service, which advised the Secretary of State for India. Rawlinson was not an academic, having led a life of active service in the East India Company's army and as a diplomat. But while an army officer in Persia he had won fame by deciphering and translating the cuneiform inscriptions which the Achaemenid king, Darius the Great, had had carved on the cliffs of Behistun five hundred years before the start of the Christian era.

Yule, too, had served in the army of the East India Company. Though probably best-known as the co-author of a handbook of Anglo-Indian colloquialisms, *Hobson-Jobson*, he had devoted himself in retirement chiefly to a study of medieval reports of China, *Cathay and the Way Thither* (1866), and an account of Marco Polo's travels in the East, *The Book of Ser Marco Polo the Venetian, Concerning the Kingdoms and the Marvels of the East* (1870). The experiences of both men were a further source of inspiration to the earnest young Hungarian student, which he later gratefully acknowledged in the dedications of two of his books.[10] By the time he left England, Aurél had accumulated letters of recommendation from a variety of impressively influential well-wishers.

At last, in the autumn of 1887, the steady work of the past two decades paid off. Still with no European position in sight and with his funds running low, he heard through Rawlinson and Yule of a dual post in India, combining the position of Registrar at the Punjab University with that of Principal of Oriental College in Lahore. It was an opportunity to gratify his elderly father; to practise at last what he had prepared himself for over so many years; and to do what few orientalists had done, begin work in India itself.

He had the example of his old professor, Bühler, before him as an indication of how high academic standing in Europe could be preceded by less prestigious but useful work in the East. It was not an ideal solution because India was far from the academic circles of the West. But perhaps the adventurous spirit in Aurél, which was soon to demonstrate its power, spoke to him now as he stood on the edge of his future, looking uncertainly forward.

He had had a cloistered childhood and youth in which diligence had come easily but originality had so far eluded him. He had learnt self-reliance but not independence; and he had pored over the topography of Asia only in his imagination. His uncle and brother had directed his studies with a devotion which was admirable but which had circumscribed his actions and retarded his own sense of direction. Perhaps an intimation of how his life might change passed through his mind, even while he continued to hope for a return within a few years to the kind of position for which he had been groomed. His generous patrons awaited his answer: he decided to go to India in the hope of securing the dual post.

Aurél's departure was clouded by the death of his mother only a few weeks beforehand. His father had organized a family party on the eve of his journey, but the atmosphere was muted. Ignaz could not bring himself to attend. Ernst came to Budapest to say goodbye to his brother, but his wife Jetty (as she was known in preference to Henriette) stayed in Jaworzno with their first baby.

As Aurél left the bleak atmosphere of a Budapest November, he was equipped not only with a letter of introduction from his uncle to a diplomat in Bombay, but also with the knowledge that some members of his family regarded his next step as risky, if not downright foolish. Ignaz had already emphasized that he should not feel compelled by pride or shame to stay in India if (or perhaps when) he felt there was nothing for him there.

But his father's immense pride in his 'Benjamin', and the memory of his mother's faith in her youngest child, counted for more than the reservations of his guardians. With his mother's last letter to him in his pocket, Aurél left Budapest on 16 November 1887 for Brindisi and the boat to India.

2

First Taste of the British Raj

———————————

FROM THE DECKS of the steamer approaching Bombay, newcomers received their first sight of India. Beyond the clutch of white and grey buildings at the water's edge, the slopes of the Western Ghats swept up to peaks of more than four thousand feet, green and luxuriant after the monsoon and beautiful in the bright, hot weather of early December. Behind the mountains stretched the Deccan plateau and, beyond that, the rest of that vast subcontinent of India which, over the best part of three centuries, the British had gradually been taming, ordering and colonizing.

By the time Aurel Stein arrived,* in the late 1880s, colonization was largely complete. Spacious cantonments lay a safe distance beyond the bazaars of many an old town, and few places remained on the map that had not been visited by some intrepid Army officer or dedicated district official. The imposition of order had become an Anglo-Indian art-form.[1] Through myriad offices across the land, paper passed from clerk to clerk, from department to department, ordering village squabbles and affairs of state with the same thoroughness and authority.

If in parts of the country there was sometimes resistance to this relentless process, it was not because of a lack of determination among the white ruling classes. Since the Mutiny of 1857, their methods had

———————————

* Stein's first name became Anglicized at this period and the accent therefore disappeared.

become more rigorous, their institutions more formal. Cautious coloni-
als might still take their guns with them to church on Sunday mornings;
but the British had in fact created conditions for themselves which were
as safe and familiar in many ways as those they had left behind at home.

It was a world which was easily recognizable, despite its exotic
setting, to any young man raised in the public schools of the British
Isles, where most of India's administrators had received their early training. And in its respect for integrity, decency and a sense of duty were
similarities, too, with the moral code of the serious young Hungarian
academic who disembarked in Bombay that December.

Stein had by then already had opportunity during the two-week sea
voyage to observe a little of Anglo-Indian manners among his
fellow-passengers.[2] But his diffidence made him a reticent travelling
companion. Even after living in India for many years, he was to find
these journeys something of an ordeal and once remarked in a letter that
only the presence of his dog 'introduced his master to pleasant acquaintances which he, with his unfortunate reserve would surely have otherwise missed'.[3] Though his mother had instilled in him civility and
consideration, he had little aptitude for conventional social life.

Stein was 25 when he arrived at Bombay. He stood only five feet four
inches tall, was sparely built but broad-shouldered and fit. His
dark-brown hair was neatly parted on the right and he wore a mous-
tache. His height and build might have made him an unremarkable
figure had it not been for the deep-set eyes and strong, square jaw-line
which suggested a degree of determination that, as yet, he scarcely
knew he possessed.

He left behind in Europe no group of friends outside his own family
and, once in India, seems to have used his letters to his brother as his
only outlet for private thoughts. Other correspondence was mainly with
patrons and well-wishers, influential older men who might be helpful in
his search for an academic career. These were the people who had told
him what little he knew of India. He saw the country through older eyes
and he was intent upon using his time there to win the respect of
European academics. In that way, he would be able to return home to
a comfortable university post and a life of scholarly research and
recognition among his peers. With this aim he took the train north to
the Punjab (a three-day journey) in February 1888 to begin work at
Lahore's Oriental College and, later, at the Punjab University too.

He was fortunate in his posting. From Lahore he could easily reach the area on which his interests were concentrated: the Indo-Iranian borderlands whose ancient languages and religions he had studied, and over whose mountains and deserts the hero of his boyhood, Alexander the Great, had marched. Lahore, too, had its attractions. It had been the capital of the Punjab for hundreds of years under successive rulers of India: Mahmud of Ghazni, the Mogul emperors and now the British. The Moguls Akbar, Jahangir, Shah Jahan and Aurangzeb had all left monuments to their dynasty in the form of mosques, forts, tombs, palaces and gardens. The British added a variety of buildings in their ponderous 'Mogul Gothic' style and built broad, tree-lined thoroughfares.

As a result, Lahore was a mixture of the exotic and the prosaically colonial. Marble pavilions, finely carved sandstone, glazed tilework and floral frescoes co-existed with white cantonment bungalows, clubs and government offices. The unifying element was the gardens, originally so exquisitely laid out by the Moguls, now neglected and invariably dulled by the fine dust that settled everywhere; but still imparting a sense of romance and luxury to the city.

There was another reason for the convenience of such a base. Lahore lay relatively close to the kingdom of Kashmir where, Stein knew, the mystery of a missing manuscript was waiting to be solved. Thirteen years earlier his old professor Georg Bühler, while employed by the Bombay Education Department, had visited Kashmir in search of Sanskrit manuscripts. Bühler had been particularly interested in copies of *The Chronicle of the Kings of Kasmir* (or *Rajatarangini*) by Kalhana, a twelfth-century scholar-poet.

The qualities of the *Chronicle* distinguish it from almost any known work of old Sanskrit literature. Other Sanskrit texts had been written for didactic or religious purposes and there was no tradition of narrative history from which modern historians could draw useful information about India's past. But Kalhana had set out in the *Rajatarangini* to give an account of the history of Kashmir, from earliest times to the period in which he lived. His work could be likened to the medieval chronicles of Europe and, as such, was of vital interest to Indologists.

That it existed had been known for some time. But it was not until the nineteenth century that descriptions and translations of its contents began to appear. They were full of misunderstandings and mistakes, however, because of the necessity of taking them from later copies or transcripts which had been made in the modern, Devanagari script. The original *Rajatarangini* would have been written in the old S'arada script of Kashmir; in transcribing it into another script, the copyists had all too often debased its style and obscured its meaning. Moreover, since few of the copyists had any knowledge of the topography of Kashmir which features so prominently in Kalhana's story, they could often make no sense of his descriptions. European scholars recognized that they would know the true importance of Kalhana's *Chronicle of the Kings of Kasmir* only when they could lay their hands on an old S'arada manuscript.

Such a manuscript had, in fact, been found in 1823 by the traveller William Moorcroft, though he was unaware of its full significance. He too had had it transcribed into Devanagari, with the same unsatisfactory results. Not until Georg Bühler reached Kashmir in 1875 did someone with adequate knowledge and academic training try to locate an unadulterated copy of the *Chronicle*.

Bühler's research was more successful than any so far. He established that all the extant Kashmiri versions of the *Rajatarangini* derived from a single manuscript, and that it was the same one that Moorcroft had used as his source fifty years earlier. He even succeeded in establishing its whereabouts, only to find that it was jealously guarded by the family who owned it. He had followed the scent to its source; but he was obliged to leave Kashmir having enjoyed no more than a glimpse of the elusive manuscript.

This much Stein knew before he went to India. He knew also that Bühler's work on Sanskrit manuscripts had gained him an honoured place among orientalists in Europe, and a prestigious university professorship on his return home. Wisely, the younger man kept to himself any thoughts he may have had on taking the pursuit of the *Rajatarangini* further. When he obtained the position at Lahore, it was in the full knowledge that Kashmir lay only a short distance to the north, and that his long summer vacations would give him the chance to play his own part, perhaps the most important part of all, in the search for *The Chronicle of the Kings of Kasmir*.

In the meantime, there was the more prosaic matter of his new work to consider. The posts he held, of Registrar of the Punjab University and Principal of the Oriental College, were responsible ones for a man of 25, but his youthfulness was not as surprising as it might have been in Europe. India attracted relatively few academics, and those who came tended to be more adventurous, more impecunious, or less conventional than those who stayed at home. Without having to fight their way through phalanxes of ambitious scholars competing for a restricted number of posts in the West, newcomers were able to acquire sonorous academic titles on the basis of little experience.

This did not necessarily mean that positions would be easier to find when they wished to return home; but it was an opportunity which they considered worthwhile for a time, in the hope of better things to come. By the late 1880s, improved communications had brought India and Europe within two or three weeks' sea voyage of each other and the sense of colonial isolation had lessened: there was no need to commit oneself to long periods on the subcontinent. Many of the academics whom Stein met in India intended their stay there to last only a few years.

The University of the Punjab was one of five similar institutions in India. All were of recent origin, the earliest having been created in 1857. Their primary aim was the training of well-born Indians to form the vast regiment of civil servants without whom the empire could not function. But the university founders also intended that this educated class would show by example the desirability of Western ideas and culture, which would thus be disseminated throughout the country.[4] (The policy was to backfire on the country's colonial administrators before the end of the century, by which time growing numbers of Indians educated in this way lacked work and coveted the higher positions which the British doggedly reserved for themselves.) The universities were examining bodies only: teaching was done by affiliated colleges, of which Oriental College was one.

Stein lived in the heart of the old British part of Lahore in the cavernous Charing Cross Hotel which was built, in the Anglo-Indian tradition, with heavily shaded verandas and small windows high up under the eaves to shield its sensitive northern occupants from the force of the sun. Its other European inmates and his professional colleagues (all Indian at the college) were his earliest acquaintances. The day began early, to avoid the heat which in summer was extreme, with office duties followed by private study and then lectures – for Stein also taught Sanskrit.

He was diligent and responsible, but his heart was rarely in his official work. References to it in his private letters and professional correspondence over the next decade frequently describe it as 'heavy', 'onerous' and 'exacting'. His students are conspicuous by their apparent absence from his thoughts. He was not a natural teacher; his interest lay in research rather than in the communication of information to classrooms of pupils. Within a few months of his arrival in Lahore, he was developing ideas for a private project more suited to his temperament and his career.

Stein's plan was to spend his first long vacation in Kashmir, following the example of Bühler by searching for Sanskrit manuscripts; and Uncle Ignaz's influence is evident in the preparation of this first independent project. Indeed, an appreciation of the value of good connections was to become a hallmark of Stein's dealings with officialdom. Before he left Lahore in the summer of 1888, he had secured letters of recommendation from the Secretary of State for the Punjab, the Vice-Chancellor of the University, Dr William Rattigan,[5] and the British Resident in Kashmir, Colonel W. F. Prideaux. He entered the kingdom of Jammu and Kashmir in the knowledge that he had access to some of the highest authorities in the land.

At home in Budapest, Stein's uncle and brother watched their protégé's progress with a mixture of enthusiasm and scepticism. Both considered his appointment at Lahore to be a matter of luck as well as ability; but Ernst could not share Ignaz's generally benign view. Suddenly bereft of the brother in whom he had invested so much, he tried to disguise the pain of separation. 'I shall be pleased to be relieved soon of any responsibility for Aurel's choice of profession,' he claimed defensively.[6] In one respect, however, he thought Aurel's new life had compensations: he was pleased to note the effect of the first trip to Kashmir on his literary style. Perhaps if Ernst had seen, or been able to visualize, the mountain kingdom to which his brother travelled that summer, he would have been less surprised by the sudden warmth and fluency of his writing.

Kashmir in the 1880s seemed, in many respects, unchanged since the days when Kalhana had written his *Chronicle*. Surrounded by lofty mountains, it was accessible from the Punjab only on foot or horseback and in winter was cut off by heavy snowfalls. The journey from Lahore lasted a week: by train to Rawalpindi, then along the road that passed through the hill-station of Murree, with a transfer at Baramula from tonga (a two-wheeled horse carriage) to boat. This last stage took the traveller past floating gardens and groves of chinars, or oriental planes, up the Jhelum River to Srinagar.

Few British visitors ventured there, preferring well-known and more convenient hill-stations for their holidays. Bordered to the north and east by the barren lands of Baltistan and Ladakh, the valley of Kashmir was an oasis of lakes and meadows within its protective circle of peaks. Fruit, flowers and crops grew in abundance; though its fertility belied the wretchedness suffered by its inhabitants during periods of oppressive rule. It had been occupied by a succession of foreigners, including tyrannical Afghans and Sikhs, and had only recently begun to experience settled conditions again under the Singh dynasty whom the British had recognized and supported in 1846, after receiving Gulab Singh's help in the defeat of the Sikhs. The government of Gulab Singh's grandson, Maharaja Sir Pratap Singh, was just beginning to introduce modern methods of administration after years of disorder and the devastation of famine in 1877. For a visitor in search of evidence of its past, Kashmir was a treasure-trove.[7]

Stein's first step on arriving in Srinagar was to visit the Governor, Dr Suraj Bal, to enlist his help in the acquisition of manuscripts. As a result of this meeting, he was introduced to Kashmir's pandits, the learned Hindus in whose families the traditions of philosophy, religion and Sanskrit literature had been handed down from generation to generation. He conversed with them in Sanskrit and soon gained their confidence. Within days he found himself attended, at his camp at Chinar Bagh on the edge of the town, by a stream of men eager to show him their manuscripts (and to sell them). This was a good start to his visit; and soon he received reports of the S'arada text of the *Rajatarangini* itself. But the owner who had refused Bühler permission to examine it had died, and the document had been divided – literally – among three of his heirs, none of whom was interested in letting Stein see their portion.

Any frustration Stein may have felt at this early rebuff, however, was dissipated by his enjoyment of Kashmir. The climate was a welcome relief from the oppressive heat of Lahore and the scenery reminded him of the Alps. He hired a tent in order to make a short tour in the mountains, and familiarized himself with enough of the Kashmiri dialect to be able to converse with Pir Baksh, his *shikari* (hunter) and guide, who was to remain a faithful attendant in later years. With the pandits in Srinagar he discussed the literature which their ancestors had known, and explored with them the monuments of that distant past which, crumbling and sometimes obscured by later Muslim accretions, still stood, nonetheless, as testimony to a history which the *Rajatarangini* could unravel.

It was an experience both satisfying and tantalizing. Stein was delighted by the beauty of the place and happy simply to be there. But at the same time he was impatient to find the manuscript which would reveal knowledge lost for so long, even to the pandits.

If the pandits inspired in Stein at least some of the affection for the valley which he felt during this first visit, one pandit in particular had greater influence still. It is not an exaggeration to say that Pandit Govind Kaul of Srinagar informed Stein's entire attitude to India and the East. Stein had been raised in a family in which warm, close relationships were normal, where admiration for the accomplishments of others was part of his education and where the paterfamilias figure of his uncle watched over him. When he met Pandit Govind Kaul in August 1888, he was young, far from his family and without close relationships of any kind. The friendship he formed with this erudite Brahmin filled many of the gaps in his new life.

The pandit was sixteen years older than Stein, scholarly, wise and honourable. Through association with another pandit family he had come into contact with the court, which had given him a breadth of knowledge and interests not always found among his peers. Moreover, he possessed what Stein later described as 'a power of humorous observation' which meant his erudition was never indigestible. The young academic was immediately attracted to him, and quickly came to regard him as a mentor, as well as a friend and colleague who understood and shared his interest in Kashmir.

When they met, Govind Kaul was without employment, having previously worked in the state translation department and as a teacher. By the time Stein left Kashmir in early October, he had arranged for the pandit to join him in Lahore to work on various Sanskrit manuscripts. It was the beginning of a partnership which lasted until Govind Kaul's death, nearly eleven years later.

Before he returned to Lahore and the university, Stein had an appointment in Jammu, the capital of Kashmir state which lies to the south of Srinagar, beyond the Pir Panjal mountain range. Thanks to his impeccable references, he was received by the Maharaja and his brother, Raja Amar Singh, who was Chief Minister, and from them gained permission to examine the manuscript collection in the library of the Raghunatha Temple.

The Maharaja's father had established the collection for the use of the Sanskrit school he had founded there; but it had not been shown to Bühler in 1875. It contained nearly 5,000 items and, after several days spent examining samples, Stein delightedly concluded that many of them were unknown in the West. His enthusiasm and knowledge impressed the Maharaja and his brother, and the following year the Jammu and Kashmir State Council sanctioned his compilation of a catalogue of the library's contents, at the state's own expense. Stein and his assistants, including Pandit Govind Kaul, carried out this work during the course of four years and the catalogue was published in 1894.

To secure such a project shortly after arriving in India was a considerable achievement for the young academic. This 'scientific work' as he always referred to it, to discriminate between it and his more mundane responsibilities in Lahore, would help to distinguish his name in academic circles at home in Europe. He returned to the cold-weather season in the Punjab in optimistic mood, knowing he could look forward to the company of the learned Govind Kaul during his spare hours over the months to come, and a return to Kashmir the following year.

———————◆◂——————

Stein was not to know that this first sojourn in Kashmir during the summer of 1888 was merely a foretaste of many years to come. But no doubt he caught a sense of the independence that was now his to develop as he pleased. The Aurel Stein who organized the visit to Kashmir, instigated a fresh search for manuscripts and undertook a hill-climbing tour, seemed a different person from the one who, as a frustrated student only a couple of years previously, had relied on others to present him with opportunities and had become depressed and disheartened when they failed to do so. In letters to Ernst in the late 1880s, Uncle Ignaz referred to Aurel as 'sedentary' and 'a hothouse plant'; but his image of his nephew was already outdated. Stein was no less of a scholar than he had been in Europe; but he was beginning to see possibilities beyond the end of his desk and recognize abilities in himself which the 'hothouse' atmosphere of his home surroundings had repressed. Now that the plant had been moved to the favourable climate of India, it was beginning to throw out new shoots.

One indication of this was the proposal he made to his brother on his return to Lahore, that the letters he had sent to Jaworzno describing his Kashmir visit might find a publisher in Germany or Hungary. Until recently, that sort of suggestion was more likely to have come from Ignaz. Ernst approved of the plan, now that he felt able to read his brother's accounts without wincing at his German grammar, and especially since the articles could not be presented to a newspaper without having first benefited from Ernst's own editorial pencil. But the project had not borne fruit when, on 12 May 1889, Stein received a telegram bearing the shocking and unexpected news that his father had died two days earlier.

Alone and thousands of miles from home, he could do nothing but transfer his grief to his letters. 'Forgive me, dearest uncle,' he wrote on 14 May after covering five pages with his distress, 'if I'm pouring out my pain to you; it's so difficult to grasp at all when the most bitter sorrow reaches one unexpectedly in a strange land.'[8] His first thought was of returning home. But Ignaz advised strongly against it, considering his nephew's original plan for the summer, of wandering in the mountains of Kashmir, a far better remedy. Stein accepted his advice. Meanwhile, between August and October 1889, his account of his 1888 visit appeared as a series in the Munich newspaper *Allgemeine Zeitung*, entitled 'Eine Ferienreise nach Srinagar' ('A Holiday Trip to Srinagar'). It was dedicated 'To the memory of his dearly beloved father who departed this earth in the distant homeland on 10 May 1889, in deep sorrow, by the author'.

The memory of his father accompanied Stein into Kashmir that summer. But whereas in Lahore he dwelt on the 'catastrophe' of his loss, now he drew consolation from the serenity of Kashmir's landscape and the vividness of its history. Later in his life, he often mentioned the profound solace he derived from remote places where he felt 'in touch' with the past.

Since leaving Kashmir the previous October, Stein had been trying to gain permission to see the divided *Rajatarangini* manuscript. Towards the end of 1888, he approached the father of one of his pupils at Oriental College who was a pandit and member of the Kashmir State Council and, with his support, was able at last to win the owners' confidence and borrow the 326 precious leaves that made up the eight books of Kalhana's *Chronicle*.

In the notes to his translation of the *Rajatarangini*, Stein wrote that his own repeated attempts and negotiations 'proved fruitless but were instructive to me in a small way of the methods of eastern diplomacy'. This was a lesson he learnt carefully. Without that sensitivity for 'eastern diplomacy', which he proved to have in abundance, he would undoubtedly have been less successful in his later expeditions and would probably have failed entirely to secure his best-known and most controversial haul. While such skills could seem calculating and self-serving, they also demonstrated genuine empathy: the more he learnt about a region's past, the more intuitive his ability to communicate with its people.

With the *Chronicle* temporarily in his possession, Stein could at last begin work. He planned first to produce a critical edition of the Sanskrit text (published in 1892 under the patronage of the Kashmir Durbar) and then to prepare something more ambitious. Georg Bühler gave him the only extra encouragement he needed for the latter when he told him that a new edition was 'indispensably required' and that he hoped to see Stein complete it as soon as possible.[9]

Stein's work on Kalhana's *Chronicle of the Kings of Kasmir* was to occupy much of his spare time for the next decade (during which period he learnt of the deaths of both Bühler and his revered 'master', von Roth). When he was not occupied with official duties in Lahore during term-time, or working with Pandit Govind Kaul and other assistants on the catalogue of the Jammu library, he and Govind Kaul pored over the manuscript together. When university and college closed during the hot weather, he travelled to Kashmir where he spent weeks at a time on topographical peregrinations, verifying Kalhana's descriptions of buildings and geographical features, extracting useful information as he went from conversations with local people well-versed in the traditional lore of Kashmir, and amassing an encyclopaedic knowledge of the valley. The result was a translation of the text into English complete with commentary, notes, geographical memoir and maps, which finally appeared in two volumes in 1900, and which is still consulted by scholars today, nearly a century later.

———————◆ ◀———————

During this period, Stein studied another source of information which was later to become a familiar name to anyone who followed his expeditions and read his books. This was Hiuen Tsiang (Xuanzang), the seventh-century Chinese Buddhist monk who travelled across Central Asia to India and whose account of those travels had been translated into French in the mid-nineteenth century.[10]

Hiuen Tsiang set off in AD 629, aged 27, in order to visit the country in which his faith had originated and to collect Sanskrit texts of Buddhist teachings and philosophy. After a remarkable journey across Chinese Turkestan and through what is now northern Afghanistan, he reached Kashmir by 'crossing over mountains and treading along precipices'.[11] There he stayed for two years in order to study under an eminent Buddhist philosopher, before travelling through the Punjab to Bodhgaya, where the Buddha is said to have achieved enlightenment. He then spent several years at a monastery nearby.

On his return to China in 645, the relics and books which he had brought home were paraded through the streets of the capital and Hiuen Tsiang settled down, under the patronage of the Emperor, with a team of assistants to twenty years of translation work. One task which he completed shortly after his return was a description of his travels; and it was this work, known as the *Record of the Western Regions*, which became a permanent source of inspiration for Stein and a constant companion on his travels in Central Asia.

He had encountered Hiuen Tsiang's *Record* while still a student, for this and similar accounts of India by other Chinese Buddhist monks were the only available record of India's early history. But it was not until he reached the East that its extraordinary topographical accuracy became clear, and it was in Kashmir that he first had the opportunity to put its descriptions to the test. He described Hiuen Tsiang as his 'Buddhist Pausanius': and to the many who were then familiar with classical history and the importance in historical topography of the *Itinerary* of Greece written by the second-century antiquary, Pausanius, no more graphic a description was necessary.

Now that he was in north-west India, Stein became increasingly aware of the Buddhist element of its history. Hiuen Tsiang's factual descriptions of the landscape and people he encountered there during the seventh century told of Buddhist civilizations in decay. But only a few centuries before his time the area had been at the heart of a dynamic Buddhist culture. First promoted there in the third century BC by the Mauryan king Ashoka, whose empire stretched from Bengal to the Hindu Kush, Buddhism had also been adopted by subsequent rulers of this part of the subcontinent. Bactrians swept in from north-western Afghanistan not long after Ashoka's death, and they were followed by the Scythians or Sakas from Central Asia, by Parthians and by the Kushans.

The extent of the kingdoms of these conquerors varied from century to century but all included the Peshawar valley, known then as Gandhara. Under the Kushan king Kanishka, who ruled during the first century AD from his capital at what is now Peshawar, Gandhara became the centre of a flourishing Buddhist culture. Monasteries and stupas sprang up and were still there, neglected and dilapidated, when Hiuen Tsiang passed through five hundred years later.

Besides lying in the path of successive waves of invaders, Gandhara also straddled trade routes linking the East with the Mediterranean. Its history was densely layered and historians and linguists in the West had only recently begun to understand its complexity. Stein had as good a grounding as any orientalist; but that merely emphasized the limitations of his learning. Here in Gandhara itself, however, he was introduced not merely to the past that he knew from books, but to the material legacy of that past.

The Buddhist art of Gandhara gave tangible expression to the fusion of cultures from East and West which had taken place there. It drew together the strands of Stein's interests and stimulated a curiosity in him which would lead him to the deserts of Central Asia and their forgotten history. For it demonstrated the assimilation of Greek art forms with Eastern culture to an astonishing degree. The Bactrians who conquered Gandhara in the second century BC included men of Greek descent, heirs of men whom Alexander had left behind. Though remote from their homeland and intermingled with the native population of Bactria, they preserved their artistic traditions and adapted them to the demands of Buddhist statuary, friezes and temples. The beauty and vigour of this art reached their apogee later, during the dynamic Kushan era, gracing thousands of buildings throughout the region.

Stein had not yet seen the remains of those buildings that still stood in the northern hills of Gandhara. But he had his first taste of their delights when he encountered the contents of the 'Wonder House' of Lahore, the Central Museum, described here by Anglo-India's most famous literary son:

> In the entrance-hall stood the larger figures of the Greco-Buddhist sculptures done, savants know how long since, by forgotten workmen whose hands were feeling, and not unskilfully, for the mysteriously transmitted Grecian touch. There were hundreds of pieces, friezes of figures in relief, fragments of statues and slabs crowded with figures that had encrusted the brick walls of the Buddhist stupas and viharas of the North Country and now, dug up and labelled, made the pride of the Museum.[12]

Thus did Rudyard Kipling describe, in his novel *Kim*, the museum whose curator was his father, John Lockwood Kipling. Lockwood, depicted in the novel as white-bearded, wise and gentle, with an innate understanding of Buddhism, had come to Lahore in 1875 to take up the dual position of Principal of the Mayo School of Art and Curator of the newly established museum. Stein met him soon after arriving in Lahore, by which time Lockwood Kipling, then aged 51, had been in the Punjab long enough to have become an authority on Gandharan art. He willingly shared his knowledge with his young friend.

During Stein's early years in India, when he had few friends, he spent many evenings with the Kiplings: perhaps the warmth of their household reminded him of home. Rudyard Kipling had left India in the year that Stein arrived, but the parents remained until 1893. By then, Stein had formed, through them, a friendship which would last the rest of his life.

In 1890, a young vice-principal called Fred Henry Andrews joined Lockwood Kipling at the School of Art. He was a friend of Rudyard in London and the son of a printer and publisher, Arliss Andrews. His younger brother, George Arliss, became a well-known actor, while he himself trained in the studio of a stained glass craftsman. He was an intelligent, personable artist, enthusiastic on the subject of handicrafts and industrial design and possessed of an appreciative eye for form which complemented Stein's archaeological approach to objects.

The two young men met at the Kiplings' house early in 1890 and were destined to remain friends for fifty years. By early May they were planning a short archaeological expedition to Murti, in the Salt Range of the Punjab, where Stein had discovered a Jain temple during his winter vacation which he had identified as one mentioned by Hiuen Tsiang. With what was already becoming his customary efficiency, Stein approached the authorities, armed with a letter of support from Bühler, and obtained a grant of Rs 500. At the same time as the civil servants in his hotel were leaving for Simla (where the Punjab state secretariat, like the Government of India, spent the summer months), he and Andrews set out for the hills.

Stein told his brother that Andrews was 'an assistant whom an archaeologist in India would find it difficult to match'.[13] The two worked together: while one excavated 'marvellous ornaments, capitals and architraves', the other took photographs of the finds, delighting in the richness of their forms. It was on this trip that Andrews initiated his friend into the art of photography, which Stein was later to use to such effect on his major expeditions.

Here, also, both witnessed the way in which India's ancient monuments were gradually being destroyed, for the sculpted stones on the site were being removed by contractors who found them useful in the construction of a nearby railway bridge. Stein later saw the same thing happening in Kashmir and used his acquaintance with the Maharaja to make a plea for the preservation of the kingdom's antiquities.

After Fred Andrews' death in 1957, an obituarist claimed that Stein adopted oriental archaeology and exploration as his main interests as a result of Andrews' influence. But this seems unlikely. Andrews had no training in the history or languages of Asian civilizations, and met Stein long after the influences of the latter's youth had already drawn him to the East. Undeniably, however, he proved an enthusiastic, supportive and devoted assistant, helping to equip his friend's expeditions and spending long periods of his career compiling catalogues of the finds brought back from Central Asia. His initial excitement over the classically influenced temple at Murti no doubt led him to encourage his friend in other, similar projects, and such encouragement was bound to be valuable to a young man just embarking on original research.

Perhaps the fact that he was younger than Stein (he was born in 1866) and admired his talents also boosted the latter's confidence. Certainly it seems a little precocious of Stein at this early date to describe himself by implication, in his letter to his brother, as an archaeologist. His university studies in Europe might be said to have prepared him for archaeology, in so far as anyone received such preparation – for archaeology did not exist as an academic discipline and the only training was in the field. But his expeditions so far in India had been limited to topographical observation. Nevertheless, he was no less qualified for the work than many others who excavated sites elsewhere at the same period. He had, in fact, been considering gaining more practical experience by applying for a position as archaeological surveyor, though the low pay discouraged him.

The salary was an indication of the cautious approach to archaeology in India at the time. The Government of India first formed an Archaeological Department in 1862 and appointed General (later Sir) Alexander Cunningham as its Director. His task was to make a record of ancient remains and, initially, the project went well. His role was redefined in 1871 as Director-General of the Archaeological Survey of India and he produced twenty-three volumes of reports covering the same number of years of work.

But the repair of ancient monuments was not part of his brief and local governments, whose responsibility it was, were rarely inclined to take it seriously. The combined lack of will, funds and staff soon rendered India's meagre archaeological authorities ineffectual: the Director-General who succeeded Cunningham in 1885 resigned in 1889, only one or two archaeological surveyors remained in their posts and no one produced any reports of value after 1885.

Had the classically trained European scholars of the time found more to their liking in the art and architecture of India as a whole, the fact that the country had no organized survey department would have been less significant. Her monuments would have attracted wealthy amateur archaeologists and the sort of attention that the excavations of Heinrich Schliemann at Troy and Mycenae, for example, were enjoying in Europe at the time. But the incomprehensible and disconcerting sculpture of Hindu temples repelled some, and bored others. They preferred the familiar territory of Greece and Rome, and the legacy of the Old and New Testaments. Insofar as his interests in the art of northwest India sprang from his fascination with Greek influence there, Stein clearly belonged to that same cultural tradition. But the spirit of enquiry was to lead him far from conventional paths.

During the early 1890s, however, his thoughts still concentrated on finding a position back in Europe. On home leave for the first time in 1890, he took the *Chronicle* manuscript with him as visible evidence of his achievement. During the crossing to England from Ostend, where he visited Helene, his sister's daughter, it nearly met a watery end. The porter carrying the box which contained it dropped his load overboard into Ostend harbour. It was retrieved with difficulty but the manuscript, despite being soaked, dried without a trace of its immersion. It was a narrow escape from what would have been a singularly inappropriate end: for it is part of the creed of the Brahmin caste (to which the owners of the manuscript belonged) that they should not travel across water. Had Stein been of a superstitious nature, he might well have been unsettled by the incident. His brother Ernst, on the other hand, was irritated by what he saw as an irresponsible attitude to other people's property, and by the fact that Aurel's luggage was not insured.

Stein returned to India in October, leaving his uncle feeling lonely in Budapest. It was the last time they would see each other, for Ignaz died the following year, on 11 November 1891. The loss of this father-figure intensified Stein's own feelings of loneliness which often surfaced in his letters during the next few years. Despite his friendship with Andrews and a few others (including a spinster, Miss Francis, who was an inspector of schools), despite social events and evenings at the Punjab Club, Stein continued to lead an essentially solitary life. He sent photographs and descriptions home to Ernst and Jetty, and told them of continuing frustrations with his work and his efforts to save money. He went on solitary trips to sites and monuments; and he spent his thirtieth birthday in 1892 sitting in the grounds of one of Lahore's Mogul monuments reading Horace and the French nineteenth-century literary critic, Sainte-Beuve. His self-sufficiency gave the impression that he was content with his own company. But he missed knowing that there were one or two close relatives nearby – or friends who could replace them – to whom he could return from his wanderings.

A pattern soon evolved to the year. During term-time Stein worked conscientiously at the university and college, revelling in the cold of winter while others sat in overcoats in front of their fires. Like other Europeans, he felt far less comfortable in the sweltering heat that built up before the rains arrived, or during the monsoon when floods covered parts of the city, the atmosphere was muggy and there were infestations of ants, lizards and frogs. Summers in Kashmir became the high point of his year.

He was never content with his positions in Lahore. His letters to Ernst often mention his dissatisfaction and he soon began to apply for other posts: a professorship in Bombay in 1890 and an inspectorship of schools in 1892, neither time with success. His apparent lack of commitment to his job, however, did not prevent him from making strenuous efforts to secure a salary increase (from an initial Rs 700 to Rs 1,000 per month), an extended contract, longer furloughs and pension rights (the latter being a particular concern, since he was outside the Indian Education Service and its pension arrangements).

Nor did it, apparently, impair his efficiency. When Sir William Rattigan resigned as Vice-Chancellor of the University in 1895, he recorded his satisfaction in a testimonial for Stein's benefit, writing that he 'displayed great business capacity, marked ability, and considerable tact and judgment in dealing with men and things. When he joined us everything was more or less in a chaotic condition, and he has helped me always in the task of reorganization with a zeal and devotion which I cannot praise too highly.'[14]

This organizational ability was a characteristic that nobody who knew Stein could fail to notice. His belongings were always tidy, his books and papers filed and catalogued, the letters he received annotated according to the date received and the points to be made in reply. Indeed, there was something almost obsessive about the way in which everything was kept, not haphazardly, as if he were simply reluctant to throw anything away, but deliberately, as a record to which he could refer at any time. The papers he left at his death ranged from reports on his expeditions to sheaves of his cook's accounts and lists of the recipients of letters written fifty years earlier.

Comments in his letters over the years testify to his love of domestic order, whether he was living in the Charing Cross Hotel, college rooms in Oxford or in a tent in the mountains of Kashmir. They help to explain how he was able later to set about, practically single-handed, the enormous task of preparing for his first, year-long expedition. And where that desire for order faltered in the face of wearisome responsibilities, such as the sorting of archaeological finds in uncongenial surroundings, the powerful sense of duty inculcated in him since childhood took over.

———————➤ ◄———————

Stein's life was not entirely one of solitary study and lonely vacations. Despite the fact that he was not gregarious, he made friendships during his years in Lahore that lasted all his life. The earliest friend of all seems to have been Edward Maclagan (1864–1952), a member of the élite Indian Civil Service, who was destined to become Governor of the Punjab in the early 1920s. Born in the Punjab, he first met Stein in Oxford in 1886 and was living in the Charing Cross Hotel when Stein arrived in Lahore. Though the two men saw comparatively little of each other in later life, Maclagan was always a staunch supporter and admirer of his friend's achievements.

Another friend from these early days in India who won Stein's lasting affection was a good-humoured young officer in the Indian Army, Lionel Dunsterville (1865–1946). He had been at school in Westward Ho! with Rudyard Kipling and was the model for the character Stalky in Kipling's tale based on their schooldays, *Stalky and Co*. When Dunsterville invited a Hungarian aristocrat of his acquaintance, Sigismund de Justh, to India, de Justh, apparently rather taken aback by the hearty character of Anglo-Indian club life, sought refuge with Stein. Dunsterville later wrote in his memoirs that de Justh then introduced him to Stein 'with a view that when he should have returned to Hungary, I should have some influence to counterbalance the rougher side of my character'.[15]

Stein made many acquaintances, both civilians and military men, over the years and probably seemed to them a strange figure. He was not anti-social, visiting the Club and observing the many unwritten rules of Anglo-Indian social etiquette with his customary care. But his regard for his pandit friend and the hours he spent with him at work on the Sanskrit manuscripts of Kashmir marked him out as something of an oddity; as Lockwood Kipling and his sharp, witty wife, while popular, were considered 'artistic' – in other words, eccentric – because of their enthusiasm for the early Buddhist art of the region.

In October 1894, Stein made a change in his living arrangements which brought him closer to English friends than he had been so far in India, and thus influenced his plans for the future. At his own suggestion, he moved into the spare rooms in the house which Fred Andrews – now Principal of the art school and Curator of the museum – occupied with his wife and small daughter (house-sharing being common practice in India).

Mayo Lodge, as it was called after a former viceroy, was a large bungalow quietly situated on the western edge of Lahore near the Ravi River and the Mogul monument, Anarkali's Tomb. Stein had a bedroom, bathroom and sitting-room on the west side of the house overlooking the garden. The relaxed and friendly atmosphere of the house and the company of gentle, educated and academically minded friends gave him his first sense of a home in India.

The other 'home' which he came across for the first time the following summer in Kashmir, was of a different kind. Though it offered no European companions, it gave spiritual satisfaction of a kind Stein could not find on the plains and perhaps had experienced nowhere else, not even at home in Hungary. For he was now no longer simply the youngest member of a family far away; he was a man of 32, single, independent, in need of a separate identity. The weeks he spent in the summer of 1895 encamped on Mohand Marg, an alpine summer pasture 11,000 feet above sea-level, sowed the seeds of a desire for its tranquillity and purity which would bring him back year after year, until the name of the meadow became synonymous with that of its summer visitor.

Mohand Marg (*marg* meaning an alpine grazing ground) lay hidden in the mountains to the north of Srinagar, about fifteen miles along the road to Leh from the town. A steep path led from the road through a number of small hillside settlements and fields, then up past rocky crags. Above these, the *marg* opened out across the mountainside, giving views of the Sind valley far below in one direction and the Vale of Kashmir in the other. Massive, snow-bound peaks dwarfed the distant rivers and lakes. Trees skirted the *marg* and clothed the slopes below, flowers filled it in summer and rocky outcrops hung above it.

Snow usually prevented Stein from arriving before the first days of June, and by mid-October the onset of winter forced him unwillingly down to the valley again. He always took with him enough tents and equipment to support himself, his small retinue of servants and the occasional visitor. Supplies were brought regularly from Srinagar. Sometimes the *marg* was enlivened by *gujars*, or shepherds, who brought their animals to the summer grass. Otherwise it remained Stein's private world where he could be at peace: alone but never lonely. He called it his kingdom, and he loved it with a devotion that could scarcely have been matched by any king.

During the early summer of 1895 and again in 1896, Stein spent longer than usual in Kashmir. In order to work on his translated edition of the *Chronicle* he obtained extra leave from the university, and his correspondence at this time makes it clear that he was pinning his hopes for a European post on the publication of the book. Printing must be completed by the autumn of 1897, he told his publishers Constable, for it was then that the eleventh International Congress of Orientalists would be held at Paris. He had another furlough due in 1897, and he meant to be there.

At the same time, the attractions of the East increased little by little. He was so engrossed in his work that perhaps he did not notice the way in which India, his friends and his summers in Kashmir in particular were subtly changing his life. In 1896 he found time to take down the Kashmiri folktales recited by a professional storyteller, Hatim Tilawon, in order to record the language of the Sind valley and its folklore. And in the same year he acquired a dog, a fox-terrier called Dash. Ostensibly this was to keep rats away from the Mohand Marg camp, but Dash quickly became an indispensable companion, travelling everywhere with his master and enlivening otherwise lonely periods with antics which Stein described affectionately in letters. Animals had played no part in Stein's urban upbringing, but perhaps he had been influenced by his old friend Lockwood Kipling, who wrote in his own book, *Beast and Man in India* (1891), that 'the companionship of a good dog will teach more effectively than the words of any philosopher'.

Shortly before he was due to take his furlough in 1897, Stein became involved in new research when a fellow-scholar arrived from France. The influence of the French on Indian and oriental studies was formative: it was they who first translated the travelogues of Hiuen Tsiang and other early Buddhist pilgrims to India. Stein was to become a close colleague of the Sinologists who worked on these translations, including

Sylvain Lévi and Edouard Chavannes. But in 1896 it was Alfred Foucher whom he met.

Stein and Foucher had corresponded, and Foucher had recently come to India to study Gandharan art, accompanied by his aunt, Mme Michel. Stein joined them to travel north to Swat, the ancient land of Udyana which Alexander the Great had subdued on his way from Bactria to the Indus. Swat was now a border district in the sensitive area between British India and Afghanistan, under the command of Major Harold Deane. But Deane was an enthusiastic amateur epigraphist, as well as a political officer, who knew that the valley was full of as yet undeciphered inscriptions and many Buddhist remains.

Stein had time on this short trip only to recognize that there was much to be learnt from the Swat valley. He was due to leave for Europe in a few months' time, to try to arrange a move that would take him far from the Indian subcontinent. It was not the time to be contemplating further tours on the North-West Frontier; nor to be enjoying too much the company of his friends at Mayo Lodge or the blissful serenity of his Kashmir mountain retreat. And yet these things were in the back of his mind as he set out for Europe yet again.

3

Ambition Finds a Way

───────────◆───────────

Y THE TIME Stein reached Europe in 1897, far older and stranger
manuscripts than the one he had traced in Kashmir had found their
way to India. They came from the remote region of Chinese Central
Asia, where once the Silk Road had run between rich oasis settlements.
In 1890 a British army officer called Lieutenant Bower arrived in
Kucha, an oasis town on the northern edge of the Taklamakan Desert,
in search of the murderer of another British traveller.[1] While there he
was offered an ancient birch-bark manuscript, which he bought and
sent to the Asiatic Society of Bengal in Calcutta. It was examined and
eventually deciphered by Rudolf Hoernle, a noted philologist and
Principal of the city's Madrasah, or Muslim college.

Hoernle recognized the language on the birch-bark leaves as
Sanskrit, written in the Indian Brahmi script in about the fifth century
AD. He published his findings in 1891, and they sent a ripple of excitement through orientalist circles. For the birch-bark leaves which Bower
had bought – henceforward known as the Bower Manuscript – were not
only far older than any other known Indian document; they were also
evidence of the spread of Indian influence into the old, pre-Muslim
civilization of Chinese Central Asia, all trace of which scholars had
assumed lost.

Two years after Bower's find, a Moravian missionary in Leh called
Weber bought other, similar manuscripts, this time of paper, and sent

these, too, to Hoernle. More were bought by the Russian Consul in Kashgar, the most westerly oasis town in Chinese Turkestan, and sent to St Petersburg. It later became clear that all these manuscripts had been found at the same site, a ruined Buddhist monastery near Kucha. Hoernle appreciated the potential importance of his position as the recipient and interpreter of these documents but recognized also the possibility that the Russians, ever in competition with the British, might try to siphon off any finds in the direction of their own scholars. He therefore persuaded the Government of India to encourage its agents to buy manuscripts wherever possible and to send them to him. As a result, he soon accumulated enough material in Calcutta to be able to form what he called the British Collection of Central Asian Antiquities.

Rudolf Hoernle had spent most of his life in India. He was born at Agra in 1841, the son of an ordained member of the Church Missionary Society, and began his career at Benares as a professor of philosophy after attending university at Basle and studying Sanskrit in London. Early work for the Asiatic Society of Bengal established his reputation as a philologist and this was further boosted when he deciphered a birch-bark manuscript from the North-West Frontier.

It was while he was in Vienna during 1886, to give a paper on that manuscript at the International Congress of Orientalists, that he and Stein first met. Stein kept in touch with Hoernle's work through the journals of the Asiatic Society of Bengal. So at the time he returned to Europe in 1897 for the International Congress in Paris, he knew that Hoernle was hard at work trying to decipher the latest batch of manuscripts to have reached the British Collection as a result of his demand for material from Chinese Turkestan.

These had been sent by the British representative in Kashgar, George Macartney. Once it was known in the region that Macartney would buy antiquities, he had been supplied with a stream of items by local treasure-hunters eager for reimbursement. The latest manuscripts, said to have been found in the Taklamakan near Khotan, a town to the south of the desert, were written in unknown characters and were proving a far harder nut to crack than the earlier finds.

At the same time as Hoernle was labouring over the Macartney documents, yet another manuscript came to light which assumed greater significance for Stein than any of the other finds. It too consisted of fragments of birch-bark and had recently been found among

the papers of Jules Dutreuil de Rhins, a French explorer who had travelled through Chinese Turkestan and had been murdered by villagers in
eastern Tibet in 1894.[2] Unlike the Bower and Weber manuscripts,
however, these leaves contained writing in Kharosthi, the ancient script
of north-west India which, with Brahmi, was used in the third century
BC edicts of Ashoka.

Both scripts had been deciphered some fifty years earlier by James
Prinsep, an official of the Calcutta Mint. But Kharosthi was so far
known only in inscriptions and coins: no manuscript using its alpha-
bet had ever been found. Nor was this the only significant fact about
these birch-bark leaves. The French scholars who deciphered them
found that they contained a sacred Buddhist text written in the Pali
dialect of northern India, the language favoured as a medium for
teaching by the Buddha, and that they probably dated from a period
no later than the second century AD. They, too, had been found near
Khotan, once an important centre along the trading route between
China and the West.

Here was clear evidence of the diffusion of the Buddhist culture of
Gandhara into the old Silk Road cities of Chinese Central Asia. Scholars
had known for some time, from French translations of the early
Chinese pilgrims such as Hiuen Tsiang, that Buddhist communities had
existed in the region. But they had had no inkling that evidence of those
communities still remained, nor that the languages and scripts of northern India had travelled intact through the formidable mountain ranges
separating Gandhara from that vast desert tract to the north.

Stein was gripped by the implications of the desert discoveries. He
had seen for himself the legacy of Gandharan culture in the ruins of the
Punjab and the North-West Frontier. With images of Graeco-Buddhist
art in his mind, he realized that the desert might yield much more than
simply manuscripts. He was also growing increasingly suspicious of the
mysterious Macartney manuscripts to which Hoernle was devoting so
much time.

An idea came to him, improbable at first but which quickly developed, for an expedition to that remote northern desert which would
apply Western methods of investigation to its sites and test the truth of
the native treasure-seekers' claims. He had as many qualifications for
such work as any orientalist: the right philological background,
first-hand knowledge of the art and inscriptions of Gandhara and a

decade's experience of detective work in historical topography among the mountains of Kashmir. Why should he himself not undertake such an expedition?

A paper given at the 1897 International Congress by the French scholar M.E. Senart on the Dutreuil de Rhins manuscript only fuelled his determination. He tentatively discussed his idea with fellow orientalists, and particularly with his old teacher, Georg Bühler. There was one element of the plan, however, which neither man could properly assess, and that was the country itself, the desolate deserts and mountains of Chinese Central Asia.

———————▶ ◀

The region known in Stein's day as Eastern or Chinese Turkestan, and later as Sinkiang, had been ruled by the Chinese for centuries. But it lay thousands of miles from the centre of power and its people were of Turkish, rather than Chinese, origin. The Buddhist pilgrims who wrote of their journeys westward across its parched and forbidding landscape from the fifth century AD onward, in search of the origins of their faith in India, were concerned mainly with shrines and points of doctrine. They mentioned only briefly the oases that fringed the Taklamakan Desert, the thriving monasteries there and the cities that had already been swallowed by the encroaching sand.

Consequently, little was known about the lost civilization of the Silk Road, which had once passed along the northern and southern edges of the desert. Modern accounts of the area were rare, since few travellers ventured into such inhospitable terrain. However, Anglo-Russian rivalry and the expansion of the Russian Empire eastwards had recently focused attention on the region. In particular there was interest in its western boundary, where the extremities of India, Afghanistan, Russia and China collided in the massive Pamir mountain range.

Since 1890, a British representative, George Macartney, had been stationed at Kashgar in the far west of Chinese Turkestan. Officially his role was 'Special Assistant to the Resident in Kashmir for Chinese Affairs', but in practical terms this meant keeping an eye on the activities of the powerful Russian Consul there, Nikolai Petrovsky. It was through Macartney that Hoernle had added to his Central Asian collection. Several European explorers had also recently been in the area: the unfortunate Dutreuil de Rhins with his companion, Fernand Grenard;

an English army officer called Captain H.H.P. Deasy; and, most important of all from Stein's point of view, an intrepid Swedish geographer,
Sven Hedin.

Hedin had first encountered the Taklamakan Desert in 1895, when
he nearly lost his life in its empty, waterless expanses. In the following
year he was taken by local guides to the site of a ruined city in the desert
north-east of Khotan, where he found not only the remains of buildings, orchards and avenues preserved in the sand, but also Buddhist
stucco figures and wall-paintings. Hedin was no archaeologist but he
realized that he had been brought to one of the old cities of the Silk
Road and that, in the brief time he spent at the site, he had already seen
more evidence of a lost civilization than any scholar in the West had
dreamed existed.

The first reports of his travels and finds appeared in the Journal of
the Royal Geographical Society. Stein scanned the Journal for news of
these and other explorations, including those of Deasy and a party of
Russians, and added them to the store of information he was accumulating as he developed his idea.

At the same time, however, he had to consider the work to which he
had dedicated the past nine years and his ambitions in Europe. He could
not afford to abandon the latter simply because of an extraordinary plan
which might come to nothing. His hope that the two-volume
Rajatarangini would be off the presses in time for the 1897 Congress was
disappointed (it was not published until 1900); but he was able to give
Congress members an advance copy of the first volume, paying full
tribute to Bühler's part in it as he did so. He also saw his uncle's old
friend, Ármin Vámbéry, the Professor of Oriental Languages at
Budapest. And through him it seemed, at last, that a career in Europe
was about to materialize. Vámbéry told him he was planning to propose
the creation of a new chair in Indo-Iranian philology at Budapest
specifically for Stein's benefit.

By the time he returned to India early in October 1897, therefore,
Stein knew he was well on the way to realizing the ambition which had
preoccupied him since early youth, and which had long been his
brother's hope. Before the following spring was out, he would know
whether he was to become a university professor in his home town.

And yet he found himself happy to be back in the East. Before travelling to the Punjab, he spent a few days on an archaeological tour in Kathiawar (a region of princely states north of Bombay) with the scholar Sylvain Lévi, who had worked on the manuscripts brought back by Dutreuil de Rhins. Back in Lahore, he felt so settled that he soon began to doubt the wisdom of leaving India. The imminence of change suddenly cast his youthful ambition in a less attractive light. A decade away had given him a different perspective on the Western cities he had once frequented and on the life an academic would lead there.

Budapest had grown into a big, bustling metropolis with double the number of buildings it had had during his childhood, many grand boulevards, huge new railway termini and the largest stock exchange in Europe. There were new river walls and quays, new bridges, even the royal palace on Buda Hill was being rebuilt. Vienna, Paris, London, all had seen an explosion of growth. Though he was a sophisticated child of mainland Europe, Stein had become used to a different way of life during his first years of independent adulthood and one which suited his temperament. The simple pleasures of summer camps in the mountains had developed a new side to his character.

Moreover, there were clouds on the political horizon in the Austro-Hungarian Empire for anyone of Jewish origin, even if he were baptized and middle-class. Assimilation was proving no shield against bigotry. The urbane Jews of Vienna and Budapest who dominated the world of finance, many professions and much of cultural life, were the objects of anti-Semitic agitation just as their co-religionists were who continued to move westward from the ghettoes of Russia and the eastern edges of the empire. In 1883, when Jews were accused of murdering a Christian peasant girl in eastern Hungary, there had been riots in Budapest and Uncle Ignaz had told Ernst that he preferred not to consider what might happen to Aurel in the future. Things had been calmer since then, but in Vienna the Christian Socialist party was growing powerful with its anti-Semitic, anti-patrician manifesto.[3]

By comparison India, despite occasional tensions, seemed a gentler place, where Stein felt socially at ease. And when he returned to Mayo Lodge in early November 1897 and met its new occupant, Percy Stafford Allen, his attachment to Lahore only increased.

P. S. Allen arrived in Lahore from England in the spring of 1897 and, like Stein, lived first in the Charing Cross Hotel. Then Andrews and his wife, Alice, invited him to move to Mayo Lodge, where he occupied Stein's rooms while the latter was away on leave. He was 28 years old and had just been appointed Professor of History at the Government College in Lahore. He was one of those who were in India for want of the right opportunity at home: he would have been happy to settle in Oxford from the day he graduated from Corpus Christi College. Gentle, unworldly and studious, he already knew that he wanted to devote his life's work to collecting and editing the letters of Erasmus. But he had no private means at the time and no fellowship from his college, so he took to teaching, initially at Magdalen College School in Oxford.

There was an austerity about him which no doubt made him difficult to know. As one of his pupils later recalled, however, 'there was nothing more delightful than the way in which this manner of his used to melt into everything that was human to those who were privileged to be his friends'.[4] He was regarded by those friends as the most faithful and selfless of men. Stein, never likely to be discouraged by mere austerity, quickly warmed to this serious but sympathetic newcomer. Far from his family environment in Hungary and unsure where to put down his own roots, he was ready for the warmth and affection of a close friendship – something he had not yet experienced. His devotion to Allen and later, by extension, to his wife, developed quickly and remained one of the most important features in his life.

The convivial life which Andrews, Allen, Stein and, later, others led at Mayo Lodge is vividly described in letters which Allen's cousin, Helen Mary Allen, wrote to her mother when she visited Mayo Lodge in 1897–8. Helen Allen was not only Allen's cousin but also his fiancée – indeed, the two were related even more closely than most cousins, since their mothers were sisters and their fathers were brothers. In later years, Helen's personality seemed to merge with that of her husband. But at the time of her trip to India, she was a lively, intelligent, fairly conventional girl from a closely knit family, fresh from England and keen to report all her experiences to her mother. She was unnerved by the 'sea of dark faces' round her at railway stations, dismayed by her Anglo-Indian brother Basil's plans to travel home second-class, and comforted by the fact that the Mayo Lodge 'chummery' – as shared, mainly bachelor, houses were called – was better equipped than many, having good glass, china and table linen. But she was also enthusiastic about and fascinated by India; and she was delighted to find her fiancé in good company.

'This varied house-hold seem to live in great peace & harmony & Perkle [one of several nicknames she used for Percy Allen] really is fond of them,' she wrote. It was 'so refreshing in the midst of Anglo-Indian society to meet people with such an exceptional amount of furniture to their brains'.[5] Her mother had made some remark about the young bachelor Stein in connection with the imminent arrival in India of Percy's sister, Catherine; but Helen told her that Dr Stein was 'a bright active little man with vigour enough for 10 giants & a fund of learning, not at all the sort who would think twice of any girl he met'.

To judge from her descriptions, the Andrews coped less well with life in India than Stein. 'Mrs Andrews is small & neat & sallow looking as though she has been much tried by the climate for her hair is quite gray though she cannot be very old. Her whole heart is wrapped up in her little girl [Nora] who is at home & the poor mother does nothing but talk of her. He is also dark & small & sallow, with many gray hairs & a very quiet manner.'

Helen went riding with Percy and later with Stein, who showed her a variety of sights on the outskirts of Lahore and regaled her with their history. One of his favourite social activities was a picnic, especially when he organized it himself, and the one he gave at Shahdara, the tomb of the Mogul emperor Jahangir, was a particular success. Helen noted his 'love of & capacity for making arrangements & everything was done in a delightful style. The little man himself rode out in the early morning to see all was ready' and the guests arrived later, seating themselves on cushions round a cloth spread across the balcony of the tomb.

There were other entertainments: tennis parties (which Stein joined reluctantly), walks and rides in the cool of the evening, and badminton tournaments which Percy's sister, Catherine, enjoyed when she came out. She and Helen went as Stein's guests to Ladies' Night at the Club, and with Percy hosted a dinner party at Mayo Lodge which was judged a triumph. When Stein heard that Percy and Helen were hoping to go to Kashmir, he offered to show them the places of historic interest, or to provide them with a detailed itinerary and the services of Pir Baksh, since Percy was 'far too kind' to manage coolies all by himself. 'Dr Stein is most amusing', Helen commented, '& evidently thinks it quite unnecessary for Perkle & me to need a chaperone, which I call a sensible view of the case.'

Shortly afterwards, Helen met Thomas and May Arnold – 'the Tommies', as Percy called them – a couple who had recently come to Lahore and were later to move into Mayo Lodge. She found him charming, 'but his outer man is so peculiar that I had not time to get over it. He is short & small in every way, save for gigantic teeth which protrude like a walrus'. Add to this that he has a mass of light brown hair combed on end like a German & that he wears gold spectacles & talks in a small, high voice & you may imagine that it would take some time to grow accustomed to him . . . She looks much older than her husband, indeed she can be no chicken as she has been round the world 4 times.'

Thomas Walker Arnold was Stein's junior by less than two years. He and May (who was, indeed, some years older than her husband) arrived from Aligarh in the United Provinces (now in Uttar Pradesh), where he had taught philosophy at the Muhammadan Anglo-Oriental College. A modest, scholarly man with a bright enthusiasm for life and an engaging sense of humour, he had become interested in oriental studies while an undergraduate at Cambridge. At Aligarh he had energetically espoused its rationale, whereby Muslim intellectuals and enlightened Englishmen aimed to provide an education combining Muslim culture with Western educational methods, along lines laid down by the college founder, Sir Syed Ahmad Khan. By the time he arrived in Lahore he had already written one book, *The Preaching of Islam*, and was to write several more.

Arnold's dedication to the Aligarh ideal, and his affectionate understanding of Indian Muslims, paralleled Stein's own feelings for the pandits of Kashmir. An immediate empathy sprang up between the two men which Stein acknowledged, many years later, by adding Arnold's name to his own in the title of the exploration fund he established.

Along with Arnold's high spirits went a reticence in the matter of private emotions which was probably well understood in this small group of like-minded friends. A colleague later wrote of him something which might equally have applied to Stein: 'Of his innermost feelings it was difficult to learn anything though he always made very clear his own views on general subjects. I believe he had a religion all his own, but I don't think anyone ever discovered what it was. He was slow to bestow friendship, but having bestowed it was as true as steel'.[6]

Life in the Mayo Lodge chummery added a new dimension to Stein's existence. Perhaps to the three Englishmen its conviviality seemed normal; but it was a novel delight to the reticent young Hungarian. So much of the character of his friends' lives appealed to him that he could hardly resist when they decided that each should have his own nick-name. His amusement at the idea and gratification at being considered one of such a fraternal band overcame any doubts about such levity. P.S. Allen had already become used to fellow-undergraduates address-ing him as Publius, because of the initials he shared with the Roman general Publius Scipio Africanus. So the designation went ahead, as Andrews later described:

> About this time a few local enthusiasts started a scheme to form a volun-teer body to be called the Panjab Light Horse, of which I became a member. Volunteering being thus in the air, it was, I think, Allen, with his delightful sense of humour, who suggested that there should be a Mayo Lodge con-tingent of volunteers (non-military) with Stein as CO. As we were all desirous of contributing such help as we could in promoting Stein's work, this seemed appropriate enough. Eventually we each acquired a designation or nom-de-guerre. Allen was Publius, Arnold was the Saint, or alternatively he and Mrs Arnold became the Hierarchs, my wife and I were the Baron and Baroness, and Stein, of course, the General: names by which we always thereafter addressed each other.[7]

The recognition of seniority implied by the title General (later expanded to Beg General because of Stein's Turkic connections) was yet another sign of how Stein's life had altered. Beyond the confines of home, he was no longer a submissive brother and nephew but rather the oldest member of a band of friends. In early letters to P. S. Allen he used his new title self-consciously, prefacing it with remarks such as 'if I must'. But soon he shortened it to BG, and BG he remained. His adoption of his friends' titles was no less complete, and Helen Allen soon acquired one of her own, becoming – and remaining – Madam to them all.

Stein had a high regard for the sisters and wives of his friends. He admired May Arnold for her extensive travels and knowledge of orien-tal art. And Helen Allen immediately won his loyalty. But, as she guessed, he seems to have been uninterested in the female sex in any other way. The cold-weather season which saw an influx into India of marriageable young girls such as Catherine Allen (known collectively as the fishing fleet) might have introduced him to potential wives. But if he ever felt more than friendly affection for a woman at this time – or later – it is not recorded.

His attitude towards the opposite sex, like his view of a conventional social life, was coloured by his commitment to work. As Andrews wrote later, his 'principle of regarding his work as the first consideration under all circumstances governed his life'.[8] Clearly, the sort of life he enjoyed in Lahore and Kashmir might have proved more difficult to arrange had he been married. He was also cautious about money, more concerned to save than to spend. He may have felt, as Ernst had done during the 1870s and much of the 1880s, that he could not afford to marry. But there seems to have been something more fundamental than this about his feelings for women.

He had grown up in a male-dominated world, with a mother who, in a role more akin to that of a grandmother than an authoritative parent, had been beyond reproach and whom he had adored. Women occupied a quite different world from the one in which he was raised by his uncle and brother. They were distant, difficult to know, easier to revere from afar, perhaps rather disconcerting at close quarters if they displayed anything other than conventional, public, womanly virtues. Had he been born several decades later, when social conventions were more relaxed, he might have had relationships with women; perhaps, more likely, he would have preferred male company whatever the circumstances.

If there was ever any likelihood of his regarding male friends or assistants in anything other than a genuinely asexual light, it was overruled by his extremely well-developed sense of the nobility and morality of the highly cultured man, inculcated in him since early childhood. Though robustly heterosexual men may disagree, it seems perfectly possible that a man such as Stein experienced no sexual passions. He had an affectionate nature and placed great importance on the companionship and loyalty of both like-minded friends and the various servants and surveyors who accompanied him on his journeys. At the time in which he lived, when the code of physical behaviour between men and women was comparatively strict, the expression of warm affection for members of the same sex was unlikely to cause comment as, ironically, it might in the more liberal climate of today;

and it provided Stein with the emotional outlet he needed in his otherwise self-contained life.

———————➤ ◄———————

During the winter vacation of 1897–8, an unusual opportunity presented itself to Stein. Throughout the year, the volatile North-West Frontier region had been in turmoil following an uprising at Chitral in 1895 encouraged by a mullah known to the British as 'the mad fakir'. For some time, imperial policy there had been one of conciliation based on a deep knowledge of the country and its people, and some of the empire's most talented men had devoted themselves to the task. But lately they had been handicapped by the cumbrous administrative processes of the state of Punjab, to which they were subject.

By the end of the century the system had weakened. The British found themselves with a large-scale revolt on their hands and the Army mobilized – much to the delight of its officers, who admired the warlike Pathans and treated an excursion to the Frontier as a light-hearted adventure. In late 1897, troops were poised to make a punitive foray into the Swat valley and, after that, into Buner, where no European had been since the arrival of Alexander the Great.

Stein knew enough of Swat from his brief visit in 1896 to want to return. And he recognized that he could use the impending invasion as a means of getting there. With characteristic efficiency he arranged, in the space of a few days, leave from the university, a grant of Rs 500 from the Punjab administration (supplemented with Rs 100 by his friend Maclagan out of interest) and preparations for the trip. By 5 January 1898 he and his small team of a surveyor, two other men and several mules had caught up with the staff of the commander of the entire operation, the splendidly named General Bindon Blood,[9] and with them entered Buner.

During the punitive foray into Buner, Stein recorded in his notebook the looting of villages, the appropriation of grain and stores, and the swords, shields and other belongings that were strewn about the hillsides. This was the policy known to the troops as 'butcher and beat it' which, Stein knew, threatened to damage or destroy ancient remains. Despite his concern for the sites, however, he seems to have accepted entirely the necessity for such action by the Army.

His work prompted a less sympathetic reaction from the natives than he usually received from his friends in Kashmir. Lionel Dunsterville, who was also on the Buner expedition, later recalled the opinion of the Pathan NCO in Stein's official escort, which had been provided by Dunsterville's own regiment. At the end of a day judged satisfactory by Stein, the Pathan told Dunsterville that the sahib had had no luck in his search for gold. When Dunsterville replied that Stein was looking not for gold but for evidence of how men had lived two thousand years ago, the Pathan retorted: ' "Nonsense, he only pretends that. If people dig in old ruins, it is to find treasure and nothing else. Every one knows that. How can you find out how men lived 2,000 years ago by digging in the ground? And who wants to know how they lived? For myself, I would sooner find a bag of gold that would help me to live." '[10]

Stein was back in Lahore by early February 1898 and his report on the trip was published later that year. Meanwhile in Mayo Lodge there were several changes. In March the Andrews left for England, where Andrews was to become head of the art department at the East London Technical College; and in August, P. S. Allen went home to marry his cousin Helen, returning with her in October. At the same time the Arnolds moved into the house with their small daughter, Nancy; and the household expanded yet further when another family, the Haileys, joined it in the autumn.

Malcolm Hailey was another Corpus Christi man, beginning what was to be a glittering career in India. As a colonization officer in the Punjab, he worked with peasants newly settled on land which had been reclaimed from the desert by irrigation. Later he became a member of the Viceroy's Executive Council, Governor of the Punjab and Governor of the United Provinces. But his private life was full of tragedy. His daughter Gemma, who was a young child when he brought her to live at Mayo Lodge, died of cholera in 1922; his vivacious Italian wife, Andriana (known as Andi), died in 1939, and his son Billy was killed during the Second World War. He was, by all accounts, an exceptional man and a charming friend, and Stein kept in touch with him long after they ceased to see each other regularly.[11]

News from Budapest came early in the year. Vámbéry wrote to say that the faculty had voted in favour of Stein's appointment, and that the Minister would approve it. Soon the matter would be settled. Outwardly, Stein appeared delighted at this apparent fulfilment of his hopes. Privately, however, he was hoping for something utterly different. When he travelled to Mohand Marg in June 1898 for a final period of 'special duty' in which to complete his introduction to the *Rajatarangini*, he was also planning the project that would take him far from Kashmir, far beyond the known limits of Sanskrit scholarship, and farther still from a chair in Indo-Iranian philology back in Europe.

He was convinced that there was a trail to be followed from India into Chinese Turkestan. Until an archaeologist explored the Taklamakan Desert, many questions would remain unanswered – including those he had been asking himself privately about the texts in unknown scripts on which Hoernle laboured, which he suspected were forgeries. Gradually he had been preparing to undertake an expedition himself, and he was almost ready now to submit his proposal to the critical gaze of the authorities.

One of his most valuable sources of information was Sven Hedin's book, *Through Asia*. He took copious notes on the names of hills, deserts and towns; stories and superstitions; the price of camels; the use of iron tanks for water; the need for spades and ropes, and sesame oil for feeding to camels in the desert; the height of sand-dunes and the temperatures at different times of the year; Turki words for the various items he would need to buy; the names of the men engaged by Hedin and of the local officials in different towns; the difference between the expected and the actual length of marches; the amount of provisions taken and the number of men needed; the location of water; the usefulness of snow-spectacles and of cigarettes to stave off thirst.

At last, in late August, he wrote to Sir Mackworth Young, Lieutenant-Governor of the Punjab, to obtain his preliminary sanction. Then, on 10 September 1898, he submitted to the Punjab government his formal proposal for an expedition, to take place in the following year. He envisaged limiting himself to the Khotan area, and he was careful to mention the possibility of other expeditions being planned by the Russians and by Hedin, in a shrewd attempt to stimulate the imperial bureaucrats' competitive instincts.

———◄———

At the same time as Stein was working on plans for his expedition, he was in correspondence with Rudolf Hoernle in Calcutta. Hoernle had helped organize the Asiatic Society of Bengal's funding of the maps that were to appear in Stein's translation of the *Rajatarangini*, and he was impressed by the younger man's abilities. Ever since Stein had shown an interest in the collection from Chinese Central Asia, they had been in close contact and on his return to India in late 1897, Stein turned to Hoernle as an adviser and confidant in the development of his proposals for an expedition.

Knowing Stein's desire for a better post than his present one at Lahore, Hoernle became eager to see his young colleague succeed him when he retired in 1899 as Principal of the Calcutta Madrasah, where the long holidays gave ample opportunity for private work. Stein had no knowledge of Arabic; but Hoernle's recommendation would carry weight, and he leapt at the opportunity. Though he was planning an expedition, he still needed a job which would provide him with a salary, during his absence as well as on his return. And he was longing for a change from his positions in Lahore.

During the winter vacation at the end of 1898 he went to stay with the Hoernles in a house they had taken in Simla. It was there, while they sat at Christmas dinner, that a letter arrived from the Bengal government offering him the position. Initial pay of Rs 800 per month would rise in five years to Rs 1,000; there would be free residence in the Principal's house, worth, he calculated, another Rs 250 per month, and several personal allowances. Best of all, there would be pension rights since the position made him a member of the Indian Education Service, giving him security he had previously lacked. Hoernle had also played down Stein's lack of Arabic to good effect, emphasizing instead the good relations he enjoyed with Muslims in Lahore.

As he walked in the snowy hills surrounding Simla that winter, Stein had good reason to feel ebullient. After a decade in India, during which he had frequently felt frustrated by an apparent lack of opportunity, he was on the verge of undertaking an expedition which could make a major contribution to oriental studies. Moreover, the problem of employment had been solved. Given that he had no opportunity to work full-time on archaeology, the Madrasah position seemed as suitable as any.

When they heard of his promotion, a few well-wishers offered muted warnings about the difference in climate between Lahore and Calcutta. But Stein was too preoccupied to give much thought to such a minor matter; nor to the rather more serious consideration of how it would feel to be a thousand miles from his friends in the Punjab. As to the specially created university chair that awaited him in Budapest, it had still not been confirmed. In fact, the university seems later to have announced Stein's appointment. But by then he was on his way to Central Asia and had put all thoughts of a return to Europe behind him.

Ernst Stein's reaction was, perhaps, to be expected. He had waited for years to hear that his brother had become a university professor. When he learnt that Aurél was instead planning to cross the Karakoram Mountains and lead an expedition into the Taklamakan Desert, he was dismayed, seeing only danger and disaster ahead. Stein tried to allay his worries. He had always responded gently to Ernst's over-protective fussing, and he could afford to be patient still. He knew that nothing his brother could say or do now would stop him from carrying out his plan.

With only a few weeks left before he had to leave to take up his new position, Stein had much to do. His application for permission to undertake his expedition was still making its laboured way through the machinery of three administrations: the governments of the Punjab, India as a whole, and Bengal, where he would shortly be working. He had to sell the furniture from his rooms in Mayo Lodge, correct proofs of the *Rajatarangini* and, most important of all, plan his expedition. There was simply insufficient time, and he soon had to accept post-ponement of the expedition while he put in a year of work at the Madrasah. To compensate, he heard on 24 March 1899 from Hoernle, who had been lobbying hard on his behalf, that 'the Viceroy is rather keen on the subject, and I think you will find him ready to do everything to further it and make it successful'.[12]

An opportunity to test viceregal support came soon afterwards. Lord Curzon, *en route* to Simla for the first time since his appointment as Viceroy the previous August, stopped in the Punjab to discuss the administration of the North-West Frontier (which he was soon to reorganize). As part of the reception, Stein was given the job of guiding him round the Lahore Museum's collection of Gandharan art.

No Indologist could have hoped for a more receptive ear. The strong personal interest of this dynamic young Viceroy (he was only three years older than Stein) in the archaeology of India presaged well for the country's neglected monuments and its moribund Archaeological Survey – and for anyone energetic enough to have formulated his own plans for research. Stein also had in his favour the fact that Curzon had travelled in the region through which his projected journey would take him. He prepared well for their meeting and made sure Curzon knew he had nothing to do with the museum, so that he would not be held responsible for its poor presentation of the collection. At the end of the visit, Curzon volunteered his support for Stein's expedition. Perhaps at that point Stein spared a thought for his uncle Ignaz, whose example in the matter of getting things done he had followed to such good effect.

Hoernle, too, continued to be active in his support for Stein's expedition. But in his mind the proposal underwent a strange metamorphosis. In the letters of support which he wrote on Stein's behalf, he began to describe himself as 'the originator of the expedition' and 'the intellectual father' of the idea. In one letter he claimed: 'The idea of that expedition was first conceived by myself during my work in Simla on the existing British Collection of Central Asian Antiquities. Dr Stein, than whom there is none in India better fitted to carry it out, heartily responded to my suggestion to be the leader of the expedition.' In most of his letters, which are now in the Stein archive in Oxford, he used some such expression – and on the copies which he evidently gave Stein for his records, Stein marked every such reference in the margin with one neat stroke of a red crayon. For nowhere in Stein's own writings, either private or for publication, is Hoernle described as the originator of the scheme.

Stein clearly felt irritated by Hoernle's appropriation of his idea, for he went to some lengths to correct the impression his colleague was creating. In his introduction to *Sand-Buried Ruins of Khotan*, his 'popular' account of the first expedition, he concentrated on paying tribute to Hoernle's help and support (it was Hoernle who suggested that he write such a book in addition to a scholarly report) and mentioned the origins of the expedition almost in passing. But in a letter to Thomas Holderness, Revenue Secretary to the Government of India, written three days before setting off for Khotan in May 1900, he made his position clear. However grateful he felt to Hoernle, he could only think that he was suffering from 'deficient recollection' in considering himself the originator of the idea. Making clear his appreciation of the methods of the Indian bureaucracy, Stein pointed out that, had the plan not been the result of his own initiative, the form of his application to the government would have been 'distinctly incorrect'.

Hoernle was conciliatory when Stein broached the subject. But he seems to have been determined to win as much recognition as possible for his part in the plan. He was about to retire and return to England, and the thought that some other scholar might be given the responsibility of processing Stein's finds evidently haunted him. There is a note of desperation in his repeated assertions that the finds should come straight to the British Museum, rather than to India, and that he should be the first to see them, because of his work on the British Collection of Central Asian Antiquities.

There was another reason for his anxiety. He too had suspicions about the Macartney manuscripts in his collection; and he knew that Stein's work in Khotan might reveal them to be forgeries. If this were to happen, he had to be the first to know, so that he could control the way in which the information was then released to the academic world. Otherwise, his reputation would be at stake.

In the meantime, Hoernle's enthusiasm for the expedition knew few bounds. He envisaged Stein as 'the leader of an expedition which is to furnish results to various branches of science' and by August 1899 was advising him: 'Get other surveys to join and help you. It will add to the general interest and the kudos of our project.' This was not at all what Stein had in mind; and Hoernle's ambitions alarmed him for another reason. One of his chief concerns was to keep his plans concealed from others for as long as possible, for he badly wanted to be the first archaeological explorer to reach Khotan. The more Hoernle discussed the project, and expanded his vision of what it should encompass, the more likely it was that news of it would reach possible competitors.

———————◆◀———————

While his plans were developing, Stein made the move to Calcutta. In his diary for April 1899 he noted the activities of his last month in Lahore: walks through peach avenues and rides along the city walls, dinners on the veranda and coffee taken at night on the roof. By contrast, when he emerged from Howrah Station in Calcutta early on 6 May, and made the short journey across the Hooghly Bridge into the city, he felt as though he would be swamped by the heat and humidity. The Great Eastern Hotel, he wrote in his diary, smelt 'like a slave ship'.[13]

It was a bad time of year to make the acquaintance of Calcutta. It had been hot in Lahore – 80° Fahrenheit in his room at the end of March, he had noted – but that was nothing compared with the oppression of the Bengali climate just before the arrival of the monsoon. The next few entries in his diary were punctuated by appalled observations: 'Horrible night', 'Terrible heat', 'No breath of air', 'another dreadful night'. He was aghast, too, at the congestion on the streets and the difficulty of getting a carriage when making a journey. 'Wished I had some Pathans,' he wrote ruefully.

The Calcutta Madrasah, of which he was now Principal, was a school of distinction. Founded for Muslim boys in 1781 by Warren Hastings, it had two departments: the Arabic, in which only the traditional curriculum was followed, and the Anglo-Persian, where pupils were trained for the matriculation examination of the university (Persian had been the official language of government in India until 1837, and was the language of Muslim tradition in the country). Most students lived at home, and their training lacked the dynamism which had so enthused Thomas Arnold at Aligarh. Edward Denison Ross, who succeeded Stein as Principal of the Madrasah in 1901, wrote later that education there was 'mainly a question of getting the texts by heart. There was no scope for original thought or initiative.'[14]

The Principal's quarters at 19 Wellesley Square consisted of a large, bare Anglo-Indian bungalow which Stein disliked. Perhaps the spirit of a series of discontented bachelor principals inhabited the place, for Denison Ross also found life lonely there. Considering that he was in Calcutta for a year, however, Stein got off remarkably lightly from a job and a place he never enjoyed. His life there was a series of escapes.

Only three days after his arrival in Calcutta he set off again for Darjeeling, the summer refuge of the Bengal government, where the file on his expedition was currently entombed in some departmental office. One of his first acts on reaching the hill-station was to seek out the grave of Kőrösi Csoma, the Hungarian whose travels in Asia had been part of his early education on the East. Now as never before there was reason to feel an affinity with that lonely scholar's hopes and goals. Csoma had never reached the lands beyond Tibet where he had hoped to find clues to the origins of the Magyar people, and it was those lands that Stein, albeit for different reasons, now planned to explore.

The Governor of Bengal, Sir John Woodburn, agreed to allow Stein a twelve-month 'deputation' from his official post, beginning at the end of the long vacation in July 1900. The Government of India's formal approval followed soon afterwards. Funding would be shared by the Government of India and the governments of Bengal and the Punjab, and amounted to a total grant of Rs 9,000 (around £27,000 now). An extra Rs 2,000 came from the Survey of India to support a native sub-surveyor – for Stein was keen to map what was largely an unsurveyed region. The finds would be examined first in London, and their allocation to specific museums decided later. The Foreign Office was to arrange his Chinese passport, and obtain permission for him to travel to Europe through Russian Turkestan after completing his work at Khotan.

Knowing that his project was now secure, Stein took Dash with him to Sikkim, walking through bamboo and rhododendron forests until he caught his first sight of Mount Everest, Nepal and Kanchenjunga, and plucked his first orchid. He was beginning to experience the contentment of his days on Mohand Marg when a more shocking reminder of Kashmir arrived in the post. News came that Pandit Govind Kaul had died of typhoid at the age of 53. The pandit had been a representative of so much that Stein admired, and had been such a close companion during otherwise lonely years, that his death left a deep impression. At intervals during the rest of his life, he continued to be reminded of his old friend and to mourn his loss.

On his return to Calcutta, Stein began to prepare properly for his expedition. He engaged a servant, Mirza Alim, from Russian Turkestan, with whom he could learn to speak Turki, and rounded off his evenings of study with walks round the Maidan with Mirza and Dash. At the same time, he managed to arrange several more trips away from the 'tropical suburb of London'.[15] One, a tour of Bihar, introduced him to a local tax collector and amateur antiquarian who became a lifelong friend, C.E.A.W. Oldham. The two men visited Bodhgaya and other Buddhist sites, and Oldham never forgot the way in which these brief visits demonstrated Stein's grasp of topographical detail, his ability to trace the steps of Hiuen Tsiang and his memory for descriptions written by the Chinese pilgrim.

Apart from these respites from his work at the Madrasah, Stein felt that nothing good had come of his move to Calcutta. His hostility to the city and the climate overshadowed any benefits of the position that Hoernle had held for eighteen years, and he was already plotting a course that would lead him back to the Punjab after his expedition was over. The post he had in mind, as an inspector of schools, though not ideal would at least involve him in travel through an area of great relevance to his studies. The earliest available vacancy was likely to arise in 1901 at Rawalpindi, and in March 1900 the Bengal government gave him permission to apply for the job.

In the longer term, Stein's hopes still lay with the prospect of a position which would involve him full-time in archaeology. His interest in Lord Curzon's pronouncements on that subject was correspondingly intense. Before leaving Calcutta, he heard Curzon make what was to become a famous speech to the Asiatic Society of Bengal on the preservation of antiquities, signalling the dramatic changes he was about to make in the government's attitude towards archaeology. Stein noted rather patronizingly in his diary: 'Too good for such an audience. Whether anyone really could grasp him? Shall watch the deed to follow the word.'[16]

At last the time came to leave Bengal. The threat of plague closed Calcutta's colleges earlier than usual in 1900, giving Stein welcome extra time. He planned to set out for Chinese Turkestan at the end of May from Kashmir, where he could gather together his equipment and attend to a number of outstanding matters in peace. But his initial destination was Lahore. As the air turned cooler during the two-day train journey, his mood lightened. 'Tired but happy', he wrote in his diary on the night of his arrival. There were friends, music in the open air and fireworks on Thomas Arnold's birthday a few days later; then the journey to Kashmir. Snow still lay low down the mountains, the valley was filled with the colours of spring and Stein approached his old haunts joyfully after an absence of two years.

Ever since he submitted the proposal for his expedition in 1898, he had been accumulating information and stores from various sources, little by little. He had already provided Ernst with a list of addresses to use over the coming year. He had written to the British representative in Kashgar, Macartney, for information on the climate of Khotan, the addresses of the main dealers in manuscript finds, approximate prices paid, the availability of translators, the best items to bring as presents, and the market for ponies and mules. He had arranged a loan from the Rawalpindi arsenal of two carbines and two revolvers. Certain supplies, such as clothing, he had found in Calcutta, but more had had to be ordered, often from England, and most had been sent to await his arrival in Kashmir.

He had listed the books he wanted to take, among them Hiuen Tsiang, Hedin's *Through Asia* and Curzon's *The Pamirs and the Source of the Oxus*, Yule's *Cathay and the Way Thither*, an anthropological handbook, Moore's *Family Medicine*, Hoernle's reports on the Central Asian Collection and a guide to Turki and Hindu Kush dialects. In a notebook he had reminded himself of the destinations for various pieces of kit: saddlery to Lahore, tents straight to Kashmir, heavy articles to leave Calcutta for Rawalpindi on 1 April and so on. There were also lists of the equipment he would need: a green Willesden canvas bath, a rot-proof ground-sheet for his wool-lined tent, folding candle lanterns, rot-proof canvas buckets, meat lozenges, compressed food tablets, chocolate, jam, camel blankets. He wrote down estimates of how much food would be eaten and how much it would cost.

Important details came from Ram Singh, the Gurkha surveyor from the Survey of India who would be accompanying him to Khotan. Together with his cook, Jasvant Singh, Ram Singh had accompanied Captain Deasy on his travels in Tibet and Chinese Turkestan, so was able to provide information on the number of marches between the towns and villages *en route* to Khotan, the likelihood of supplies being available, whether transport could be hired along the way, what sort of equipment Deasy had found particularly useful and what survey work he had done.

Wherever supplies from England were concerned, Stein could rely on the assistance of Fred Andrews. Andrews arranged for a British firm to send samples of tinned food, and investigated the merits of various types of camera. He looked into the weight and cost of a portable well-sinking apparatus, reported on dessicated vegetables, ink powder and binoculars, and chased an order for a Burroughs Wellcome medical chest which had been held up, the suppliers said apologetically, by 'extreme pressure of business put upon us by the war [in South Africa]'.[17] Stein warned his friend that 'distance is no protection from me'.[18]

All Stein's closest friends did valuable work for him. At the same time as Andrews was inspecting, buying and shipping assorted expedition equipment (and, incidentally, designing the cover for Stein's book),

Arnold was helping with the apparently interminable task of getting the final proofs of the *Rajatarangini* checked and returned to the publisher in London. The Allens were later to do the same for other books.

Stein himself, on reaching Kashmir at the end of April, went first to his old camping ground, Chinar Bagh at Srinagar, in order to meet the traders and craftsmen who were used to providing for Europeans and their camping trips. He ordered mule trunks and *kiltas* (leather-covered storage baskets), fur coats and clothes for his assistants. There were also late additions to his kit to accommodate, such as the copy of the *Eastern Hindukush Gazetteer* sent by the Survey of India and marked 'secret'.

Then he left the town and pitched his tents in a grove of chinars beside the Sind River – as near Mohand Marg as he could get so early in the year. There was still work to do on the *Rajatarangini* before he could leave. The introduction remained to be written, in which Stein would lament the loss of Georg Bühler (who had drowned in a boating accident two years earlier) and the fact that fate had thus denied him the satisfaction of giving his patron the completed, published *Chronicle*. And there were letters to write in search of patronage for the book to satisfy the publishers, who had told him that the cost of printing had risen dramatically because of its size and massive index. The book had cost the 'enormous' sum of £552 to print, of which no less than £117 had been spent on author's corrections and alterations to proofs.

During the last week of May, Stein's men assembled at his camp-site. Mirza Alim had travelled with him from Calcutta and the surveyor, Ram Singh, appeared punctually on the 24th. His cook, Jasvant Singh, had already come up from Lahore where he had been waiting for last-minute supplies to arrive. His high caste prevented him from preparing food for a European, so Stein had arranged through Macartney in Kashgar for another cook to come from Chinese Turkestan to join the expedition. This was Sadak Akhun, whose arrival in rough fur cap and coat and huge leather boots, after the best part of two months on the road, gave the camp a touch of Central Asian colour.

Stores and equipment were packed and repacked until everything was ready. Then they were loaded on to a small flotilla of boats which would take them down the river to Bandipur on the northern shore of the Wular Lake, the starting point for the expedition. On 29 May, as Stein was preparing to leave, the Srinagar post-master arrived in triumph with the Burroughs Wellcome medical chest which had been given up for lost. That same evening, Stein and his party set off along the river, under the old bridges and past the ghats where his pandit friends were waiting to wish him well. They travelled through the night, and by the following morning had reached Bandipur, beyond which rose mountains covered with a fresh fall of snow. Another day was spent there weighing, numbering and packing loads. On the following morning, 31 May 1900, the loads were transferred to sixteen ponies and the small party set off along the road to Gilgit and the north.

4

Birth of a Great Adventure

T HE REGION OF Chinese, or Eastern Turkestan was – and remains – one of the most remote and least hospitable in all Asia. Massive mountain ranges isolated it from neighbouring countries; and the arid conditions of the Tarim Basin, in its midst, restricted its population to scattered oases on the fringes of the vast Taklamakan Desert. Its chief towns were thousands of miles from the seat of national authority, and communication between them was by means of roads whose condition had barely changed in centuries.

This was the territory across which camel caravans had once travelled, dwarfed by the immensity of desert and mountain, in pursuit of trade between China and the Mediterranean. But the lonely wastes had long since witnessed the demise of that overland route and its people possessed no written records of their own history. Nor were foreigners much wiser about this obscure tract of Asia for few had contemplated, let alone undertaken and survived, the gruelling conditions of a journey across its natural defences. On its southern border marched the Karakoram Mountains, the Kun-lun range and the bleak, high-altitude plateaux of Tibet. Along the north-western boundary ran the T'ien-shan, or Celestial Mountains; and to the west the huge, spiked and splintered peaks of the Pamir range, the Roof of the World, separated Eastern from Western, or Russian Turkestan.

Travellers from China proper had no less an intimidating introduction to the area, for they were confronted by the barren expanses of the Gobi and Lop deserts, where spirits were said to lure men to their deaths. This was the land which Westerners had once called High Tartary, and which the Chinese had known as the Western Regions. By the time Stein arrived there, recent events had led to its being renamed the New Dominion, or Sinkiang.

Eastern Turkestan had slipped in and out of Chinese control several times over the centuries. By the 1860s it seemed on the point of becoming a separate Muslim state. An adventurer called Yakub Beg, who had spent his early life unpromisingly as a dancing boy in Khokand in Russian Turkestan, took advantage of Muslim uprisings against China's Manchu dynasty to seize power for himself. By the end of the decade he controlled most of the main cities and towns of the region and sought recognition as an independent ruler from both the Russians and the British, playing them off against each other with some success, initially at least.

But the Russians feared that Muslim rule east of the Pamirs might rally the population of Western Turkestan, the conquest of which they had not yet completed. So, while their aim was certainly to extend their influence into Chinese territory, they were not sorry to see the Manchus quell the revolt and unseat the upstart Yakub Beg, who died (whether by his own hand or at someone else's is unclear) in 1877. The Manchus administered their reconquered province by means of a small Chinese minority of civil and military officials, who kept apart from the native Uighur people and left their traditional feudal structures intact.

This arrangement suited Stein's own purposes, for it was among the Uighurs that he would find the treasure-seekers who had provided Hoernle with material for his collection. All he needed from the Chinese administrators was permission to go about his business unhindered.

Certain facts were already known about the early period in which he was interested, either from Chinese annals or from the accounts of pilgrims such as Hiuen Tsiang. The Chinese had first contemplated extending their influence westward in the second century BC, in search of allies against the Huns who threatened their northern borders. The sixth emperor of the Han dynasty, Wu-ti (Wudi) (140–87 BC), hoped to enlist the help of the Yueh-chih (Yuezhi) people. These nomads and horsemen had once lived on the western fringes of China proper but the Huns had driven them far away, beyond the Pamirs.

As his envoy the Emperor sent an officer called Chang Ch'ien (Zhang Qian), but the message took more than a decade to reach the Yueh-chih. Chang Ch'ien fell into the hands of the Huns on the way and spent ten years as their prisoner before he could complete his journey westward. When at last he reached the country of the Yueh-chih, in the Fergana region of Western Turkestan, he found that the people had no desire to return to the east and confront the Huns.

The information he took back to the Emperor, however, about the civilized lands that lay beyond the wastes of the desert, and the handsome horses that thrived there, fired Chinese determination to drive the Huns back from the approach to the West. By the beginning of the first century BC, they had succeeded in this. They began to send political missions to the states in and beyond the Tarim Basin and to promote the superior industrial produce of their country. So it was that the fine fabric made from the cocoons of the silkworm was first brought from China along the routes to the West, giving those routes, many centuries later, the collective name of the Silk Road.[1]

Chinese control in the Tarim Basin broke down in the early years of the first century AD, and alternately grew or receded thereafter until it retreated before the White Huns in the third century. Three centuries later, Turkish tribes overran the area, and only the writings left by passing Chinese pilgrims tell anything about the Buddhist culture of the oases at that time. China's T'ang (Tang) dynasty succeeded in reasserting power in the seventh century but, again, this was challenged, this time by Tibetans in the south and by Arabs advancing from the west under the banners of Islam.

In response to the latter, the Chinese undertook an extraordinary military expedition, the only recorded instance of a force of comparatively large size crossing the formidable territory between Eastern and Western Turkestan. In AD 747, a Chinese general led his 10,000 men over the icy passes of the Pamirs and the Hindu Kush and down into Yasin and Gilgit, in what is now northern Pakistan. His victory there did little to stem the relentless flow of Islam into Chinese Turkestan; but it deservedly has a place in the annals of daring exploits. Stein was fascinated by the episode and made two detours, in the course of separate expeditions, in order to see more of the area that witnessed such heroics.

Not until the relatively stable rule in the thirteenth century of the Mongol Genghis Khan and his successors did conditions again favour trade across the Tarim Basin. This was a better-documented period, since it was in the thirteenth century that perhaps the best-known of all Central Asian travellers, the Venetian Marco Polo, wrote of his life and travels in the empire of the Mongols, or Tartars as they were known in the West (though there is now some doubt among scholars as to whether he ever set foot in Central Asia). A translation of the book he wrote on his return accompanied Stein wherever he went during his first expedition, no matter how restricted the space in his baggage. It had the dual merit of being an indispensable guide and having as its translator and editor one of Stein's old mentors, Sir Henry Yule.

China in Marco Polo's time was as much of an enigma as it had been to the citizens of ancient Rome. The goods that travelled along the Silk Road were handled by many different traders in the course of their long journey, and the Persians and, later, Muslims who monopolized the central sections of the route guarded their privileges jealously. The people who bought and wore Chinese silk when it first reached the West had no concept of the methods by which it was made, nor of the place from which it came, and this ignorance of the East remained long after the secrets of silk manufacture first escaped westward from China, probably during the fourth century AD.

Marco Polo claimed to have begun his travels in 1271 as a boy of 17 in the company of his father and uncle, both adventurous Venetian merchants. He spent the following twenty years travelling in the empire of Kublai, Great Khan of all the Tartars, which stretched thousands of miles across Eurasia, from the Yellow Sea to the Mediterranean. Polo crossed territory never before seen by a European, witnessed events never before recorded in the West and lived in the mysterious country of the Seres (silk), as China had long been known. His descriptions were no doubt limited by his mercantile viewpoint, and his estimates of distance based on the unscientific measure of a day's journey. But the information contained in his account was to provide Stein with many geographical clues in an otherwise uncharted expanse of shifting sands.

───────────◄─►───────────

However much Stein enjoyed eliciting valuable information from centuries-old sources, he was no pedant. Up-to-date local knowledge of the area was vital, hence his careful study of Hedin's book and reports of any other expeditions to the area. Of the latter there had been a number in the past few decades, among them the British diplomatic mission of Sir Douglas Forsyth to Yakub Beg in 1873; the explorations of Nikolai Mikhailovich Prejevalsky, a Russian aristocrat who gave his name to the breed of wild horse he discovered there;[2] and the visit of a Russian scholar, Dimitri Klementz, to the Turfan area. No travellers in the region had been practical archaeologists, however, and Hedin was the only person known to have crossed the Taklamakan Desert in recent times.

The most immediate information on the area Stein knew he could gain from only one source, and that was George Macartney, the British representative in Kashgar. Macartney occupied a position that was precarious and isolated even by the challenging standards of the far-flung British Empire. Supposedly an assistant in Chinese affairs to the British Resident in Kashmir, six weeks' journey away across towering mountain ranges, he had lived in Kashgar for a decade as a guest of the Chinese. He had no recognized status there and no hope of being supported by the Government of India if his situation became difficult.

Macartney was phlegmatic about his position in this remote place. To him it was, perhaps, only another aspect of what had always been an irregular life. His father, Sir Samuel Halliday Macartney of the Chinese service, had defied the unwritten rules of the British in the East by taking a Chinese wife, and had brought up his four children in Nanking. After George Macartney's death, his obituarists were to seek comfort in the fact that his mother had at least come from an aristocratic family, even if she were an oriental. Macartney himself never mentioned his Chinese blood, not even to his own children. Nevertheless, it was precisely this background that gave him such appropriate credentials for his work in Kashgar, which he was to pursue for twenty-eight years.

He first arrived in the town in 1890 as a 23-year-old Chinese translator for Francis Younghusband, a young intelligence officer whose uncle, Robert Shaw, had been the first Englishman to visit Kashgar in 1869. Younghusband was sent north by the Government of India to investigate the Pamir Gap, a fifty-mile-wide undemarcated area between the frontiers of Afghanistan and Sinkiang which the British feared might be seized by the Russians. He already knew the region, having crossed Chinese Turkestan from Peking to India in 1886. He and

Macartney spent the winter of 1890–1 in Kashgar and when he left the following summer to confront the Russians in the Pamirs, Macartney remained behind.[3]

Macartney's tasks were to keep an eye on the Russian representative in Kashgar, Nikolai Petrovsky, to cultivate friendly relations with the Chinese and try to bolster them against Russian influence, and to encourage trade between Sinkiang and India. In all these he was remarkably successful despite pitiful resources, only grudging recognition from his distant superiors and a dire paucity of companions.

The only other Westerners in Kashgar at the time, apart from Petrovsky and the small staff at his consulate, were one or two Swedish missionaries and a Dutch Roman Catholic priest called Father Hendricks with whom Macartney, for all his knowledge of languages including Chinese, Hindi, Persian and Turki, is said to have conversed in Latin. Despite this handicap, he found in Hendricks a close companion, as well as an invaluable source of local gossip and information, and the priest shared his house for several years. Indeed, it was this friendship between the two men that prompted the Russian Consul to break off relations with his British rival.

Petrovsky, who had been in Kashgar since 1882 and was elevated to the rank of Consul in 1895, was a difficult man: vain, high-handed and domineering, but cultivated, clever and shrewd. Single-handedly, except for occasional help from his small force of Cossacks, he represented the power of Russia in the region and worked tirelessly to increase its already considerable influence. He was deeply unpopular, but had so successfully intimidated the local Chinese officials that they had become little more than spectators at his games of manipulation and obstruction. When Macartney, in anticipation of his new wife's arrival, tried to find Hendricks another home in Kashgar, Petrovsky did his best to obstruct him. Having failed, he instead severed all communications with his rival in late 1899, resuming them only three years later.

At the same time, Stein and Macartney were corresponding on the subject of Stein's forthcoming expedition. It was on Macartney's recommendation that Stein decided to visit Kashgar before beginning work in the desert. Diplomatic approaches to the Taotai (provincial governor), Macartney suggested, would sooth suspicions among people 'to whom the word "science" is an empty sound' and who would probably interpret his work either as a search for hidden treasures or an attempt to disturb ancient graveyards.⁴ He advised a clear statement of objectives in Stein's passport. But when Stein received the passport from the Government of India, he found that his description of his activities, including the conduct of surveys and acquisition of antiquities, had been reduced to a far more general statement.

'The yamen [official residence] call upon the local authorities along the line of route', it ran, 'to examine Dr Stein's passport at once whenever he presents it for inspection, to afford him due protection according to Treaty, and not to place any difficulties or obstacles in his way.' The accompanying letter from the office of the British Minister in Peking explained: 'In the application to the Yamen it was not thought advisable to ask for the special facilities asked for by Dr Stein . . . [he] will probably find no difficulty in executing the surveys he mentions. As to the excavations and the purchase of antiquities, it is considered that any reference to them here would hinder rather than assist his objects.'⁵ Stein would have reason to recall this prescient remark in years to come.

———————◆——◆———————

The morning on which Stein set out from Bandipur in Kashmir on the last day of May 1900 was a fine one. Wild flowers were beginning to blossom beside the lake, and there were fresh falls of snow on the mountain-tops, as he set out for Gilgit, 200 miles and two weeks' hard travelling to the north. Along the valley the small, stone-walled fields were sprouting their first rice shoots and the chinars and walnut trees were in full leaf.

Within a few miles the track began to climb away from the lush hamlets, and by the next day he had already crossed the first pass at Tragbal and was high on the Gilgit Transport Road. This was the old route out of the Kashmir valley and across the mountains of Baltistan to the Indus. It had recently been upgraded by the British; but by today's standards, the term 'road' seems an absurdly exaggerated description of what was no more than a rough, stony track that plunged into gorges and clung to the edges of precipices, and which was open to pack animals for only three months of the year. Compared with lesser paths through the mountains, however, it was an enormous improvement which, together with a new telegraph link, brought the small British force at Gilgit into relatively close contact with Kashmir and the Punjab. Its use was restricted, and Stein had needed permission from the Government of India's Foreign Department in order to take his party that way.

The North-West Frontier had held Stein's interest for so long that it now seemed natural to be there. In the wild, craggy mountains where Afghanistan and India met, and where the Indo-Iranian and Greek influences of antiquity could still be traced, he loved to lose himself in the distant past, in thoughts of tribal culture and conquering Macedonians. That he was free to travel in so much of this remote area was a happy accident of fate for, had he come to the East before the late 1880s, his wanderings would have been more circumscribed by the limits of British control. Apprehension about Russia's expanding power in Western Turkestan, and her influence in Afghanistan, had recently encouraged the Government of India to push deeper into the tribal territories of the north-western border lands, and the British flag now flew in both Gilgit and Hunza.

The atmosphere of high adventure and espionage which attracted so many young officers to the Frontier, and which gave rise to the romantic notion of the 'Great Game' – a term popularized by Rudyard Kipling[6] – seems to have had little effect on Stein. If his views on politics ever found expression in his letters or books, they were generally conventional, supportive of the imperial venture and complacent in their assumption of the benefits of British influence. What really absorbed him in the mountains of the north-west was the past, not the present.

On the second day of his journey to Gilgit, for example, his thoughts were not of military campaigns but of ethnographic history. Noting the 'ethnographic boundary' between the people of Kashmir and the Dards, who populated the area northwards as far as the Hindu Kush, he wrote: 'I can never see a Dard without thinking of the thousands of years of struggle these tribes have carried on with the harsh climate and the barren soil of their mountains. They . . . have seen all the great conquests which swept over the North-West of India, and have survived them, unmoved as their mountains.'[7] He strongly believed in the study of ethnic inheritance as a key to understanding the past of a people, and was to devote time on each of his expeditions to anthropometric measurements and observations of the inhabitants of regions he passed through. The photographs which he took in the course of these investigations feature in most of his books.

This highly developed sense of history contributed to his matter-of-fact attitude towards his own travels. He tended to regard any hardships he himself suffered as insignificant in relation to the continuity of life in these ancient places (a view that contrasted sharply with his resentment of the difficulties he believed he endured in his official employment). Besides, he was not one to dramatize the rigours of mountain travel. He preferred simply to concentrate on achieving his aims as efficiently as possible, and his written descriptions of his travels reflect this attitude. He minimized hazards because he knew them to be inevitable, whereas writers more concerned with histrionic effect might well have adopted a more colourful style.

The journey to Gilgit took him twelve days. At high altitudes, he rose soon after midnight in order to move on before the sun's rays melted the snow and made the going exhausting, if not dangerous. Swollen streams threatened to wash away the snow-bridges which sometimes provided the only crossing-points. At one of these, on the descent from the Tragbal Pass, one of the laden ponies fell into the torrent, taking Sadak Akhun with it. Neither was hurt, but stones had to be laid along the narrow ledge of snow in order to get the remaining animals across, and heavy rain throughout the operation meant that everyone was soaked.

During that day, the party took seven hours to cover eleven miles and Stein called a halt the following day so that the men could rest and the baggage be dried. Before they set off again, he transferred the more fragile loads, containing surveying equipment and cameras, to a few locally hired coolies in anticipation of worse conditions to come. On 5 June the party reached the Burzil Pass.

It was very cold and not yet light when they got to the summit, 13,500 feet above sea-level. But the snow was hard and they covered the six miles to the top from the rest-house, where Stein had spent the previous evening, in three hours. On the far side stretched an 'arctic waste' of glittering snowfields, its only inhabitants large, ginger marmots which sat at the mouths of their burrows, taunting Dash with their loud whistling and disappearing immediately at his approach.

The little dog remained unperturbed by the hardships of the march, as happy to accompany his master across mountain passes as he had been to follow him through the jungles of Sikkim or the dusty fields outside Lahore. Stein's servant, Mirza, had given Dash a Turki name,

Yolchi Beg, meaning Sir Traveller, and Stein noted that his Turki servants, 'being untrammelled by the caste conventions of India, never hesitated to show their affection for my faithful companion'.[8]

From the Burzil, Stein moved on to Astor. This meant a drop down to lower altitudes and warmer temperatures, but also to a harsh environment where small patches of cultivated land struggled amid the bleak surroundings of sun-scorched rocks and naked mountain faces. In the distance ahead were glimpses of the grey-brown River Indus and, beyond, shadowy mountains falling back in rank after rank to the north. With Gilgit only a couple of days away, he broke his journey in order to visit the camp of Captain John Manners Smith, the Political Agent at Gilgit who was on his way back from a shooting expedition.

Manners Smith was one of the heroes of the 1891 Hunza campaign. He was famous for having defied the expectations of the enemy by scaling a massive precipice beneath their feet, winning himself a Victoria Cross in the process. Now, in the position of 'Warden of the Marches', as Stein liked to call such postings, he and his wife were defying native expectations yet again with their typically British approach to camp life.

Their tents had been pitched on the shoulder of a slope high above the road where the ground was thick with violets and forget-me-nots, and Mrs Manners Smith had invested the scene with the 'true refinement' which, Stein observed, Anglo-Indian ladies knew so well how to achieve 'even at the most distant points of the Empire'.[9] He also admired the presence in camp of the Manners Smith children. His opinion that 'the British Baby' was a pioneer of empire and civilization (the two amounting to the same thing in his eyes) punctuates his writings, both private and published.

From the high alpine meadow to which Stein's hosts took him for 'afternoon tea', the Indus valley could be seen stretching south towards Chilas. There the river moves through a vast and lifeless expanse of rock and sand where the heat is intense and man's imprint minimal, dwarfed by the great, blasted landscape. Even today, when the Karakoram Highway runs alongside the river there, vehicles are few and travellers can go for hours without sight of another human being. In 1900, the country from Chilas downstream almost as far as Peshawar was still in the hands of independent tribes, uncharted territory which no

European had penetrated. Stein could not know then that he himself would be the first European to see it; though perhaps he hoped, even then, for the opportunity to explore its precipitous mountainsides and hidden valleys.

In contrast to the bleak expanses of the Chilas area, the broad, gently sloping valley in which Gilgit lies is green and productive. Fields and orchards spread across it, from the foot of the mountains to the lip of vertical cliffs that have been created over centuries by the river cutting deep into the alluvial plateau. The streams which thread their way across the plateau slice through the edges of the cliffs as they drop down to join the river, creating the impression of massive bastion walls lining the path of the inexorable Indus.

Stein stayed three days in the small cantonment at Gilgit, admiring its order and cleanliness and warming to the genuine interest in the area displayed by its British residents. Making good a few defects he had detected in his outfit over the past twelve days, he was even given by one of the officers' wives strands of her own hair for use in his photo-theodolite. Then, having rested and arranged fresh transport, he set out again on 15 June for Hunza and the road to China.

The newly improved bridle-path which he followed up the Hunza River wound its way along a succession of deep gorges, cutting into the walls of rock wherever possible, projecting far above the foaming waters elsewhere by means of *rafiks*, narrow galleries built out from the rock face with stones and the branches of trees. Beyond Hunza the proliferation of these galleries, and the terrifyingly precarious footholds they afforded, dictated that loads were carried only by coolies. Even the sure-footed Dash had to be carried where *rafiks* took the form of ladders, held to the cliff-faces only by interwoven branches which one of the frequent earth tremors could effortlessly dislodge and scatter into the gorge below. Travellers approaching Hunza today in the relative comfort of buses or jeeps may still glimpse the remnants of such routes, threading their way along the mountainside above the Karakoram Highway. Away from the new, metalled roads, they will find them still in use.

Earlier in his journey, hazy weather had denied Stein a view of Nanga Parbat, above Gilgit. But at Hunza the massive, ice-bound peak of Rakaposhi glittered against clear skies, rearing above the other mountains that surround and dwarf this hidden kingdom. Pausing at the Nilt gorge to identify the 1,000-foot-high cliffs scaled by Manners Smith and his native soldiers in 1891, he met local men who eagerly showed him the place, their pride in the British exploits undiminished by the fact that they themselves had been fighting for the Mir of Hunza at the time.

The Mir had fled to Sinkiang after the British stormed his palace at Baltit, and had been succeeded by his more pliable half-brother, Muhammad Nazim. Stein visited him, conversing in Persian since the local Burisheski tongue is peculiar to the Hunza valley and bears no resemblance to either Indian, Iranian or Turki languages. Farther up the valley a few days later, he was delighted to find the people of Ghulmit speaking a language resembling the ancient tongue of eastern Iran. He noticed, however, that the Punjabi tongue had made rapid inroads among the Hunzakuts during the few years in which troops from that region had been stationed, under the British, in what had previously been a remarkably isolated place.

This was a trip to gladden a philologist's heart. Stein noted that, while still in Hunza territory, his party consisted of Wakhi guides and coolies, Hunza coolies speaking Burisheski, an orderly from Gilgit who used a Dard dialect and personal servants whose language was Turki. Ram Singh, the surveyor, communicated with his Rajput cook in Hindi. Stein himself spoke Turki to his servants, and Persian to the Wakhis and better-educated villagers, and regretted that the absence of any Kashmiri attendants prevented him from practising that tongue too.

On 26 June, the party reached the point at which the local coolies returned home. Behind lay the fertile valley of Hunza, its orchards and cornfields watered by an intricate network of watercourses, its mulberries and apricots ripening in the heat. Ahead lay the final climb through a boulder-strewn landscape to the Kilik Pass and Chinese Turkestan. Here, at least, Stein could use ponies again. Here also he was met by a cheerful young soldier from Sarikol, the region immediately on the far side of the border, who had been sent to inquire after his progress, for George Macartney had made sure that the authorities knew of his impending arrival.

Three days later, on 29 June, Stein and his party reached the Kilik Pass, 15,800 feet high, and camped for the first time in China. What neither he nor the authorities in Sarikol yet knew, however, was that the country whose frontier he had just crossed after a month of hard travelling was at that very moment engaged in a bitter struggle against international domination which threatened the life of every European in China.

————————▶ ◀————————

The Boxer Rebellion of 1900 came after more than half a century of Chinese concessions to foreigners during which the Chinese received precious little in return. The resentment fuelled by the demands of the foreign powers finally exploded under the leadership of one of China's many secret sects, the Society of the Harmonious Fists, or Boxers, who began to attack Christian missions and foreign importations such as telegraph lines. Supported by the enfeebled Manchu dynasty's Dowager Empress for her own purposes, the Boxers then assaulted the foreign legations in Peking, and provincial governors were ordered to expel all foreigners.

The uprising was eventually put down by an international expeditionary force in August 1900, with the loss of many Chinese lives. But in June, the situation was still dangerous and the outcome by no means certain. Stein's safety was the responsibility of the Government of India and his presence in China caused a flurry of telegrams. The British Resident in Kashmir, Macartney's official superior, wired the Foreign Department asking for orders in view of the 'disturbances' and was told to rely on Macartney. 'Stein should be warned not to proceed unless Macartney can assure him there is no real risk,' ran the telegram. 'Where is Stein, ends.'[10] The Kashmir Resident sent a copy of this telegram to Manners Smith in Gilgit, asking for urgent news of the archaeologist's whereabouts, and Manners Smith sent copies on by mail-runner. Stein was finally located high on the plateaux of the Pamirs.

His reply on 7 July characteristically played down the dangers and neatly contrived arguments favouring the course of action he himself preferred. The information received by Macartney's representative in Sarikol, he said, showed that Kashgar was quiet. Moreover, the fact that a consignment of revolvers and ammunition had been entrusted to him to deliver to Macartney was a further reason for the completion of his journey. Stein had in fact heard of the Peking uprising: a messenger from Hunza had already brought Reuters telegrams to his camp, for delivery to Macartney, on 2 July. But he merely trusted the 'time-honoured decentralisation' of China to minimize the likelihood of trouble in this westerly extremity of the empire.[11] And in the event he was right. Sinkiang did not erupt.

The part of the Pamir range into which Stein crossed at the end of June is known as the Taghdumbash Pamir. Here, where Pakistan (or India as it was in Stein's day) and China meet, the boundary is a natural as well as an official one. From the south, the approach is up rocky gorges and mountainsides occupied only by marmots – and, nowadays, the occasional wretched road-gang. On the northern side the view opens on to wide, gently sloping plateaux, reminiscent of steppe but bounded by the fantastic, jagged peaks of the Pamirs as far as the eye can see. Small streams water the grasslands, producing bright patches of wild flowers.

These great stretches of country are still home to the nomadic Kirghiz people whom Stein encountered there. But their presence remains infinitesimally small in that vast, silent landscape, one of the last magnificently empty places on earth. No one who goes to the trouble of getting there, even today when it is a relatively easy matter, could fail to be exhilarated by 'the Roof of the World'. For Stein the exhilaration was particularly intense since he was within a few miles of a place which had long held significance for him: the watershed of the Oxus River.

The Oxus – now known as the Amu-darya – forms the northern boundary of Afghanistan as it runs westward before turning north to the Aral Sea. 'All the interests of ancient Iran cluster in one form or the other round the banks of the great stream,' Stein wrote later.[12] Also looming in his mind was the figure of Alexander the Great, who crossed the river during his Bactrian and Sogdian campaigns in the winter of 330–329 BC. He was nearer the Oxus than he had ever expected to be when, as a boy, he had dreamt of it in a library beside the Danube. A two-day detour would take him nearer still: so while his surveyor was busy at work in the area of the Kilik Pass, he made the journey through snow in order to know that he had stood near the head of the Wakhan valley and the source of the river.

Afghanistan itself, however, was forbidden territory to an archaeologist employed by the Government of India; besides, the demands of his expedition called him back. An official reception party awaited him in Tashkurgan, the chief place of Sarikol, five days' ride away. There he was accommodated in a yurt (a traditional felt tent) while he organized fresh supplies and transport, and explored the ancient walls of a town that had been a key point on old trading routes. In 1900, its status was merely that of an administrative centre – though the ability of the local people to speak not only their own language but also Persian and Turki testified to its former role as a major trading crossroads.

When Stein arrived, he found little more than a recently built Chinese fort, for an earthquake in 1895 had reduced the rubble-built houses of the town to ruins and the people, encouraged by the peaceful conditions, had moved to outlying hamlets to tend their animals. Today, rubble and ruins still cover a large area on top of the fortified crag. A few small, unpaved streets below, a single dusty avenue and a large, gaunt guest-house and compound are all that qualify for the name of town. There is more life on the surrounding plain, where calling voices and the tinkling of bells on animals' collars carry for miles, and minute figures can be seen far off, walking with their goats or working outside their huts.

Stein was anxious to survey the site of the town, but suspected that the commander of the Chinese garrison would object. Not one to be discouraged by mere rules and regulations, he and Ram Singh waited until midday, when the soldiers were asleep. Then they went about their task while Macartney's representative there, an enterprising former pupil of the Oriental College in Lahore called Sher Muhammad, occupied the local Amban (chief magistrate) with discussions concerning the party's journey. On 10 July, Stein and his men again moved on, this time aiming for Mustagh-Ata, 'the father of ice mountains'.

On the inaccessible heights of Mustagh-Ata, according to Kirghiz tradition, lived an ancient saint. Hiuen Tsiang had heard a similar story, featuring a giant looming among 'brooding vapours'. Stein had eagerly awaited his first sight of the massive snow-capped mountain. But by the time he reached it, heavy rain had brought a superabundance of vapours, and these were followed by snow. He was intent on surveying it, however, pressing the local Beg (headman) to provide the necessary yaks and making concessions only in leaving Dash safely in camp when he started the ascent. Lying in his tent high on the mountain's shoulder during the next few nights, he could hear the sound of the wind, and of avalanches crashing down the far side of the Yambulak Glacier.

Several men set off in his party, but they fell out one by one until he was left with only two from Hunza who had crossed the border with him. At 20,000 feet, the three men stood in the soft snow and gazed at the panorama before them: range after range of mountain peaks that seemed to span the entire breadth of the Pamirs. Stein wrote afterwards of the gleam he thought he detected in the eyes of his companions. The hillmen of Hunza had long been known as raiders and brigands in Sarikol, where the wide plains offered far richer grazing grounds than they could find in their own narrow valleys. The flight of the old Mir and the arrival of the British in Hunza had changed all that; but Stein had noticed how talk of past raids animated all classes of Hunzakut. With little prompting his two men broke into happy recollections of raids and aired their contempt for the peaceful, nomadic Kirghiz.

Stein's sympathies were firmly with the Hunzakuts. They had 'pluck', he wrote of them later; and this was a high accolade, since pluck was one of the human qualities he most admired. They also held an impressive record of speed in crossing these mountains. Stein had earlier witnessed with astonishment and admiration the feat of a messenger sent from Hunza to Tashkurgan. He had left Hunza on the morning of 18 June and, on his way back from Tashkurgan, met Stein on the 25th. He had covered about 280 miles in the intervening week, across the Pamir passes and along the dreadful *rafiks* of Hunza.

Stein could not equal such a performance. But he was capable of marches that tested the endurance of even experienced guides. Leaving the great ice-mountain on 23 July, he pushed on down the massive rocky gorges that lead to the Tarim Basin and arrived in the oasis of Tashmalik late on 28 July, after a fourteen-hour walk and ride. He was up the following morning with the first light, determined to reach Kashgar that same day. There were fifty miles to cover. Leaving most of his party to follow, he rode out at six o'clock with Sadak Akhun and a couple of pony-men.

The willows and poplars that line the roads in the oases of the Tarim Basin delighted him after the wilderness through which he had ridden. The hamlets were thick with luxuriant vegetation: fruit trees, vegetables and huge melons grew in profusion, and irrigation channels sparkled in the fields. Men worked on their crops and women and children came to the doors of their mud-walled homes to hear the songs of Stein's men. Beyond the oases, sandy wastes and tamarisk clumps gave Stein a hint of what lay before him in the desert.

He was now on the main route into the Kashgar oasis, and the high-laden donkey carts thronging the road created thick clouds of dust. Sadak Akhun assured him that Chini Bagh, the Macartneys' house, was close at hand. But he repeated his assurances so often, over so many hours, that they soon ceased to be encouraging. At last, in failing light, the old mud walls of Kashgar city appeared ahead through the shadowy poplars. There were no lights and no sounds, for the city gates were already closed.

Chini Bagh lay outside the walls. Sadak Akhun led the way down a short avenue and there, at last, were the gates of the Macartney house, lit by a single lantern. Stein dismounted from his tired pony, walked down some steps from the courtyard into a terraced garden and found his hosts waiting for him. He had been on the road for two months, and he was the first archaeologist ever to set foot in Kashgar.

5

Lost Cities of the Silk Road

K ASHGAR IN 1900 was an isolated place. It lay a thousand miles from the capital of Sinkiang, Urumchi, and the peasants, petty traders and artisans who occupied its oasis had little need for communication with the outside world. It was precisely that outside world, however, which in the past had made Kashgar a major staging and trading post. Routes ran eastward round either side of the Taklamakan Desert, westwards to Samarkand and Bokhara, and across the Pamirs to Afghanistan and Iran.

At the beginning of the twentieth century, the city's position was still significant, but the emphasis had changed. The most important road now was the one that led to Russia and the railhead of the Transcaspian Railway at Andijan, on the far side of the Alai passes. The Tsar's armies had gradually conquered all the independent khanates of Western Turkestan during the preceding decades, and the railway that followed in the soldiers' wake brought new influences to the Chinese border: not only modern communications but also Russian-made goods at a price with which traders from India could barely compete.

The proximity of the railhead meant that the Russian Consul could enlarge his small force of Cossacks at short notice. And since Russian Turkestan had extended its hospitality to two pretenders to the ruling seat in Kashgar – one the son of Yakub Beg, the other a descendant of Kashgar's patron saint, Abakh Hoja – the Chinese administrators of

Kashgaria (southern Sinkiang) had every reason to fear the growing power of their neighbour. Even the ordinary people expected their country to fall into Russian hands sooner or later. By 1900, a Russian bank had opened in the city, the currency of exchange was the rouble and there was talk of the Russians building a proper transport road to Andijan (which they did six years later).

Living in Kashgar under such circumstances, George Macartney had little in common with British representatives elsewhere whose positions were founded on the strength of empire. He had the confidence and friendship of the administrators of Kashgaria and did his best to protect the interests of British trade. But in ten years there, he had been unable to combat the influence of Russia and was pessimistic about the prospect of ever doing so. Indeed, his wife wrote many years later that, had it not been for the fact that her father-in-law, Sir Halliday Macartney, was at that time Secretary to the Chinese Legation in London, and that the Chinese Minister there had personally recommended George Macartney to the Taotai of Kashgar, the situation would have been untenable in the face of Russian hostility.[1]

So it was no grand British establishment that welcomed Stein on 29 July 1900. The Macartneys' home, Chini Bagh – meaning Chinese Garden – was a simple native house, built of mud and brick round three sides of a courtyard and standing in an orchard. Inside the thick, single-storey walls, the rooms were lit only by skylights. But a certain amount of 'Europeanizing' had gone on. The low platforms which usually fill much of the floor-space in the rooms of Turki houses had been levelled, and Russian stoves had replaced open fireplaces. Macartney had even been lent a framed piece of glass by Petrovsky, with which to make a window, but after their disagreement it had had to be returned. The furniture was rudimentary, for most of it had been made by Macartney and the Dutch priest, Hendricks, in the 1890s, when the only alternatives were boxes or the floor.

The arrival of Macartney's new wife, Catherine Theodora, in 1898, had brought some changes. There were now bright carpets, cushions and lampshades, a rocking chair and some Austrian bentwood chairs, a bed with a box-spring mattress which Macartney had bought from a Russian officer, and a piano which Theodora had had sent from England. Stein, in any case, was an undemanding visitor and declared that the house had 'all the comforts of an English home' – a judgement which may have pleased his hostess but doubtless would have shocked many other house-proud ladies who had never ventured out of England.

Theodora Macartney ventured farther than most. She had known George Macartney since childhood and had been engaged to him for two years when they married in 1898. The leave he was granted on that occasion was so short that their honeymoon was spent returning to Kashgar on the Transcaspian Railway. She claimed later to have been 'the most timid, unenterprising girl in the world' with no desire to travel and 'no qualifications for a pioneer's life, beyond being able to make a cake'.[2] In reality, her strength of character must have been considerable, for she not only survived the initial journey across the mountains from Russia to Kashgar, but also made her life in Chini Bagh for the next seventeen years. There she raised three children, coped with many inconveniences and enjoyed the experience of an unfamiliar culture.

It was the sights and sounds of Kashgar that first impressed most visitors to Chini Bagh. The house stood on the brink of a loess cliff at the north-western edge of the city, looking out across the Tuman River to belts of poplars and willows, beyond which rose the far-off mountains. On the unpaved roads that crossed the flat, fertile land, cavalcades of carts and donkey-riders raised clouds of dust as they made their way into the city, and the shouts and songs of the people wafted across the fields. Melons and rice, cotton and lucerne all grew in profusion, watered by a carefully maintained network of irrigation channels.

In summer, when the distant snows melted, the water levels rose. The hotter the weather, the better the water supply and the more abundant the crops. Rainstorms were unwelcome, since they battered the fields. But the dust storms of summer were worse. Theodora Macartney wrote later of the 'uncanny stillness' and darkness that preceded the arrival of a shrieking wind and dust that penetrated every crevice, coating everything and making even breathing difficult.[3]

━━━━━◄►━━━━━

Chini Bagh suited Stein. It fulfilled his requirements in providing the company of genial, civilized Europeans without the 'bustle and outside interference' that he disliked in an 'ordinary European existence'.[4] The only demands on his time were self-imposed and concerned almost exclusively with his work: either the impending journey into the desert, or the final proofs of the *Rajatarangini* which had followed him relentlessly to Kashgar.

The postal services that made this possible very rarely failed him, during either this or subsequent expeditions. Mail sent via India was taken to Gilgit whence the *dak*, or mail, runners travelled fortnightly across the Karakoram Mountains to Kashgar. They delivered letters regularly throughout his eight-week journey from Kashmir to Kashgar, and were to keep him similarly well-supplied during the following ten months, whether he was camping in Khotanese orchards or deep in the desert. Mail also reached Kashgar from Europe across Russia, taking about one month to complete the journey. Stein's expeditions to remote places over the years were to make him an authority on postal services; and it was often a source of irritation to him that publishers and other business correspondents failed to master the system as he had done.

He stayed in Kashgar throughout the month of August. The temperature, which often reached 100° Fahrenheit in the shade, did not bother him: the only climate that ever elicited from him strong complaint, as opposed to merely comment, was the oppressive humidity of Calcutta. He rose at dawn, to the call to the faithful that floated across the roofs from the Idkha mosque, and by six in the morning had settled down to work in the shade of Chini Bagh's poplar groves and heavily laden fruit trees. A mullah from the chief *madrasah* of Kashgar taught him Turki, and local artisans repaired his kit; though they were not as skilled at imitation as their Indian counterparts and had to be carefully supervised.

Each morning, Stein and Macartney carried out a tour of inspection round the courtyard of Chini Bagh where the craftsmen worked. Then, during the hottest part of the day, Stein retired to a dark-room he had improvized to develop the many photographs taken over the previous two months. Later, after tea, he would join his host for a walk or ride through the lanes. After dinner, he sat with the Macartneys on the roof of the house and listened to songs – reminiscent to his ear of Hungarian airs – sung by Kashgaris returning from picnics in their orchards beyond the river.

Sometimes Cossack music wafted through the still night air from the Russian Consulate not far away. But Stein had to wait till his return from the desert before he could meet Petrovsky. In his popular account of his expedition, he wrote tactfully that the reason for the delay was the 'indisposition' of the Russian Consul. The truth was that Petrovsky simply refused to see him.

Petrovsky's hostility towards Stein's presence in Kashgaria threatened to impede his entire expedition. As Macartney had explained to Stein in 1899, the support of the Taotai in Kashgar was necessary before any work could be done in the Khotan area. But already, before Stein himself called on this Chinese official, Macartney had heard from the latter's lips a pathetic confession. Explaining that he hesitated to give his permission in the face of Russian disapproval, the Taotai told Macartney that he 'knew he might be accused of cowardice; but he was a coward and a fool, and he fully admitted this fact, as well as his fear of Petrovsky'.[5]

Macartney managed to allay his fears, reassure him as to Stein's intentions and extract from him the appropriate recommendations. But Stein left nothing to chance. Characteristically arming himself with plenty of information on the correct etiquette for such meetings, he called on the Taotai, behaved impeccably and sprinkled his conversation liberally with references to his 'Buddhist Pausanias', the pilgrim Hiuen Tsiang, knowing this would lend credence to the expedition. Privately, he noted in his diary that the Taotai was 'a typical burlesque Mandarin, but good-natured'.[6]

If Stein's approach seems disdainful to modern eyes, it should be remembered that this was a period when judgements far more glib and presumptuous than his most private reflections could be published and go unremarked. The way in which Captain H.H.P. Deasy, another European visitor to Chinese Turkestan whose book of travels appeared in 1901, dismissed traditional events, local culture and the deaths of servants makes Stein's attitude to the region and its people seem a picture of humanity. Unfortunately, this humanity, and a dislike of unpleasantness in any form, translated into such measured prose that Deasy's outspoken criticism of Petrovsky, for example, remains more interesting reading than Stein's tact.

One person to whom Stein warmed was Father Hendricks. The old priest had been nicknamed 'the newspaper' because of his habit of collecting all the news and rumours of the day. Wearing a battered old clerical hat and a dirty Chinese coat, he would trot busily from one place to another throughout the day, entirely dependent on his friends for meals.

He read mass to himself each morning in front of an altar assembled from a packing case covered with a grubby lace cloth, and appeared to have made not a single convert.

Stein regarded him as embodying 'the principles of international amity'.[7] Probably he preferred his eccentric ways to those of the Swedish missionaries, the Raquettes, whose 'foolish display of apprehension' over reports of the siege of the legations in Peking he noted privately in his diary.[8] The bazaars were awash with rumours of ferocious fighting and massacres in the capital, and there had been some tension between the native people and the Chinese garrison. But the people of Kashgar were not much inclined to rebellion and Stein preferred to trust to their peaceable natures than to fret about unsubstantiated rumours.

While Westerners were all too familiar a sight in China proper, in Kashgar they were still rare and the city when Stein first saw it was little affected by European ways. There were, in fact, two cities, an old and a new, lying seven or eight miles apart. The residents of the 40,000-strong old city were an exotic mixture. There were Uighurs, the descendants of the Turkish tribes that overran Chinese Turkestan centuries before, Kirghiz from the uplands, Aryan-featured Tajiks from Sarikol and Afghanistan, Pathans, traders from the Punjab and some ethnic Chinese. The common language was Turki, from which modern Turkish comes, but Persian was also spoken.

Most of the residents were Muslims, but comparatively lax in their observance and notably casual over marital arrangements. The streets of their bazaars were narrow and generally muddy from the water that slopped out of the water-carriers' panniers, and the small shops that lined them were often shaded completely from the sun by reed awnings. Despite the gloom of the lanes, however, the old city was (and still is) made colourful by the bright clothes of the people and the overflowing fruit stalls heaped with melons of all sizes and shades, apricots, peaches, mulberries, grapes, and black and yellow figs.

In the much smaller, new city to the south the colours were more muted, for this was where the Chinese garrison was housed, and where the Taotai had his official residence. The shops sold Chinese goods, jade, *cloisonné* and silk brocade, and this was where Stein shopped for presents for his family. He was always rather embarrassed to admit to this occupation, but clearly indulged in it often on his travels, because he never failed to bring back silks and furs for his sister-in-law and the wives of his friends, as well as a variety of other items, such as brass-work and carpets (the Chinese coats he gave Helen Allen are now in the Ashmolean Museum in Oxford). The tidy ways of Kashgar's Chinese shopkeepers won his approval immediately: he admired the way in which their correspondence was addressed, docketed and kept in pigeon-holes.

Stein was set to start his journey to the desert sites by the beginning of September. He had had difficulty in obtaining more water-tanks to supplement the two brought from India, and eventually had had four battered iron kerosene tanks from Russia adapted by a local blacksmith. He had acquired reliable baggage animals, eight camels and twelve ponies, at modest prices; and he had hired four more men. Three of the main members of his party remained the same: the cook, Sadak Akhun, the surveyor Ram Singh and his own cook, Jasvant Singh. But Stein's personal servant, Mirza Alim, had proved unequal to the rigours of the journey from Kashmir, and was left behind in Kashgar. Sending most of this small force of men and animals ahead on 10 September, Stein left Kashgar on the following morning for Khotan and the Taklamakan Desert.

His route lay via Yarkand, the chief trading centre and largest city in Chinese Turkestan: Sven Hedin had estimated its population, together with that of nearby villages, to be 150,000. Like Khotan beyond, it lay on the old Silk Route skirting the southern side of the Taklamakan, and the road that led there from Kashgar was well-used. Stein chose instead a route slightly to the east that would take him into a stretch of desert and past a Muslim shrine the exact position of which he wished to fix.

At least part of the reason for this detour was to test himself and his equipment. He saw how the ponies' feet sank into the soft sand of the dunes and how continual ascents and descents of forty-foot slopes tired them and made each mile covered a laborious achievement. Dash was similarly afflicted and had to suffer the indignity of travelling in a camel basket, with only a hole in the lid from which to survey progress. The party reached Yarkand on 17 September.

It was important for Stein to call at towns, if for no other reason than to keep himself supplied with cash. He had arranged to receive his government salary in Chinese money through Macartney, and to obtain funds from his expedition grant by cashing Government Supply Bills and cheques with local merchants. But in towns he could also enquire after desert sites known to treasure-seekers, and look out for interesting old items to take home as gifts, which the traders were only too pleased to bring for his inspection.

Like Deasy and Hedin before him, Stein had to attend more than one official Chinese dinner during his time in Sinkiang. And like them, he found such occasions severe endurance tests. Hedin had been overwhelmed by the liberal doses of fiery spirit and the forty-six courses through which he had been obliged to sit, and Stein was similarly intimidated, though aware that he had escaped lightly by being given only sixteen. He recorded in his diary no more details of the food than to note that he was 'glad when rice came . . . Revived by tea.'[9] But in his own book, *Through Asia*, Hedin described a few dishes typical of such feasts: 'the skin, fins, and cartilage of different varieties of fish found in the seas and rivers of the Chinese empire, fungi, salted mutton fat cut into long strips, lizards (salamanders), ham with a great variety of widely different adjuncts, besides a multitude of strange preparations, the real constituents and names of which remained mysteries to me'.

There was little opportunity for archaeological investigation in the oases themselves: centuries of irrigation had covered the fields with several feet of silt and rotted any old wood that survived beneath. After ten days in Yarkand, Stein set off again for Khotan, with pack animals refreshed from the rest. Four of them had spent the period in especially favourable conditions, in woods south of Yarkand, having developed sore backs on the first leg of the journey. Stein, disliking both the cruelty and the inefficiency involved, was angry with the camel and pony men who had tried to hide the injuries from him. But his threat, to deduct from their pay any expense incurred by having to replace unfit animals, ensured that the offence did not arise again.

The appalling complications of his accounts made an unequivocal, if not ruthless, approach to such problems essential. The Indian government insisted on the periodic submission of accounts in return for their funding of the expedition, and he was too methodical and responsible to evade his duties. But the vagaries of currency arrangements in Sinkiang made them an intimidating and time-consuming business. Calculations were done in both local and Chinese units, neither of which converted easily to the other. Moreover, local *tangas* were worth more in Khotan than they were in Kashgar. Items imported from Russia were priced in roubles, and it was the rouble which determined the exchange rate for Indian rupees. Stein grappled diligently with the jumble of figures that resulted, but he resented the time spent on such calculations.

One task, by contrast, he was anxious to tackle. The mysterious blockprints in unknown languages which were part of the British Collection of Central Asian Antiquities, and which had so puzzled Rudolf Hoernle, were said to have been found in the desert between Karghalik and Khotan, near a place called Guma. They had been sold to Macartney by a local man called Islam Akhun, and had aroused Stein's suspicions as soon as he heard of them. In Kashgar, he received information from Macartney which only confirmed those suspicions.

Two years previously, in 1898, a Swedish missionary stationed in Yarkand had heard from a servant boy that someone, almost certainly Islam Akhun, was manufacturing 'old' books to meet the demand from Europeans. The blocks were made from pear-tree wood and the characters copied from genuine old documents. After printing, the paper was hung in chimneys until brown, then fastened together into books which, dampened and sprinkled with sand, soon acquired the sort of appearance which fooled buyers into thinking they were centuries old.

In April of the same year, Islam Akhun agreed to lead Captain Deasy to one of the buried cities where he claimed to have dug up such books, but their short expedition into the desert ended in complete failure after Deasy realized that none of the local men in his party knew where they were. At his insistence, Islam Akhun was later arrested and sentenced to a month of wearing the cangue, a large square board weighing about thirty pounds which fitted round the neck like a mobile version of the stocks. But the matter ended there, as far as Deasy was concerned, and his account of it did not appear until his book was published in 1901.

En route to Khotan, Stein stopped at Guma to investigate the many nearby sites which were supposed to have yielded Islam Akhun's old books. The local begs recognized only two of the names, and nowhere was there evidence of antiquities, buried or otherwise. At Khotan, however, unmistakable proof of forgery appeared. A Russian Armenian, hearing of Stein's presence and interest in antiquities, brought him a birch-bark manuscript which he had bought for 40 roubles, evidently hoping to sell it for a larger sum.

The characters on the birch-bark looked very like those in Hoernle's blockprints. But when Stein applied what he called 'the water-test', dabbing the leaves with a wetted finger, the ink dissolved – as he knew it would not have done had it been genuinely ancient. At last he had proof of the deception in his hands (he did not record the reaction of the Armenian to the sight of his investment disappearing before his eyes). Islam Akhun's whereabouts were not then known, but Stein seems to have been confident that he would be able to catch up with him later.

From genuine local 'treasure-seekers' he was anxious to hear about items found at old sites beyond Khotan. These men had learnt to make money out of the recent demand from European travellers for antiquities. Like gold-washing and jade-digging, treasure-seeking offered, as Stein put it, 'a kind of lottery to those low down in luck and averse to any constant exertion'.[10] But they had no idea of the significance of their finds, and were unable to describe accurately the places where they had found them. So he gladly accepted an offer from Badruddin Khan, the head of the Afghan merchants in Khotan, to organize 'prospecting parties' who would go to the desert in order to bring back examples from specific, identifiable sites. During the month that this prospecting would occupy, Stein would go south into the Kun-lun Mountains to survey the area containing the headwaters of the Khotan River, a task he had set himself at the start of his expedition.

In the arrangement of both this and his forthcoming journey into the desert, he had the support of the Amban of Khotan, Pan, a gentle, elderly mandarin who evidently understood and appreciated scientific work. Like the Kashmir pandit, Govind Kaul, Pan seemed to Stein to personify all that was good in an ancient culture which he deeply respected. But here, unlike in Kashmir, Stein was handicapped by his lack of Chinese and dependence on an over-confident and stupid interpreter. There were to be many occasions when he bitterly regretted his ignorance.

With native Turki speakers, communication was simpler – as was the finding of accommodation. According to the tradition of the region, he could approach the owner of whatever garden pleased him for permission to make his camp there. In Khotan the garden he chose belonged to a dignified old man called Akhun Beg, whom he disturbed reading a Turki translation of a Persian epic which Stein knew in the original language, and thus he found another friend.

————————➤◀————————

While autumn had only just come to the Tarim Basin, weather conditions changed swiftly as Stein and his ten-pony party made their way into the foothills of the Kun-lun range on 17 October. Measuring the height above sea-level with a boiling-point thermometer, he recorded an early morning temperature no higher than freezing point, only two days' journey from the oasis. On 23 October, a fine, freezing cold day, he climbed a high ridge in search of a good surveying station and suddenly found himself gazing at a glittering panorama of snowy ridges, spurs and glaciers, with the gorge of the main branch of the Khotan River plainly visible.

Despite the intense cold, Stein immediately began to take a complete circle of views with the photo-theodolite while Ram Singh worked at his plane-table. Darkness was almost upon them when they left. Their path to the Karanghu-tagh valley below led down three thousand feet of precipitous rock faces, and by the time they reached the bottom and crossed the chasm where the river lay, they could see nothing but the white foam of the churning water. Even Stein's dispassionate descriptive style could not disguise the tension of that journey, nor the aptness of the name given to the valley, which means 'mountain of blinding darkness'. It seemed appropriate that the hamlet of the same name was used by the Khotan authorities as a destination for banished criminals, and Stein was glad to leave its bleak surroundings for the next stage of his survey work.

He had hoped to find a route up through the gorge of the Khotan River, but this was not to be. After much hard scrambling across boulder-strewn ground, up crags and along ledges, he was forced to admit defeat and return to the dismal penal colony, wishing he had a hot-air balloon or 'man-carrying kite' at his disposal.

Stein's hope throughout this journey into the Kun-lun was to reach a point from which he would be able to see the peaks already triangulated from the Ladakh side, so that his own positions could be fixed with absolute certainty and Khotan connected for the first time with the Indian Trigonometrical Survey. Early in November he reached that point, on a high ridge after an exhausting climb. The same night, as he sat looking at the moonlit sea of mountain peaks before him, he experienced a curious illusion. The reflection of moonlight on the dust haze that hung over the distant desert suddenly brightened, and he found himself looking at what seemed to be the lights of a huge city far below on the plains. The effect was intense, almost mystical, drawing from him a yearning for someone to share it with. He scribbled a simple postscript to his latest letter to Percy Allen: 'I wished you were near to keep me company.'[11]

In his absence from Khotan, the treasure-seekers had done their work. The party led by the most experienced among them, an old man called Turdi, brought fragments of fresco showing Indian Brahmi characters, stucco objects of Buddhist worship and a small piece of paper on which was written something in Central Asian Brahmi. The site where these antiquities had been found, nine or ten marches north-east of Khotan, was known to the men as Dandan-Uiliq – 'the houses with ivory' – and its location corresponded to that of the buried city which Sven Hedin had visited, and which he had called simply Taklamakan. Having first explored Yotkan, an ancient site within the oasis where items lay buried beneath the soil of heavily fertilized fields, Stein reduced his supplies and animals to the minimum and, taking with him the two men who had guided Hedin to the site, set out for his first destination in the desert. It was 7 December and winter had come to the Taklamakan. Stein had abandoned his tent for a house during his last few days in Khotan. But now he had to rely on his thick felts and furs, his serge-lined tent and his Stormont-Murphy Arctic Stove to keep him warm in the deadly cold of the desert, where the temperature dropped to $-10°$ Fahrenheit at night and scarcely rose above freezing point during the day. He revelled in the pure desert air while working, but it was more difficult to get used to sleeping conditions. These necessitated the wearing of a fur-lined balaclava, wrapping himself in heavy blankets and rugs on top of his outdoor wear, pulling his fur coat over his head and breathing through the sleeve in order to protect his face. In amongst the layers of his bed snuggled Dash, wearing his own, specially made, Kashmiri fur coat.

After three days, Stein stopped at an outlying oasis to hire labourers for his intended excavations. Without the example of his two robust local guides, he would have been hard-pressed to overcome the people's dislike of winter conditions and their superstitious fear of desert jinns or spirits. He managed to assemble thirty men and hire a dozen donkeys to supplement his seven camels. There was enough food for four weeks, a small amount of fodder for the donkeys and rape-seed oil for the camels, which could survive on only half a pint of the liquid every other day.

In the desert the only vegetation to be found was tamarisk scrub, round which great hollows had been worn by the wind. In these hollows an advance party dug wells and built fires from dead roots. Guided by Turdi's unerring instinct, Stein's expedition moved through the lifeless wastes until, on 18 December, it suddenly found itself amid the bleached stumps of dead trees and the ruined houses of Dandan-Uiliq.

Where the sand had blown away, the ruins of wattle-and-plaster walls stood exposed. Though much damaged by the careless digging of treasure-seekers, they still bore faded representations of Buddhas and Bodhisattvas. Rows of posts sticking out of the sand elsewhere showed the existence of other wood-framed buildings as yet unopened. The men picked Chinese copper coins from the ground on the very first day which showed by their eighth-century date that Dandan-Uiliq had still been occupied in Hiuen Tsiang's time.

Had Stein's written accounts of his desert discoveries not been governed by his scholarly reticence, he might have penned a more dramatic account of his arrival at this first site. His predecessor at the same spot, Sven Hedin, had had no qualms about stating the historic importance of his visit five years earlier. 'No explorer', he had scribbled in his notebook as he stood among the ruins, 'had an inkling, hitherto, of the existence of this ancient city. Here I stand, like the prince in the enchanted wood, having wakened to new life the city which has slumbered for a thousand years.'[12]

If Hedin wakened Dandan-Uiliq, Stein breathed fresh life into it. For it was he, and not Hedin, who had studied the old Chinese annals and learnt the historical topography of the Tarim Basin so well from the descriptions of Hiuen Tsiang. Hedin had made intelligent guesses about the significance of the ruins; now the real work began.

During the next two weeks, Stein and his men excavated fourteen buildings, both temples and houses. The temples typically had an inner, square cell in which would have stood the stuccoed pedestal of a colossal Buddha, the size of which could be estimated from the statue's feet, which were all that remained. Between the cell and the outer walls was a corridor which would have been used for ceremonial processions, and which was decorated with larger than lifesize paintings of Buddhas, or smaller rows of saints and representations of legends. Stucco reliefs of Buddhas, Bodhisattvas and gandharvas, a kind of angel, lay on the floor where they had dropped from walls higher up. At the feet of the central Buddha images rested painted panels of wood, just as they had been left by pilgrims as offerings more than a thousand years earlier.

There was a strange lack of reality about the buried city. In the still air of the desert, it emerged with so many details intact that its civilization seemed almost recreated. Yet it was dead, desiccated, shrivelled. The extreme aridity of the conditions in which it had lain had preserved it, but also emphasized its utter lifelessness. Trunks of poplar avenues and orchards stood as bleached and blasted reminders of a thriving town that had gradually been abandoned to the forces of the desert. The sand had trickled in through cracks in walls, whipped along streets and blown through doorways during storms. Gradually it had filled all spaces with its slow, insidious stream, until it washed over the crumbling walls and collapsing roofs and spread in smooth undulations above, softly erasing all trace of the buildings beneath save for a few tall, ragged stumps.

The desolate atmosphere of the site unnerved the two Hindus, Ram Singh and Jasvant Singh, when they arrived straight from the mountains; but for Stein it possessed an almost magical attraction. It was as close to reliving the past as he could get and he was absorbed by its revelations. With each discovery came further evidence of the Indian character of the art: on each document were inscribed Buddhist texts in Sanskrit, or Brahmi writing in an unknown language. There were scraps of Chinese notes and instructions which revealed the old name of the place, Li-sieh, and the period at which it had been abandoned, in the late eighth century. There were even brooms made from grass stalks which the people of Li-sieh had used to brush the invasive sand from their houses, monasteries and shrines.

One painted panel showed a rat-headed figure, the hero of a Buddhist legend in which the king of the sacred rats saved Khotan from invading Huns by leading his followers in chewing through the harnesses of the aggressors' horses. Stein, using Hiuen Tsiang's description as a guide, had visited the shrine outside Khotan where these rats had once been honoured. It had long since been adopted by Islam to honour pigeons accredited with similar heroic qualities.

The paintings on other panels remained a mystery for some time. One, depicting a Bodhisattva strongly Persian in appearance, Stein understood fully only when he came to work on the south-east border of Persia, fifteen years later. Another, he later realized, told the story of how a Chinese princess, on her way to marry a ruler in the Western Regions, smuggled silkworm eggs out of China by hiding them in her hair. He packed all these panels, together with stucco reliefs, fragments of frescoes and a small statue, into cases padded with cotton wool and soft paper for transport back to the West.

During this first excavation in the desert, he formulated his ideas on the reasons for the abandonment of such settlements. Sven Hedin had suggested that the Keriya River once ran past the town and that, when its course shifted eastward, the people could no longer survive without its water. Stein politely refuted this theory. He argued that the late eighth century was a time of great upheaval, when Chinese authority in the region succumbed to invaders from Tibet, and that outlying oases would have been the first to suffer, since they were dependent on firm local administration for the maintenance of irrigation canals. With Tibetan hordes at large in the Tarim Basin, the people of Li-sieh took fright. Gradually they left their homes for the safety of larger oases and more reliable sources of water. Sometimes they visited their shrines to leave votive offerings; but gradually these too they left to the mercy of the desert.

That future generations never returned to recolonize such places, once the Tibetan danger had passed, Stein was later to attribute to a reduction in the volume of the rivers. The high glaciers would have shrunk gradually over centuries, he believed, under the effect of a milder climate. It was a less dramatic theory than local stories, current in Hiuen Tsiang's time as they were in 1900, that told of cataclysmic onslaughts of sand. Such tales interested Stein only as examples of local folklore; as perhaps did another legend, concerning Dandan-Uiliq, which Hedin heard in 1895. 'Among the ruins of its towers, walls and houses,' he was told, 'gold ingots and lumps of silver lay exposed. But if a caravan went there and loaded its camels with gold, the drivers would become bewitched and would walk round and round in a circle till they collapsed ... Only by throwing away the gold could they break the enchantment and be saved."[13]

Stein left Dandan-Uiliq on 4 January 1901. He had spent Christmas Day happily enough, sharing his dinner with Dash in the bitterly cold tent and thinking of the friends and relations to whom he had been careful to send greetings well in advance. But he had also experienced the potential danger of the desert when, having stayed behind in the dusk as his party returned to camp after the day's digging, he lost his sense of direction and was guided back to the tents only by the shouts of his men. A lesser problem, toothache, he had treated himself in a process made laborious by the cold. Having been woken by pain, he had had to melt a lump of ice in an aluminium tumbler over a candle before he could dilute the chlorodyne which would dull the throbbing nerve. He did not dwell on such discomforts, however, for the desert had yielded treasure.

———————►◄———————

Between visits to desert sites, Stein had to return to one or another of the oasis towns for money and stores, to rest animals and men, and to keep on good terms with the local authorities. Both during these stays and while out in the desert, he worked methodically at his camp desk, writing not only notes but also letters to friends and officialdom. There were also always new labourers to recruit, and Ambans to whom he would bring gifts of some kind, according to the custom of the place: highly scented soap, perhaps, tins of sardines, or Russian sweets.

En route to the next potential site in early January 1901, he received startling proof of its age. His quick-witted camel-man, Hassan Akhun – who was to work for him on all his Central Asian expeditions – introduced a man who owned two inscribed tablets taken from the site. On them Stein recognized immediately the ancient Kharosthi script of north-west India, and saw with delight that the writing appeared to be far older than any, apart from inscriptions, ever found in India itself. He immediately engaged the local treasure-seeker who had found them, a young miller named Ibrahim, and moved his large party, now numbering more than forty men, out into the desert. On 27 January, ninety miles north of the Niya oasis and beyond the point at which the Niya River dies away in the desert sands, he again saw the tell-tale timbers of a buried city protruding from the ground.

Before the first day was out he had found, barely hidden beneath the sand, several finely carved pieces of wood displaying ornaments typical of those seen on early Gandharan sculptures, and the following sixteen days produced much more. The work of the first day alone disclosed more than a hundred wooden tablets, written by different hands but all showing clearly the Kharosthi writing that was in use in the Punjab and adjacent trans-Indus areas during the Kushan era, the first three centuries AD.

They were the first specimens ever discovered of Indian records on wood: the materials commonly used in India, palm leaf or birch bark, would not have been available to the people of Turkestan. But Stein's excitement was tempered by reservations. Here was a cache that equalled, if it did not exceed, the total amount of Kharosthi material currently available either in or outside India. But what if the tablets revealed nothing more than repetitions of the same sacred Buddhist writings? He could ascertain that much only by examining the texts. Many would have shelved all their other plans in order to concentrate on such an extraordinary discovery, but not Stein. Following his strict daily routine, and despite the fact that the ink froze in his pen, he methodically wrote up a detailed account of the day before allowing himself to turn, with fingers numbed by cold, to the intriguing tablets.

Thereafter, he could indulge in a justified sense of triumph. For the Kharosthi script, though difficult to read, revealed that the language used was an early Indian Prakrit, probably also from north-west India; and that the contents were not sacred texts at all, but a wide variety of official orders. The tablets were wedge-shaped and fastened together in pairs, with the writing running from right to left on the inner face of one and a clay seal on the outer side of the other, which served the purpose of an envelope and kept the ink beneath it as black and fresh as if penned only a day or two earlier.

That such tablets had come to light on the very first day at Niya was extraordinary enough. But they also recalled persuasively an old tradition, recorded by Hiuen Tsiang, that Khotan was conquered and colonized by Indian immigrants from Taxila, in the north-western Punjab, in the last two centuries BC. The dating of the tablets to a period no later than the third century AD was verified by other finds: another tablet written in Indian Brahmi characters of the Kushan period, Chinese coins of the second century AD and wooden tablets inscribed with

Chinese characters, one of which proved later to be dated precisely to the year AD 269.

Many more wedge-shaped tablets came to light during the excavations at Niya, as well as others that were oblong in shape, carefully dated and covered with 'envelopes', tied together with string and sealed with clay. Wood had clearly been the stationery of this ancient place, despite the fact that paper had been invented in China at the beginning of the second century AD. More remarkable than the tablets themselves, however, were the seals that fastened them together. For there, pressed into the clay, were the unmistakable images of Greek figures: Heracles, Eros standing or seated, and Pallas Athene with aegis and thunderbolt, all made from engraved stones that closely resembled Hellenistic or Roman work of the first centuries AD.

There was no better evidence of the contact between the oases of Eastern Turkestan and the civilizations of the Mediterranean, thousands of miles away. And it was appropriate enough that Stein should be the one to uncover it, drawn to the East as he had been by a fascination with Alexander the Great and the intermingling of cultures. As if to demonstrate this fusion, one of the tablets he found bore two seals side by side: one a Western-style portrait-head, the other a set of Chinese characters.

From the style of the Kharosthi writing, and the dates of coins and of a Chinese tablet (later deciphered by a French Sinologist), Stein estimated that the site had been abandoned towards the end of the third century AD, when the withdrawal of Chinese authority from the area after the death of Emperor Wu-ti caused great instability. Among the ruined buildings of the dead city, he found the remains of fences that had once surrounded orchards; layers of dead leaves that had fallen from trees planted when emperors still ruled in Rome; fragments of carpet, part of a guitar, chopsticks, a boot last and a mousetrap, and a finely carved armchair with arm-rests in the form of Hellenistic monsters. The arrangement of the houses, with low platforms on which to sit and sleep, and posts in the centre of rooms to support raised roofs and skylights, was similar to the design that Stein knew well, and which prevails in traditional homes to this day. Nearby, in a rubbish heap whose pungency, when disturbed, belied its age, lay several Kharosthi documents on leather, still folded as their owners had left them, in small, neat rolls.

After sixteen days, Stein's labourers needed rest. Digging in the desert was exhausting work, the sand streaming back into the hole from which it had just been lifted even as the digger drove his spade in again. Besides, the atmosphere among them needed leavening. Stein's interpreter and the camel-man, Hassan Akhun, had come to blows and Sadak Akhun had complicated matters by joining in. Stein separated them with difficulty, using an ancient walking stick which he happened to have in his hand at the time. But the interpreter made a play for further attention by attempting suicide by self-strangulation; and Sadak Akhun soon afterwards fell into a depression brought on by *charas*, a local drug. Only by keeping him under constant observation was Stein able to get any useful service out of the man. Later, when fully recovered, Sadak Akhun explained that he had been under the influence of the evil spirits of the sand dunes at the time.

The winter which made work possible, despite its numbingly low temperatures, would soon be over and there were other sites still to inspect. Having left Niya on 14 February, Stein moved on to Endere, about 100 miles farther east. Work continued over four days, sometimes by the light of bonfires after darkness had fallen. Paper leaves bearing Tibetan writing – the oldest yet known – indicated that the inhabitants here had left only when raiders from the south arrived in the late eighth century. In an old temple, Stein found stucco sculpture, paper manuscripts and a central pedestal on which rested the legs of what had once been four seated images. By the time he left Endere, on 26 February, the frozen desert streams were beginning to melt and a distant haze presaged the dust-storms of summer.

During this last, busy phase of the expedition, while Stein hurriedly inspected two further desert sites, one of his pony-men arrived with a mailbag bringing letters and newspapers from India and Europe. It was one of Stein's pleasures in the desert to hear from friends and family, their letters all the more welcome for arriving at unpredictable intervals. But the mailbag which reached him now as he travelled along a gritty road contained unhappy tidings. From hopeful contemplation of the difference his discoveries might make to his life and work, he was wrenched by the news that Percy Allen and his wife were leaving India forever.

The news was not wholly unexpected. Both had suffered ill-health while living in the Punjab, and Publius's desire to devote himself to Erasmus could not be satisfied at such a distance from the European libraries in which he would have to do his research. In 1900 his father offered him a modest allowance of £250 a year which made life in Oxford possible.

Stein knew and supported his friend's hopes. But the announcement that they were so soon to be fulfilled took him by surprise and cast a shadow on the plans he had been nurturing for a return to the Punjab. The Allens intended to revisit India in 1908, and Publius wrote reassuringly that 'there are stronger things than distance'; but Stein, reading his words amid a sea of sand, suddenly felt disorientated. 'I have realized only too late what I lost when I allowed myself to be drawn away from that magic circle which you and Mrs Allen know to hold your friends,' he replied from an overnight camp by the Keriya River. 'Now it seems as if I [have] lost you a second time. For though I am quite in the dark about my own return to the Punjab, I could always hope for happy days with you as long as we were both on Indian soil . . . Vale, amicissime, Yours ever, the BG.'[14]

There was no time for idle contemplation of his loss, however. And when a firm offer of the inspectorship of schools in the Punjab arrived from India, in the second week of April, he accepted. There seemed, for the time being, no alternative.

Sand-storms were now a daily occurrence. Sand penetrated clothes and goggles, blew into eyes, throat and lungs, and created a yellow fog through which the sun beat down, creating a reflective glare which intensified the increasing heat. Back in Khotan, the fruit-trees were already heavy with blossom and the temperature during the day was high in the eighties (though still below freezing point at night). It was time for Stein to leave the Taklamakan and head for home. But before he left, there was one important matter to sort out in Khotan: the forgeries of Islam Akhun.

Among all the documents Stein had found in the desert, not a single one carried 'unknown characters' such as those found on the blockprints in the Calcutta collection. Nor did the sites he had excavated bear any resemblance to those described by Islam Akhun. Convinced that a spectacularly successful imposture was waiting to be uncovered, he enlisted the help of his favourite Chinese official, Pan, the Amban of Khotan, and Islam Akhun was duly brought to Khotan on 25 April.

Islam Akhun had whiled away the winter in an outlying village by practising as a *hakim*, or medicine man. His equipment for this role included some pages from a French novel and fragments of a Persian text, though it was never established whether these were meant as incantations or medication to be taken internally. He had already been punished for misleading Deasy and forging his signature, and Stein had no wish to see further retribution meted out. He felt, in any case, that the Indian authorities and their representatives had invited deception by their thoughtless enthusiasm for buying anything answering to the description of 'old books'. He was simply interested in discovering the truth from a man he could not help admiring for an intelligence and versatility that was far above the average in the oases of Chinese Turkestan.

The ensuing interviews, spread over two days, proved highly entertaining. When he came to describe them in his book, Stein curbed his amusement for the sake of what would surely be Hoernle's wounded pride. But the humour of the situation was not lost on his readers: the Kiplings, father and son, no doubt echoed the thoughts of others when they remarked on it at the time of publication.

Islam Akhun claimed at first to have been simply the agent of others. But the details of his own elaborate defence eventually betrayed him, for he also claimed never to have seen the places in which the 'old books' were dug up. At this, Stein was able to confront him with the exact reproduction of the stories he had told Macartney about his alleged discoveries, as printed in Hoernle's 1899 Report. Islam Akhun was so impressed by seeing his own words enshrined in print that the temptation to explain how he had perpetrated such a magnificent fraud proved irresistible. He was even able to identify among the illustrations in the Report the block-printed pages which he himself had manufactured.

His idea of making what was evidently popular with Europeans had sprung from a reluctance to go to the trouble of visiting sites where the real thing could be found. As he quipped to Turdi, Stein's guide, the weather-beaten old treasure-seeker was living proof that 'there was nothing to be got out of the desert'. Instead, together with several accomplices he had begun by creating books by hand, sometimes even copying genuine Brahmi characters seen on fragments of old manuscripts. Confidence soon triumphed over caution, however, and he had turned to mass production in order to satisfy demand; for, after all, none of the people who bought 'old books' could read them, regardless of whether or not the books in question were genuine.

The people who worked in his 'factory' were given a free rein in inventing their own writing. The paper, easily available since Khotan was the centre of the Turkestan paper industry, was dyed yellow or light brown, and the leaves, once block-printed, were hung over fireplaces whose smoke stained them until they looked appropriately antique. They were then bound into books in crude imitation of European volumes (a detail which was inexplicably overlooked by those who should have known better) and the finished products were sprinkled with sand, as Deasy had heard three years earlier.

News of Islam Akhun's confession spread quickly through the bazaars and his humiliation seemed to cow him; but not for long. Stein had joked to him during the course of their conversations that he was too intelligent to remain in the oases of the Tarim Basin, and Islam Akhun had drawn the obvious conclusion. Shortly before Stein left for Kashgar, the wily forger came to him and made an unsuccessful plea to accompany him to Europe, where he evidently felt his abilities would be better appreciated.

There was much leave-taking to observe before Stein could quit the Khotan oasis, for thanks and gifts of cash had to be given to all who had helped him. From Pan, he parted with regret. To the guide, Turdi, he gave a sum far greater in value than anything the old man had ever found in the desert, which was received with tears of gratitude. The troublesome Chinese interpreter was left in the arms of someone whom Stein poetically described as 'a captivating Khotan damsel of easy virtue', having rid himself of his family in Kashgar by divorcing them through the post.

Stein left Khotan finally at daybreak on 1 May. At the Pigeon Shrine, where in Hiuen Tsiang's time the sacred rats had lived, he threw a handful of corn in sentimental recognition of the old belief that the birds, and before them the rats, would grant the wishes of those who paid their respects. Back in Kashgar, the Russian Consul, Petrovsky, newly reacquainted with Macartney and other British nationals, deigned to grant him an audience. Stein's nationality, however, was something of a mystery. He had renounced Hungarian citizenship at the start of his career in India. But on applying to Simla for a passport for his journey home through Russia, he had been sent a certificate of identity instead and told that a passport could not be provided since it was unclear 'whether you are a naturalized British subject'.[15]

Exactly a year after leaving Srinagar, Stein set out for Russia on 29 May 1901. He took with him only the six ponies that carried his antiquities, two more for personal baggage, the pony-men and Sadak Akhun, who had sobered up considerably since his outburst in the desert. His Indian men returned home the way they had come, taking Dash with them to spare him quarantine in England.

The journey across the Alai passes to Osh normally took eighteen days; Stein did it in ten. At the border, where he was immediately ushered into the comfort of Russian official quarters, it seemed to him that he had stepped suddenly into Europe. And though his journey involved more riding, through the lush valley of Ferghana whose horses the Chinese had coveted so many centuries earlier, he was soon being transported across Russian Turkestan by the Transcaspian Railway. He had covered more than four thousand miles between leaving Kashmir in May 1900 and reaching Osh. His finds had been greater than he had dared hope; and he was already determined to return for more.

6

A Fight for Freedom

———————————◆———————————

S TEIN WAS NOW set on a collision course with the representatives
of authority in India. He had no difficulty imposing order and discipline on himself, but he strained at the leash of employment. Official
duties had become simply a means to an end. He could not afford to do
without the financial security of his salary and pension but, beyond
those necessities, his aim was freedom.

His first journey into Chinese Turkestan merely whetted his appetite
for exploratory work. But further expeditions could not be undertaken
without a continuous effort to overturn the expectations of the bureaucrats of the Indian Civil Service (ICS). To a man at a desk in Calcutta or
Simla, Stein's frequent requests for special treatment may well have
seemed irrelevant and self-indulgent. He was, after all, a government
servant with a job to do. That he almost always achieved his objects was
due partly to his own indomitable will and partly to the fact that the ICS,
despite its shortcomings, contained many men of ability and vision who
sympathized with his aims.

In his blackest moments, Stein sometimes chose to believe that the
entire ICS was against him; but usually he reserved his scorn for the
babus, or clerks, whose ranks filled the back rooms of the administration. Most of the leading men of India attracted from him nothing but
admiration, and his respect for them only increased if they chose to
interest themselves in his maverick ways.

Returning to Europe in the summer of 1901, he could look forward to seeing the few friends and relatives with whom he was close. Publius and his wife had been in England since mid-May, staying with her parents in Chislehurst, Kent, and with his father at Teignmouth in Devon, prior to moving to Oxford. The Andrews had taken a house in Hampshire.

One colleague, however, deserved his attention before anyone else. Rudolf Hoernle, the first scholar to work on the early manuscripts from Chinese Central Asia, the man who had devoted so many hours to the study of the mysterious blockprints, must be told the unhappy truth: that his work had been in vain, that he had been duped by a wily but uneducated Khotanese forger and that his published work on the subject would now be utterly discredited. It was not an easy message to convey kindly and Stein, probably deliberately, left little record of the meeting, which took place soon after his arrival in England in early July, at Hoernle's house in Oxford.

Hoernle's deep disappointment and embarrassment soon found expression, and he told Stein he wanted his report on the forgeries destroyed. But by then it was too late. The first part of the report had been published by the Asiatic Society of Bengal in 1899 and was probably by now on the library shelves of every orientalist in Europe. Part Two of 'A Collection of Antiquities from Central Asia', however, had not yet gone to press. It was due to appear in the Journal of the Asiatic Society of Bengal later that year; by acting quickly, Hoernle could use it to rectify his terrible mistakes.

He chose, understandably, to gloss over his own gullibility. At the time that Part One was published, he declared, it was unclear whether the Calcutta collection included forgeries. But since then, 'Dr Stein has obtained definite proof that all "blockprints" and all the manuscripts in "unknown characters" procured from Khotan since 1895 are modern fabrications of Islam Akhun and a few others working with him.' Then, avoiding mention of the fact that in 1899 he himself had dismissed rumours of Islam Akhun's fraudulent activities and had concluded that 'the scripts are genuine', he turned to an examination of those parts of the collection that were indisputably genuine.[1]

Thus was honour salvaged. And Hoernle made a remarkable recovery. A few years later he was able to reveal the origin of the non-Indian language in Brahmi characters which appeared on many of the documents found by Stein in 1900–1. It was a hitherto unknown tongue of Iranian origin, known thereafter as Khotanese and studied in depth since Hoernle's death in 1918 by several European scholars.

———————◄—————

At the British Museum, Stein was lent a room by the Department of Indian Antiquities and began the task of recording the details of the two to three thousand objects that formed his collection as they were unpacked: precisely where and at what depth on the site they were found, their numerical order and so on. He saw to the development of nearly a thousand photographic plates, and helped a member of the manuscripts department unfold rolled documents and place them between sheets of glass. He started work on his preliminary report of the expedition, a succinct resumé which covered forty-odd pages and was published later in the year by the Government of India.

Keeping in mind his hopes for a return to Chinese Turkestan, he was also careful to inform the India Office of the help he had received from the Chinese ambans of Khotan and Keriya, and to pass on Macartney's suggestion that the Viceroy might send a letter of thanks to the Fo-tai, or Governor of Sinkiang, in order to 'facilitate further research'. Macartney himself he praised in fulsome terms, as did most European travellers who passed through Kashgar.

It was at this early stage in the preparation of Stein's first finds that his friend Andrews took a formal role in his work. His initial appointment was as a temporary assistant at the British Museum, for the preparation of a complete inventory of the collection. Subsequent positions rarely offered much more security or status than this; but Andrews seems to have accepted his modest part with little complaint. His interests overlapped with Stein's, and his abilities as an artist meant he could illustrate items that had not been photographed. (His vignette of Pallas Athene decorates the title page of most of Stein's books.) Moreover, he was assiduous in checking details and, generally, in acting on Stein's behalf.

In the early days, before the first expedition, Stein had felt slightly ill at ease with their relationship. To each written request for help he would attach an apology for asking so many favours. But gradually the two settled comfortably into their roles: Stein leading an adventurous life with the prospect of dramatic discoveries, while Andrews loyally provided support. The latter enjoyed the opportunities to work on new material, the gifts of handiwork that Stein brought back for him, and the many letters sent to him from the desert, including one in the form of a wooden tablet, like those found at Niya. Through his vicarious experience of archaeological exploration in the Taklamakan Desert, perhaps, he found expression for a side of his character not fulfilled by the more mundane work of a teacher.

There were other demands on Stein's time before he returned to India. He had not seen his brother since 1897 and knew that both Ernst and his wife Jetty were anxious that he should spend his leave with them. On the way back from Kashgar to London, he had broken his journey at Krakow and travelled the short distance to their home at Jaworzno in order to steal a couple of days there before work on his collection began. In mid-August he returned to spend a fortnight with them in Bad-Nauheim, a spa town to the north of Frankfurt.

Ernst was just about to celebrate his fifty-eighth birthday, his wife was 47. Their son, also called Ernst, was nearly 10; Theresa, their first child, was four years older. They were a conventional family and Ernst, who had always been middle-aged in outlook, now seemed to belong not only to a different generation but also to a different world from the one Stein inhabited.

Fourteen days among the holiday-makers of a German spa were hardly Stein's idea of a pleasant rest. But the spa was better than the seaside, which Jetty had originally proposed, and the mixed feelings of affection and brotherly duty which underpinned his relationship with Ernst made him content to play the role required of him for the period. That he felt himself 'in my brother's watchful presence', as he wrote in a letter from Bad-Nauheim to Publius, suggests that little had changed in Ernst's attitude towards him.[2]

Stein managed to secure an extension to his leave in order to complete his preliminary report before returning to India to take up his new position in the Punjab. He also obtained permission from the India Office to write a 'personal narrative', a popular account which would be based on the descriptions he had written for Ernst, and which had been suggested to him back in 1898 by Hoernle as a useful way of publicizing his work. Busily working on his various papers as he travelled back to the East, he sailed from Naples on board the Rubattino Navigation Company's SS *Raffaele Rubattino* on 19 October.

———————►◄———————

How alluring the Punjab had seemed during his months in the desert, with his application to return there still unanswered and his memories of picnics with friends in old Mogul gardens. Now he was returning to a post he wanted, and his short spell in Calcutta was already a fading, unhappy memory. But part of the reason for his return had disappeared when the Allens' last packing case was removed from Mayo Lodge; and there were other changes which further qualified his enthusiasm. Responsibility for the sensitive Frontier region between British India and Afghanistan had just been taken from the Punjab government and given to a newly created province, the North-West Frontier, in order to free the border from bureaucracy.[3]

Stein probably sympathized with the reasons behind this decision. But he was dismayed by its effects on his own position. The chief attraction of the role of Inspector of Schools in the Punjab, as far as he was concerned, had been the opportunity it offered for visiting areas of the Frontier which were full of antiquarian interest. The creation of the new province meant that some of the most interesting of those areas had been removed from his circuit – unless, that is, he could rearrange matters to his own advantage.

He had one important card to play, his friendship with the first Chief Commissioner of the new province. This was Harold Deane, now a colonel and later to be knighted: the man who had encouraged Stein to explore Swat in 1898 and whose own interest in the Graeco-Buddhist culture of the border lands made him one of Stein's keenest supporters. Almost immediately after his return to India in November Stein paid a visit to Deane at Peshawar, where the administration of the North-West Frontier Province was to be based, to discuss the possibility of transferring to the new province.

The inspectorship in itself was not a bad way in which to earn a living, he told Publius: 'I like the marching and do not mind the inspecting – perhaps because circumstances permit it being done in a somewhat amateur – and Sahib-like fashion.'[4] He did not suffer from worry and fatigue as he had in Lahore; and he was learning Pushtu, the language of the Pathans, from an orderly. But working under Deane would be better, and might lead to an even more satisfying outcome. For the Archaeological Survey of India, since its revival by Curzon, had taken the first tentative steps towards proper organization, though its funds were still minimal; and Deane, with his knowledge of Frontier archaeology to carry weight in official quarters, thought a part-time archaeological post might be created in his province.

At the same time as he was plotting not only to transfer his inspectorship but also to secure this, as yet non-existent, archaeological post for himself, Stein was also planning a return to England to write a detailed, scholarly report of his expedition. He seems to have been utterly unaware of the impression he might create in trying to secure for himself quite so many favours. Unabashed, he lobbied all his contacts in the provincial and national governments, observing that the nature of his new job left no time for his 'scientific' work. Like a boy citing good behaviour as reason for a treat, he pointed out that the total cost of his expedition had been very low. And, surprisingly, he had his way. His visit to England was approved, and a grant provided to cover expenses and the cost of his passage to and from England. He booked a first-class cabin on the hurricane deck of the P & O mail steamer SS *Arabia* from Bombay on 3 May 1902.

In the midst of these arrangements, yet another project was forming in his mind; the most important of all to Stein himself. The longing he had had since early youth to see Bactria, the ancient northern region of Afghanistan which Alexander had conquered and colonized, had only intensified during his expedition to the dead cities of the Silk Road. If the influence of Greece could be found so far away in Central Asia, what fascinating evidence of its Graeco-Buddhist past might Bactria reveal to someone who knew what to look for and where to find it?

Bactria had been famous as a centre of Buddhism since the second century AD, when it was ruled by the same Kushan tribes whose kingdom included Gandhara. In the seventh century Hiuen Tsiang had visited the capital, Bactra – now known as Balkh – and described its splendid New Monastery. Stein's discoveries of 1900 and 1901 showed that the once-vibrant Buddhist culture of the Tarim Basin had clearly been inherited from north-west India. In that case, the inheritance would have come via Bactria, since it was through that region in early times that the most commonly used route ran between Eastern Turkestan and Gandhara: Hiuen Tsiang himself had used it. Bactria was the missing link between what Stein knew of Gandhara and what he had discovered in the Taklamakan.

An idea had only to lodge itself in Stein's mind to be developed, tested and fully organized by the time he came to mention it to anyone else. He was determined to get to Bactria; and he saw an opportunity to sell the idea to the most influential person of all, Curzon himself, when the Viceroy paid his first official visit to the newly created North-West Frontier Province in April 1902. Stein obtained permission to meet him in Peshawar in order to show him some specimens of his finds from Khotan, and organized his presentation for maximum effect. Bactria came naturally into his speech. The Viceroy, he noted in his diary, 'recognizes strength of my argument about the time now to secure those sites for India or B. Mus. [British Museum]. Seems to appreciate proposal & not to shrink from polit.l. difficulty.'[5] To Publius he wrote excitedly, 'It seems like the fulfillment of a dream I had since I was a boy & only the Gods know whether it will all come right.'[6]

He had extra need of exciting professional prospects, for the news from home was dispiriting. In January 1902 his brother had a 'paralytic attack', probably a stroke. Stein told Publius that he 'passed miserable days' when he first heard of it, and the thought of visiting Ernst in his claustrophobic home in Jaworzno probably added to his depression. There was talk of retirement to Italy or the Adriatic, but it was to Vienna, Jetty's home town, that she and Ernst decided to move. Stein went there as soon as he reached Italy in mid-May. He found Jetty busy house-hunting, and the children sick with measles. Ernst was still at Jaworzno, weak and listless, sunk in memories of the past, and Stein's stay of five days only confirmed his fear that his brother was failing.

His pocket diary for the summer of 1902 is punctuated with melancholy comments on Ernst's condition. In late August he described his brother's decline as 'a deep-cutting sorrow . . . His drooping head, his languishing eyes – Alas.' Only the presence of little Ernst and Theresa lightened the gloomy atmosphere. But they could not help him when he travelled to England and yet more sorrow, news of the death of 'my poor little dog', Dash, who had followed him across thousands of miles in Chinese Turkestan, only to die far from him, in India. 'Thought of his 6 years' companionship,' he wrote mournfully. '*Requiescat in pace.*'

Again in the latter half of September he returned to his brother's side, but every hour there cost him increasing effort, for everything about the situation cast him into deeper gloom. 'E. suffers much from breathing difficulty,' he wrote in his diary on 26 September, '. . . Worked on book but without peace or concentration. Feel uselessness of my sacrifice of time . . . Scarcely in the open all day. E. in sleep or silence all day. Thoughts of ties that have snapped already. Devotion of J. [Jetty] . . . A wretched day & no good from sacrifice.'[7] On 1 October he returned to London, where he was scarcely happier, for he felt obliged to visit his sister's daughter, Helene, now living in Hampstead, whose talk of illness, nerves and other troubles was all that awaited him at the end of an Underground journey which he loathed. From 5 to 22 October, the pages of his diary are blank, for it was then that Ernst's health collapsed and he died.

The companionship of his friends in England during this period provided Stein with the support he needed, and sealed the knot that bound him to them, their homes and their way of life. The Allens' home at Longwall Cottage in Oxford – 'a tiny little place with a tinier garden, carved out of the old Magdalen College Schoolhouse', as Publius described it to a friend[8] – quickly came to symbolize all that was attractive about England; her history, her old buildings, her learning, her gentle summers and green gardens.

This image transferred with the Allens when they moved to other houses in Oxford, as if they carried with them a light which burned night and day, showing Stein the way home whenever he wanted the reassurance of such a place. For after Ernst's death had severed his closest links with central Europe, it was England he had in mind when he used the word 'home'. It was to the Allens that he wrote weekly, sending them the 'personal narratives' of his journeys and expeditions which he would otherwise have composed for his brother.

The question of whether the Allens would have chosen Stein as such a close friend, had he not chosen them first, is difficult to settle. Had he been a less avid and devoted correspondent, would they have written once a week to him for more than forty years? The friendship was in some ways unequal and unbalanced. He lived mainly apart from society, while they were surrounded by friends, family and colleagues. His attitude towards them was totally uncritical, and the veneration in which he held them required a response. The qualities of faithfulness and selflessness which others noted in Allen, and which his wife shared, made it natural that they should provide for their friend what he so obviously lacked.

To his sister-in-law Jetty, Stein remained a faithful correspondent. But she surrendered herself to reclusive grief and mourning after her husband's death and her letters alone, bordered with black for nearly twenty years, could not have sustained him. After Ernst's death, Stein went on a journey which, though it conjured up his past, also laid it to rest. *En route* to Vienna to spend Christmas 1902 with his dead brother's family, he returned to Dresden for the first time in many years. At the place where he had been a boarder, the old Frau Direktor, perhaps sensing some of the reasons for his visit, handed him letters which had been written nearly thirty years earlier by his mother.

In Vienna, storms lashed the city during the Christmas period, and Stein frequented the graves of his brother and sister, one fresh, the other dug there long ago. Just before he left the city, news came which seemed to close a door on all the memories and complex emotions that haunted him. In the town of Jaworzno there had been a great fire, and the mine had been flooded. Fire and water, lightning and thunderstorms seemed to exorcize the spirits of the past, a past dominated by his brother and the ties that had bound them together. Something inside him had been set free.

━━━━━◄►━━━━━

The work which Stein had hoped to complete during eight months in England could not be dispatched in such a short period, and twice he had to apply to the India Office for extensions to his leave. Each time, his application was successful, undoubtedly helped by support from the Royal Geographical Society, where he read a paper in June 1902, and the thirteenth International Congress of Orientalists which, meeting in Hamburg later the same year, passed a resolution thanking the Viceroy and the Government of India for their support of Stein's work. Consequently, he spent the whole of 1903 based in England, speedily finishing his popular account of the first expedition, *Sand-Buried Ruins of Khotan*. The book was published in the summer of 1903 and 500 copies, or two-thirds of the print-run, sold almost immediately. (He later recovered the publishing rights by buying the printing blocks from the publishers for £24, and arranged for another firm to publish a cheaper edition which appeared in 1904.)

This was the first and one of the most readable of his books on Chinese Turkestan. Lockwood Kipling read and approved it, and advised Stein to 'cultivate that pleasant vein of observation and personal appreciation of things seen and experienced that seems to come naturally to you. Dry as dust archaeology is out of date entirely.'[9] But Stein was not a natural raconteur. Each time he returned to the desert, his accounts of his journeys grew longer, and after the second expedition he gave up writing 'popular' books in favour of massive scholarly tomes.

Unlike Sven Hedin or Deasy, he never succumbed to the idea of preceding his text with a portrait of himself posing in Central Asian costume. The frontispiece in this first book showed one of the statues he had unearthed from the desert, and on the dedication page was a mournful tribute: 'To the memory of my brother, whose loving care ever followed me through life, this account of my journey, first recorded for him is inscribed in unceasing affection and sorrow.' His friend Thomas Arnold, writing to congratulate him on the book's appearance, observed 'how cruel fate had been to you, in that this book, like your translation of the Rajatarangini, had never met the eyes of him whose approval and sympathy you most valued'.[10]

Stein's detailed report of his expedition was still to be written; and he was able to begin it at the house Andrews had taken at Clanville, near Andover in Hampshire, where he stayed for most of 1903. It was a congenial environment. The house dated from the early eighteenth century and stood in an area of old-fashioned villages and quiet lanes. When the weather was fine, Stein worked at his camp table at the end of a lime avenue in the garden, picked wild flowers in the meadows and sallied out with Andrews on evening bicycling tours. The bicycle, however, was not his preferred method of transport, as Andrews later recalled:

> Conversing as he rode, Stein forgot that the machine was not a horse and that it needed continuous guidance and attention. The result was a somewhat wobbly and erratic line of progression, varied by occasional mild collisions with a stone or tussock or even with me if for a moment I was off my guard. At last Stein decided to abandon the 'shameless thing' as he called it, because, as he said, he could not 'spare time to have a broken leg'.[11]

Almost all his time was devoted to his work. He had managed, again, to secure Andrews' help at the British Museum by contributing £50 from his own expenses allowance towards an honorarium of £150 for his friend. But the detailed report, *Ancient Khotan*, proceeded slowly. It was an ambitious project: a scholarly account of the ancient associations of all the places through which he had passed on his way to Chinese Turkestan in 1900 and of the oasis settlements there, as well as a painstaking description of his discoveries. Andrews compiled a list of all the antiquities and various scholars contributed special reports: the French Sinologist Edouard Chavannes on the Chinese documents, the Hungarian geographer Lajos Lóczy on the sand and loess in which the antiquities had been found, two members of the British Museum on Tibetan manuscripts and coins, a professor of chemistry on the stucco fragments.

However much Stein disliked the sedentary labour involved in recording the results of his work, he regarded it as unprofessional to shirk such a duty. In this he was more conscientious than some of his colleagues, in a period when archaeology was in its infancy as an academic discipline. He also had a grasp of archaeological method which has stood up well to changing standards in the half-century since his death. He kept abreast of developments such as those described by Flinders Petrie in his *Methods and Aims in Archaeology* (1904); but his grasp of stratigraphy predates that book, as the results of his first expedition clearly show. He seems to have had an innate sense of system and a genuine interest in all the items recovered from a site, not merely the glamorous ones; an approach which, if not unknown at the time, was notably rigorous and thorough.

While still in England, and with what he felt sure was Curzon's encouragement, he submitted his official proposal for an expedition to Balkh. The text was carefully composed so as to give prominence to the relevance to India of work in Bactria:

> There is abundant historical evidence to prove that this region, one of the most important in the history of Asia generally, has from early times exercised a very powerful influence on the cultural development of ancient India. From Bactria, the traditional home of Zoroaster's religion and one of the oldest centres of civilization in Asia, there were derived those elements of unmistakably Iranian (Old-Persian) origin which meet us in the earliest extant historical remains and records of North-Western India. After the invasion of Alexander the Great, Bactria, under Greek rulers, became the seat of a remarkable Hellenistic culture, which flourished for centuries in that distant part of Asia, and from there triumphantly entered the Indus Valley and the neighbouring parts of the Punjab.[12]

The ruins of Balkh, the 'Mother of Cities' in Eastern tradition, had already yielded chance finds of coins, he pointed out, and much more could be revealed if a trained orientalist were to carry out archaeological exploration there. But he added that he would also use the opportunity to carry out topographical surveys, hoping that the promise of such useful information might act as a lure to otherwise unenthusiastic government servants.

It might have been tactful to put this audacious proposal to his employers in the Punjab before sending it to higher authorities, since it demanded yet more time away from a post he had barely occupied in the two years he had held it. But Stein did not see things that way. Having made his initial approach directly to the Viceroy, he ignored his superiors in the Punjab and submitted his proposal directly to the Foreign Department of the Government of India. Curzon himself applied to the Amir of Afghanistan on Stein's behalf; and the Amir, equally promptly, replied with a firm refusal.

The failure of his plan seemed to Stein a harsh blow, only partly compensated for by the fact that Colonel Deane in the meantime had succeeded in poaching him from the Punjab. The position newly created for him was unique: as from the beginning of 1904, he was to become Inspector-General of Education in the North-West Frontier Province and Baluchistan, the adjoining province to the south, as well as part-time Archaeological Superintendent in both regions. This not only improved his standing in the educational service but also linked him officially, for the first time, with the Archaeological Survey. But he showed as little respect for his new role and employer as he had done previously. Demonstrating a remarkable insensitivity, he put in yet another request for special treatment, before he had even begun his new work.

This time it was Tibet that he had in his sights. A British force led by Francis Younghusband was about to advance into the country. Ostensibly a trade and frontier mission, the expedition was in fact an effort on Curzon's part to impress the Tibetans with the power of British India and discourage them from forming alliances with the Russians, a development which he believed was imminent. Unlike the few intrepid independent travellers who had already managed to journey into the hostile interior of Tibet, Stein was not interested in the competitive and, so far, fruitless struggle to reach the capital, Lhasa. He merely wanted the opportunity to conduct some research in a land notoriously inhospitable to strangers.

His appeal elicited a reply of the sort several ICS men were probably itching to deliver. On 9 December 1903, Deane's secretary wrote:

As Colonel Deane has just succeeded in getting you appointed to the North-West Frontier Province on the ground of the necessity for the services of an European officer to supervise the educational work, he is sorry that he cannot forward your application to Govt. It would be obviously inconsistent and illogical for Colonel Deane to recommend the officer for whose services he had so recently applied, to be sent away indefinitely to work outside the Province, before that officer had even joined his appointment in the Province. The natural inference would be that there was little real necessity for your appointment here. The most Colonel Deane can do is to mention demi-officially to the Foreign office that in the event of an archaeologist being required for the Thibet Mission you are anxious to go.[13]

Even after such a rebuff, Stein tried again by writing to the Foreign Department a few months later, when Younghusband had been in Lhasa for some time. The reply was brief and dismissive. The government apologized for not letting him know sooner how things stood. As there were three men with the Mission who had 'made a special study of Tibetan language and antiquities', it was not possible to send him as well.[14]

Stein reacted bitterly to the rejection of his plans for Tibet. His scepticism concerning administrative bodies of all kinds now reached out to embrace the Viceroy despite the fact that, only months earlier, Curzon had supported his plans for Balkh. He was now resigned to 'long years of waiting in wasteful routine work', he told Publius,[15] and he took a grim pleasure in the curt reply Younghusband wrote in response to photographs Stein had sent him of Tibetan sgraffiti from Endere. Younghusband, passing on what Stein described to Publius as 'a truly silly attempt at deciphering [the sgraffiti] made by one of the "experts" of the Mission', remarked simply: 'They do not appear to be of much value.'[16]

Over the next couple of years, Stein was to coin a variety of uncomplimentary phrases in letters to Publius to describe government authorities and their methods: 'a mixture of red tape, classical dilettantism and – whitewash!' he wrote on one occasion, or, on another, 'that centre of intellectual sunshine'. He delivered similarly caustic judgements on his friends' behalf too. Any position denied to them as they tried to establish themselves at home in England he treated simply as proof that those in authority could not be expected to make sensible decisions. Someone who beat Thomas Arnold to a post at Oxford, for example, he damned as the 'distilled fine product' of the Government of India's 'mummified' system of language examinations, and 'living proof of its intellectual futility'.[17]

———————◀————————

During 1904, as he journeyed from school to school in the NWFP and Baluchistan, Stein wrote weekly to the Allens. He told them of the landscapes of the Frontier; and they responded with accounts of their own tours, either on the Continent in search of Erasmus manuscripts or through southern England on bicycles. Stein, knowing a little of the English countryside from his own travels and from visits made with them, followed their routes on a map and developed an affection for the places they loved purely through their evocative descriptions and from a desire to share the things that made them happy. His attachment to 'home' was only strengthened when Thomas Arnold, the last of his close circle of friends, left Lahore to become assistant librarian at the India Office in London (and later Professor of Arabic at London University).

When, a few months later, Stein took the oath of allegiance that made him a British subject (having completed the required five years' service to the Crown), it was not simply in order to sort out his uncertain status. He knew now that it was England he would always turn to, for comradeship and comfort. He felt at ease with the British character as he saw it manifested in India, and he had easily adopted the aims and ideals of the British Empire. The beautiful Kaghan valley, north of Rawalpindi, was an appropriate setting for the private ceremony that formalized this relationship. He regarded the site he had found there as a substitute for Mohand Marg, a place where he could make his camp, with a few servants and a secretary, during the hot summer months when his inspection tours ceased. He lived there, in carefully chosen isolation, on his own terms; but he was touched, nonetheless, by the 'patriotic and personal warmth' of the official sent to preside over the swearing of the oath.

In 1904, the Royal Geographical Society awarded Stein its Back Grant for his survey work in the Kun-lun Mountains. This was encouraging recognition for an aspect of his work which had developed as his interest in exploration had grown, and which he had come to regard as an essential complement to historical research. He used the money from the award to found a prize for historical geography at his old school in Dresden (where his nephew had just been sent on his advice).

Then, as if to demonstrate how the two disciplines were interrelated, he paid a brief visit to Mount Mahaban to conduct one of his hunts through historical topography. Mahaban, lying in tribal territory north of Peshawar, was one of several mountains contending for the identity of Mount Aornos, where Alexander had defeated the Indians on his way from Udyana (the Swat valley) to the Indus. Stein had visited another, Swabi, north-west of Rawalpindi, some years earlier. He had concluded then, as he concluded now, that the mystery was not yet solved, and his search for Aornos, though conducted only spasmodically between other projects, was to span many years. But this trip, which Stein was obliged to undertake in the company of a political officer, P.J.G. Pipon, provides an insight into his methods on such outings.

> Experience on past occasions has shown me that ... for doing my task *thoroughly*, I must have absolutely free disposal of the available time. This may lead to a good deal of personal inconvenience as regards marches, food, etc, which often cannot be avoided, nor in fact, need much be thought of, where scientific aims are concerned.[18]

If Pipon wanted things 'in picnic fashion' (as Stein described it in a letter to Publius), he had better stay behind, since Stein was not prepared to compromise on such matters. Later in life, Stein suggested more than once that his habit of travelling only with native surveyors and servants was due to lack of sufficient funds to pay a European. But the truth was that he liked to have things his way, and feared that the presence of another white man would make the exercise of his authority a less simple matter. His expedition to Chinese Turkestan had been ideal in that respect. He had taken only a small staff and had run things to his own liking. But it was not for this reason that in 1904 he became preoccupied with the idea of a return to Central Asia.

In the three years since the successful conclusion of that first expedition, his very success had worked to his disadvantage. The recognition which the International Congress of Orientalists had accorded him in 1902 may have helped him win more leave from the Indian government; but it had also, inevitably, publicized the secrets of the long-lost sites and fired the imagination of other orientalists. Why should not they, too, dig in the distant Taklamakan Desert for buried treasure? There was more than enough room for all of them and it was only fair that other European countries should share in the discoveries which otherwise, if left to Stein, would all end up in the British Museum.

One German expedition had already visited Chinese Turkestan in 1902, led by Professor Albert Grünwedel of the Berlin Ethnological Museum. Originally inspired by what the Russian, Klementz, had found in 1898, it had confined its work to the Turfan area, north-east of the Taklamakan, and brought away a variety of antiquities. Finance had been provided mostly by the industrialist Friedrich Krupp, and Stein knew that there were fresh funds available from the Kaiser himself to enable Grünwedel to resume work at any moment. There was also talk of a Russian expedition; and the French could not be far behind. The leading French Sinologist, Edouard Chavannes of the Collège de France, was intimately acquainted with Stein's work through his translation of Chinese texts from the first expedition. Though not an expedition leader himself, it would hardly be surprising if he encouraged such ideas in the minds of some of the other orientalists at work in Paris and at the Ecole Française d'Extrême-Orient in Hanoi, where Stein's friend Foucher was now Director.

Stein could not blame his colleagues. He had been grateful for the recognition they gave his work in 1902, he respected their scholarship and he envied them the patronage, financial and moral, that they seemed to enjoy. But neither could he repress the desire to have the desert sites to himself. He could achieve nothing, however, without permission and resources from the Government of India. He had no other patron. So, once again, he began the time-consuming business of seeking support for another expedition – this time to include sites farther east than the Khotan area – from any friend or acquaintance whose help he thought might be influential.

'All this writing and pleading', he told Publius, 'makes me feel only more than ever how petty a thing Government machinery is compared with personal independence or the money which secures it.'[19] His lack of independence was a source of constant irritation. But by now he was adept at using arguments in favour of his ambitions which he knew would strike home with the authorities. This time, in September 1904, it was 'the spectre of Russo-German competition' that he called up in his formal application to mount a second expedition. Moreover, he observed presciently, it seemed 'scarcely possible to foresee whether such favourable conditions [in Chinese Turkestan] will prevail for a prolonged period and whether political changes may not arise which would close that field to researches from the British side'.[20]

Optimistic as ever that the authorities would immediately appreciate all his points, he was predictably disappointed when they, equally predictably, responded to his application with something less than enthusiasm. He could not be permitted to return to Chinese Turkestan in 1905, as he wished, unless he had completed the work associated with the first expedition. This involved not only the detailed report, *Ancient Khotan*, but also proposals for the partition of finds between the British Museum and the museums of Lahore and Calcutta, on which the government insisted because of the joint funding by itself and the governments of the Punjab and Bengal.

Stein had written only half the report and had not even begun to tackle the partition proposal. Even for him, with his immense capacity for work, any hope of simultaneously completing these two tasks, carrying out school inspections and preparing for another expedition was clearly fantastical. Reluctantly, therefore, he put back his proposed starting date to 1906, and asked to be relieved of official duties as soon as possible in order to meet the conditions. His old friend Maclagan, reporting on the progress of his application, gently pointed out to him: 'Of course the view we had to contend against was that there was enough archaeology in India itself to spend money on without going outside Indian limits – but all your friends have stood by you manfully & we hope for the best.'[21] At last, a telegram reached Stein from England. Dated 14 April 1905 and sent by Thomas Arnold – who worked at the India Office and had seen Stein's file – it bore a single word which needed no interpretation: 'Rejoice'.

Again confounding Stein's dim view of them, the authorities had met all his requests. He could abandon his normal duties in order to finish work associated with the first expedition and start the second in 1906;

and the British Museum would join the Government of India in funding the second to the tune of £5,000. Despite this cheering news, however, he did not rejoice for long. He was oppressed by the magnitude of his tasks, by the threat of competition in Chinese Turkestan and by what he saw as his constant struggle for recognition. While the French set up orientalist schools in the East and the Germans eagerly supported more expeditions, he was forced to watch his proposals inch their way through the slowly grinding machinery of the Indian government until they reached the desk of someone who might or might not be interested enough to assent to them. His frugal style of life and careful way with money meant that he was gradually building resources; nevertheless, he could not envisage self-sufficiency for at least another decade.

Gradually the idea formed in his mind that nothing less than a unique appointment would safeguard his scientific interests, and allow him to pursue them without having to go into battle to justify each project. The appointment he visualized was Archaeological Explorer to the Government of India, a title of his own invention. Absorbed by work and his own predicament, he put it before his employers, convinced that it was the obvious solution. In the circumstances, official reaction was bound to be disappointing. And when he found himself in disagreement with the head of the Archaeological Survey as well, his low opinion of those in authority began to harden into a grim cynicism which overshadowed for the time being the memory of all the assistance he had received from a great many friends.

The Archaeological Survey of India, on whose behalf he undertook his duties as part-time archaeological inspector in the North-West Frontier Province and Baluchistan, was run by a young Director-General called John Marshall. He had come to the East straight from Greece in 1902 at the behest of Lord Curzon, aged 26 and with no experience since leaving Cambridge beyond three years at the British School in Athens. His task in India was immense, his resources minimal, and his officers in the field few and far between. He needed all the help those officers could provide; and Stein, struggling to be free to pursue his own archaeological interests beyond the boundaries of India, cannot have seemed a very helpful colleague.

Stein had already refused, politely but firmly, to undertake a couple of tasks outside his normal duties which Marshall had proposed.

Perhaps Marshall felt that this incident demonstrated a genuine need to find a replacement for Stein on the Frontier; or perhaps he was motivated by less altruistic feelings. Many years later, one of his successors in India, Sir Mortimer Wheeler, told how he had heard Marshall described as 'a beech tree under which nothing grew' and how, long after Marshall had retired from the Survey, he was still regarded by his followers as 'a remote king-god of whom his worshippers had no intelligent comprehension, and sought none'.[22] His autocratic approach may have affected his behaviour towards a fellow-archaeologist who was plainly not prepared to fall in with his plans.

Certainly it seemed to Stein, when he received an unexpected letter from Marshall in June 1905, that he was the victim of an attempt at public humiliation. Marshall wrote on the subject of Stein's forthcoming absence from his official archaeological post on the Frontier. Who was to know when Stein would settle again to educational work? he asked.

And even if you revert after, let us say, another four years to your educational duties, will there then be any better prospects of your being able to devote more time to the archaeological needs of your Province than you have done during the last eighteen months? I feel, and I think you will agree with me, that the prospects are very small. I fully appreciate, of course, that it is only due to force of circumstances that Archaeology has not been able to profit, as fully, as the Government had hoped, by your scholarship and enthusiasm during these eighteen months; but will not the same force of circumstance compel you to devote yourself even more exclusively (if that were possible) to education when you return?[23]

The separation of Stein's two posts, which would have to occur during his absence, should perhaps be made permanent, suggested Marshall, since no good man could be expected to take up the archaeological post merely for the three or four years that Stein was away.

The suggestion threw Stein into an uncharacteristic state of panic and distress. He could not believe, after all his struggles, that the Director-General should deliberately misinterpret his aims and threaten to take from him the only part of his normal employment that linked him to his true interests. Without his part-time archaeological role, he would be back where he had started, in education. 'I have always undertaken these duties conscientiously and, I believe, efficiently,' he wrote in his pained reply; 'but I have never ceased bitterly to regret the loss which my scholarly activity has suffered through the necessity of devoting myself to duties so widely distant from my scientific aims and interests.'

His aim, he told Marshall, was to be appointed Archaeological Explorer on his return from his second expedition. But until that appointment was confirmed, he wanted to know that he could return at least to the dual position on the Frontier which had been created specially for him. Otherwise, he wrote, he would 'suffer disadvantages which I should feel keenly and which, I think, would be wholly undeserved' – not least of which would be a reduction in salary.[24] Another flurry of letters left his writing-table, aimed at anyone he knew in government who might be able to restrain Marshall.

The offensive brought no positive conclusion. The Government of India told Stein they were deferring a decision on the creation of the post he proposed until after his return from Chinese Turkestan. Thomas Arnold wrote in encouragement: 'It was good to see how you arose and smote [Marshall] hip and thigh, so that his machinations are, I trust, thwarted for ever.'[25]

In early October 1905, Stein left his Kaghan valley camping ground to cross the mountains to Srinagar. There he could spend the winter writing, and gathering supplies for the next expedition in readiness for a starting date in April 1906. The return to Kashmir – his first in seven years – involved a week's journey and revived his spirits so that he was in almost playful mood when he met a group of village officials inquisitive about his luggage. Offering them a rumour which his water-tanks had prompted in Khotan, he told them that he carried compressed soldiers in his book boxes.

The pleasure with which he had anticipated a return to his beloved camping ground turned briefly to elation once he reached Mohand Marg. But it was impossible to stay there so late in the year and the cottage he rented instead provided comfortless surroundings. It was desperately cold, even with a fire, and his day was so dominated by twelve to fourteen hours of work that he barely saw another European. One afternoon, while out for a short walk, he glimpsed through the window of a colonial bungalow a cosy domestic interior which seemed to him like a scene from another world. He suffered from colds and indigestion, and his usually clear writing deteriorated to a blotchy scrawl with which he wrote terse entries in his diary, all too often variations on the same theme: 'Weary and longing for rest.'[26] Only the weekly letter from Publius kept him company, and the news that Helen Allen was expecting a baby at the end of March gave him a tenuous connection with the family lives of his friends far away.

Macartney's reports from Kashgar during the same period were hardly encouraging. The German expedition which had left Berlin in late 1904, under the leadership of a linguist called Albert von Le Coq, had been at work near Turfan. But it was now in Kashgar awaiting Grünwedel's arrival before undertaking further excavations. An American geographer named Ellsworth Huntingdon, whom Stein had met in Peshawar the previous year, was surveying in the desert; and there was news of a new French expedition, to be led by a young and capable Sinologist called Paul Pelliot. Macartney sent Stein copies of his confidential 'news reports' for the Indian government regarding 'your rivals & meddlers', as he called the competition.

'There is a good deal of jealousy between Grunwedel & Lecoq [*sic*],' he wrote in November 1905, 'and Lecoq tells me he is not anxious to work with Grunwedel . . .'. After the latter finally reached Kashgar, Macartney commented: 'Grunwedel is ill, can't go on horseback & has to be looked after like a big baby . . . No doubt had [the other Germans] known that you also were on the war-path, they would have dragged Grunwedel off, ill or not, long before now.'[27]

The fact that the Germans did not seem to know of Stein's plans was at least reassuring, though it did not allay all his fears. However, in one respect his circumstances were eased for, in response to his urgent pleas and Macartney's warnings about foreign competition, the Indian government agreed to allow him to finish work on the proofs of his detailed report once his expedition had started. Freed from some strain, he was at last able to concentrate fully on arrangements for the expedition.

These were in some respects easier than they had been in 1899–1900, for this time he knew exactly what he required and which parts of his equipment needed refinement. Tents that were lighter, medicine bottles that were more secure, dried vegetables that were longer-lasting: all were ordered, received and prepared for the final packing. By the end of March 1906 Stein was ready to leave his winter exile and descend to the plains, where he could make final preparations for the expedition and renew contact with the human race. The day before his departure, he received a telegram from Publius which he had eagerly awaited, and which promised a heartening message to accompany him out of his isolation. But the telegram brought only sorry news. There were a mere three words on the paper: 'Stillborn Helen well'. He wrote immediately to Publius:

> What is uppermost in my mind is gratitude for the assurance which that news brought as to Mrs Allen. If she is well – and I cling anxiously to the full truth of the telegram – your continued happiness is assured, and as I know, you both never felt the need of seeing it increased beyond what a kindly dispensation had made it already. I hope, you will forget before long what might have been and the anxieties through which you have passed, no doubt. Is there need to say more than that I hope from all my heart that Mrs Allen will be as bright and strong again as she was? Do assure me on this point, and I shall be able to find peace for all thoughts that turn to the incomparable 'Cottage' and its dwellers. Have you not both that genial warmth of feeling, the completest devotion to each other, which will keep you ever young? Happy, indeed, you are both already, and what we must ask from Providence first, is that your health should keep strong with your spirits.[28]

Stein's letter sounds strangely like a plea. That the child had died was a deep sadness; but that Publius and his wife should forever be scarred by its death was a prospect that hardly bore contemplation. On their happiness, tranquillity and support he had come to depend; to their devoted partnership he could turn for vicarious enjoyment of domestic and emotional contentment. Whatever else happened in his life, he needed to be able to rely on things changing only for the better in theirs. And never was this more important than when he was about to cast himself out into the desert for two years, with little but Publius's weekly letters to anchor him to any mooring.

7

Race to the Desert

———————◆———————

THERE WERE FEW times in Stein's life when he felt glad to leave
Kashmir; but his journey to the Punjab in the first days of April 1906
was one. Though he was delayed by landslips and broken bridges as he
travelled down the Jhelum valley, his overwhelming sensation was one of
relief. He had emerged from his winter imprisonment, and his expedition beckoned like a holiday after the past few desk-bound months.
There were wild flowers and bright shoots of new grass at the roadside,
and the train to Lahore seemed full of friends and acquaintances: 'probably twice as many people than [*sic*] I had talked to for nearly a year!', he
noted with pleasure.[1] To his surprise, he thoroughly enjoyed his visit to
Lahore, despite the absence of his old circle. He stayed with Edward
Maclagan, now Chief Secretary to the Punjab Government, and prowled
round former haunts in between visits to the dentist.

His most important engagement, however, was in Peshawar, with the
new Viceroy, Lord Minto. Peshawar was *en fête* to welcome Minto to the
North-West Frontier Province, busy with point-to-point races and
garden parties, and Stein enjoyed the atmosphere. His opinion of
Curzon had soured, but he had hopes of his successor. Making no intellectual claims and lacking Curzon's personal interest in architecture and
archaeology, Minto might have seemed less useful from Stein's point of
view. But Stein, like most others in India, warmed instantly to his unaffected and charming personality.

Stein had secured his interview through a friend, Colonel James Dunlop-Smith, who had helped him in the past and was now Minto's private secretary. It took place on 14 April and seemed promising. Minto agreed to look at the file on his proposal to become the Indian government's Archaeological Explorer and to send it to the India Office. 'He quite endorsed my view as to the advantage of a clear settlement', Stein recorded, 'and a clear course for me to future explorations. His questions showed that he was not posing as an expert in matters Central-Asian, but ready with plain common sense to grasp my fitness for work there . . . '.[2] The Viceroy also showed a sympathetic interest in the forthcoming expedition and in his visitor's keenest ambition, to dig at Balkh.

Mixing calculation with genuine enthusiasm in his talk with Minto, Stein likened his longed-for goal to the excavations on Mediterranean soil by Heinrich Schliemann which had captured the public imagination during the 1870s and 1880s. 'Lord Minto understood what I told of my hope for another Troy,' he wrote afterwards, 'and did not seem to mind that I could not promise there a pendant to the Elgin Marbles, only perhaps the earliest products of Graeco-Buddhist art and relics of Zoroastrian antiquity.'[3] Though the interview was inconclusive, Stein was heartened by the friendly treatment he received. It was proof, he felt, that he was right to strive to keep his ideas and proposals constantly before the eyes of the influential.

One of his last calls in Peshawar was to the man who was perhaps his greatest supporter on the Frontier, Colonel Deane, lately elevated to KCIE. He wrote at the time, 'I felt the parting from his protective aegis, perhaps for longer than my journey,' and his instinct was prophetic, for he was never to see him again.[4] Deane was as true a friend as Stein could have hoped for in high places. No other administrator or officer in British India would watch the progress of the second expedition with more genuine interest than he; but he did not live to see Stein return from Central Asia, dying in 1908 while still in his mid-fifties.

Part of Stein's preparations for his second expedition involved packing and sending things away, as well as having them sent to India from England. In his small office in Peshawar, where he had hardly spent an hour, he packed his books into tin-lined cases to save them from the depredations of white ants. To the Allens he sent his collection of carpets, Turkestan brasses, photograph albums and Sanskrit manuscripts, with instructions that the carpets should be used by friends and the manuscripts deposited, in his name, in the Indian Institute at Oxford. His letters to Publius were to combine with notebooks and other jottings to form his 'Personal Narrative' which would later be worked up to book form, and he had given his friend a deed box in which they could be stored. He had also ordered birthday presents for friends well in advance.

He had arranged to borrow certain surveying instruments from the Royal Geographical Society and the Survey of India;[5] measuring calipers and tapes from the Royal Anthropological Institute for his ethnographic enquiries into the different tribes he would encounter along the route; arms and ammunition from the Rawalpindi Arsenal; and a variety of items from the Sappers and Miners depot, including ropes, leatherwork tools for repairs and bamboo poles for his tent. He had a copy of the confidential *Gazeteer of the Eastern Hindukush*, and a number of other maps bought from the oriental bookseller Harrassowitz of Leipzig; and he had accumulated small turned wood and metal boxes, envelopes, elastic bands and labels for the storage and identification of his finds. There were quantities of miscellaneous items such as tabloid medicines, bandages, needles and safety pins. He had also taken the precaution of packing his morning coat, in order to make the proper impression at formal meetings with the mandarins of Chinese Turkestan.

One vital thing he still lacked, however, and that was help in surmounting the first serious physical obstacle along his route. He had decided to travel north by the fastest way, via Chitral and the mountains of the Hindu Kush, in order to waste no time in reaching the desert sites. The Indian Foreign Secretary, Sir Louis Dane, had managed to secure permission from the Afghan government for him to cross into the Wakhan corridor, the strip of land that extended between Russian Turkestan and British India to the Chinese border. But the initial stages of the journey involved negotiating the difficult Lowerai Pass into Chitral, and the political agent in whose patch the pass lay, Major S. H. Godfrey, was extremely reluctant to provide the necessary assistance, in the form of baggage animals and extra men, which Stein would need.

Throughout the early months of 1906, Godfrey stuck firmly to his view that Stein's proposal to cross the infamous Lowerai in late April or early May was unacceptably dangerous, and that he must wait till later in the year, or else go to Chinese Turkestan by the longer route through

Ladakh. Even the fact that his chief, Sir Harold Deane, wished to help Stein did not alter his view. After all the time and effort it had cost to persuade government of the need for a swift return to the desert, Stein was exasperated by such obduracy.

It was already mid-April, and there was still no sign of Godfrey succumbing to his counter-arguments, when Lord Minto arrived in Peshawar with Dunlop-Smith. To the latter Stein privately described his predicament and, a couple of days later, he heard from Godfrey that arrangements could, after all, be made for the journey. Once again, he had reason to be grateful for the intervention of his friends. When, three years later, he came to write the popular account of his second expedition, he recorded that gratitude in his Preface; but Godfrey's name was noticeable by its absence from an otherwise comprehensive list.

Stein made final preparations at the hill-station of Abbottobad and then at Chakdara Fort in the Swat valley, from which he watched his expedition caravan file out at the end of April on its way north. He took pleasure in the knowledge that he had managed to restrict the baggage for this longer trip to fifteen mule-loads, one fewer than in 1900. Three loads not needed until the autumn had been sent by the slower route through Ladakh; the rest were here, in the care of his small team of followers. In addition to the surveyor Ram Singh and his cook, two Turki caravan men, Muhammadju and Musa, and some pony-men, another trained Indian now accompanied the party. This was Naik Ram Singh, a Sikh corporal of the First (Prince of Wales's Own) Sappers and Miners who had volunteered for the work in return for a salary at least five times his normal pay. His carpentry skills were exactly what Stein wanted, and he had had additional training, at Stein's request, in the development of photographic negatives and the drawing of plans.

In vain Stein had tried to find for himself a cook as efficient as Jasvant Singh – or Just One Thing, as he was affectionately known. The man he eventually acquired proved incapable and was soon sent home. This was a surprising piece of bad luck, for Stein could hardly be described as a demanding diner. Indeed, it was his indifference to food that contributed, in the opinion of his friend Andrews, to his recurring dyspepsia. Andrews based his judgement on first-hand experience, for he once inspected the kitchen arrangements in the Mohand Marg camp. 'I never went near it again,' he remarked long afterwards, 'and I have often marvelled at his immunity from typhoid.'[6] Stein's lack of discernment in the matter of nourishment was no doubt an advantage during expeditions, when meals might not be cooked until midnight, or when water was so scarce that there was no cooked food available at all. But, despite his pride in his robust health, such eating habits did not help a constitution already prone to indigestion.

His physical fitness, however, was unquestionable as he set out in April 1906, aged 43, on his second expedition. Imposing double marches on his party, he reached the small capital of Dir in two days and waited impatiently there, at the foot of the Lowerai, while heavy clouds moved slowly across the mountains. As soon as conditions allowed, he set out for the pass. Each load was lightened to a maximum of forty pounds; the carriers were divided into three detachments in the charge of himself and the two Ram Singhs; and four men carrying only spades and ropes accompanied each detachment. Gaps of fifteen minutes were to elapse between each group, to limit the pressure on snow which threatened to slip from beneath their feet; and the crossing was to take place at night, while the surface was frozen and relatively stable.

The operation proceeded with military precision. Three groups of lanterns, tiny points of light on the mountainside, moved slowly up the snow-filled gorge leading to the summit until, by dawn, the first men braved the icy wind on the saddle of the pass, more than ten thousand feet above sea level. Beyond them on the northern side, a sheer snow wall dropped a hundred feet to the almost equally precipitous mountainside. The way down was marked by steps trodden into the snow at three- or four-foot vertical intervals by indefatigable *dak* runners.

From the brink of this precipice, Stein directed his carriers down the treacherous drop with shouts and gesticulations until they had negotiated the first, most dangerous stretch. Then he descended after them, past signs of an avalanche which, he learnt later, had plummeted down only the previous afternoon. Other avalanches earlier in the season had buried men and ponies beneath the path he now followed. In the circumstances, the ludicrous sight of the incompetent cook being carried down, 'more like a log than an animate being',[7] was a welcome distraction.

The most hazardous part of Stein's journey to Chinese Turkestan was now over and he could begin to enjoy being on the road again, savouring the racial and linguistic characteristics of the people, the antiquarian remains and the historical associations of the region. But it is clear from letters he wrote at this time that he regarded the beginning of the expedition as a definite separation from his friends, despite the fact that it was normal for them to be thousands of miles away.

Their letters would continue to reach him, albeit much more slowly than usual, and he would continue to write long epistles in reply, however busy, cold or tired. But the knowledge that he would be farther from them than usual made him feel the distance as though he were experiencing a physical parting. Friendship was a thing he prized most highly. He always took care to mention how he used presents such as gloves or books. And wherever he went, he never forgot to send birthday greetings, gifts and special notes from places particularly interesting to the friend in question.

Now, as he trekked towards the desert, the weekly letter from Publius assumed greater importance than ever. 'I shall long for your letters in the desert as I did for the mails that would bring me news from my brother,' he had told Allen earlier in the year, anticipating the isolation and loneliness he knew he would feel at times.[8] Publius did not let him down. During this expedition and for years to come, the letters left his hand regularly, opening with *Amice charissime* and concluding with the expression of affection he and Stein came to use habitually to each other, *Vale, charissima.*

In these circumstances, Stein treasured the knowledge that his friend's career as an Erasmian scholar now seemed secure. Having completed the first volume of Erasmus's collected letters, Publius had at last received a commitment from the publishers, the Oxford University Press, to the publication of as many volumes as necessary to complete the project. The decision meant that he could devote himself unreservedly to a lifetime's work, even if his financial situation required him to spend part of his time marking examination papers and doing other mundane tasks in the university. 'It is long since a letter filled me with such joy as your great news,' Stein had told him, and he meant it.[9]

Thoughts of friends, however, could not allay anxieties about the competition now confronting him in Chinese Central Asia. The threat of being beaten to a site by rival archaeologists constantly nagged at him, detracting from the pleasure of the expedition and depriving him of any serenity of mind. 'If a rush to the east is imperative', he had written to Macartney earlier in the year, 'I shall not hesitate to make it as early as possible after seeing you';[10] but it was hardly an ideal frame of mind in which to approach his old hunting ground. How much easier things would be if only he were independent and able to undertake expeditions at his own expense, 'then recover it by offering the collection to the highest bidder!' as he had once fantasized in a letter to Andrews.[11]

The German, von Le Coq, had told Macartney that the archaeological survey of Chinese Turkestan had been 'partitioned' between different nations by the Congress of Orientalists, and that Turfan, in the north, had been allotted to the Germans. He 'appears to be rather hazy as to the British sphere', Macartney had remarked laconically.[12] But Stein swiftly rebutted the assertion. He was not aware of the Congress having made any such arrangement, he said. It was possible that it had been suggested by the International Association of Central Asian Archaeological Exploration. But that was a Russian creation, with no English committee, and it was hardly likely that the Government of India would agree to such a partition without safeguarding British claims in the southern part of Sinkiang.

This was partly bravado on Stein's part, since the one thing of which he felt he could never be certain was adequate backing from the Government of India. If such a partition were arranged, he was, in fact, far from confident that the Indian authorities would protect his right to work in the southern regions. The best he could do to defend his own interests was to approach Chinese Turkestan as quietly as possible and hope that the Germans had not been galvanized into further activity by reports of either his or others' arrival.

His French rival, Pelliot, was another serious threat. Stein admitted to Publius early in 1906 that he was 'wicked enough' to hope that travelling difficulties might delay the Frenchman's party, and had even envisaged contributing to that delay, if Pelliot travelled via British Indian territory, by 'a hint to the Foreign Dept. [which] would prob. suffice to keep them to the Ladak [*sic*] route which is slow & difficult'.[13] Delays did indeed hamper Pelliot, though they were caused by the loss of his heavy baggage on the way through Russian Turkestan. He was held up for two months and did not reach Kashgar until the end of August 1906.

In the meantime, Afghanistan beckoned to Stein. He allowed himself a diversion near the Darkot Pass in order to see the point where the Chinese general had crossed in AD 747, on his way to invade Gilgit. During this brief, exhausting foray, he managed to find the energy to write to Edouard Chavannes, the friend and colleague through whose scholarship the story of this extraordinary invasion had first been revealed in the West. Then it was only a couple more marches to the Baroghil Pass and entry into the upper Oxus valley and Afghan territory. According to orders from the Amir of Afghanistan, the colonel commanding the Wakhan frontier garrisons was waiting to meet him.

Colonel Shirin-dil Khan appeared in full uniform, riding across the barren landscape at the head of a band of horsemen. His distinguished bearing, bluff manner and knowledge of and affection for his country were bound to appeal to Stein. After a lifetime of military service elsewhere in Afghanistan, he had returned seven years previously to the place of his birth, Badakhshan, and the neighbouring region of Wakhan, and had much to tell of these lands high on the Oxus which Alexander the Great had known as Bactria. The two men held long conversations in Persian, which left Stein elated and hopeful that the foundations for a longer visit might thus have been laid. He wrote to the Amir, couching his letter in the elaborate terms required of an address to the ruler and interweaving self-interest with flattery. Afghanistan, he wrote, 'in historical interest and in antiquarian remains of a famous past is not surpassed by any other ancient countries of Asia'. Results such as those described in *Sand-Buried Ruins of Khotan* – a copy of which he was sending to the Amir – could equally well be obtained in Afghanistan 'under guidance of a duly qualified scholar' and would make other scholars throughout the world grateful for the Amir's 'enlightened and firm rule'.[14]

The last stage of the journey to Kashgar passed swiftly. Stein rode ahead of the baggage and covered in six days a distance usually reckoned to take ten. Dash II, a fox terrier he had acquired two years earlier to replace the first Dash, proved a spirited member of the party, quickly learning to jump on to the pommel of his master's saddle when necessary and flagging only on the Wakhjir Pass, between Wakhan and Sarikol, when his subdued whines voiced everyone's thoughts. A brief halt at Tashkurgan allowed Stein to dine with the Russian officer in charge of a Cossack garrison recently established there. Then it was on again until, on 8 June, he rode into Kashgar in a dust-storm at the end of a day's ride of sixty miles.

———————▶ ◀——

There had been some changes at Chini Bagh, 'this dear old place' as he thought of it.[15] The most obvious was that there was now a new Macartney generation: Eric, who had been born in England in 1903 and had travelled across Russia to Kashgar while still an infant, and Sylvia, a few months old at the time of Stein's arrival. Stein was fond of babies and had already endeared himself to Eric, whom he had first seen in London, by arranging for presents to be sent to him each Christmas (the choice of which he usually left to Helen Allen).

George Macartney's new role as a father had had more effect in a domestic sphere than recent promotion had achieved publicly. Early in 1904 he had been appointed British Consul in Kashgar, a development his friends and admirers had long hoped to see. As he told Stein at the time, however, 'the British government have created the post without reference to the Chinese government' and the latter reacted to the news by refusing to recognize the appointment.[16]

Relations with the Russians, on the other hand, had improved. Petrovsky had left Kashgar and events had forced Russia to divert her attentions away from this corner of China. Humiliating defeat in the Far East at the hands of Japan had been followed by revolution at home. The next man to become Russian Consul-General in Kashgar, Kolokoloff – who had held the same post at Mukden in Manchuria, until the Russo-Japanese War drove him out – was a much more genial colleague. Good relations between Russians and British were never more evident than on the occasion of Father Hendricks' funeral, which took place in late June after the old priest had succumbed to cancer. His coffin was borne by Cossacks and followed by every European in Kashgar. 'About the man and his queer hermitage there reigned a *chiaro obscuro* which would require a Rembrantesque pen,' Stein told Publius sadly.[17]

The expedition party left Kashgar the same day. It was 23 June and Stein had been there only two weeks; but quiet days on the shady terraces at Chini Bagh were luxuries he could not afford this time. He had learnt from Macartney of Pelliot's delay, and of the German party's activities near Kucha on the northern arm of the Silk Road, and he was

anxious to move eastward in order to get well ahead of both. He had
several places in his sights and feared that Le Coq and Pelliot might aim
for them too. Apart from his old hunting grounds in the vicinity of
Khotan, he wanted to reach a site in the Lop Desert, east of the
Taklamakan, which Sven Hedin had visited in 1900 and 1901. From
there he would move on to Tun-huang on the border of Kansu, the
north-west frontier province of China.

On the outskirts of that town, he knew, lay a shallow valley overlooked by cliffs that were honeycombed with hundreds of grottoes. For
centuries they had been venerated as sacred temples by Chinese
Buddhists and they were decorated with frescoes and sculptures. The
Hungarian geologist Lajos Lóczy had first described these 'Caves of the
Thousand Buddhas' to Stein when the latter was in Europe in 1902; but
the information was no secret and it was only a matter of time before
other European archaeologists arrived there too. In fact, Le Coq had
planned to do precisely that, back in the autumn of 1905, and it was only
a succession of unlucky delays that prevented him from setting out long
before Stein even left India.

Le Coq had an additional reason for reaching the caves, for he was
armed with information which did not reach Stein's ears until the latter
arrived in the Tun-huang oasis in March 1907. Le Coq had heard a
rumour which suggested that an enormous cache of ancient manuscripts had recently been discovered, hidden in one of the grottoes.
Unlike the paintings that decorated the still popular cave shrines, these
manuscripts were, of course, portable. He had intended to go to Tun-
huang in order to inspect and, if appropriate, acquire these documents
when he received instructions from his superior, Grünwedel, to meet
him in Kashgar in October 1905. There he was kept waiting for more
than a month while Grünwedel slowly made his way towards the city,
during which time Macartney had ample opportunity to learn something of his plans (though not of the hidden manuscripts) and pass the
information on to Stein.

When the German party returned to the Kucha region in early 1906,
Le Coq again hoped to be able to continue eastward to the sacred caves;
but this time he was incapacitated by illness. Leaving Grünwedel and
his assistant to complete the excavations without him, he turned for
home, passing through Kashgar only a month after Stein had left. Le
Coq was to return to Chinese Turkestan once more, but was never to

achieve the success which the Tun-huang manuscripts would undoubtedly have brought him if only he had been able to get to the caves in
time.

———————————◀━━

Unaware of what lay in store at Tun-huang, Stein settled happily into
the old pattern of expedition life. He often felt more comfortable in
Central Asia than in India. No matter how strong his affection for
Kashmir, and despite the fact that he knew more than most of Sanskrit
and the ancient traditions of the subcontinent, he felt that a European
could never be totally at ease with 'ever-inscrutable India'.[18] In the
mountains of the North-West Frontier and beyond, however, the cultural and spiritual differences between himself and the inhabitants
seemed only superficial compared with the understanding that could be
swiftly established.

The contrast between India and Central Asia was highlighted by
many small incidents, such as his party's first meeting with the advance
party of Afghan border guards in the Wakhan corridor. Stein sat down
with his hosts to a meal which his two Ram Singhs – one a 'Hinduized
Gurkha', the other a Sikh – declined to share lest they break their caste
rules. Stein did not feel this sense of separateness in his relations with
non-Indians, whether Chinese ambans or tribal chieftains, with whom
he so often enjoyed an immediate rapport. He would not have attributed the contrast simply to religion, and his close friendship with Pandit
Govind Kaul was proof that he entertained no bias in the matter. But
in general he felt, regretfully, that an ultimately unbridgeable cultural
divide lay between India and the West.

No such divide came between him and Chiang, the Chinese secretary
who accompanied him on this second expedition. During his first foray
into Sinkiang in 1900–1, he had been painfully aware of his deficiency
in Chinese, and every document that emerged from the desert bearing
Chinese characters reminded him of it. This time, he was determined to
be better equipped, for he was going into territory where Chinese
writing would probably provide the only indication of the age and
meaning of each antiquity or manuscript. The fact that his French rival,
Pelliot, was a gifted linguist and Sinologist (and was at that very moment
profiting from an enforced halt in Russian Turkestan by learning Turki)
was an added incentive.

Chiang was the solution to his problem. He had been summoned to Chini Bagh by Macartney, who had heard of him through his own Chinese secretary, and he made an immediately favourable impression. He was lively, intelligent, good-natured and honest, and had worked as a clerk in Sinkiang for seventeen years (leaving wife and child at home far away in Hunan). He was happy to act as Stein's interpreter, assistant and guide in matters Chinese. Equally important, he had no misgivings about travelling in the 'Great Gobi', unlike most of his compatriots who dreaded the desert. The only potential problem appeared to be the question of communication between the two men. Chiang had managed to avoid using the native Turki tongue throughout his career, with the result that his knowledge of it was minimal and his pronunciation almost impenetrable. But Stein brushed this difficulty aside. They would muddle along and, besides, he intended to begin to learn colloquial Chinese immediately, so that before long they would be able to converse in that language alone.

Stein's plan was to go first into the Kun-lun Mountains and continue the survey of the headwaters of the Khotan River which he had begun in 1900. He would return to the Tarim Basin when the cooler autumn weather made work in the desert practicable. At Yarkand he bought himself a good-looking young horse which he named Badakhshi, after the animal's supposed origin in Badakhshan. He had equipped himself with eight camels and twelve ponies while at Kashgar, and assembled a small retinue of followers including some who had worked for him six years earlier, such as a pony-man, Tila Bai, and Hassan Akhun the camel-man, whom he liked for his sense of adventure as well as his reliability.

His surveyor Ram Singh seemed less amenable than usual, at times sullen and unhelpful. However, Stein's Chinese passport promised to compensate for any deficiencies in his own party. On Macartney's recommendation, he had asked the Indian government to secure for him a document that would describe him in more detailed and imposing terms than the one he had used during the first expedition; and in this, at least, the authorities had not disappointed him. His passport identified him as a 'great official', putting him on the same footing as the highest territorial authorities in the Chinese Empire. He could be fairly certain that the local ambans would welcome him to their districts and make available whatever he needed, whether labourers, accommodation or supplies.

By early July, he was in the foothills of the Kun-lun, where he stayed for a fortnight in order to complete, at last, the correction of proofs for *Ancient Khotan*, his massive full report on the first expedition. During the following four weeks he and Ram Singh studied the terrain stretching away towards Tibet and tried to identify the difficult route which W. H. Johnson of the Trigonometrical Survey of India had followed when he crossed the Kun-lun from the western Tibetan plateaux to Khotan in 1865. Back in Khotan by early September, he checked the baggage which had arrived via the Ladakh-Karakoram route and made final preparations for his desert campaign. There were also many friends to see in this town where he felt so comfortable. Badruddin Khan, the head of the Afghan traders, gave him an impressive welcome and the new Amban threw a large garden party in his honour. Pan, Amban in 1900–1, had been promoted to Taotai of Aksu on the northern arm of the Silk Road; and Akhun Beg, in whose garden Stein had stayed in 1900, had left on a pilgrimage to Mecca – from which his family feared he might never return. Happily, Stein was to see both these old friends before the expedition was over.

The buoyant mood of his time in Khotan did not last. When Hassan Akhun returned from the mountains where he had been resting the camels in good grazing grounds, he was distressed to report that two of the animals had died. He ascribed the loss to poisonous plants and there was no one with veterinary knowledge to provide a more scientific explanation. By the time the baggage train reached Keriya in early October, three more had succumbed and Stein was convinced that an infectious disease had caused their deaths. There was nothing for it but to buy others, and this meant a loss of about a thousand rupees from a grant that needed careful husbanding.

At the same time, he was depressed at having to finalize 'the loathsome distribution proposals for my old collection on which the GI [Government of India] had set their heart'.[19] He explained in his proposals that the more fragile antiquities simply would not survive the Indian climate, and therefore must remain in the British Museum. The others he divided between London, Lahore and Calcutta only with the greatest reluctance, for he was convinced that they should all remain together in order to retain their full significance.

News had also reached him from Macartney of Pelliot's arrival in Kashgar; and no news at all had come from India on the matter of his employment after the expedition. Deane wrote a friendly letter suggesting that his worries were unnecessary. 'There is such a strong backing of influential people interested in your work behind you', he reassured his friend, 'that you may feel pretty easy in your mind.'[20] Stein refused to be consoled. 'It is pleasing to learn that I have "influential friends", but I have so far found their voice rather inarticulate and do not expect to hear it raised with any emphasis in future,' he commented ungraciously to Publius.[21]

The irony of his situation as he wrote this, on deputation from a full-time post in order to do precisely what he wanted in Central Asia at the expense of the Indian government, seems not to have occurred to him. It was not surprising that the view from the other side was rather different. William Foster, who was Assistant Registrar at the India Office and had often had contact with Stein over one request or another, remarked in a letter to the secretary of the Royal Geographical Society: 'Our fascinating traveller generally gets the best of any bargain he makes – though one must own that he makes a worthy use of his encroachments.'[22]

Stein also felt dejected at reading Publius's descriptions of the late summer tour, part work and part holiday, that he and Helen had just made in Switzerland and Germany. They prompted recollections of places he had known in his youth. He wished the Allens had been able to visit Tübingen, though the people he associated with the place (principally his old tutor, von Roth) were long dead. 'It seems hard at times to have lost practically all who taught and guided me in my work,' he wrote, indulging his tendency to maudlin sentiment whenever old memories or attachments were concerned. 'But why complain of this when those who were dearest to me, have all been torn away?' He took comfort in the knowledge that Publius so often thought of him and that there were always letters on their way to him in the desert. 'Besides my work & its interest there is little else left, as you know, to encourage me.'[23]

The long-term prospect was certainly clouded. There was no knowing what the Government of India might decide about his proposal to become Archaeological Explorer. And he had no idea what he would do if, in the meantime, Marshall at the Archaeological Survey deprived him of his archaeological surveyorship on the North-West Frontier. The thought of returning to a purely educational position after two decades in India, two expeditions and many years of frustration was hardly bearable. Had he been younger and less experienced, or a more carefree optimist, he might have hoped that the results he would take home after this second period in Chinese Turkestan would bring him more respect and therefore more bargaining power. But he had decided that it was pointless expecting to make an impression on the tin gods of the administration. And if he ever considered the possibility of becoming genuinely famous as a result of his work, he never committed the thought to paper.

Instead, his eyes were firmly fixed on the prospect of financial independence as the only way to throw off the shackles of employment. After 1909–10, he told Publius, he intended to save all furlough allowances in order to be free by the time he reached the age of 53. Those two years were to be the exceptions because it was then that he intended to realize a hope cherished since he last saw his closest friends in England in 1903 – to spend holidays with them in Europe. 'I am often thinking at my times of rest, ie. on the march, of plans for the summer and autumn, 1909,' he told Publius in one of his many references to the subject. 'How glad I shall be for the real rest which I can hope to find only near you!'[24]

Stein would not have felt able to enjoy the prospect of such rest without having earned it. At the two sites he visited first on leaving Khotan, Khadalik and Niya, he worked relentlessly in high temperatures and clouds of dust during the day, only to stay up late into the night recording the location and condition of all the more important pieces. In a letter to John Scott Keltie, Secretary of the Royal Geographical Society, he admitted that he had rarely felt so exhausted at the end of the day. 'But I made a big haul', he added, 'and felt in my element.'[25] Relief came with the abrupt arrival of autumn. Suddenly the desert was beautiful, its river beds lined by poplars ablaze with red and yellow foliage, golden reeds and purple tufts of tamarisk. Dash hunted happily after deer, hares and foxes, and the fresh air and lower temperatures brought a lightness of step to men who had been stifled for weeks by dust, heat and glare.

Regardless of the season, and however strenuous his activities, Stein was never too tired or too preoccupied to enjoy the atmosphere of the desert sites. The character of the ancient settlements, and of the people who lived and died there, came easily to his imagination; so easily that at times his perceptions of the past overtook the present and it seemed to him that the cities were still living places, with houses and temples and orchards, and inhabitants who still used the pots and brooms and keys that he found in their homes. Beyond the splintered timber frame-work and wattle walls of the houses in these abandoned places, the bleached trunks of dead trees stretched to a sea of sand whose monot-ony was broken only by the wave-like crests of yellow dunes. It was an utterly barren scene. But for Stein it had a magnetic power. He looked at it and heard what he described as 'the Sirens' call', summoning him farther and farther into the depths of the unknown desert. The feeling of being 'a real "treasure-seeker"', which he had experienced at Niya, drew him on.[26] And there was much more treasure lying just beyond the horizon.

8

Treasures of the 'Black Hole'

A WAY TO THE east lay Stein's next goal, the forbidding territory of the Lop Desert. There, the smooth, impassive dunes of the Taklamakan gave way to a far more turbulent landscape: a desolate, unremitting expanse of clay banks and trenches that had been carved out of the earth over centuries by biting Mongolian gales and the sand carried by the blast. Nothing lived here. There were no plants, no water, no shelter, just pitted, eroded ground that lacerated camels' feet and continually forced any travellers off the line of their route as they tried to negotiate its troughs and terraces. Icy winds blew from the north-east, the temperature dropped well below 0° Fahrenheit in winter and even the thickest clothes afforded little protection from the piercing cold.

In the late thirteenth century, Marco Polo wrote:

But there is a marvellous thing related of this Desert, which is that when travellers are on the move by night, and one of them chances to lag behind or to fall asleep or the like, when he tries to gain his company again he will hear spirits talking, and will suppose them to be his comrades. Sometimes the spirits will call him by name; and thus shall a traveller ofttimes be led astray so that he never finds his party. And in this way many have perished. Sometimes the stray travellers will hear as it were the tramp and hum of a great cavalcade of people away from the real line of road, and taking this to be their own company they will follow the sound; and when day breaks they find that a cheat has been put on them and that they are in an ill plight. Even in the day-time one hears those spirits talking. And sometimes you shall hear the sound of a variety of musical instruments, and still more commonly the sound of drums. Hence in making this journey 'tis customary for travellers to keep close together. All the animals too have bells at their necks, so that they cannot easily get astray. And at sleeping-time a signal is put up to show the direction of the next march.

So thus it is that the Desert is crossed.[1]

The route Marco Polo followed through this desert linked the southern oases of Chinese Turkestan with Kansu province, the western extremity of China proper. It was passable only during winter, when the salt water of the wells froze and became fit for consumption, and was rarely used in Stein's day. More important in ancient times had been the northern arm of the Silk Road which ran from Tun-huang, in Kansu, along the foot of the T'ien-shan Mountains to Turfan and on to Kashgar. However, early Chinese annals indicated that a faster route from Tun-huang to the northern oases opened in about 110 BC cutting directly across an inhospitable expanse of salt-encrusted prehistoric sea-bed. The remains that Sven Hedin had stumbled across stood at the north-western edge of this ancient sea-bed, and they suggested that evidence of China's first advances westward still lay in that harsh terrain.

Hedin had described his discovery in his second book, *Central Asia and Tibet*, published in 1903. In the last three months of 1900, he had undertaken a voyage by boat down the Tarim River into the heart of the Taklamakan Desert. But he had been prevented from reaching Lopnor, the salt lake into which the Tarim empties itself, by the river freezing over. To pass the time while waiting for the thaw, he and his party set out across the desert on foot until, at the end of March 1901, they came upon the strange sight of old wooden ruins set high on hillocks that had been created by the erosive action of wind and sand.

During a cursory inspection of the place, Hedin found coins, iron axes and wood-carvings; but the gradual melting of his ice supplies impelled him to move on. Twelve miles into the following day's journey, he stopped to dig for water and found that his only spade had been left behind at the hillocks. The man responsible returned to fetch it and, in doing so, chanced upon more ruins and a number of beautifully carved wooden boards. Hedin had no time to investigate further; but the following year he returned to the site – later identified as the town of Lou-lan. He unearthed a variety of manuscripts which, scholars later found, revealed much about the life of this long-buried town. Stein, of course, had read Hedin's account of these discoveries. He admired his colleague's ability to recognize important finds despite his lack of appropriate training; but he was also determined that he himself, rather than Hedin, would be the first to reveal the true archaeological importance of the site.

Preparations for the journey to Lou-lan took place in early December 1906 at Charkhlik. No longer the busy city of Marco Polo's time, this was a small oasis of about five hundred homesteads, populated mainly by Lopliks, the indigenous people of the area who lived traditionally as nomadic fishermen on the marshes and lakes of the Tarim River, but who had recently begun to settle and cultivate the ground. Only the fact that the district came under the authority of his old friend Pan, Taotai of Aksu, enabled Stein to accumulate, in such a small place, the large amounts of provisions and extra camels necessary for a fifty-man party spending five weeks in the desert. He was also lucky to secure the services of two men who had worked as guides for Hedin. Both were hunters with the characteristic Mongolian features and thick, archaic dialect of the Lopliks, and their presence in his team helped to persuade other, less intrepid locals that they might, after all, return alive from a winter journey into the dreaded Lop. The footsore camels were resoled in the traditional (and painful) way, with ox-hide soles sewn to their footpads; and the party left Charkhlik on 6 December to farewell cries of '*Yol bolsun*', 'May there be a way', from the labourers' apprehensive relatives.

Had they known the man who led the party, they might have felt more confident; for every stage of the trip to Lou-lan had been carefully calculated. Stein had arranged in advance for a ferry to be improvized (out of dug-outs lashed together) in order to get all his animals and baggage across the river beyond Charkhlik. Once this operation was completed, he established a depot at a small place called Abdal and divided the baggage and stores into those to be taken and those to be left behind. On the first, waterless stage of the journey he planned to make use of the ponies, which would then return to the depot. Thirty donkeys would be taken farther in order to carry as much ice as possible. They would also be used, together with the camels, as transport columns between advance bases so that supplies of food, ice and animal fodder could be moved along the desert route. This would allow the party to stay some time at Lou-lan without having to depend solely on what they could carry there in a single trip. The camels could survive on a little rape-seed oil until, having reached Lou-lan, they could be taken to feed on reed-beds farther north.

Stein's natural efficiency and love of order made him well-suited to the organization of such military-style operations. He had been trained by his brother to be careful with money, so the need to use every rupee of his expedition grants wisely was no hardship. He would probably have been equally precise even if he had had to account to no one but himself. His sense of responsibility dictated that none of his arrangements were vague or left to chance, and it was a matter of pride to him that he stayed within his budget, sold his animals at a profit, arrived at destinations on schedule, chose suitable routes and navigated successfully through uncharted territory. However attracted he was by wildernesses, he was never complacent about the dangers that went with them. If he made mistakes, he took care to learn from them, and any loss of animals distressed him, not only because of his fondness for them but also because it seemed to him an indication of failure.

It was not mere chance that no European accompanied him on these journeys through Chinese Central Asia. Travelling as he did, accompanied only by servants and subordinates, his authority was unquestioned. There was no one to query his decisions, criticize his methods or demand a hearing. Such a life could be lonely, and he was not immune to feelings of isolation. But it was an isolation which, by and large, he chose. The absence of a like-minded companion made him warm to those among his men who seemed to understand something of his motivation, but he did not feel obliged to make concessions to them as he would have done to a fellow-Westerner. He expected them to be as fit and resilient as he was himself and, though he made some allowances for levels of efficiency that could not match his own, he was irritated by sloppy work and lack of stamina. Eric Macartney's boyhood impression of him, recollected late in life, was that he was 'quick-tempered but very brave',[2] and his men undoubtedly felt the effects of both those characteristics.

The journey across the Lop Desert to Lou-lan took seven days. It was impossible to cover more than fourteen miles a day over the broken ground, and Stein several times retired to bed to the sound of the poor camels groaning in pain as Hassan Akhun sewed ox-hide to their badly cracked feet. Prehistoric flint arrowheads, knife-blades and fragments of coarse pottery lying on the ground were the only signs that this place had once supported human life. A bitter wind blew from the north-east, and at night Stein's men had no other protection from it than their fires, built from the dead poplars that littered ancient river-beds. Unlike him, they had no tents, and they were sometimes so numb with cold that it was several hours before they could get animals and baggage ready to move in the mornings. As they travelled across the desolate landscape, they marked their route with lumps of clay and dead wood, the only available substitutes for landmarks by which to plot a course. The sole means of finding Lou-lan was by compass and Hedin's sketch-map. But these did not fail. Late on 17 December, after three miles of what seemed like a gruelling obstacle course up and down twenty-foot-deep trenches, the party finally reached the first ruin of Lou-lan.

The relief among the men from Charkhlik was evident. It was Hassan Akhun's reaction, however, that fascinated Stein, who liked to think that his camel-man might have inherited his energy and temper from ancestors in the Classical West. Adopting a triumphant posture, one arm stretched out and resting on his staff, Hassan Akhun addressed the labourers as if, noted Stein, he were half vindicated prophet, half demagogue. 'Had he not always tried to drum it into their thick heads that under the guidance of his Sahib, who could fathom all hidden places of the dreaded Taklamakan with his "paper and Mecca-pointer", i.e. map and compass, all things were bound to come right?'[3] It was certainly something to be proud of, Stein felt later when he had thoroughly surveyed the area, that his and Hedin's calculation of the position of the Lou-lan site differed only by about a mile and a half. Equally important, there was no sign of any French or Germans, 'and thus', he wrote to Publius, 'the 1,000 miles race from Khotan (done exactly in three months including one spent in excavations) is won – for the present'.[4]

Over the next eleven days, the wind-battered ruins of Lou-lan rewarded Stein's efforts with many revelations of their long-lost past. There were small objects such as spoons, beads made of glass, paste and stone, fragments of lacquered ware, buckles and bronze mirrors, woollen slippers and what proved to be the earliest known piece of woollen pile carpet. From the items collected here by Hedin, Stein already knew that the remains dated from exactly the same period as those at the Niya site, that is, the first three centuries AD. And on the very first day of work, his men unearthed Chinese documents on wood and paper in a house built of wattle and timber, just as at Niya. Others recovered from an ancient rubbish heap a day or two later were to confirm his most hopeful speculations regarding the role of this isolated town. For when, on their arrival in Europe, Edouard Chavannes began to decipher them, he found that some were addressed either to or from no less a person than the Commander-in-Chief of the Western Regions – the chief representative of Chinese power in the Tarim Basin.

Lou-lan, it transpired, had held a garrison whose purpose was to protect the first tentacle of Chinese imperial influence as it probed its way westward through the Lop Desert, from the first century BC onwards. As if to illustrate the forces that propelled merchants and traders along that bleak and perilous road, a small bale of yellow silk emerged from the ruins: a faded, brittle and long-forgotten remnant of the commodity that made the trade routes of Central Asia famous throughout the world.

Stein had hardly dared to hope for evidence of the spread of Indian scripts and language this far east. But several wooden tablets inscribed with the Kharosthi writing of north-west India emerged from the excavation. The imperial army, it seemed, while energetically defending its lines of communication through Lop, had not disturbed the administration of local rulers whose language and culture originated far away in Bactria and Gandhara. Chinese ideas, however, were bound to infiltrate that culture, and one small item bore particular significance in this context: a strip of white silk bearing Kharosthi writing. This was the first tangible proof of an old tradition that the Chinese had used silk as a writing material before the invention of paper, and that the idea had been adopted for other scripts.

It was a torn scrap of paper, however, that bore the most puzzling piece of writing: an unknown script, recalling Aramaic. Pondering the possible origin of the western trader who perhaps dropped or threw away this fragment, Stein had it packed along with other finds, unaware that a treasure-trove of letters in the same script awaited him farther along his route. Though he did not yet know it, he had unearthed the first example of the lost language of Sogdiana, the region of Samarkand and Bokhara.

He also took away with him a more prosaic object: the metal tape-measure which Sven Hedin had used at Lou-lan in 1901 and which was still lying where he had left it on the base of a stupa. Uniquely, this was something from the desert which Stein intended to return to its owner.[5]

By the end of December, Stein's ice supplies were getting low and many of his men were suffering from the effects of prolonged exposure to the bitter weather. He himself was experiencing repeated malarial attacks, originally contracted in India. His Christmas was enlivened, however, by the almost miraculous appearance of Turdi, the *dak*-man (unrelated to the treasure-hunter of the same name whom Stein had employed in 1900–1), who trudged into camp on 24 December with a large bag of letters. Stein had last seen him on 15 November at the Endere River as he set out with a mail-bag for delivery to Badruddin Khan at Khotan. Badruddin had sent him back with more mail, this time on a pony, and Turdi had covered the distance from Khotan to Abdal, outside Charkhlik, usually reckoned as thirty marches, in twenty-one days. At Abdal he had insisted on following Stein's tracks into the Lop Desert, despite the danger of doing so with no supplies beyond what little ice he and his guide, a local hunter, could carry. He had covered 1,300 miles in thirty-nine days. And though he had spent the last day without water, his first request was that Stein inspect the seals on mail-bags from Macartney to see that they were still intact. Then he was led away to the fireside by admiring labourers, leaving Stein to spend the evening poring over four months' worth of letters from friends.

———————◄——◄———————

Stein left Lou-lan five days later. He dispatched his archaeological finds back to Abdal on four camels in the charge of the surveyor, Ram Singh, whom rheumatism had more or less incapacitated. Then, never one to travel willingly over ground already covered if there was an alternative route, he set out with half a dozen of the fitter labourers across uncharted desert, towards the marshes and lagoons marking the end of the Tarim. The terrain changed from hard clay to ridges of sand-dunes, with little in the way of dead trees or tamarisk clumps to provide fuel until, on 4 January 1907, the party reached reed-beds and found themselves on the banks of a frozen lagoon. Beneath a foot of solid ice, the water was no more than six or eight feet deep and so clear that fish could clearly be seen swimming below. As they crossed the ice-sheet, past holes cut by fishermen for their nets, Stein watched Naik Ram Singh's reaction with affectionate curiosity.

The Naik had encountered many strange natural phenomena in the course of his work, but a lake frozen hard enough for camels to walk upon was not one of them. His astonishment only intensified when he considered what his fellow villagers in the Punjab would say when he tried to explain the scene to them. By the time Stein came to relate this incident in his account of the expedition, the story was full of poignancy for him because he knew that the brown eyes of Ram Singh – whom he usually described as 'honest', the word he reserved for his favourite followers – would never again see any sight, either remarkable or ordinary. Before the second expedition was over, the Naik, the sturdiest member of the entire party, would be reduced to helplessness by the sudden and irreversible loss of his sight.

The total eclipse of the sun that followed ten days later on 14 January 1907, when Stein was taking a rare rest day in camp, passed without comment by his men, Lopliks and Indians alike. He himself was captivated by the shades of yellow, blue and green that filled the sky, the glowing silver of the sun and the strange, ethereal light that glittered on the ice-sheet of the river and the feathery brushwood of the silent surrounding riverine jungle.

For every moment of wonder, there were many more filled with the mundane details of organizing an expedition. Before Stein could set out for his next goal, he had to send a trusted messenger, Ibrahim Beg, to Kara-shahr, 330 miles to the north, to collect the next instalment of Chinese silver sent by Macartney. At the same time he sent a message, to be conveyed from Kara-shahr to Kashgar by the Chinese telegraph and then by post to the Surveyor-General in India, asking for a replacement for the surveyor Ram Singh, whose rheumatism now seemed too severe for him to continue. Only then, in late January, could he start for the next site, Miran, which had been brought to his attention by one of his hunter-guides.

He had arranged for Chiang to establish camp there, and the familiar sight of his devoted Chinese secretary, clad in dark silk jacket, yellow silk overalls, small cap and slippers warmed Stein's heart as he rode up out of the darkness. Chiang had not accompanied the expedition to

Lou-lan, and there had been no communication with him in the meantime, for want of a common written language. Stein had missed Chiang, and not simply because he had felt the need of a translator. Despite his independence and his distrust of working with anyone other than subordinates, he had come to rely on Chiang's sympathetic companionship and what Stein regarded as his 'gentlemanly' qualities. In many ways, Chiang's company was as important as the weekly letter from Publius. Letters might arrive at two-month intervals; Chiang could be by his side every day.

<hr>

Miran was the scene of some of Stein's most exciting discoveries. They have tended since to be overshadowed by the antiquities he was to find later at Tun-huang, a location that did more to capture the popular imagination than a few half-buried ruins scattered about a barren plain. Those scattered ruins at Miran, however, provided the most startling proof of the inheritance of Western artistic styles and techniques in that farthest corner of Central Asia.

They also contained quite the filthiest rubbish that Stein had so far encountered in his excavations in Chinese Turkestan. Twenty-five years and many more excavations later, he still vividly recalled the sight and stench of the rooms in the Tibetan fort which his men began to excavate on the morning of 24 January 1907. 'I have had occasion to acquire a rather extensive experience in clearing ancient rubbish-heaps', he wrote in 1932 when he was nearly 70, 'and know how to diagnose them. But for intensity of sheer dirt and age-persisting smelliness I shall always put the rich "castings" of Tibetan warriors in the front rank.'[6] The cells were piled high with sweepings, straw, scraps of clothing, broken implements and, Stein implied but was too fastidious to state, age-old human excrement.

Digging in the howling wind that persisted throughout the three weeks of their stay at Miran, the labourers could not avoid inhaling and choking on the dust of this detritus. Stein had a choice. He could either stand on a rampart of the fort in order to watch the different excavations that proceeded simultaneously and be blasted by the icy gales; or he could descend to the diggings where he was engulfed by the blinding fog of disintegrating filth. Wherever he turned, there was no relief from the vicious climate. Work occasionally came to a standstill when all his men, bar Chiang, fell sick. Only the camels and ponies found relief, grazing a few miles away in the belt of scrub and reeds surrounding a stream which had once been used to irrigate Miran. 'Truly,' he told Publius, 'this part of the country is dying and its conditions a foretaste of what "desiccation" will make of our little globe – if things run long enough that way.'[7]

What the conditions imposed by way of physical suffering, however, they more than balanced – at least in Stein's view, if not that of his miserable labourers – by yielding antiquities that were wonderfully preserved. From the fort came miscellaneous office papers written in everyday Tibetan of the eighth and ninth centuries, the mere fact of their existence being as interesting as their contents to scholars who had so far had barely any access to early secular Tibetan documents. A packet of papers in Runic Turkish was a reminder that the Western Turks shared with the Tibetans the conquest of the Chinese-held Tarim Basin in the eighth century; but, interesting as these finds were, it was Miran's art remains that gave Stein the greatest thrill.

These came to light in mounds which had once been Buddhist shrines, but which Stein concluded had fallen into ruin long before the Tibetans built their fort nearby. As item after item emerged from the debris, each seemed to outdo the last in the beauty of its form, its completeness and its extraordinary resemblance to the art of the ancient, Classical West. First came a colossal stucco head, seventeen inches across, then the huge seated torsos to which it and others had once been attached; and then a delicately painted fresco that took Stein completely by surprise.[8] As digging progressed, winged angels began to appear on the wall until he found himself looking at what appeared to be representations of early Christian cherubim. Eagerly he swept the earth away from the dimpled, vivacious faces and gazed on figures with smiling eyes and mouths, pink cheeks and round faces, whose origins lay far away in the cupids of Classical mythology.

That these faces decorated the dado of a Buddhist temple in the Lop Desert could be explained by the fact that Buddhist mythology includes a class of celestial attendants known as gandharvas. These were sometimes represented in the Graeco-Buddhist sculpture of Gandhara by the figure of the winged Eros. Clearly, the artist who had painted this Miran dado had been thoroughly versed in that Graeco-Buddhist tradition. But he had also been gifted in the use of colour and of chiaroscuro, a technique never before observed in Indian, Central Asian or Far Eastern early pictorial art. From other finds nearby, Stein dated the fresco to the third century AD. It was a find of great significance, for in India no pictorial work correspond-ing in date and origin to the sculpture of Graeco-Buddhist Gandhara had ever been found. More digging revealed other wall-paintings depicting typical scenes from Buddhist iconography; and yet more in another ruin that were frankly secular and Classical in design, with a festoon of flowers and wreaths, and figures who carried objects such as decanters, goblets and a guitar.

The link with the Classical West which so fascinated Stein was con-firmed by the discovery of a short inscription on one of the religious scenes. It recorded the payment the artist received and his name, written as 'Tita'. No such name could be accounted for etymologically in any Indian or Iranian language; it could only be the Sanskrit or Prakrit version of the Roman name 'Titus'. Here was the signature of a man who must have travelled east early in the Christian era, probably from the Roman Orient, until he came to a Buddhist settlement deep in the heart of Asia where he found employment, and where he left his name as a memorial for others to read 1,500 years later.

The contrast between the bright colours and vivacity of the frescoes, and the freezing, wind-battered desolation of the gravel plain in which Miran stood, emphasized the conflicts in Stein's view of the desert. Having spent several months in the wilderness or in the primitive settle-ments of the oases, he was spellbound by the beauty and the atmos-phere of enjoyment conjured up by the paintings, and reassured by the promise they seemed to give of a region where such things existed, far from the 'cares and discomforts of desert labours'.[9] But he was also elated by what had been achieved, and by the number of antiquities he had managed to remove and pack.

The removal of the frescoes was a 'ticklish' operation. Some of them had slipped down from their original positions, and large fragments, in some cases several feet tall, stood leaning in layers against the part of the wall that still remained. They were no more than half an inch thick and extremely brittle: a mere touch could cause them to break off at the edges. Stein had his men make boards from dead poplar trunks brought from near the stream, and on these he laid layers of cotton wool covered with tough Khotan paper. Then he took a large sheet of tin, improvized by Naik Ram Singh from empty cases and stiffened with thin iron bands, and slid it down behind the first broken panel, taking care not to damage the one behind on which the first rested. Using this tin sheet he could tilt the panel forward on to the padded board, on which it lay flat and could then be moved safely.

A different method had to be used for the dado of angels, since it was still in its original position on the wall of one of the shrines. Its plaster was thicker and less brittle than the other frescoes, however. There was scarcely any wall left above it, and a window flanked it on one side, so it was relatively easy for Stein to cut out the panels with a large flexible steel saw. They too were laid on padded boards; then the boards were put together with the painted surfaces facing each other, but separated by more layers of cotton wool. Each pair of panels was padded with reeds cut carefully to size. When several of these pairs had been made into a packet, they were tied with ropes, laid between planks and placed in cases made to fit them exactly. Stein was unable to take with him as much as he would have liked, since the frieze signed by Titus was too brittle to be removed from its wall in the limited time available. He took photographs instead. The excavations were refilled, the antiquities sent off on their two-month journey to Kashgar; and Stein resolved to return to Miran later to finish the task.

Now he was ready for the last lap of his journey into China. However alluring the thought was to him, it disturbed his men, Turki and Indian alike. The Indians had grown accustomed to the ease with which their needs were met in the oases of the Tarim Basin, and they had heard that they would not be made so welcome by the 'heathens' of Kansu province. The hazards of the 380-mile desert track ahead of them seemed less daunting than the unknown destination to which it led. These hazards, however slight compared with those of the waterless tract leading to Lou-lan, were considerable. Only a couple of days into the journey to Tun-huang, late in February 1907, three of the donkeys hired locally succumbed to exhaustion, having had to cover twenty-four miles without water the previous day. The trials of the next stage of the journey, across the crumpled salt surface of an ancient lake-bed, claimed three more by the time the caravan reached an ample supply of water and ice.

Suspecting that the animals' owners were neglecting them, Stein put Ibrahim Beg in charge of the fodder and offered rewards, over and above the normal hire price, to those who brought their donkeys through safely. This stratagem worked, and there were no more deaths. But the grim aspect of the landscape continued and for fully seventeen days of the trek, there was no sight of another human being. The surroundings brought to mind those earlier travellers, Hiuen Tsiang, Marco Polo and another Buddhist pilgrim, the monk Fa-hsien (Faxian), who crossed the Lop Desert in AD 399 and wrote of it: 'Though you look all round most earnestly to find where you can cross, you know not where to make your choice, the only mark and indication being the dry bones of the dead left upon the sand.'[10]

Stein was looking for other marks and indications which he had reason to believe he might find in this desolate place. In 1899, a French diplomat called Bonin had reported seeing ruined watch-towers during an unsuccessful attempt to follow Marco Polo's route across the desert. Nothing was known about these ruins, but the probability that they were connected with the original Chinese advance into the Tarim Basin, and the fact that his excavations so far in the region had been highly rewarding, encouraged Stein to hope for further revelations. On the evening of 7 March, as the party trekked across a bare gravel plateau, he noticed a tower-like mound away to the north, too far off to examine, and then another only about a mile from his path. The latter was unmistakably an ancient and well-preserved watch-tower, about fifteen feet square and twenty-three feet high and built of hard clay bricks interspersed with layers of tamarisk branches.

The next morning, he found yet another tower nearby. At first, it seemed that the building stood alone. But looking at the ground, Stein noticed a line of reed bundles protruding from the gravel soil. Following them a little way, he saw with delight that the line stretched away straight to another tower three miles to the east. A little excavating proved that this line was indeed a wall, made of reed bundles placed horizontally and at regular intervals across layers of stamped clay, with more bundles of reeds lying at right angles on the outside. There was no time to undertake a full investigation, but plenty of opportunity for observation as he made his way towards Tun-huang. The route was lined by towers and by outcrops of the wall that were five or six feet high in places. The remnants of these utterly forgotten fortifications reaching westward into the desert exerted a powerful fascination on Stein. He resolved to return, as soon as he had restocked with supplies in Tun-huang and ascertained how much work awaited him at the Caves of the Thousand Buddhas.

----------➤ ◄----------

Even in the stark dress of winter, the groves and tilled fields of the Tun-huang oasis offered a luxuriant contrast to the ground the expedition party had crossed. Stein reached the town on 12 March in the teeth of a bitter wind, three weeks after leaving Charkhlik and one week short of the time deemed necessary for the journey by traders, who still reckoned by the estimate Marco Polo had made of twenty-eight days. He found himself a camp-site in the garden of a dilapidated old house, risked freezing to death by donning his best European clothes in order to visit the Amban, and befriended the military commandant, whose presence in the town gave emphasis to its position on the frontier of China proper. He paid off the Charkhlik donkey-men, brought his accounts up to date, gathered local information from Muslim traders and made preparations for a return to the watch-towers in the desert. And then, on 16 March, he rode out to see the valley of the Thousand Buddhas.

Here, in a shallow, barren depression about twelve miles south-east of the Tun-huang oasis, stand the cliffs containing the sacred grottoes – named after a legend concerning a monk who dreamt he saw a cloud with a thousand Buddhas floating above the valley. Stein's first view of the caves as he rode across the sand and gravel revealed a honeycomb of small, dark cavities, apparently unconnected and accessible only by ropes or ladders, like the troglodyte dwellings of hermits. The flights of steps that had once linked them had long since crumbled away. Farther along the cliffs, a multitude of larger, decorated caves pierced the rock-face in irregular tiers over a distance of about half a mile, reminiscent of the rock-temples of India, whence the tradition had spread to the east. Some of the original antechapels or porches of the shrines had fallen away, so that the paintings on the inner walls could clearly be seen, their colours startling against the drab background. Two colossal Buddha images, each about ninety feet high, thrust upwards through several open halls from the cavities in which they stood. In the lower shrines, sand had drifted through the entrances and partly filled the antechambers.

There was no sign of any attendant when Stein arrived. He moved freely from one to another of the highly decorated sanctuaries, familiarizing himself with their general plan and marvelling at the continuity of tradition that linked the Graeco-Buddhist sculptural art of north-west India with these painted walls and stucco figures at the gateway to the Far East.

Beyond the antechapel of a typical cave temple a high, wide passage led to an inner cell that had been hewn from the solid rock. Because of the extremely dry atmosphere, the paintings on the plastered walls had survived remarkably well and the colours of their figures and floral designs were still bright. On a platform in the centre of the cave sat the colossal stucco figure of a Buddha, attended by symmetrically arranged groups of Bodhisattvas on either side. Some of these statues had been damaged, either by iconoclasts or by crude restoration, but the grace of the drapery and the traces of gilding that were still apparent testified to an ancient Indian inheritance. Similarly, though the legendary scenes depicted in the frescoes were Chinese in style, the faces, poses and drapery of the figures they featured were unmistakably Indian in origin.

Stein deduced that most of the larger shrines dated from T'ang times, from the seventh to the tenth centuries, when the Tun-huang oasis enjoyed a period of prosperity. But he knew that the valley had been a place of pilgrimage since the fourth century AD and that earlier work, therefore, might well exist in other, possibly less accessible cave temples.

The fact that pilgrims still devoutly attended the images, however, made him cautious. It would be foolhardy to attempt anything other than respectful inspection of the frescoes and stucco sculptures: the risk of popular resentment was too great to contemplate removal. There was no sentiment in his approach; he regarded the shrines of the Thousand Buddhas in purely pragmatic terms. If he had been able to remove their works of art without arousing the wrath of pilgrims and local people, he would have done so. But the danger of reprisals was real. Besides, he was buoyed up by a rumour he had heard since arriving in the oasis, of a secret hoard of manuscripts that had been discovered in one of the caves and which, if he could get his hands on it, would more than compensate for the self-restraint he was otherwise obliged to exercise.

The manuscript hoard was said to have been locked up in a side chapel by official order after discovery. But Stein had discussed with Chiang the ways in which the local priests, 'usually as ignorant as they were greedy', might be persuaded to open it again.[11] Once at the caves, the two men managed to discover in which cave temple the manuscripts lay. The monk who obliged them with this information also showed them a manuscript borrowed from the secret library, and its fine condition and evidently Buddhist text – albeit in a form of Chinese incomprehensible to Chiang – made Stein impatient to see more. The guardian of the shrines, who was also the person who had discovered the hoard, was a Taoist priest called Wang; but he was away on a begging tour of the oasis and, without him, there was nothing more Stein could do to further his own interests, other than hand the young monk a large tip. 'I always like to be liberal with those whom I may hope to secure as "my own" local priests . . . at sites of ancient worship,' he wrote afterwards.[12] Then he left the valley, wondering whether, when he and Wang met, the guardian would prove 'sufficiently good-natured – and mindful of material interests' to allow manuscripts to leave his closely guarded library.[13] Money was the tool he intended to employ at this particular site.

The weeks that followed gave him some of the most satisfying work he could have hoped for in all his time in Chinese Central Asia. Returning to the watch-towers in the desert on 24 March, he was in a field of study all his own, where no competitors snapped at his heels and where he could lose himself completely in the past. From beneath thin layers of earth and gravel he retrieved countless objects that brought to life the daily routine of the soldiers posted to those bleak and lonely outposts. He read their letters, collected their domestic implements, walked in the path they had worn as they patrolled the windswept wall. He grew accustomed to the arrangement of their quarters, to the orders and preoccupations of the officers, and to picking records of the time of Christ from their resting place only a few inches below the surface of the ground.

'I feel at times as I ride along the wall to examine new towers, etc., as if I were going to inspect posts still held by the living,' he told Publius on 26 April.

With this experience daily repeated of perishable things wonderfully preserved one risks gradually losing the true sense of time. Two thousand years seem so brief a span when the sweepings from the soldiers' huts still lie practically on the surface in front of the doors or when I see the huge stacks of reed bundles as used for repairing the wall still in situ near the posts . . . I feel strangely at home here along this desolate frontier – as if I had known it in a previous birth.[14]

In contrast to the callous calculation of his approach at the Tun-huang caves, his method here was a model of integrity and high purpose. There was no treasure likely to emerge from the haunts of poor soldiers, at least not of the sort to cause a sensation in Britain or to transform his status in India. The wealth of the wall lay in its abundant antiquarian evidence: details of the soldiers' lives, of the way the wall had operated and of the topographical considerations that influenced its construction. A site could hardly have been devised to attract Stein more, with his interest in both historical and geographical factors and his ability to synthesize the two. He was absorbed by a desire to understand as much as possible about the place.

He sat in the ruins of watch rooms imagining the Huns advancing across the harsh and almost featureless terrain; he found the charred evidence of fires lit by soldiers to send signals down the line. He admired the way the engineers who built the wall had incorporated natural obstacles, such as marshes and hillocks, into their line of defence; and he collected records on wood – later found to date from the first century AD, the oldest Chinese documents yet known – which showed that the garrison had been supplemented by non-Chinese soldiers, probably in many cases deported convicts. Travellers who passed on their way to and from Central Asia had also left documents behind: some of Stein's most treasured discoveries were a wooden tablet and eight folded letters (on what was later found to be the earliest known example of rag paper) written by traders in the forgotten language of ancient Sogdiana, the language he had first come across at Lou-lan.

To his great satisfaction, he also identified the remains – still boasting fifteen-foot-thick walls and standing more than thirty feet high – of the Jade Gate: the famous fort, named after the best-known product of Khotan, from which all traffic passing westward along the desert route was controlled in Han times.

The wall and its watch-towers dated from the reign of the dynamic Han emperor Wu-ti (140–87 BC), when they were built as a branch of the Great Wall itself. However, the Great Wall had been created, during the third century BC, as a barrier against the nomad hordes of the Mongolian plain, whereas this wall was also an instrument of expansion. It reached towards the western lands that Wu-ti was so eager to discover and exploit, and protected travellers along its route. Stein referred to the wall as the 'Chinese *limes*', using the Roman term for an ancient defensive road system. He found sections of it east of Tunhuang and, with Dash always at his heels, traced the line westward to the point where it ended in the natural obstacle of impassable marshes at the terminal point of the Su-lo-ho River. The materials of the wall – clay and bundles of reeds or brushwood – were almost petrified by salts in the ground and had a cohesive elasticity that had defied relentless erosive gales for two thousand years.

The climate changed swiftly, in the course of Stein's investigations, from the icy cold of winter to oppressive summer heat. Conditions became almost intolerable when swarms of mosquitoes and other insects built up on the marshes. The men from Tun-huang, whom he had managed to engage only with difficulty, were debilitated by opium and liable to desert during the night if not closely watched. Still, he revelled in his work and rode back to Tun-huang in mid-May, across gravel wastes glittering in 150° Fahrenheit of heat, with a light heart and in anticipation of another imminent discovery.

As if to demonstrate the vigour and potency of old traditions, the annual pilgrimage to the Caves of the Thousand Buddhas took place just after Stein's return. Gaily dressed parties of local people trekked to the shrines, riding in donkey carts and enjoying their holiday. Having been politely warned by the Amban that his presence at the caves would be intrusive at such a time, he waited impatiently in an oasis now bright with the spring colours of young corn and small wild irises, distracting himself with letters, notes and accounts. Then, on 21 May, he rode out again to the sandy valley that had so often occupied his thoughts during the previous two months.

Wang, the guardian of the shrines, was waiting to greet this visitor who had come, ostensibly, to study and photograph the paintings and sculpture of the caves. The diminutive priest was pleased to show off his achievements there. Though a Taoist, he was an admirer of Hiuen Tsiang, and it was the latter's connections with Tun-huang, whence he had set off on his journey to India in AD 629, that had drawn Wang to the oasis in about 1900 after his discharge from the army. There he had taken upon himself the task of cleaning out and restoring the shrines, in some cases having new frescoes painted, including one that depicted the legend of Hiuen Tsiang's journey. He financed these labours by his begging tours and by selling charms and blessings, and it was this need for funds that his visitor hoped to exploit if Wang proved reluctant to part with the contents of his locked library. Stein deliberately avoided a lengthy conversation with Wang at first. He thought him 'a very queer person, extremely shy and nervous, with an occasional expression of cunning which was far from encouraging. It was clear from the first that he would be a difficult person to handle.'[15]

In order to prepare the way, Stein sent Chiang to engage the priest in conversation and to make offers of donations as he saw fit. This resulted in Wang cautiously agreeing to show them such manuscripts as he could easily extract, but his less than enthusiastic manner convinced Stein that more persuasive tactics were necessary. He therefore paid Wang a formal visit and asked to be shown the restored cave temple in which, he knew, lay the door to the hidden library. Masking his distaste for Wang's crude additions to the decoration beneath a show of admiring interest, he was able to take in with one swift glance the fact that the side chapel's doorway had recently been completely bricked up. This was a bad sign, for it surely implied that Wang suspected the real reason for his visitor's presence there and had resolved to keep the contents of the library safely beyond reach. It was time for Stein to play his trump card.

'I knew that it would be futile to talk to him about my archaeological interests, about the need of first-hand materials for Chinese historical and antiquarian studies, and the like, as I was accustomed to do on meeting educated Chinese officials,' he recalled later.[16] But there was one subject he could be fairly certain would find favour with the dedicated guardian of the shrines: Hiuen Tsiang, the Buddhist monk whose influence had reached across the centuries to touch the lives of both these men, so far apart in every other respect. It was a gamble, for there were no other cards left to play. But it worked. The priest's shyness wore off as he eagerly discussed with Stein the travels of the old pilgrim and proudly showed him recently painted frescoes in the new loggia to the temple representing episodes from Hiuen Tsiang's legendary life. One of the scenes gave Stein another ace to keep in reserve, for it pictured

Hiuen Tsiang bringing large bundles of manuscripts away from India. He would wait for the right moment before suggesting that it would be appropriate for him to take some of those ancient manuscripts back to their spiritual home.

Leaving Chiang to press home the advantages thus won, Stein retired to his tent, which had been pitched in a grove of fruit trees in front of the grottoes. Late the same night, while sitting at his table there, he heard footsteps outside. Through the flap of the tent slipped his faithful Chinese secretary, silent but evidently elated – and carrying a bundle of rolled manuscripts. Chiang had just received a furtive visit from Wang, who had brought him the bundle, carefully concealed beneath his long robe, as the first of the specimens he had agreed to show them. The manuscripts, plainly very old, were in Chinese and again Stein silently cursed the ignorance that prevented him from being able to read them. But Chiang, sitting up all night over the rolls, came to his rescue and by daybreak was able to announce with triumph and amazement that their colophons identified them as versions of the Buddhist texts brought from India and translated by none other than Hiuen Tsiang himself.

This seemed, even to the sophisticated Chiang, too fortuitous to be anything less than an auspicious omen, and he said as much to Wang. By the afternoon of the same day, the naïve, credulous priest felt sufficiently emboldened to allow his visitors sight of the antechapel itself, and the scene almost took Stein's breath away. Behind the dismantled brickwork and rough wooden door, lit only by the flame of Wang's small oil-lamp, lay a chamber about nine feet square, in which old manuscripts lay stacked on top of one another to a height of about ten feet, barely leaving space for two people to stand in the room beside them.

It was a spectacular sight but also a daunting one, for there was no space or light to examine this treasure trove. It was, as Stein wrote in a letter to Keltie at the Royal Geographical Society, a veritable 'Black Hole'.[17] Neither would any suggestion of bringing the manuscripts into the larger area of the cave temple be likely to win Wang's consent, for he was already nervous at the prospect of word spreading that he had opened his locked library to a foreigner. A compromise was reached instead, whereby Stein began to examine a few rolls at a time in the privacy of a small room adjoining the main shrine, lit by paper-covered windows.

The discoveries that followed were so extraordinary that it was difficult for Stein and Chiang to remember to conceal their excitement for
fear of harming their cause. Trying to remain calm, they unrolled
Chinese Buddhist manuscripts dating from the fifth century AD,
Tibetan leaves from the eighth and ninth centuries, and papers bearing
texts written in Sanskrit and other indigenous languages of Buddhist
Turkestan, all of which had been preserved in near-perfect condition in
the moisture-free atmosphere of the sealed cave chamber. None of
Stein's manuscript finds in the desert could equal this magical haul. His
joy intensified when, on unrolling a large canvas package, he found
himself looking down on a heap of paintings, mostly on fine silk or
linen. From their triangular tops and floating streamers he took them
to be temple banners, on which the colours seemed still as fresh as if
they had just been deposited there.

Other, much larger banners came to light, worn from use and too
fragile to unfold, and many more pictures, papers and textiles. Stein and
his assistant barely noticed the time passing until it was too dark to work
any longer. They were able to put most of the rolls to one side 'for
further study', but the question of removal was not broached. Only at
about midnight did Chiang again grope his way to his master's tent, this
time with a large bundle of their selections under his arm. The careful
diplomacy with which he had developed his relationship with Wang
ever since arriving at the caves had paid off. Wang had agreed to hand
over the rolls, as long as nobody else learnt of the transaction while
Stein was on Chinese soil.

For the next seven nights the stealthy transfer of manuscripts and
paintings continued. By day, Stein and Chiang amassed those which
they wished to retain for the conveniently euphemistic purposes of
'closer study', and by night Chiang conveyed the increasingly weighty
bundles to Stein's camp under cover of darkness. As Wang grew more
confident that his visitors could guard their shared secret, he allowed
more and more rolls and bundles to leave his cave. By the end of the
week, Stein had to enlist his two most trusted servants, Ibrahim Beg and
the pony-man Tila Bai, to help with the midnight relay of what had now
become sackfuls of material.

At this point, Wang's fragile composure suddenly deserted him.
Locking the library behind him, he left hurriedly for the oasis, ostensibly to visit his neglected patrons but probably chiefly to discover

whether the truth about his visitors' activities had leaked out. Only after a week's stay confirmed that nothing was known of his guilty secret did he feel sufficiently reassured to return to the shrine, where his persistent guests promptly succeeded in squeezing twenty more bundles from him.

There was no time for more than the most cursory examination of what had emerged from the walled-up library. Stein could not be sure that Wang's collaboration would last, and he was anxious to pack what he had managed to obtain before there was any change of heart. The packing alone took several days and had to be done as discreetly as possible. He had anticipated the situation by bringing several empty boxes with him, and others were brought to the camp in instalments, to avoid rousing suspicions.

The manuscripts filled seven cases, the paintings, embroideries and miscellanea a further five. In return, Wang received donations in Chinese silver ingots for the renovation of his shrine which were generous indeed in his terms, but which Stein described to Andrews as 'a sum which will make our friends at the Br. Mus. [British Museum] chuckle'.[18] He persuaded himself that the little priest was almost glad to know that part of the hidden library was being taken to a far-off 'temple of learning' by a fellow disciple of the great Hiuen Tsiang.

The expedition party finally left the valley of the Thousand Buddhas on the morning of 14 June with its boxes and baggage on five horse-drawn carts. Its departure was hastened by official concern that it should leave the Tun-huang oasis before an expected outburst of unrest over revenue assessment. Stein later had reason to be grateful for the warning, for the yamen there, where he had originally planned to store his precious boxes, was attacked by the discontented local populace soon afterwards and partly destroyed.

———◆◄—

Stein had no qualms about his acquisition of the hidden library as he rode away from Tun-huang. The manuscripts, paintings and textiles had suffered what he considered 'a dismal imprisonment' before he succeeded in bringing them to light; and he had no doubt that, had he not rescued them, they would eventually have found their way out of the cave into obscurity or destruction. Wang had no conception of the importance of what he had guarded so faithfully, and Stein believed that his own duty lay in carrying as much as possible of the hoard back to Europe where it could be studied and explained by modern scholars. At the same time, a certain respect for the simple Taoist priest mingled with the disdain he felt for his superstitions and his crude additions to his beloved shrine. Stein understood his timorous reservations, his fear of losing his reputation and the support of his patrons, without which his restoration work would grind to a halt. He admired his tenacity of purpose and the fact that the not inconsiderable amounts of money that Wang collected appeared never to go into his own pocket, but to be devoted to his gaudy cave temple.

Stein himself, despite the thrill of his discovery, was glad to get away from the claustrophobic caves and the oppressive quantity of manuscripts most of which, frustratingly, he was unable to decipher. 'It has been a time of great strain though apparently there was physical rest,' he told Publius shortly before leaving the caves. 'But, of course, I prefer *plein air*, even if it be in the desert, to caves & diplomatically discreet burrowings.'[19]

9

A Hero's Welcome

―――――――•――――――――

ONCE THE STORY of Stein's discoveries at Tun-huang became known, the other achievements of his second expedition tended to merge in an unfocused backdrop to the main drama. The unveiling of a secret library that had lain sealed and forgotten for hundreds of years was a single event, plainly more memorable than the gradual exposure of a lost civilization that had left no great monuments, no gold and jewel-encrusted relics and no easily accessible sites.

Stein himself, though he may not have expected public acclaim, knew as soon as he saw the 'Black Hole' and the quantity and age of its contents that his spectacular find would astonish and excite fellow-scholars in Europe. His own interests, however, were by no means monopolized by the library. For him, the discovery at the caves was not an isolated incident, but part of a much wider search for the old culture of the Silk Road. Every manuscript, fresco, sculpture and domestic object collected from sites across the Tarim Basin contributed to that search; without the information that they furnished, the significance of Tun-huang's secret library could not be fully appreciated. So the fact of his great haul did not affect his original plans for the rest of the expedition. There was much to be done between June 1907 and his expected return to India in the autumn of 1908.

As had become his habit when in Central Asia, Stein escaped to the mountains during the hottest months. He was finding the geographical aspect of his work increasingly absorbing, though there were particular difficulties attached to it here in the Nan-shan range, south of Tun-huang.[1] Progress was continually overshadowed by the locally hired pony-men's fear of mountains, Tibetan bandits and, in the absence of any more tangible threat, dragons which they claimed to hear during the night. They were 'timorous people', Stein told Publius, 'queer products of an ancient civilization which has never encouraged pluck or "roughing"'[2] – qualities he particularly admired, and which he expected in staff.

Despite the handicap imposed by these 'senile babies', however, by mid-August he had the satisfaction of knowing that he had travelled far enough east to reach the drainage area of the Pacific Ocean. In all, he and Ram Singh mapped 20,000 square miles of a little-known region. The value of such mapping is clear when one considers that it is still in use today. By the end of the month, he had returned to the plains and reached Kan-chou, his easternmost goal, where a large bag of mail awaited him, brought by messenger on a sixty-day ride from Kashgar.

Letters from 'home', as Stein was by now accustomed to call England, were never more welcome than when they arrived like this, perhaps two hundred at a time, in deliveries separated by gaps of several months which emphasized the enormous distance between him and his friends. To judge the importance he attached to them, one has only to look at his reaction when a mail-bag reached Tun-huang in the midst of the clandestine clearing of the library. Writing in immediate reply to four months' worth of Publius's letters, Stein told him that he would not begin with news of the harvest 'rich beyond expectation' that he had found in the caves, because the 'great event of these fruitful weeks was the arrival of faithful Turdi, my Dakman . . . I cannot describe to you fitly the eager joy with which I read through all these long-expected epistles . . .'.[3]

Perhaps there was something disingenuous about the sixteen sides of effusive response to his friend's news that preceded mention of his own activities at Tun-huang. But this was the usual style of his correspondence: he had been well-trained in the polite art of replying to the points of a friend's letter before launching into his own. Besides, his letters to Publius were outlets for thoughts that ranged far beyond summaries of work done and places visited. When he wrote to his friend from Tun-huang, it was with old preoccupations still on his mind: the loss of his family (compared with Publius's continuing enjoyment of his), his pessimism regarding recognition of his work and his longing for financial independence.

Fred Andrews received similar versions of the familiar litany. But Stein's letters to him usually also contained requests of one sort or another. While at Tun-huang, for example, planning ahead as ever, he asked him to have two silver watches inscribed with messages of thanks to Chiang and Tila Bai (the one for Chiang to cost not more than £2 10s, the other to be cheaper) and sent out to him as soon as possible. 'Whenever I use any of the stoves, presents, etc., with which your unfailing care had provided me,' he told his friend consolingly, 'I think of you with true gratitude.'[4]

———————◄►———————

By this stage in his exploration of Central Asia, Stein had travelled the length of Chinese Turkestan. In 1901 he had crossed the mountains into Russia on its western border, and now he had penetrated the ancient frontier of China proper, fifteen hundred miles to the east. He had passed through every oasis of the southern Silk Route between Kashgar and Tun-huang at one stage or another of his two expeditions, and had spent many weeks in the mountains that form the southern ramparts of the Tarim Basin. But he had never seen the oases along the great northern arm of the Silk Road, nor the Celestial Mountains, the T'ien-shan, except as a faint white outline on a distant horizon. It was this region that he now intended to visit.

The German archaeologists Grünwedel and von Le Coq had effectively made it their own as a result of their work in and around Kucha, Korla and Turfan in 1902 and 1904–6 (though von Le Coq and his assistant, Theodor Bartus, had nearly come to blows in the process with two Russians, the Beresovsky brothers, who had also claimed the right to excavate at Kucha). But Stein was curious to see what his competitors had done, and optimistic that it would be possible for him to find sites in the north that they had overlooked or been unable to reach. For they were not, as he was proud to be, cast in the explorer's mould.

He could afford to contemplate visiting the scenes of their efforts with a certain equanimity. The Germans had proved, by their limited excavations, to be less of a threat than they had seemed before he set out in April 1906, and Russian competition had failed to live up to the reputation it had had in 1898. Apart from Klementz's early discoveries, the Beresovskys had been the only sign of serious Russian interest, and they had not stayed long. Others were bound to follow where Sven Hedin and Stein had led; but Stein's domination, in archaeological terms, of the southern side of the Taklamakan Desert remained unchallenged. Hedin had no interest in detailed archaeological investigation and was now in Tibet.[5] Stein knew that the Frenchman, Paul Pelliot, intended to go to Tun-huang and that, as a Sinologist, he would be a shrewd judge of the value of the many manuscripts and paintings that still remained in the hidden chapel. But nothing could detract from the fact that he, Stein, had been the first European to discover the library and would be the first to announce its existence to the world.

At the same time as he started from Kan-chou for Turfan, Pelliot was *en route* to Tun-huang from Kucha, where he had been working for several months. It was only during a diversionary visit to Urumchi, the capital of Sinkiang, that the Frenchman heard of the existence of the library. Even then, he did not realize that any Westerner had already seen it and it was not until he was actually shown the secret chapel by Wang, months later, that he understood that Stein had beaten him to it. By the time he returned to Paris in the autumn of 1909 with a large collection of scrolls and documents, bought from Wang for the equivalent of £90, every orientalist in Europe knew about the library, and Stein's status as the archaeological trail-blazer in Chinese Central Asia was secure.

———◆———

It was with pleasant feelings of familiarity that Stein returned from the edge of China proper to the autumnal landscape of Turkestan. He had lost his surveyor, Ram Singh. But even as Ram Singh prepared for his journey back to India in early October 1907, a replacement, Lal Singh, arrived. And he was not the only welcome arrival. Two hundred more bundles from Wang's secret library came to join the rest of the haul, brought by camel train travelling at night and away from the main route to avoid detection. Stein now had seven camel-loads of booty from the caves, for which he had paid a total of £130.

In the desert fringes of the Turfan area, the Germans had made some important discoveries. Notably, at Karakhoja they had unearthed remains of a flourishing eighth-century Manichaean community;[6] and at Bezeklik, nearby, they had removed many fine wall-paintings from old rock temples which, unlike those at Tun-huang, had long ago fallen into disuse. Farther west, in the Kucha oasis, there were ruins that had attracted the attentions of every archaeological party: German, French, Russian and even some Japanese travellers in 1903. During November Stein paid brief visits to the scenes of his rivals' discoveries and told Publius of the evidence he found of German excavation.

'You will understand the awkward dilemma I had to face', he wrote, 'when I found ruin after ruin of big temples, monasteries, etc., dug into with the method of a scholarly treasureseeker, yet rarely explored with any approach to archaeological thoroughness.' To make up in a few months for what the Germans had failed to do in three or four years was impossible, he said, especially without the evidence of what they had removed. Besides, 'the task of clearing up what others had neglected, was not in my line'. One site which they had not touched was surrounded, he remarked with some contempt, by what, in the Khotan area, 'we should have scarcely called . . . a "desert" . . . Still this sufficed to keep off the Germans.'[7]

At another site, known to the local people as 'Ming-oi' – 'the Thousand Houses' – Stein decided to devote a fortnight to systematic excavations. Almost one hundred shrines came to light containing many pieces of delicately carved heads, torsos and busts. It was a worthwhile exercise, he told Publius, despite freezing temperatures, icy mists and heavy hoar-frosts, since the only other visitors to have worked there, the Germans, had indulged only in

a sort of scraping. But what distressing traces they have left behind! Fine fragments of stucco sculpture flung outside on the scrap heap; statues too big for transport left exposed to the weather & the tender mercies of wayfarers, etc. I cannot guess what made them dig here with quite an inadequate number of labourers, & still less I understand this indifference to the fate of all that was left in situ. Was I really too sentimental or over-conscientious when amidst the physical difficulties of the true desert I spent time & labour over filling up again my excavations at ruins so little exposed to human destruction as those of Lop-nor & the Tun-huang desert?[8]

Stein was proud of his own thorough methods, so it was not surprising that he was shocked by evidence of apparently irresponsible 'treasure-seeking' (which, as Peter Hopkirk suggests in *Foreign Devils on the Silk Road*, may have been the work of the Germans' assistant, Bartus, rather than the far more scrupulous Grünwedel). But the injured self-righteousness of his letter suggests that he may have derived a certain satisfaction from finding such evidence of inferior practices among his rivals. Not that he publicized the evidence. He was not above grumbling privately, but a public squabble would have seemed to him deeply distasteful.

Besides, there were few reasons for him to regret the limited amount of time he was able to spend on investigating sites on the northern Silk Road. Unlike those he had excavated in the south, they were not safely isolated in the desert and had been repeatedly dug into by local people in search of manure for their fields. In addition, many months of work (and correspondingly large sums of money) would have been needed to excavate thoroughly the many layers of cellars and caves that had been created over the centuries by people escaping the fierce summer heat. He was better off in the southern desert, and it was there that he now headed, by the most direct, and potentially highly dangerous route.

Fred Andrews once said of Stein that he 'never writes a book of adventure and hairbreadth escapes, although he had plenty of these'.[9] The journey he made across the Taklamakan Desert in January and February 1908 could have been described in such terms; and would have been, no doubt, had it been undertaken by, for example, Sven Hedin rather than Stein. The contrasting styles of the two men reflected their different aims. Stein's insistence on preparation, professionalism and pragmatism made his account of this journey comparatively mundane. Hedin, by contrast, had already described in books the drama, as he perceived it, of his travels, and proved himself capable of neglecting responsibility for the romance of adventure. His first, impetuous response to the 'mysterious lure' of the Taklamakan in 1895 had led to the deaths of two men, seven camels and a dog.

In 1896 he had conducted a better-prepared expedition. On that occasion he crossed the desert from south to north by travelling alongside the Keriya River to the point where it dried up in the sand, then pushing northwards across the dunes until he reached the Tarim River flowing from west to east. It was this route that Stein now intended to use, but in the opposite direction, in order to reach several sites near the Keriya River, and then Khotan, as quickly as possible. For all his careful preparations, however, he too recognized the lure of the wilderness. In his book on the second expedition, he admitted that 'even without this specific reason, I might have found the chance of once more crossing the very heart of the desert too great an attraction to resist'.[10]

Like a son reassuring an anxious mother, he played down the risks of the journey to his friends. But he knew it was a hazardous undertaking. Whereas Hedin had known that he would reach the Tarim flowing across his route as long as he continued northward, Stein was aiming south for a river that flowed directly towards him. If his calculations were less than exact, he would miss the terminal point of the Keriya River and face many more days in the waterless desert before reaching safety. There were no maps of the territory through which he was to pass besides the one Hedin had made, and no fixed landmarks. Neither was there any way of knowing whether the Keriya River still ran where Hedin had seen it twelve years earlier. The rivers that sank into the Taklamakan often changed their courses and their terminal points were surrounded by a maze of dry beds that gave no clue as to the whereabouts of the true one.

At Shahyar, two days south of Kucha, he made final arrangements. Twenty-four camels loaded with antiquities set out for Khotan in the care of Chiang and Tila Bai, following the well-known but roundabout route alongside the Tarim and Khotan rivers. Fifteen others would carry everything necessary for the desert crossing. Reluctantly he agreed also to his Indians' requests for four ponies, for use on the far side. He hired eight local men for well-digging, loading and later excavations, and ensured that they and the rest of his team had plentiful provisions. They were twenty men in all, with a 150-mile journey across the barren heart of Chinese Central Asia ahead of them; and it is doubtful whether any of them shared Stein's pleasure in the prospect.

Leaving Shahyar on 28 January 1908, they set out through riverine scrub where they could fill eight large bags with ice, and water the camels. Then came the advance into high, rolling sand-dunes – the scene of what is probably Stein's best-known photograph and one which he found full of beauty. But the anxieties of his labourers kept him from complete enjoyment of the scene. They had an imperfect grasp of the distance to be crossed before water could be reached, and needed constant encouragement.

Stein himself began to feel seriously concerned when, on 7 February, despite having reached the ancient dried-out delta of the Keriya River, he could detect no clues as to the position of the true river-bed. For three more days he searched in vain while water supplies ran lower and lower. At last Naik Ram Singh, having been sent out to search for a place to dig a well, returned with even better news: he had seen men's footprints in the sand. The party set out enthusiastically on the trail of these unknown potential saviours. But after several miles it led away across barren dunes and the men, disheartened, turned back to the 'death-bound waste' of the dry river-beds.

Stein had now reached the point where he was counting cartridges in the holster of his revolver to make sure he had enough to put the ponies out of their misery if necessary. During the night of 11 February he placed the remaining ice in the care of the reassuringly cheerful Lal Singh, lest anyone should be tempted to raid their meagre supplies. The precaution was a wise one. Next morning, the mood of the Shahyar men had swung and was dangerously close to panic: they threatened mutiny and talked wildly of turning back towards the Tarim. With difficulty, Stein convinced them of the futility of such ideas. But in his heart he could not blame them, for their prospects were beginning to look desperate.

Taking Lal Singh with him and with Dash at his heels – the dog apparently still flourishing on little more than a saucerful of his master's tea each day – he set out southward. His plan was to part from his surveyor after a few miles so that they could search east and west for signs of the river. Even Lal Singh was dismayed by the desolate scene and had turned back to warn the caravan against further advance when Stein, climbing to the top of a high ridge of sand, suddenly saw through his binoculars four glittering streaks, about four miles distant. They were sheets of ice.

The caravan, galvanized into sudden, frantic activity, shambled across the sand, the men summoning unknown reserves of energy to clamber up ridges in the hope of glimpsing the precious vision. Eventually they reached the edge of the first ice sheet, and Stein saw to his delight that it was not simply the salt lake he had expected but the river itself, flowing clearly towards imminent oblivion along a course that had certainly changed since Hedin mapped it twelve years earlier. From here, the journey south would be straightforward, and Stein could allow himself and his men a short rest after sixteen days in the wasteland of the Taklamakan.[11]

Stein reached Khotan in early April. He stayed with his old host, Akhun Beg, safely returned from his pilgrimage to Mecca,[12] and inspected several sites recommended by local treasure-seekers. But the main work of the expedition was over. Only two important tasks remained, and to achieve the first meant a journey back across the Taklamakan Desert to Aksu, following the Khotan River route by which Chiang had only recently brought his caravan of antiquities safely to Khotan. There were one or two sites *en route* to justify what must have seemed to his placid Turki acquaintances nothing less than masochism. But the real reason was his desire to see the old mandarin, Pan, now Taotai of Aksu, whom he held in such affection and whose benign influence he hoped would help Chiang.

Chiang dearly hoped for promotion, in order to supplement his savings. Only thus would he eventually be able to retire back to his home in the southern province of Hunan, where he had left his wife and infant son seventeen years earlier. Stein's determination to help his faithful Chinese secretary towards this goal was only intensified by the knowledge that he could not fulfil Chiang's wish to be taken to England or India as a permanent secretary. Together, Chiang, Stein and Pan drew up the appropriate application and Stein later had the satisfaction of hearing that Chiang had become Macartney's Chinese *munshi*, or secretary.

On the return journey to Khotan, the small party halted for a few days in Yarkand in order to sell Stein's camels. The animals' fame, it seemed, had spread far and wide since his desert crossing. They were in fine condition, and interest was so strong that he was able to sell them at a 70 per cent profit on the purchase price, on behalf of the Indian government. The deal satisfied his passion for good husbandry, however sad he felt to part with his 'brave' animals, as he always termed them.

Before he could leave for a final survey of the sources of the Khotan River, *en route* for India, Stein had to deal with his final task and the most laborious part of the entire expedition: the repacking of all his cases of antiquities prior to their final journey to India and England. The work took a depressing six weeks. But he found that nothing had been damaged since being packed on site, and he was able to give the Miran frescoes even more protection by applying a network of narrow bandages soaked in carpenter's glue to the backs of the plaster panels.

It was while he was immersed in such tasks that disaster befell Naik Ram Singh. Stein had sent him back to Miran in March, to take more photographs and to remove other frescoes if possible. While on his way there with Ibrahim Beg, the Naik began to suffer sharp pains in his head. At Charkhlik he lost the sight of one eye, but continued doggedly to Miran and started to oversee the clearing of a temple. Then blindness attacked his other eye too. Still he refused to admit defeat and waited for a few days, hoping that the affliction might be temporary. Eventually he allowed Ibrahim Beg to lead him all the way back to Khotan; and there he was brought to his employer, pitifully helpless after so much stalwart work throughout the expedition. Stein was shocked and upset by his fate, not least because he wondered at first whether the hardships of a two-year expedition might be to blame.

The Swedish missionary at Yarkand, to whom he immediately sent Ram Singh for treatment, reassured him at least on that point. The cause was glaucoma, a disease for which there was then scarcely any treatment except where immediate recognition of the symptoms could be followed by an operation. All Stein could do was to arrange for Ram Singh to travel without further delay to Ladakh and Srinagar in the care of trusted companions, whence he was taken home to the Punjab by his brother. His condition deteriorated swiftly thereafter, and he was dead before the end of the following year. Little did Stein know, as he watched the sturdy Naik being led away, that he too would end the expedition disabled and helpless.

On 1 August, a convoy of more than fifty camels left Khotan bound for India, carrying the results of Stein's explorations. Two days later, he too said farewell to the oasis and the people who had come to represent for him a sort of home. Chiang accompanied him on the first march and the moment when they too had to part was poignant for them both. They had been almost constant companions for two years. Stein had known no comparable bond since the death of Govind Kaul nine years previously, and had set out on this second expedition with no idea of the friend he would find in his Chinese secretary, nor of the support he would derive from Chiang's jovial temper, his curious and lively mind and his steady loyalty. Even so, the parting was probably easier for him than for Chiang. Stein, after all, had reunions with beloved friends ahead of him, while Chiang faced many more years of what was effectively exile before he could hope to return to his family in the distant east.

Now the final lap of Stein's expedition began. In the weeks that followed, he achieved his aim of tracing the course of the Khotan River to its source, high in the glaciers of the Kun-lun peaks, and completed his survey of the main chain of that massive range. But his supplies and the strength of his pack-animals came under severe strain. Several ponies died, and a combination of violent winds and low temperatures made conditions unpleasant for beasts and men alike. In a vast, sterile basin more than 15,000 feet above sea-level his own handsome pony, Badakhshi, who had thrived during twenty-seven months of bruising travel, suddenly sickened and died in the space of a few hours, despite being wrapped in blankets and watched all through a bitter night. His death deeply distressed Stein. 'Often I had pictured to myself our joint delight when I might let him taste on a Kashmir Marg what real grass and Alpine flowers were like,' he wrote afterwards. 'But the Gods had willed it otherwise and let him succumb, when the goal seemed so near, in the dreariest waste I had seen.'[13]

The plight of the party had begun to seem desperate when at last, as the animals' fodder was exhausted, they reached an old route across the mountains not used for forty years, and found water and limited grazing for the animals – succour that came two days too late for Badakhshi. Stein now pushed on to his last goal, the watershed of the main Kun-lun range. On 22 September he, Lal Singh, Musa and three Kirghiz men from the valleys set out for their final ascent. Roped together to guard against crevasses on the glacier that lay between them and the crest, they toiled through softening snow until, ten hours after starting, they reached the top, 20,000 feet above sea-level.

The panorama that lay before them was overwhelmingly majestic. Great snow-blanketed peaks surrounded them, smooth and imperturbable in places, harshly serrated in others; and far away to the north, in contrast to the dazzling white before them and the pure blue above, a dull yellow light signalled the distant dust haze of the Taklamakan Desert. Stein was so elated by this culmination of his work, so preoccupied with photography and with helping Lal Singh to set up his plane-table and fix and check their position, that he hardly noticed the exhaustion from which his body was suffering, nor the temperature, which was well below freezing point.

At half-past four he finished, snatched a few mouthfuls of food and began the descent with the others, at the urgent insistence of the

Kirghiz. He had not had time to change his boots, which were wet through. At the edge of the glacier the small party mounted yaks that had been brought to wait for them, in order to get them off the treacherous moraine slopes as quickly as possible, for it was already dark. At points where they had to dismount and walk, Stein was conscious of his poor grip but attributed it to fatigue and a slippery surface. But by the time he stumbled into camp, he realized the truth. Tearing off his boots and double socks, he put his hands to his toes and felt their icy coldness. They were all badly frostbitten.

Stein did not write another letter to Publius until nearly four weeks later, by which time he was an invalid in the care of the Moravian Mission hospital at Leh, in Ladakh. In the warmth of the autumn sunshine, he lay on a veranda looking across to the little town and the massive, barren mountains that surround it, and composed a chronological account of the disastrous finale to his second expedition. 'I am very sorry for the worry this unlucky incident at the very close of my explorations may cause you,' he wrote to his friend. 'But I have told you the detail in all truth & hope, you will join me in taking a philosophical view of the whole case . . .'.[14] Now that the danger was past, the last thing he wanted was for people to treat him as though he were disabled, for he was determined not to let the loss he had just suffered interfere with future work. The fact that the operation he had recently undergone had left him utterly immobile, and likely to remain so for many weeks more, he forbore to mention.

On that black and freezing night on the mountain when he discovered the frostbite in his toes, he had set to work immediately to try to restore circulation by rubbing them vigorously with snow. His servants Aziz and Musa had helped. After some time, warmth began to spread slowly through the toes of the left foot, though the skin and flesh were clearly badly affected; but the toes on the right foot remained numb. The advice of his mountaineering manual, that 'the aid of an experienced surgeon should be sought at once', was hardly reassuring. He was high in barren mountains, with a long and arduous journey across some of the bleakest passes in the region lying between him and the nearest European doctor at Leh.

It would take four days simply to get to the point where he had arranged to meet his heavy baggage train, and another two weeks, at the very minimum, to cross the mountains and reach Leh. And what damage might frostbite and gangrene do, not only to his toes but to both his feet, in the meantime? At this point Stein confided his thoughts to no one, but it was probably with feelings close to desperation that he contemplated the coming weeks. To be forcibly immobilized was anathema to him. But to be compelled to travel thus across three hundred miles of mountain track, in the knowledge that he might be crippled at the end of the ordeal, required every ounce of 'pluck' that even he could muster.

After enduring an agonizing few hours astride a yak on the day after the accident, he managed to have a litter improvized from bamboo tent poles. Slung between two ponies, one in front, the other behind, this carried him precariously down to the place where Tila Bai was waiting with the main caravan. Somehow he got through two days there, settling accounts with the Kirghiz and Khotan men who had supplied animals during the past weeks. Then he set out, with only his few personal servants, as rapidly as possible along the skeleton-strewn Karakoram route. A messenger went ahead to request medical help. On 3 October the small party crossed the notorious Karakoram Pass, more than 18,500 feet above sea-level, and two days later reached the rocky approaches to the Sasser Pass.

At this point Stein could go no further without additional help, for his litter would not have survived the climb, and the pain in his feet would probably have made it impossible to ride. But a band of Ladakhis, sent out by the British Joint Commissioner in Leh on hearing of Stein's plight, met the party just as it faced this impasse. With their support he was carried over, and down into the first Ladakhi village where the doctor from the Moravian Mission hospital, the Reverend S. Schmitt, awaited him.

Six more days were to pass before any operation could be performed, for Schmitt saw immediately that Stein was too exhausted to undergo surgery there and then. He saw, also, that some of his toes were gangrenous beyond recovery. So, on 14 October, two days after arriving in Leh, Stein submitted to the amputation of all the toes on his right foot: three from the upper joints, two completely. Those of his left foot, though injured, were expected to heal without loss.

As he waited in Leh for his strength to return, and for the painful wounds to heal sufficiently to allow movement, Stein's main fear was that news of his accident would cause an irreversible change in attitude towards him. He was relieved to have lost only his toes. But, trapped in his hospital bed, he felt he had lost control of events and that colleagues and associates were writing off his future, just when he should have been exploiting what little influence his important discoveries might bring him. He played down the denouement of the expedition as merely an 'awkward mishap'. By the time he was able to travel in a litter down to Kashmir during the first half of November, however, he had almost resigned himself to the slower pace at which an invalid must move. He had not walked for two months, but he knew, even so, that he had reason to be thankful.

In the circumstances, he was rather dazzled by the surprising amount of good fortune that seemed suddenly to come his way. Carefully attended throughout the twelve-day journey down to the valley, he was greeted in Srinagar by Captain D. G. Oliver, the Joint Commissioner for Ladakh. He was to be a guest of the Residency (though the man now Resident, Francis Younghusband, was away) and there he enjoyed what seemed, after two and a half years in mountains and deserts, a lavish style of life.

'There is warmth & sunshine, – & bodily comfort or I ought to say luxury of all sorts around me,' he told Publius, like a child wondering at things seen for the first time.[15] The Residency had electric light and 'art furniture' and Captain Oliver looked after him as though he were a member of his own family. Stein's two Turki servants, Muhammadju and Musa, were still with him; he took daily rides to the shores of the Dal Lake in the Resident's carriage; letters arrived regularly from admiring and concerned friends and colleagues. Dunlop-Smith had written to say that the Viceroy followed his activities with interest and had granted him permission to go to England immediately on special duty to work on his finds which were being shipped there (they arrived in January 1909). Moreover, Dr Arthur Neve of the mission hospital in Srinagar assured him that his ability to walk and climb would be unimpaired once the wounds had healed. Stein was taken completely unawares by such attentions. He had expected to feel handicapped but, instead, he was being treated like a hero. (Though at least one person disapproved of such treatment. When Stein's narrative book on his second expedition appeared in 1912, it was reviewed in *The Times of India* by a vitriolic writer who claimed that Stein was 'a frail little man, of sedentary habits, without the physique that is required by the explorer'. He should give up fancying himself as a geographer, the anonymous reviewer said, and stick to working as an antiquarian for the Government of India.)[16]

The attentions he enjoyed in Kashmir continued to be showered on Stein during his remaining few weeks in India (though they were marred somewhat by news of the deaths of the Chief Commissioner of the North-West Frontier Province, Sir Harold Deane, and Theodore Duka). Being able by the end of November to hobble with the aid of a stick, he left Srinagar for Lahore where he stayed with the Maclagans for nearly a fortnight while sorting out his accounts. Undeterred by the pain he was still experiencing in his feet, he travelled on to Dehra Dun, in the Himalayan foothills north of Delhi, and settled details for the preparation of his maps with Colonel Burrard at the Trigonometrical Survey office.[17] Then he took the train to Calcutta to stay as the guest of his friend and supporter, Dunlop-Smith.

It was his first visit to the capital since his unhappy sojourn there in 1899–1900, but times had changed. Determined to press claims, not only for his own deputation to England and future status, but also for pensions or gratuities for Naik Ram Singh and the surveyors, he was continually surprised to find himself pushing at open doors. Everyone listened, everyone helped and the Viceroy himself inspected a small private exhibition of some of his finds with palpable interest and good humour.

He boarded ship on 26 December, reached Brindisi early in January 1909 and, after brief visits to relatives in Budapest, Jetty and her children in Vienna and colleagues in Paris, stepped on to English soil again on 21 January. Andrews and Arnold were waiting for him at Victoria Station. The following day, having lunched at the Royal Geographical Society with Keltie and R.E.G. Amundsen, the Norwegian explorer (and future conqueror of the South Pole), he took the 4.45 train to Oxford and reunion with his dearest friends. 'Cannot believe that I am really back at the blissful Cottage', he wrote in his diary late that night, 'where all look so young as 5 years ago . . . Sit & talk until 11.30pm, – with weary feet.'[18]

Though the sea journey had restored some of Stein's vigour, it is likely that his friends found him looking markedly older than the man they had last seen five years earlier. Two doctors' reports among Stein's papers make it clear that the punishing targets he had set himself during his second expedition had not been achieved without cost. His friend Neve, at the Srinagar mission hospital, wrote at the end of November 1908 that he was 'in a condition of nervous overstrain, owing to his prolonged exertions and hardships; and of late owing to sleeplessness, etc.' A surgeon in Lahore considered that he was 'only a shadow of what I remember him a few years ago. His health and constitution have in my opinion permanently suffered from the hardships to which he exposed himself.'[19]

In the circumstances, there was no better place for him than Longwall Cottage, where he could enjoy the rare luxury of being the object of unstinting care and affection, supplemented later in the year by the company of his beloved little dog. He had considered leaving Dash in India in order to spare him the journey and the ordeal of four months' quarantine, but had been unable, in the end, to contemplate the parting.

The life of his friends in Oxford was, of course, familiar from the many letters that had followed him all over Central Asia. But there was a particular reason to enjoy being there again in person. He wanted to share Publius's quiet delight in the research fellowship of Merton College to which he had been elected in March the previous year. Stein had long hoped for some such position for his friend, and the news that it had arrived at last had kept him 'in a state of jubilation' when he first read of it in Turkestan in May 1908.

'As soon as I saw that cover from Merton I had a clear presentiment of its joyful contents,' he had told Publius. 'If ever anyone deserved freedom from worries & petty tasks as a reward for whole-hearted scholarly devotion to a great aim it is you . . .'.[20] He had asked for more information on Merton so that he could 'read it up' before he reached Oxford. Later, while recuperating from his operation in Kashmir, he wrote to Publius about a reference to an Erasmus letter which he had seen while trying to read the journal of the Royal Geographical Society on his painful journey across the Karakoram Mountains. The letter proved to be unpublished and Publius, following up the tip, had traced it just in time to add it to the second volume of his work.[21]

Stein was no less concerned for the career of Fred Andrews: partly from altruistic motives but also because it touched directly on his own.

From the wildernesses of Central Asia he had looked towards the time when, he knew, he would have to submit himself to confinement in the British Museum in order to unpack and catalogue his thousands of finds. And the one hope that made the prospect bearable was that Andrews would be taken on as his assistant. The two men had corresponded on the subject and Stein had advised making full use of their contacts in the India Office. But his own methods did not come naturally to his friend: Andrews, he confided to Publius, was 'far too modest & shy about seeing people'.[22]

Without such a congenial colleague to share the task, the thought of being incarcerated in London filled him with dread. While he waited for the British Museum to decide how to accommodate his new collection – stored, in the meantime, at the Natural History Museum in South Kensington – he indulged in the happier but impractical thought of offering it to some other institution, such as the Ashmolean Museum in Oxford. In reality, the periods Stein spent in Bloomsbury were sporadic, at least initially, and it was Andrews, whom the Museum authorities did eventually employ on a part-time basis, who bore most of the burden. While Stein travelled throughout Europe, giving lectures and being lionized by fellow-scholars, Andrews it was who sat in the British Museum basement day after day, troubled by inadequate lighting and a lack of storage space, and later by the need to replace departing assistants.[23]

One of Stein's first public appearances on returning to Europe was at Budapest in April 1909, where he was met at the railway station by what he described as 'a grand reception'. Tickets for his lecture sold out ten days before the event, the theatre in which it was held was packed with 'the best people', and the Archduke Josef (a cousin of the Austrian Emperor Franz Josef) had him introduced in his box afterwards. 'What amused me a great deal', Stein told Andrews, inadequately concealing a pardonable, boyish pride, 'was the attitude of quasi-awe which assured perfect silence to the very end.'[24]

———— ◆ ————

Many such occasions followed during the three years that Stein spent in Europe on a combination of leave and special duty. He lectured in Paris, Vienna, Munich, Hamburg, Frankfurt, Cambridge and various other places in Britain, as well as in Budapest again. The universities of

Oxford and Cambridge bestowed honorary degrees on him and the Royal Geographical Society awarded him its prestigious Founder's Medal. He was deeply gratified by the support that this medal represented and when, the following year, he received the CIE (Commander of the Indian Empire) he told Keltie that, notwithstanding this new mark of recognition, he regarded his Royal Geographical Society award as his greatest encouragement. 'It has helped me more than anything else', he wrote, 'to bear up with difficulties encountered after my return – and to retain the hope of fresh chances of useful work in the future.'[25]

Despite these honours, however, and the welcome he received from friends and colleagues everywhere he went, he felt uncomfortable in the densely populated cities of the West. He stayed with the Allens in their cottage and absorbed something of their attachment to Oxford; he visited relatives in Budapest and renewed his acquaintance with places and sensations that had once been familiar. But nowhere in Europe felt like a true home.

During what he once called his 'life of long self-willed exile'[26] from Hungary, he had grown used to observing his native country with affectionate and often rueful detachment, and he was alarmed now by political and economic developments there. The increasingly anti-Semitic tone of populist parties in the Austro-Hungarian Empire struck a depressing note to one who had been brought up to believe in the moral force of humanism. His uncle's and brother's creed of culture, reason and integration seemed threatened by something destabilizing and divisive. And the fact that his closest relatives and colleagues there were ageing and fond of recalling the past no doubt intensified the impression that things were changing for the worse.

'Home', if it meant anywhere, now meant England, but only in the sense of the place to which one went on leave from India. For all his identification with the aims of the British Empire, his admiration of 'gentlemanly' qualities and the 'Englishness' of many of his own characteristics – his reserve, his love of action, his probity and loyalty to friends – he was an outsider there too. At the numerous dinners, meetings and lectures to which he was invited, he was a self-effacing guest, unskilled in the art of small talk though always attentive and scrupulously polite in carefully pronounced English and other languages. Perhaps the more observant among his companions detected in him a deeper, private self that was far removed from his immediate surroundings. Perhaps he in turn recognized and even envied in them a sense of belonging which contrasted sharply with his own feeling, as he once described it simply to Publius, 'of being a stranger almost everywhere outside my own camp'.[27]

One result of so many years of life in camp was that he found it difficult to work anywhere else. It was impossible to give his attention properly to written reports of his expedition as long as he stayed in London, or even Oxford. So, at the start of a nine-month period of leave in July 1909, he packed his belongings, left Dash in the care of the Allens and travelled to the Continent in search of a passable substitute for Mohand Marg. Family obligations, however, came first and he spent part of August in Carlsbad (now known as Karlovy Vary in the Czech Republic) and the Austrian Tyrol with Jetty and her children.

His loyalty to his dead brother's family was steadfast. But it was not always demonstrated without effort: not only because it was hardly in his nature to enjoy family holidays in popular resorts but also because Jetty's company was scarcely likely to raise the spirits. Stein himself could be morbidly sentimental about the death of his elderly mother and father. But Jetty, having lost a husband who had not yet grown old, easily outdid him in her regret for the past, her more or less permanent state of mourning and the depressed discontent with which she viewed her present situation in Vienna. Ernst had left her comfortably off, and Stein urged her to spend some time out of the city, either with her sister in the Austrian Tyrol or in some congenial Mediterranean town. Her dolorous dissatisfaction with her life, however, seems to have become necessary to her; she did not want a solution.

Nor were her offspring carefree companions. Ernst, the younger, approaching his eighteenth birthday, was possessed of an arrogance and lack of humour that upset both his mother and his sister Thesa, a philology student in Vienna. Neither nephew nor niece enjoyed the hikes of several miles that their uncle considered proper walks, so Stein had to suppress his inclination to stride off into the hills and put his maimed foot to the test. He spent hours rereading his uncle's letters of the 1870s and trying to do his own duty in the role of paterfamilias. He listened to the complaints of first one sibling, then the other, and silently attributed at least some of Jetty's problems with her son to the fact that she had not persisted with his early education at Stein's old school in Dresden, but had brought him home when he complained of unhappiness. When Stein finally left the family in September and moved to a hotel near Riva, on Lake Garda in the Italian Tyrol, it was with a great sense of relief. In his diary he wrote, 'Warm sunshine & bright colours recall Kashmir & India so often. A feeling of freedom & ease such as missed since long.'[28]

During the next few months in Italy, he used his leave to correct the proofs of no fewer than ninety-four map sheets, and to begin an account of his expedition. The latter was to be a book for the general public, while the maps were to accompany a far larger, scholarly report. The formula was the same as he had used after his first expedition, with the difference that increased success in the field and greater knowledge of the land in which he had worked encouraged a natural tendency to prolixity. Whereas *Sand-Buried Ruins of Khotan* had been contained within a single volume, its successor, *Ruins of Desert Cathay*, needed two heavy tomes to carry its 1,000 pages and 350 photographs, plates and maps.

That the publisher, George A. Macmillan, was a victim of Stein's powers of exhortation is evident from a letter he wrote to Keltie at the Royal Geographical Society at the time of publication, early in 1912, in which he referred to the 'somewhat excessive size' of the book, 'which the author persuaded us to adopt'.[29] The scholarly report, entitled *Serindia* – after the term 'Serinde' which French orientalists had invented to describe Chinese Central Asia – was similarly inflated. Its predecessor, *Ancient Khotan*, had dealt in detail with the first expedition in two volumes. But *Serindia* totalled five – three of text, one of plates and another in the form of a box containing the ninety-four map sheets. It was a massive work, with contributions from a number of other scholars, and was not published until 1921.

It was also a monument to Stein's dedication. He viewed with a sinking heart the prospect of recording and analysing all his finds, checking all his sources, writing thousands of words, organizing other contributors and correcting hundreds of printer's proofs. Such sedentary desk-work kept him away from what he believed was his most important task, further excavations in the field. But he knew that the results of his expeditions were of limited use as long as they were unrecorded, so the making of such a record seemed simply an unavoidable responsibility. Unlike some archaeologists – including his rival Pelliot – he wrote up every expedition he undertook and every item he found, sacrificing all personal preferences to thoroughness and doggedly pursuing every line of enquiry until he could include all the information he deemed necessary. Fred Andrews was to write of him that his capacity for work 'exceeded that of anyone I ever knew'.[30]

It also made for a life of self-imposed solitude. After a couple of weeks on Lake Garda, Stein moved to the more bracing climate of the mountains, where he stayed near the Mendel Pass until the hotel closed for the winter.[31] He rose early and retired to bed usually well before midnight, but frequently found the hotel food indigestible and suffered from painful bouts of dyspepsia. Often, too, he felt feverish; but his foot, at least, was recovering fast. 'Bad road taken with ease', he noted in his diary on 26 September; 'a hope for the future of my foot. Plenty of cottonwool is the dodge.'[32]

In the desert, Stein had often comforted himself with thoughts of the holidays he would enjoy in Europe with his friends, but their visits were all too often brief. Thomas and May Arnold came to stay in the Tyrol for two weeks and provided a welcome distraction. And later, during the winter which he spent at Portofino Kulm on the beautiful Riviera di Levante, he was joined for a short time by Fred Andrews. Together they spent Christmas in Florence with Jetty – who had been persuaded at last to part from Vienna for a few weeks – and then returned to Portofino for walks on the wooded hills and down to the quaint old towns and villages along the Ligurian coast. Andrews later recalled a particular afternoon:

It was here I realized [Stein's] faculty for acquiring foreign languages. One afternoon we were descending from the Kulm to the picturesque little fishing port of San Fruttuoso. Stein did not know Italian – one of the few European languages he was ignorant of. We overtook an old fisherman and greeted him with a word or two. I was for pushing on, but Stein by some means induced the fisherman to talk, and by the time we reached San Fruttuoso they were chatting together fluently.[33]

Stein had in fact had one or two Italian lessons, but the point of Andrews' anecdote was undoubtedly true.

———◆◄———

The question of Stein's future in India had still to be settled. Officially, he was still employed by the Education Department. There had been no further discussion of the position of Archaeological Explorer which he had proposed for himself back in 1905, and no word on whether he would be allowed to resume his part-time archaeological duties on the North-West Frontier following Marshall's attempt at sabotage. But in July 1909 came a 'very private' letter from the trusty Dunlop-Smith.

> The Secretary of State [for India] writes very nicely about you and your work and says he is quite willing that you should be transferred to the Archaeological Department. But he adds that the G of I [Government of India] have already spent as much on trans-frontier exploration as can be justified and he objects to the appointment of a 'special explorer'. He therefore leaves for future consideration the precise nature of the employment to be offered to you on your return to duty.[34]

This was followed by a formal letter from the India Office in September, proposing Stein's appointment as a superintendent in the Archaeological Department, to be regarded as supernumerary until a vacancy occurred (and on a salary of Rs 1,250 per month to match what he had earned in his previous post, which was more than other superintendents received). Stein played for time, replying with an enquiry about his pension while he sought the opinion of friends. On the face of it, the offer might have seemed encouraging. But no government employment could satisfy a man who sought to combine two incompatibles – a full-time salaried post and the freedom to do as he wished – and Stein's reaction was to suspect the very vagueness in the proposal which others might have expected him to welcome. The possibility that he would be asked to work on projects that did not interest him, or, worse still, in a region other than the north-west, seemed insupportable.

His old friend Maclagan tried to calm his fears and, seeing the matter from the government's standpoint as well as Stein's, advised him to 'practise brevity'[35] – surely more in hope than expectation, for anyone who knew Stein well knew also that brevity was a territory he showed no inclination to explore. Stein felt his own caution amply justified when, having accepted the position, he found himself in early 1910 gazetted to Bengal, the one area in India which, as he wrote to Hailey, 'is to me personally most uncongenial – or to put it plainly – distinctly hateful'.[36] He even used delicate health as a reason why he should not return there: a sure sign of desperation in one who normally refused to allow any ailment to interrupt work.

The posting was, in fact, a mere formality, owing to the need to fill a vacancy on paper. Stein was not due back in India until the end of 1911, by which time he had been given the one position in the Archaeological Department's gift that was likely to bring him at least partial satisfaction: Superintendent of Archaeology in the North-West Frontier Province. The mere thought that his career was still at the mercy of such apparently arbitrary decisions, however, renewed his determination to evade the humdrum duties of routine employment. 'I shall try to have a special task of sufficient magnitude sanctioned before I go back to India & then claim the necessity of completing it, results, etc., included,' he told Publius. 'Perhaps, the assurance that I may cease to encumber the Indian exchequer after four years more of duty in India may help to appease the conscientious Babus, big & small, who dread my "exploring".'[37]

The 'special task' he had in mind was, not surprisingly, another attempt at reaching Balkh in Afghanistan. John Marshall, whose tone had become friendly since Stein's triumphant return from Turkestan, assured him of his support. But he strongly advised him 'not to press forward any plan for trans-frontier exploration under the present regime at the India Office . . . Lord Morley [Secretary of State for India], I think, has quite made up his mind that there are to be no more expeditions at present; and I would strongly counsel you to avoid giving the Government at home an opportunity of putting this decision on record again.'[38] Stein acknowledged his point but made plain, nevertheless, his resolve to pursue his plan.

At least part of the reason why Stein cared so passionately about his role in India was because he fully recognized his dependence on employment there. However unsatisfactory it was to be obliged to feign interest in a life of government service, it was the only way in which he could secure an income and, at the same time, gain support for his expeditions. From time to time, his friends in England would try to interest him in some academic post, but the time was long past when such a career held any real allure for him. Purely scholarly activities now seemed fit only for retirement. As he told Publius when the latter suggested he might aim for a fellowship at Oxford:

Yes, My savings with a Fellow's stipend would suffice for a modest scholarly life such [as] I look forward to. But where would the money for travels & explorations come from? You know how little is to be got even by English Orientalists for work in the non-Biblical East. So I think it well to keep my connection with the IG [Indian Government] as long as they give me a chance & treat me fairly.[39]

However, he was gratified by the offer of temporary rooms at Merton College which Publius arranged for him at the end of his period of leave in the spring of 1910.

While he was obliged to be in England, the Allens were keen to spare him the conditions of the capital, which he loathed. He had refused, as gently as he could, their invitation to live with them at Longwall Cottage during the twenty months of work on his collection that awaited him between April 1910 and December 1911. 'You know my difficulties about working in a town,' he had explained, 'my need of isolation when absolute concentration is essential, and all the rest of my "indigestible" ways. It is too late to alter them.'[40] So instead, they offered a tactful arrangement which, no doubt, they sensed would answer his requirements: a set of rooms at Merton College, overlooking Christ Church Meadow where Dash could ramble while Stein divided his time between the college and the British Museum.

The period in Oxford was not without problems. He was bitterly disappointed to find his collection relegated to what he and Andrews both considered third-rate accommodation in the British Museum. But the compensations were great.[41] Having spent years reading Publius's accounts of life, both academic and domestic, in Oxford, Devon and elsewhere, he now had a chance to enter that charmed world of gentle conversation, long walks and shared delight in landscapes, ideas and Erasmian discoveries. He made friends in Oxford's academic circles, and he entered further into the concerns of his friends' families. The quiet dignity and restraint with which they met the deaths, in 1910, of Helen's mother and Publius's father only strengthened the admiration, respect and love he already felt for them. It is hard not to suspect also that he occasionally found himself reflecting on the difference between their undemonstrative faith and zest for life and the self-indulgent gloom of his sister-in-law.

In the meantime, work on his collection continued. Already the press had hailed what the *Illustrated London News*, a weekly paper with a close interest in archaeology, called 'Dr Stein's Remarkable Discoveries in Chinese Turkestan' (12 June 1909), and some of his finds were exhibited at the Festival of Empire in 1911. But the real significance of those discoveries emerged only after years of study by scholars in France, Germany and Scandinavia, as well as in Britain. Stein's five-volume *Serindia* was long in the making, though his most valued collaborator, the Sinologist Edouard Chavannes, produced a publication of his own, *Documents chinois decouverts par Aurél Stein dans les sables du Turkestan chinois*, in 1913.

By the time *Serindia* finally appeared in 1921, Stein was mourning the death of Chavannes; but others had responded to the challenge of the material, in particular the paintings and manuscripts from the Caves of the Thousand Buddhas. Arthur Waley, later to become known as a prolific translator of Chinese poetry, worked on the paintings while employed in the British Museum's Department of Oriental Prints and Drawings, reading and interpreting their inscriptions and identifying the subjects portrayed: his detailed catalogue was published in 1931. An enormous portfolio of colour plates appeared in 1921, introduced by Lawrence Binyon; and Lionel Giles published the results of his study of the Chinese manuscripts in 1944. A far larger and more comprehensive work appeared more recently by the Sinologist Professor Whitfield (see Bibliography).

The paintings certainly deserved this attention. Though few of them rise above what Waley called 'artisan quality', together they form an unrivalled picture of how the Buddhist art of north-west India reached the fringes of China and adapted to Chinese taste or was supplanted by existing Far Eastern styles. A few banners bear inscriptions that are dated, and the styles of dress on the secular figures of donors in others enabled Waley to estimate that the entire collection dated from the seventh to the tenth centuries AD.

During the early part of that period, Tun-huang would have been busy with traffic passing to and fro along the Silk Road as the dynamic T'ang dynasty sought to expand again through the Tarim Basin, after three centuries in which Chinese control had disappeared from the region. But in AD 781, Tibetan invaders seized control of Tun-huang, severing communications between Chinese Turkestan and the heart of the empire in China proper, and isolating the Buddhists of the Tun-huang area from co-religionists to east and west. So the paintings executed after that date are the work of artists, usually monks, who were working in a vacuum, producing votive banners for local people to use in the shrines and monastery temples that were the focus for their devotions.

This alone would make the paintings a rich source for scholars. But their value is magnified by the fact that in the mid-ninth century, when some were being painted and others were perhaps already being stored away, Buddhism was outlawed and suppressed in China, along with other 'foreign religions', and much of its art was undoubtedly destroyed. The paintings of Tun-huang escaped this fate. At some point in the eleventh century, it seems, a statue was removed from one of the Caves of the Thousand Buddhas and its place was taken by a massive store of thousands of manuscripts and paintings, some of which were already old at the time of deposit. The entrance to the cave was then sealed; and so it remained until Wang, the self-appointed caretaker of the caves, dis-covered it by chance more than eight centuries later. Stein believed that the store had been hidden away to save it from Tangut invaders. Modern scholars, however, consider it more likely that the orderly fashion in which the scrolls and bundles were packed into their 'library' signifies that the disposal was made deliberately, as a way of reverently depositing items that were no longer needed but which could not be thrown away.

Most of the paintings are tracings or copies of older originals, and the number of times such copies were made often resulted in smaller details being rendered unrecognizable. A conventional representation of a certain scene from a legend of Buddha's life would undoubtedly suffer distortion in its passage, over many years, from north-west India to the western fringes of China. A monk in Tun-huang who had the job of copying such images had no knowledge of their distant origins to which he could refer. The messages contained in the images therefore tended to be distilled to the point where only their essentials remained.

Nevertheless, the influence of Gandhara was clearly visible in the tones of light and colour used, as were the traditional Chinese artistic styles with which the copyists, and the worshippers who commissioned their work, were familiar. Individuals would commission banners which they would then donate for use in the monasteries that once thrived in

Tun-huang, and often these donors were depicted at the bottom of the paintings, clothed in contemporary, secular dress. Landscapes were also used as background, especially where paintings dealt with a narrative theme.

The painted banners did not cover as wide a span of time as the wall-paintings in the caves, for the earliest grottoes in the valley of the Thousand Buddhas were carved from the cliffs in the fourth century AD and devotees began to decorate them not long afterwards. But the widely varied manuscripts that Stein recovered from the secret library proved to be more representative of the long history of the shrines, and of the diverse origins and creeds of the people who passed through the oasis. Lionel Giles, who worked on the manuscripts at the British Museum, pointed out that with, on average, a dated document for more than every alternate year between AD 406 and AD 995, the collection provided an unbroken sequence hardly rivalled in any other literature of the past.[42]

The majority of the manuscripts were Chinese versions of Buddhist texts and there were many copies of the most popular ones; but there were also fragments of early secular works and a large, block-printed roll dating from AD 868 which proved to be the oldest known example of a printed book, a copy of the popular Buddhist work, *The Diamond Sutra*, which is now one of the British Library's prized possessions. There were Manichaean texts in Chinese, Buddhist documents in Tibetan and Sogdian, a small book in Runic Turkish, and manuscripts in Indian Brahmi script which were found to have been written in no fewer than three distinct languages: Sanskrit, Khotanese and another 'lost' tongue from the north of the Tarim Basin which Rudolf Hoernle designated Kuchean. Lionel Giles wrote later that the length of sheets that had been unrolled and then rolled up again during cataloguing must have totalled between ten and twenty miles. Stein and his colleagues merely initiated the study of these documents; many more decades of work lay ahead.

Such studies had no place in Stein's plans for his own future work. Neither by qualification nor by inclination was he bound to the basements of the British Museum. After three years in the West, he was straining at the leash. Once, during his second expedition, he had scribbled in a notebook thoughts which no doubt passed through his mind many more times after arriving in Europe in January 1909:

The traveller whom a mail train carries like a whirlwind past mountains, rivers, towns & finally deposits in the vortex of a strange city, must feel far more up-rooted & separated than a person of average observation who has marched from place to place & whom slow gradual change has prepared for new milieu [*sic*] . . . To peep into every house & hut along the road is better than to see towns in electric illumination flit past like fireflies.[43]

Nor was this unease with Western civilization the only reason for his desire to return to India. The 'special task of sufficient magnitude' – in other words, his revived hopes for an expedition to Balkh – seemed to be meeting with a favourable official response, and he was anxious to return to the Frontier, so that he could set out as soon as permission came. Moreover, during 1911 news of a series of uprisings against the exhausted and decrepit Manchu dynasty reached the West from China. What the outcome would be was unclear; but at least one of the contributory causes appeared to be a violent animosity towards foreigners.

In previous expedition proposals, Stein had warned the Indian government that changing circumstances in Chinese Turkestan might, sooner or later, make archaeological excavations difficult, if not impossible. At the time, these warnings had acted as a spur and thus served his purpose. But now he feared that political and social turbulence would be enough to dissuade the British Indian authorities from sponsoring further explorations. He wanted to be able to return to the region, sooner or later, and now, when he was determined to resist routine employment, such a prospect was particularly important.

It seemed to him unlikely that the passive Turki people of Sinkiang would rally to this new revolt; but reaction among the Chinese who lived in the region was less predictable. Macartney was the best source of information on such matters. However, Stein had not heard from him since learning of the events in China. Whatever happened, he felt uncomfortable being so far from areas that interested him so closely. By mid-December 1911 his three years in Europe were over and he was on board a steamer bound, once more, for India.

10

Escape from Civilization

A S HE TRAVELLED eastward, Stein's sights were firmly set on Afghanistan. It was nine years since he had first tried to enter the country, with Lord Curzon's help, and more than six since he had enjoyed a tantalizing few days on Afghan soil in the Wakhan corridor, *en route* to Kashgar. That he had set foot there at all was something, for few Westerners had visited that mysterious country. British experience was mostly confined to the conflicts of the First and Second Afghan Wars (1841–2 and 1879–80). No one with more than an amateur interest in archaeology had ventured into the interior, and Afghanistan's ancient sites lay forgotten behind the massive mountain ramparts of the Hindu Kush.

The inaccessibility of those sites taunted Stein. The fact that none of his orientalist colleagues and rivals had seen them either merely intensified his desire to be the first to reveal the secrets of Balkh and its lost inheritance of Graeco-Buddhist culture. His experiences in Chinese Central Asia had made him keenly aware of the need to act immediately on his intentions, for fear that 'foreign competition' would get there first. So the continuing reluctance of the Amir, Habibullah, to allow him into the kingdom was not only frustrating but a nagging worry, too. Undoubtedly it stemmed from the ruler's hostility towards British India; and that meant, in turn, that he could not be relied upon to dismiss applications from archaeologists untainted by British connections.

It seemed likely that the Amir had been influenced in his decision to allow Stein into the Wakhan in 1906 by the prospect of an enjoyable visit to India the following year, at the invitation of Lord Minto. Stein aimed, therefore, to time his next proposal to coincide with similar circumstances: the 1911 Delhi Durbar in honour of King George V, which he imagined Habibullah would attend. In fact, the Amir did not come to India. But Stein found that his application, nonetheless, met with a response favourable enough to encourage persistence. With his reputation enhanced by the achievements of 1906–8, he found support among the most eminent men in India, including Sir Spencer Harcourt Butler, recently appointed the first Education Member of the Viceroy's Council.

'His interest in my work & plans', Stein told Publius, 'is an asset of value such as never fell to my lot in Olympian circles; for his influence with the Viceroy is known to be great.'¹ Another influential patron was Sir Henry McMahon, who became Indian Foreign Secretary in 1911. McMahon had been a member of a mission to Kabul and of two boundary missions on Afghanistan's borders, and the resulting friendship he formed with the Afghan rulers made him an incomparable ally for Stein. Through an indirect connection, Stein also made sure that he had a personal introduction to the new Viceroy's personal secretary, Sir James du Boulay – a plan which he outlined in a letter to Publius, prefacing it, apparently without irony, with a description of himself as 'not an expert in self-advertisement.'²

Making careful use of all these contacts, he met the new Viceroy, Lord Hardinge, at Peshawar in early April 1912 and received a sympathetic hearing for his plans. A few days later he submitted his official request to McMahon. He hoped to start from Kashmir in the summer of 1912 and work at Balkh and then at Bamian – whose two gigantic Buddhas, carved from the rock-face of the valley walls, attest to its position on the ancient route from the Oxus to the Indus – before returning to India some time in the following year. McMahon replied that he had written to the Amir, with the Viceroy's permission. But he warned Stein against expecting an immediate response from Habibullah. 'He is not, as you know, a very methodical correspondent, & some considerable delay occurs at times in his replies.'³

In the meantime, Stein began work as Superintendent of Archaeology on the Frontier. Like all the posts he had held since leaving

Lahore in 1899, this one was to claim him for only a few months. These he spent as far as possible in camp, in contrast to his predecessor who, he told Publius, was not keen on camp life and had equipped the superintendent's office with tents 'almost entirely of the type which requires an elephant or a bullock cart to move it'.[4] One night in March his camp received a visit from thieves who carried off a gold watch that had belonged to his father, and to which had been attached an enamel locket containing the portraits of both his parents.

Perhaps if Dash II had been there, the raid would have failed. But Stein had left his terrier in Oxford in the care of Publius and Helen Allen, feeling that he was too old for further Central Asian adventures. His letters to the Allens were punctuated by enquiries after Dash's health and messages of affection for his beloved companion. Once he apologized for being so solicitous about his pet, excusing himself on the grounds that the loss of so many 'dear ones' over the years had made him apprehensive. His dog had become as important to him as his closest friends or relatives, and Dash II, or Dash the Great as he occasionally referred to him, had a special place in his affections.

But the prospect of life in India and further expeditions without a canine comrade was bleak. It was not long before he arranged to buy another fox-terrier puppy, to continue what had by now become a tradition. The new puppy was, of course, also called Dash.

One thing, above all, Stein longed to do without delay and that was to return to Mohand Marg, where he had last had his summer camp in the far-off days of 1898. The Marg was not only his true home, but also his retreat from the disappointing realities of the outside world which confronted him in the East just as they had in London and Hungary. Violent demonstrations of disaffection with British rule in India were increasing. Helen Allen's brother, Basil, had been the victim of one in Bengal in 1908 and there had been disturbances in Lahore too.

For Stein, the rioters were 'members of the insect class'. Writing to enquire after the recovery of Helen's brother, he observed, 'usually it needs the sword to cut such Gordian knots'.[5] The assassination attempts on Lord Minto at Ahmadabad in 1909 and on Minto's successor, Lord Hardinge, in December 1912, widened the cracks in the edifice of order and certainty that the British had tried to build in India, and they shocked Stein. Instinctively he favoured discipline and stability, and he disapproved of an education system that Westernized young Indian men but left them discontented with their lot. If only India could offer them a higher standard of education in their own languages and culture, he thought, youthful energies could be more positively directed.[6]

His opinions interested Sir Harcourt Butler to the extent that he often consulted Stein during this period while formulating his own policy on education. Stein, for once on the receiving end of the sort of persistence he himself had often inflicted on others, found the demands on his time rather irksome. His respect for Butler, however – and, perhaps, his susceptibility to the flattery of being asked – overcame any reservations. He was soon to discover that Butler's friendship could have surprising results.

At the end of May 1912, Stein made the longed-for move to Mohand Marg, having been given special permission to work on *Serindia*, his scholarly report of the second expedition. At last he could enjoy again the dazzling views and breathe the pine-scented air, 'the avalanche perfume'. He sent Helen Allen a bunch of edelweiss picked on the climb up and exclaimed, 'How grateful I am for the kind dispensation which has allowed me to return here – on my own feet!'[7] With him came young Dash III and two assistants: a secretary, Nilakanth Kaul, who was the son of his old friend Pandit Govind Kaul, and a draughtsman, Afrazgul Khan, a young Pathan sepoy from the Khyber Rifles who had already acted as his assistant at excavations on the Frontier earlier in the year. Several old retainers welcomed him back to his 'kingdom', including Pir Baksh, the *shikari* who had accompanied him on his earliest Kashmir hikes in the 1890s.

Things seemed just as they had been fourteen years earlier. And yet the very familiarity of it all emphasized how much his own life had changed in that time. When a visit by Hatim, the storyteller, revived memories of the summer of 1896, Stein felt as though the period when he had made his record of the old man's tales belonged 'in a former birth'. But he was happy and relaxed – more so than he had been for a long time. Then, on 16 June, he received some unexpected news, as he wrote to Publius the following day:

Late last night a heavy Dak bag arrived & to my utter astonishment brought a letter from the Viceroy's hand announcing the K.C.I.E. [Knight Commander of the Indian Empire], with a bundle of congratulatory telegrams from Simla. I scarcely believed my eyes; for how could I as a simple man of research foresee this more than generous recognition, the due otherwise only of men who have worked hard for the State. It seems in some ways an overwhelming attention almost. I know of course, that I owe it mainly, if not solely, to Sir H. Butler's friendly interest in my labours and to the Viceroy's personal kindness.

All night my thoughts were turning to those dear ones who would have rejoiced so greatly in this acknowledgement of my efforts and who have all left me long ago. But if anything can console me for this it is the happy assurance that a kindly Fate has given me such incomparable friends as you both are, and that you share my feelings.[8]

Publius, in replying, did not forget one detail which he knew would please his friend. In his minute, careful hand he wrote the following on behalf of Dash the Great:

Many congratulations, dear Master. Am wearing my collar of achievement.
If I had known this was coming, I should not have cried on the Wakhjir.
Whip the young one, & keep him in order.
Bow wow
SIR DASH, K.C.I.E.
(Have assumed this title).[9]

Stein's fight for recognition was won. It had been brought to a triumphant conclusion during the traumatic finale of the second expedition, though he had not guessed it at the time. Now, official favour marked him as one of the elect, his path had been swept clear and, though he was too modest to parade his new status, he could not deny that he found its effects pleasant enough.

Perhaps the fact that he was now Sir Aurel – he had decided immediately to continue using the name by which his family had always known him – helped when he decided to press a claim to Mohand Marg. Usually, when he described the mountainside as 'my own' or 'my kingdom', he excused himself by putting the expressions in self-deprecating inverted commas. But in November 1905, when he had climbed up to enjoy a few hours there, he had heard from the local people that others had recognized its advantages as a camping ground during his

1. Nathan Stein (180?–89): fond father but inept man of business

2. Anna Hirschler Stein (*circa* 1817–87): Aurel sailed for India with her last letter in his pocket

3. Ernst Stein with his wife Henriette and children, Ernst and Theresa. Ernst's 'watchful presence' dominated Aurel's early years

4. Aurel Stein shortly before he set out on his second expedition to the
Taklamakan Desert

5. Lahore days: (*from left*) Fred Andrews, Alice Andrews, Dash I, Percy
Allen, Helen Allen (?) and Stein, in 1897

6. Stein's private 'kingdom', Mohand Marg, 11,000 feet up in the
mountains north of Srinagar, Kashmir

7. A house fit for a British consul, Chini Bagh in Kashgar, as rebuilt by the Macartneys *circa* 1912

8. In a Chinese garden: the Macartney family (*from left*), Robin, Sylvia, Theodora, Eric and George, with George's brother Donald standing behind

9. A tamarisk cone in the Taklamakan Desert forming the backdrop for members of the second expedition team: (*from left*) Stein's assistant Ibrahim Beg, secretary Chiang, Stein with Dash the Great, cook Jasvant Singh (*standing*), surveyor Lal Singh and Naik Ram Singh

10. Forgotten city: an ancient house at the Niya site with decorated double bracket, retrieved from the sand

11. Hassan Akhun, Stein's spirited head camel-man, photographed during the second expedition

12. Turdi, the *dak*-man or postal messenger, who carried letters to and from Stein the length and breadth of the Taklamakan Desert

13. Stein's favourite mandarin, Governor Pan, when Taotai of Aksu on the northern arm of the Silk Road

14. Chiang, Stein's secretary during the second expedition, wielding calligraphy brushes and looking frail after a short illness

15. One of Stein's baggage carts loaded and ready to leave a village in Kansu province

16. Old walls at Yarkand, an important city on the southern arm of the Silk Road

17. A good example of a stupa, or Buddhist commemorative monument, in the desert in Kansu

18. In search of the Keriya River: Stein's camel train crossing the Taklamakan Desert in 1908

19. The temples and crumbling porches of the Caves of the Thousand Buddhas as Stein first saw them in 1907

20. Wang, the Taoist monk, who unblocked the secret library and sold its contents to Stein

21. Secrets revealed: Tang-period painted silk banners representing Bodhisattvas, from the walled-up library

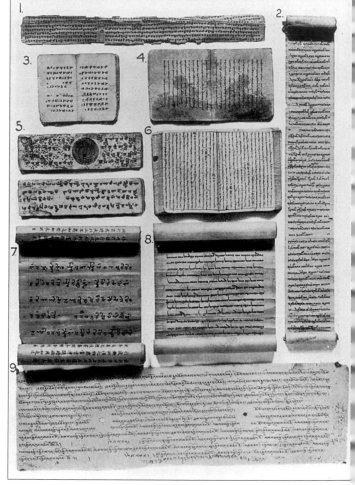

22. Voices of Tun-huang: manuscripts in (1) Sanskrit, (2) Manichaean Turkish, (3) Runic Turki, (4 and 6) Uighur, (5 and 7) Central Asian Brahmi, (8) Sogdian and (9) Tibetan

23. Angel of the East: one of the classically inspired 'cherub' faces that greeted Stein at the cheerless site of Miran

24. One of hundreds of stucco fragments from Stein's desert sites, in this case from Ming-oi, 'the thousand houses'

25. View of the main Kun-lun mountain range from one of Stein's survey stations at 18,612 feet

26. The sort of river crossing Stein rarely bothered to mention: rope and pulley on the left, rope bridge on the right for animals and laden men

27. Stein with his great friend 'the Saint', Thomas Arnold, shortly before the latter's death in 1930

28. Inappropriate companions: Stein's unwanted escort during his first expedition in Iran, 1932

29. 'Old Odysseus': Stein in a photograph taken in Lahore, 1933

absence; and their intrusion had prompted feelings of proprietorial indignation.

A 'party of gregarious vandals' had been there, he told Publius at the time, a 'band of western barbarians', a 'locust swarm'. They had dug out areas for tents and built platforms projecting from the ridge, huddling together (on the very spot where his own tent was always pitched) when there was room nearby 'big enough to camp a Brigade on!' If he could get hold of the man who had guided them here, he vowed to Publius, 'he will learn that there may be reasons for not doing it again'.[10] Of course, there were no real reasons, and Stein had no time in 1905–6 to create any before leaving on his second expedition. But he knew how it could be done and now, in 1912, back in residence on Mohand Marg and hoping to embark on another expedition soon, he was anxious to reserve the place for his exclusive use, even during his absence.

Ten-year leases were available from the Kashmir authorities on land on which bungalows or huts were to be built; accordingly he applied to build a hut on the ridge, though with no immediate plans to do so. The site was reserved for him in July 1913. In the meantime, when the Dunstervilles came on a short visit, he made them promise not to reveal the whereabouts of his camping ground to anyone when they returned to Gulmarg, a popular holiday area on the far side of the Kashmir valley.

In the peace of Mohand Marg, Stein thought often of 'the Baron', Fred Andrews. It was a recurring source of sadness to him that his friend seemed so dissatisfied with his life in London, where he was now Director of the art department at the Battersea Polytechnic. Stein longed to see him removed from 'the depressing smoke, dirt & banality' of the capital, to a position that would make full use of his talents and expertise in the applied arts of India.[11] So, when the idea of a new technical arts school in Srinagar was mooted, he determined that Andrews should be its first director.

Encouraged by the prospect of support from an Indian government newly enthusiastic about native education, Stein discussed the idea with Stuart Fraser, the British Resident in Kashmir, early in 1912. On Fraser's recommendation, he then took the proposal to the Kashmir home minister, Dr Mittra, who was sufficiently interested to invite Andrews to draw up a scheme. 'The post will not be a bed of roses exactly', Stein told Publius, 'but there is infinite scope for congenial work, & life in Srinagar under the Resident's protecting shadow is after all easy.'[12] All the same, he was anxious that his friend should make his decision on a sounder basis than simply disgust with Battersea. He knew Andrews' impatience with bureaucrats and administrators, his tendency to fretful exasperation when things did not run exactly as he felt they should, and feared that the idiosyncratic and 'quaint' ways of a native state might discourage him – and his wife, Alice, too.

The couple had moved home several times since their return to England. Alice was of a nervous disposition and seems to have been as difficult to please in her domestic arrangements as her husband was in his professional milieux. They would need to stick at the post for ten or fifteen years, Stein felt, instinctively making financial calculations, in order to save enough for retirement; and to make the move worthwhile in other ways too, for it would be difficult for Fred Andrews to find another position in Britain afterwards. Early in 1913, the Kashmir Darbar offered Andrews the position of director of the new college at Rs 1,000 a month and, after much deliberation, he accepted. Stein noted with satisfaction that the marriage of the Andrews' daughter Nora, soon afterwards, obviated the need for too many expensive 'flittings' home. He awaited the arrival of his friends in happy anticipation of the beneficial effect Kashmir's climate and natural beauty would have on them.

News from Afghanistan, for which he had waited throughout the summer of 1912, arrived in September via McMahon. The Amir had sent a reply to his letter, wrote the Foreign Secretary.

> After stating that he takes a personal interest in archaeology and express-ing gratification at the receipt of your *Ruins of Desert Cathay*, His Majesty says he must have the book translated into Persian, in order that he may read and understand it, before he can decide whether or not to permit you to visit Afghanistan. The Amir adds that the work of translation will take a long time and I am afraid we must construe his letter as being an indirect refusal of my request.[13]

The fact that Stein did not appear much disheartened by this 'true touch of Oriental diplomacy' seems proof enough of his contented state of mind that summer. He told Keltie at the Royal Geographical Society that, though the response had been negative, 'it is far more polite than the reply given ten years ago, – and I can well understand that regard for the present disturbed conditions in the world of Islam must make him specially cautious about anything that the Mullahs might easily represent as authorized "idol-seeking".[14] The fighting in the Balkans which Stein had in mind, where Serbs, Bulgarians and Greeks had united temporarily to drive back the frontiers of the Ottoman Empire, could easily have repercussions in Islamic countries such as Afghanistan which were sympathetic to Turkey.

When Stein met the Viceroy later in the year, he found Lord Hardinge 'rather tickled' by the Amir's reply but looking forward to the time when Habibullah next wanted to visit India, or even Britain. For the time being, however, Stein had to return the 'secret' books he had borrowed from the library of the Foreign Department and once more postpone plans for the longed-for adventure. There was no period of mourning, however, for he had another project to hand which he took up without delay. 'I can now with a good conscience turn all my attention to the plan of another Turkestan journey,' he announced to Publius. 'You know that it is an old one, with the outline fixed before I said goodbye to Khotan in 1908.'[15]

That outline began in Sistan, the region where south-east Iran meets the southern border of Afghanistan and adjoins Baluchistan. It was a desert area which Stein described as a 'miniature edition of the Tarim basin', where he hoped he might unearth evidence of an Iranian-Hellenistic past. No archaeologist had so far investigated its arid ground; but Sir Henry McMahon retained an interest in the ruins he had seen while there in 1902–5, and he could be counted on to support Stein's hopes. The Viceroy, too, approved of the expedition when Stein discussed it with him in October at Srinagar, shortly before the investiture ceremony where he was presented with his KCIE. In late November he submitted his formal proposal. By then, however, news from Kashgar had prompted him to modify his plans.

The revolution which had begun in Peking in 1911, three years after the death of the Manchu Dowager Empress, had reached the New Dominion slowly. Even then, its reverberations were felt chiefly in the north, almost a thousand miles from Kashgar. But in early 1912, the Manchu Prince Regent abdicated, a provisional republic was declared and the Kashgar Taotai cut off his queue, the sign of imperial servitude. His conversion did not save him. When a Chinese mob rampaged through the old city in May of that year, he was one of their first victims, and many ambans in other oases suffered the same fate.

The rebels were no more attached to republicanism than to any other creed. Opportunism and revenge informed their actions and they were uninterested in foreigners. But their control of Kashgar prompted the Russians to send 700 troops across the border from the railhead at Osh, and Macartney, the British Consul-General, considered this a more ominous event than Chinese lawlessness. He feared that Sokov, the 'gentlemanly and smooth-tongued' Russian Consul who had arrived in the city three years earlier, aimed to extend his country's influence yet farther through Kashgaria.[16] And the presence at the Russian Consulate of the grandson of Yakub Beg, the Muslim rebel of the 1870s, hardly allayed his suspicions.

Russian ambitions did, however, have the effect of strengthening relations between the British Consulate and the Chinese. By late 1912 Macartney could tell Stein: 'As a matter of fact, never have the Chinese – those here at least – been more friendly towards the British than at the present moment . . . '.[17] A new governor of Sinkiang, Yang Tseng-hsin (Yang Zengxin), had already recalled the troublesome Chinese rebels – or 'gamblers' as they were known – to serve in the army in the far north, and this was only the first of many wily and often ruthless moves by which he gained control over the various factions in the region and resisted Russian infiltration.

Ever mindful of the possibility that Chinese attitudes towards 'foreign exploitation' (as he himself called it) of their ancient remains might alter at any time, Stein was anxious to profit from this period of good relations. He was also troubled by the old spectre of competition. Both the Japanese and the Russians had been in the Tarim Basin since his last visit: the former in the shape of monks from Count Otani's Buddhist monastery in Kyoto (whom the British were convinced were spies) between 1908 and 1911; the latter in 1908 and 1910. Now he learned from Macartney that another expedition from the Berlin Ethnological Museum under von Le Coq was on its way. Had the German foreign office not been unnerved by alarmist reports in the Russian press about conditions in Chinese Turkestan, it would have arrived in Kashgar already.

If the Germans were to stick to the Turfan area, where long periods of digging within an oasis were necessary, Stein would not mind, he told Publius, since such work was hardly his line.

> But from Berlin, where systematic organization is easy and the accustomed way, they always go out hunting in packs, and though L. [Le Coq] is not the man for the desert he is likely enough to take out this time some young man with geographical ambitions who might well be guided by *Desert Cathay* to anticipate the few interesting tasks left for me.[18]

That was not all. He had recently received an enquiry from the museum of the University of Pennsylvania about exploration in Chinese Turkestan: indeed, the Director had asked Stein if he would be 'personally interested in such an undertaking'.[19] And he had heard that Count Otani planned another expedition.

In his formal proposal to the Indian authorities, he pointed out that such competition was a particularly serious threat in that region. 'Chinese Turkestan is not like Egypt a great storehouse of things of the past,' he insisted; 'its sites of importance are far-scattered and for the most part quickly exhausted.'[20] Pressing for early approval of his plans, he altered his itinerary and applied to go directly to Kashgar, reaching Sistan at the end of his expedition instead.

While he waited for an answer, Stein settled down to a winter beside the Dal Lake. He was expected to complete *Serindia* before beginning another expedition, and the only proviso Marshall had stipulated, when granting him special permission to devote himself to this, was that he should go down to Peshawar for two weeks in the New Year to inspect the museum there, of which he was honorary curator as Superintendent of Archaeology. He moved back into Dal View Cottage at Gupkar, the house in which he had spent a cold and comfortless winter in 1905–6 while struggling to finish *Ancient Khotan* before his second expedition. History seemed to be repeating itself.

'Well,' he wrote to Publius, 'Fate has willed it that I should always have to work in a "rush". Perhaps it knows why. To get the maximum output without regard for the instrument's comfort, while its fitness lasts?'[21] In fact, by the time he penned that comment he was enjoying considerable comfort, for he had moved into a larger and warmer house for the coldest months, November to April. Kaplas Villa, the house he chose, was also at Gupkar and had previously been occupied by the heir to the Kashmir throne and his tutor.

Despite the civilized surroundings, however, Stein clung to the notion that his ties to such a conventional dwelling were no more than those of a bird of passage to a feeding ground. When Publius offered to send him a Jaeger dressing-gown he declined, saying he preferred to work either in his Norfolk jacket or in a fur 'sitting-bag' which he had used during his expeditions. 'And then kindly remember that I love to feel "in camp" and unencumbered, and how out of place a dressing gown is in my style of existence!'[22]

One of the arguments Stein employed in favour of a third expedition was that he ought to go again to the desert while still physically fit. On 26 November 1912 he marked his fiftieth birthday, with little sign of the passing years. His hair was greying, he sometimes wore spectacles (though hardly ever for photographs) and, of course, he lacked a few toes. But he had overcome the potential difficulties posed by his 1908 operation and exuded physical and mental vigour. Fitness and good health had been granted to him all his life and he relied on them in order to carry out his work. But they were more than simply useful. For Stein, to be fit and healthy had become a matter of pride, part of his resolutely independent image of himself.

Whereas in the past he had not needed to take precautions, however, he was now more careful. He could not afford to neglect his feet and asked Keltie, early in 1913, to consult his 'Arctic or Antarctic friends' on footwear for use in freezing conditions and biting winds. Nor could he be cavalier about his diet. Food had never interested him but he was aware of the debilitating effects of dyspepsia. Though he seemed to suffer far less from that complaint in the East than in the West, he now heeded Andrews' advice on the necessity of eating well.

'You will be glad to know', he announced to his friend shortly before setting off on the third expedition, 'that I have, this time, two tried Indian servants who are both capable cooks.'[23] (One of them had accompanied Prince Louis d'Orléans to Kashgar in 1902, and was keen to go again.) He promised Publius that he would pay attention to food and warmth, and reassured him as to the efficiency of his new, fur-lined boots, which had been made with 'isolating layers of birch bark inside' to his own design.

The expedition was due to leave by the end of July 1913. Final approval from the India Office in London came through only in mid-May, and it was decided not to apply to Peking for a passport, since the government there might make difficulties on the grounds of local disturbances. Macartney could be relied upon to arrange matters instead. There was little time for preparations but, with two major expeditions behind him, Stein had honed his organizational skills to an impressive sharpness. He had gained permission to defer completion of *Serindia* because of the urgency of reaching sites before the Germans. Now he immediately gave orders to local tailors and leather-workers and, as usual, made full use of Andrews' presence in London to arrange the ordering and shipment of necessary items, undeterred by the knowledge that his friend had much to do in organizing his own imminent move to Kashmir.

The Andrews were due to arrive in the valley shortly after Stein left, which was regrettable. But Stein contented himself with the thought of the enjoyment they would derive from the 'quiet unassuming' English character of Kashmir in the winter and the glory of its springs. Having stayed in the valley long enough himself to be able to fill his villa with vases of acacias, roses and lilies, he moved back up to Mohand Marg at the end of May to finalize arrangements.

These included a novel approach to Chinese Turkestan which showed all the characteristics of a typical Stein proposal. It gave him everything he wanted while appearing practical and useful from an official point of view. His idea was to reach the Pamirs via the Darel and Tangir valleys on the North-West Frontier, which no European had yet entered and which were, consequently, unsurveyed.

The valleys, running roughly from north to south to join the Indus about thirty miles west of Chilas, were in the turbulent and often fanatically Muslim tribal region, beyond British control. Lately, however, they had submitted to the harsh but stabilizing rule of a chief from farther north, Raja Pakhtun Wali, son of the infamous Mir Wali of Yasin whose men had murdered the British explorer George Hayward in 1870. Pakhtun Wali had recently established friendly relations with the Gilgit Political Agency and Stein saw that he might benefit from this situation. By travelling through Darel and Tangir and surveying the country as he went, he could act as an unofficial ambassador for the British Indian authorities, provide the Survey of India with useful information and enjoy a new, direct route to Chinese Turkestan and the experience of being the first Westerner on historic territory – for the valleys were well-known to the old Chinese Buddhist pilgrims.

Moreover, as he pointed out with satisfaction to Publius, if he could use this route, 'no practicable approach to the Chinese Pamirs or Kunlun will remain which I have not followed'.[24] The Indian Foreign Department fell in with his plan, and the Raja agreed to extend his hospitality.

On Mohand Marg, Stein gathered his men. Amongst them were all his favourite followers: his old servants, Musa and Tila Bai, from Chinese Turkestan, the surveyor Lal Singh (now 51 years old) and his cook Jasvant Singh, and Stein's latest assistant, the young Pathan, Afrazgul Khan. Besides these, the Survey of India provided a second surveyor, Muhammad Yakub Khan; and a corporal called Shams Din came from the First (King George's Own) Sappers and Miners – the late Naik Ram Singh's regiment – to act as general handy-man.[25] With these and his own two cooks, Stein descended from his mountain in late July to take up an offer from the Kashmir settlement commissioner, Walter Talbot, to use his bungalow as a final 'mobilization' point. 'Never have I mobilized under such conditions of luxurious ease,' he commented to Publius from the Residency at Gulmarg, where he had been invited to spend his last couple of nights.[26]

In the same letter he explained the provisions he had made in case of his death, something he had never before mentioned on the eve of an expedition. Perhaps the troubled conditions in both China and the world of Islam prompted these precautions. Or perhaps the tragic fate in late 1912 of Captain Scott, whom he had met at the Royal Geographical Society in 1909, made Stein more aware of the risks of exploration.[27] For whatever reason, he told Publius that his will (dated November 1911) was with his solicitor, Alexander H. Wilson (son of Horace Hayman Wilson, Oxford's first Boden Professor of Sanskrit) in London. His trustees were Arnold, Publius and Helen Allen's brother Ernest.

His notebooks from the 1906–8 expedition, which would be needed for the completion of *Serindia*, were with the Punjab Bank's agent in Srinagar, and were to be sent either to Publius or to William Foster at the India Office in the event of Stein's death. He hoped that Publius's former pupil, John Johnson (who worked at the Oxford University Press and later became Printer to the University), would take on the task of finishing the scholarly report, with the support of a qualified orientalist. He left all his manuscripts and written records to the Indian Institute in Oxford (now part of the Bodleian Library).

The third expedition began late on 31 July 1913 with an overnight boat journey down the Jhelum to Bandipur, as the first had done thirteen years earlier. There it divided, the bulk of the baggage going ahead to Hunza under the supervision of the second surveyor while Stein took Lal Singh and Afrazgul Khan with him north-westward. They left Kashmir along the gorges of the Kishanganga and its tributaries, dropping down to the scorching valley of the Indus at Chilas which he had seen from afar, *en route* to Gilgit in 1900. Stein made most of the journey on foot in order to get into training for the steep climbs that lay ahead in Darel and Tangir and it was a wise policy: the 'primeval tracks' and stiff passes in the Raja's domain were to prove as taxing as anything he had tackled hitherto.

The Raja had insisted that Stein should not be accompanied by anyone from the Gilgit Agency and Stein was happy to comply. He told Publius he had 'no wish to examine all the grievances which those he tyrannizes over, may have against him. He will be a most interesting specimen to study, the last successful usurper who built up a petty throne for himself with truly traditional methods.'[28] In any case, the British frontier chiefs knew how to profit from Stein's visit without being there themselves. In a telegram that provides an interesting glimpse of their methods, the assistant to the Kashmir Resident, Fraser (whom Stein liked and held in high esteem), explained to the Political Agent in Gilgit that Stein would give the Raja a gift and distribute money to the headmen. If the Raja was helpful, the Resident was prepared to consider any recommendation Stein might make as to a cash grant afterwards:

> Sir Aurel has been told that there is no objection to his hinting his intentions in this matter to Pukhtun Wali (without mentioning any amount or unduly raising his expectations) but Mr Fraser considers that it would be unwise for you to mention the topic of rewards to Pukhtun Wali before the visit, since the Raja should not be led to consider that in admitting this visitor to Darel he is confering [*sic*] a favour as the result of bargaining or in return for a pecuniary consideration.[29]

Stein's party reached Darel from Chilas by skin raft, travelling several miles downstream on the tossing currents of the Indus. On the border of the Raja's territory they were met by his nephew, Shah Alam, and a large escort comprised in the main of outlaws from Swat, Chitral and the independent Dard areas on the Indus who had thrown in their lot with Pakhtun Wali. The wild but cheerful company and the magnificent, unspoilt scenery of alpine meadows and valleys clothed with pine, fir and deodar forests were very much to Stein's taste. Though the climbing left him too exhausted each night even to make notes – a rare event – he was exhilarated by the visit. He was also highly relieved to find his feet up to the challenge.

He and Lal Singh mapped 1,200 square miles of ground. There were plentiful ruined, pre-Islamic fortified settlements to verify the accounts of early Chinese pilgrims who had travelled that way *en route* from the Oxus to Swat and had described thriving Buddhist communities. Stein managed to identify the site of a sanctuary which they all mentioned in their accounts (and which, not unusually, remained a holy place, having been adopted as the tomb of an Islamic saint). He also noticed here in Darel something he had first seen in Chitral in 1906: decorative carving on the woodwork of houses, mosques and graves which used motifs in the ancient Gandharan, Graeco-Buddhist style.

After meeting Pakhtun Wali in the castle he was building himself near the ancient capital of Darel, Stein climbed to the high spur dividing Darel from Tangir. From this vantage point, he could see the gap between mountains away to the west where he knew the Indus dives into a treacherous, narrow gorge as it turns southward. It was a place the Chinese pilgrims had known and feared, for the only way through in their day was by fearsome rock ledges and 'iron chains' hung across the chasm and the torrent below. Stein longed to see it. But the independence of the tribes of Kohistan, the region in which it lay, had so far kept outsiders at bay.

On 21 August, Stein crossed the 14,000-foot Sheobat Pass and left Pakhtun Wali's territory. Travelling north through the Yasin valley (where Hayward had met his death in 1870), he reached the Darkot Pass eight days later. This was the route the Chinese had used in the mid-eighth century AD in their daring attempt to thwart both Tibetan and Arab enemies. Stein had been up to the pass from the northern side in 1906; now he was able to cross it from south to north and gauge the scale of the Chinese achievement, more than 1,100 years earlier. While there he discovered a Tibetan inscription on a rock nearby, made, he had no doubt, at the same period, when the Tibetans were pressing westward.

By the time Stein and his men reached the border with China, they had already crossed fifteen passes at heights of more than 10,000 feet, and had covered over 500 miles, mostly on foot. They moved rapidly through Sarikol to Tashkurgan, where the party split into three. Lal Singh headed for the Kun-lun Mountains, via Yarkand and Khotan, to extend his triangulation of 1906 eastwards; the heavy baggage was dispatched directly to Kashgar; and Stein and the second surveyor, aiming also for Kashgar, followed a route never fully explored before, down a valley running away from the eastern glaciers of the great mountain, Mustagh-ata. It was a difficult and dangerous descent but Stein emerged unscathed on to the plains on 19 September, and was in Kashgar two days later.

Conditions had changed not only in Kashgar's public life, but also at Chini Bagh, the Macartneys' home. George Macartney was made a KCIE in 1913 (partly, his biographers suggest, on the strength of the warm recommendations Stein made to the authorities after his trips to Kashgar).[30] He and his wife had for some time been planning a new house that would reflect his status as British Consul-General; and by the time Stein arrived, it had just been completed. The old native building which Macartney and Younghusband had first occupied in 1890 had been demolished and replaced by a house designed by the local Swedish missionary, Högberg. This was mostly single-storey, like its predecessor, but with a couple of rooms on the flat roof which overlooked the garden and surrounding countryside. The cliff on which it stood had been strengthened, a high wall enclosed the whole property, and there were spacious quarters for the staff and servants, with avenues of acacia trees decorating the compound. A furnace in the basement provided an efficient heating system and the European fittings extended even to wallpaper in most rooms.

Stein did not comment on such changes. One suspects he may have preferred the simplicity of the old Chini Bagh. He was certainly dismayed by the sudden enthusiasm for Western dress which the revolution had spread among the Chinese. Even Chiang, his devoted secretary, had discarded his elegant silk clothes in favour of the new fashion.[31]

However, it gave Stein satisfaction to tell Publius that reports of upheaval in the region had been greatly exaggerated in the West. 'The Russians have tried their best to create the idea of the country being disturbed,' he wrote. 'In reality all is quiet, – and the private murders & squabbles among the Chinese which followed the so-called revolution have ceased.'[32] His assessment was based partly on his habitual, hopeful underestimation of any political unrest threatening to interfere with his own activities. But it was also encouraged by Macartney's characteristically unruffled view of events. After the third expedition was safely over, however, Stein admitted that his friend had warned him at the outset not to put too much faith in the support of local ambans, as on previous occasions.

It was this change that Stein regretted most. 'Some of the best qualities of the old local Mandarin world,' he wrote later, 'including regard for scholarly aims and labours, had manifestly been discarded, while the beneficial effect hoped for from "Western learning" and republican methods was still conspicuous by its absence.'[33] Of course, what he meant by 'regard for scholarly aims and labours' was acquiescence in the wholesale removal of antiquities. But he saw nothing in Chinese Turkestan to persuade him that those antiquities would be saved for posterity if left alone. The administration was corrupt and the local people had only a quick profit in mind when they dug into old sites. There seemed to be no interest in archaeological work except among the few cultivated ambans of the scattered oasis towns. With such men – and with Pan, above all – he had enjoyed discussing his work and had had no reason to disguise his conviction that his finds would be safer in the West than in the desert. They had never suggested that they disagreed. But many of the ambans had been slaughtered or ousted in recent months, and a new breed of administrator was now in charge.

With or without their help, however, Stein had to get started quickly. The German expedition was already in Chinese Turkestan and von Le Coq, despite having had dysentery, planned to go to the Lop region that winter. 'L. seems to be bent on getting those fine Miran frescoes I discovered in 1907 & which poor Ram S.'s blindness prevented from being added to our collection,' he told Publius.[34] This time he had to set out without Chiang's intelligent and cheerful company. His erstwhile secretary had been suffering in recent years from deafness, which Stein had tried to alleviate by sending him an expensive electrophone from India. His condition had improved recently, but he was not fit for desert travel.

Stein had to make do with his assistant, Li, whom he described bluntly afterwards as a 'shrivelled-up weakly young man' who was 'absorbed in the task of treating his ailments, real and imaginary, with every Chinese quack medicine he could lay hold of, and as taciturn and inert as a mummy . . .'.[35]

Stein's plan was to reach Lop as quickly as possible via Khotan. Keen to try new routes, however, he decided to travel east from Kashgar as far as the oasis of Maral-bashi before cutting southward across the desert to the Mazar-tagh hills on the lower Khotan River. Sending all but the bare minimum of baggage on by the caravan route, he started from Maral-bashi on 25 October 1913 with a small party of men and camels and large quantities of water. They were soon out among the huge, lifeless dunes of the true desert, with ridges two to three hundred feet high tightly packed in diagonal lines across their path, and scarcely a patch of level sand between. It was by far the most forbidding ground Stein had ever encountered in the Taklamakan. He told Publius: 'You know that this nature in death torpor is familiar to me and has its attractions. But never had I seen it in such contortions.'[36]

This was the ground through which Hedin had fought his way in 1895 on his first foray into the Taklamakan, when he had lost almost all his animals and two men, coming upon water only when all chance of survival had seemed lost. Stein's own hired camels were on the verge of exhaustion by the end of the third day and there was nothing ahead but 'the same expanse of formidable sand ridges like huge waves of an angry ocean suddenly arrested in movement.'[37] He decided to turn back; and a violent storm a few days later proved his decision a wise one.

The difference, which this incident highlighted, between his caution and Hedin's recklessness was interestingly described years later by Hedin himself in his autobiography:

He [Stein] still had eighty-five miles to go, from his turning point, to the little mountain of Masar-tagh, on the western shore of the Khotan-daria [river]. It was no doubt fortunate for him and his companions that he turned in time. In a similar situation I should never have made such a decision. I should have continued through the desert. It might have been the death of me and my men. I might have lost everything, as in 1895. But the adventure, the conquest of an unknown country, the struggle against the impossible, all have a fascination which draws me with irresistible force.[38]

Stein reached Khotan by a safer route on 21 November and found a most welcome piece of information awaiting him. Macartney, in the oasis briefly on an official tour, told him that von Le Coq had abandoned his plan to reach Lop and had turned back for Kashgar. Armed with this knowledge, Stein could afford to indulge in further absorbing excavations – albeit in bitterly low temperatures – at familiar sites along the 700-mile route to Lop-nor, including Niya which by now he thought of as 'my own little Pompeii'.[39] By the end of the year he had got as far as Charchan, about 200 miles east of the Niya site, accompanied on the track into that town by a sparkling view of the snow-clad peaks of the Kun-lun far away to the south.

There, his path suddenly seemed barred. A band of revolutionaries (Stein preferred to call them 'loafers' and 'undesirables') had captured the Amban of the next town eastward, Charkhlik. No one in Charchan knew how things stood, let alone how Stein and his party would be received. Nevertheless, he decided to go on, armed with two introductions thoughtfully provided by the Charchan magistrate: one for the hapless Amban, should he be restored to office, and one to whichever 'revolutionary' had, more likely, taken his place. During the week which the party took to reach the outskirts of Charkhlik, a military detachment ended the uncertainty by slaughtering most of the revolutionaries – though not before they themselves had murdered the Amban.

After a week spent raising supplies, Stein was rejoined by Lal Singh, who had spent the previous four months surveying in the Kun-lun, under difficult conditions but with excellent results, extending the net of carefully fixed stations eastward beyond Lop-nor. Stein always paid tribute to the part played by his surveyors in the success of his expeditions (and the Royal Geographical Society also took note of their contributions, acknowledging them on published maps and presenting them with grants and awards).

Then, on 15 January 1914, the entire party set out for Miran. Stein hoped to retrieve the frescoes which Naik Ram Singh had been forced to abandon there when blindness overtook him in 1908. But a sad disappointment awaited him. Making straight for the shrine where the frescoes lay, he found only shattered fragments of plaster littering the ground. Despite Ram Singh's careful refilling of the excavation with sand and debris, someone had dug down to the wall-paintings and had crudely hacked them out.

The jagged remnants were harsh testimony to the fact that, as he had feared, his own reports had led others to exploit the sites before he himself could return. He was in no doubt as to who those 'others' were. The person who had visited Miran was 'a young Japanese traveller who lacked preparation, technical skill and experience equal to his archaeological zeal', as Stein described him in a later lecture:[40] namely, one of Count Otani's monks, Tachibana.

Tachibana's inexperience had, at least, limited his activity. He had investigated no further than the first fresco he had found. So the painted dado beneath, with its graceful figures celebrating the secular joys of life, remained intact and ready for Stein himself to remove. While he supervised this task, he prepared for another foray into the desert of Lop, where he planned this time to trace the ancient Chinese route from Lou-lan to Tun-huang. But before he could embark on this journey, ominous information reached him.

A letter from Macartney reported that the provincial government at Urumchi had ordered the district authorities to prevent Stein's party from carrying out any survey work. Urumchi claimed that Lal Singh had broken Peking regulations forbidding foreigners to map strategically important points. If the surveying continued, the expedition members would be arrested and sent to Kashgar 'for punishment under treaty'. Macartney felt the order was the work of some power-hungry official in Urumchi. He had telegraphed the British Minister in Peking to ask the Chinese government to recommend Stein to the Urumchi authorities as working 'solely in the interests of science'. But it might be months before this process could take effect. In the meantime, the best that could be expected from local ambans and their minions was passive obstruction.

Stein watched anxiously for signs of unhelpfulness among the local population near Miran. Not until later did he discover that, in the confusion in Charkhlik following the murder of the Amban, the orders from Urumchi had remained unopened in the yamen. But he knew that the timing was fortunate for another reason. He was on the point of disappearing into the desert for many weeks where no edict could reach him, and no official would follow. If he could leave before relations with the people deteriorated, he could hope that the matter would be resolved by the time he reached Tun-huang. Accordingly, he started on 1 February 1914 with a large column of labourers and thirty camels, besides his own men, bound for the Lop Desert 'where Boreas and all his family are at home'.[41]

———————◄►————————

The fact that Stein was threatened with arrest at this time seems to have been more a matter of chance than a campaign specifically against him. He was only one of several foreigners who had carried out surveys in Chinese Turkestan in the decades leading up to 1914; he simply happened to be the one doing so at a period when xenophobia was becoming an official policy in China. That he had not obtained his passport from Peking before arriving perhaps also weighed against him.

His claim that his survey work was 'purely in the interests of science' was only partly genuine. It was true that he never lost an opportunity to emphasize the interplay of geography and history, and the importance of studying the two together. But in stressing its scientific nature, he was probably deliberately turning a scholarly blind eye to the uses it could have for those with less academic interests. Once he had handed over his results to the Survey of India, the maps that its draughtsmen produced had uses far beyond the illustration of his own books and lectures. On more than one occasion he was asked by Survey or Army officers, on an informal basis, to provide information about tracks or passes that he used in remote areas; and he himself had access to confidential gazetteers and private Foreign Office libraries during preparations for his expeditions.

This probably seemed to him a perfectly normal arrangement. He had spent all his working life on or near the North-West Frontier, where secrecy and undercover operations were the norm, and where, amongst the ruling classes, there was nothing but support for the aims of British imperialism. In such an environment, it was not unusual to be drawn, however tangentially, towards the sphere of the secret services. All this was understood in India. When the Chinese failed to appreciate his point of view, Stein's impatience was increased by his disrespect for their motives. He saw only chaos and opportunism resulting from the revolution and was determined not to let it interfere with his work.

The expedition party rode into Tun-huang late in March, five weeks after starting for the Lop Desert. They had spent two weeks in and around Lou-lan, the old Chinese station which Stein had excavated in 1906, finding further evidence of the life its lonely colonists had led seventeen centuries earlier. Out of one ancient burial ground he drew not only documents on paper and wood but also household implements and a variety of silk fragments, the colours still fresh and vibrant. The contents of another spoke even more eloquently of the forgotten past. For in the graves here, on a windswept clay ridge, lay the bodies of men and women wonderfully preserved, only the parched look of their skin indicating that they were long dead, rather than simply asleep. Their hats still bore feathers, wooden pins still clasped their woollen clothes, and woven baskets lay where they had been left, filled with food for the dead.

For Stein this was a thrilling and haunting discovery. But for his labourers, the sand-storm which broke soon afterwards was a sign of the wrath of the dead whom they had disturbed. The party left the ridge the next day, and Stein set out with Afrazgul and Shams Din in search of the ancient route across the empty, salt-encrusted desert which the Chinese would have used on their first advance into Turkestan. Planning for this part of the expedition was as vague as anything Stein had tackled, for it was impossible to foresee what obstacles might delay them beyond the estimated time needed. Indeed, there was no guarantee that they would even find the route. But luck was with them. Barely had they started, guided only by compass, when they came across various small metal and stone objects. Then, on the third day, they saw a trail of coins scattered on the clay, lost from a bag or pocket centuries earlier and still looking as bright as if just minted. By such signs they were guided across the ancient, petrified Lop sea-bed.

'If I were inclined to be superstitious I might have thought myself led by the spirits of those brave patient Chinese who had faced this awful route for four centuries, with its hardships & perils,' Stein told Publius. Despite his practical approach to the desert, he was still susceptible to the romance of such evidence of the past. 'One or two incidents of this sort', he wrote, 'made me suddenly feel as if I were living through in reality some of the experiences which I remember having read as a little boy in one of Jules Verne's fascinating stories, the "Journey underneath the Earth" or whatever it was called . . . I wished, I could read that story again now!'[42] Increasingly his own experiences seemed to match the fantasies of the French novelist: a few days later, returning to the ancient fortified wall west of Tun-huang, he found his own footprints and those of Dash II still clearly visible where they had followed the soldiers' tracks seven years earlier. 'Time seems to have lost all power of destruction on this ever-dry ground which knows no drift sand nor erosion,' he commented wonderingly.[43]

The fantastic nature of his journey across the Lop Desert did not drive all other thoughts from his mind, however. A letter he sent shortly afterwards to Fred Andrews, who had referred in a letter of his own to Stein's official position as archaeological superintendent on the Frontier, shows that, as usual, he had worked out a congenial future timetable.

> You speak of 'my' office. Well, *entre nous*, I much doubt whether it will see me again in charge of its affairs. After my return to India, hoped for about the beginning of 1916, I propose to 'demobilize' and write my RGS lecture at Srinagar and then to go home with 4–5 months of special duty followed by 15 months of privilege leave combined with furlough. This would bring me just to the time (Nov 1917) when I could retire on pension under the age limit rule. Of course, I should be quite willing to continue my service, provided the extension were granted on special duty to work up the results of my journey – or to take up fresh explorations, say in Seistan.[44]

The hut which he now had permission to build on Mohand Marg was also in his thoughts. He sent his friend a sketch-plan showing an alpine-style building with living-room, study, two bedrooms and two low attic rooms. For a man who prided himself on his unfettered life under canvas, it was a surprisingly domestic vision.

———◆———

In Tun-huang, Stein was reunited with Wang, the guardian of the Caves of the Thousand Buddhas. Wang had entertained another Western visitor since Stein's own fruitful sojourn in the valley. The French Sinologist Pelliot had carried off yet more manuscripts and paintings and, passing through Peking on his return home, had alerted the Chinese authorities to the treasure trove that lay on their north-eastern doorstep. As a result, Wang had been ordered to send all the remaining items from the library to the capital for safe-keeping, though he had received none of the compensation that was supposedly his due.

Stein made it clear in later writings that he thought the transfer had been careless and destructive. In various places in Sinkiang and Kansu he was offered rolls of texts which he felt must have escaped from the secret hoard. But he skated over the fact that 'somehow' a considerable quantity of manuscripts remained at the caves. To Publius he was a little less oblique, reporting that Wang had kept back 'abundant souvenirs' – no doubt hoping for the return of one or another of his wealthy Western friends.

As a result of this precaution by the wily monk – whom Stein, apparently in all seriousness, chose to describe as 'honest' – four more cases full of manuscripts left the walled-up library, and Wang gained additional finances for his restoration work. Stein left the Tun-huang oasis soon afterwards, tracing the ancient Chinese wall eastward for nearly 250 miles before turning to Su-chou in early May in order to prepare for another journey across uncharted ground.

This time it was the Pei-shan, or Gobi Desert, that he planned to explore, by following the course of the Etsin-gol River north. Part of the attraction lay in the resemblance of the region to the part of Turkestan he knew so well. Like the Tarim River, the Etsin-gol gathers its waters from the mountains – in its case the Nan-shan range to the south – but loses them eventually in a great basin from which nothing drains. But Stein also wanted to see the spectacular ruins of Khara-khoto, the 'Black City', to which the river led. The site had been discovered in 1908 by the Russian explorer Colonel Petr Koslov, and Stein was sure it formed the remains of Marco Polo's city of Etzina. So he set out from Su-chou on 10 May, armed with a recommendation to the Mongol chief of the Etsin-gol delta and trying to learn a little Mongolian as he went. He reached Khara-khoto towards the end of the month.

The still massive walls of the old city reared up out of the gravel desert before the expedition party. They were thirty-eight feet thick at the base and thirty feet high, built of a combination of clay and timber that had endured centuries of harsh winds and storms. Stein had never before in Central Asia encountered such large and imposing ruins. Each face of the square which they formed measured about a quarter of a mile, and huge sand-dunes had been heaped against the north and west walls by the relentless prevailing winds. The setting was one of utter desolation, a bleached and desiccated landscape relieved only by scattered tamarisk cones and the empty, long-dead beds of two branches of the river.

Within the fortifications, most of the buildings that had once filled the city had crumbled into dust. But evidence remained of many

Buddhist shrines and stupas, in one of which Koslov had found marvellously preserved paintings on silk, linen and paper.[45] Searching the others, Stein came upon manuscripts, reliefs, frescoes, fragments of glazed pottery and other objects. He also looked for evidence of the abandonment of the city, which he calculated had occurred about a hundred years after Marco Polo visited it in the thirteenth century. But he did not record the story which the local people had told the Russians – that the Chinese had forced the city's surrender by diverting its water supply.

It was now July 1914. Far away in Europe, the clouds of war were gathering. On 28 June in Sarajevo, a young Bosnian terrorist had assassinated the heir to the Austro-Hungarian throne, Archduke Franz Ferdinand, and his wife. While tensions rose among the powers of Europe, Stein was high in the alpine grazing grounds of the Nan-shan, overseeing more survey work (regardless of Chinese objections). Though letters now took only ten days to reach Kashgar from England on the Russian railway, they still spent many weeks crossing the Tarim Basin in the bags of postal runners. As a result, he knew nothing of recent developments in the Balkans. He was absorbed in plans to extend the mapping done in 1907 near the sources of the Su-lo-ho and Su-chou rivers when, in mid-July, his stallion reared, slipped and fell backwards on him, crushing his left thigh and then kicking his left hip in its struggle to regain its feet.

Stein was completely immobilized. Though his leg was neither fractured nor dislocated, it gave him excruciating pain and, once more, he had to take refuge in a litter on which Lal Singh and Afrazgul carried him back to camp. After two weeks, he forced himself to move about with the use of crutches. Then he got himself carried down from the mountains and into Kan-chou, where he knew he could seek treatment from Belgian missionaries. And there, news of the war reached him from Peking.

'So the great conflagration has come which has threatened for years,' he wrote to Publius on 14 August; 'and yet at a time when the nation in England, judging from the papers, can have been little prepared for it . . . May only the Navy prove adequate to its tasks and save the country from a fatal invasion!'[46] Stein had been a member of Lord Roberts'

National Service League for several years.[47] The letters he wrote at this time show that he believed Britain was paying the penalty for not having prepared her people for war long before a crisis occurred.

'In you', he told the Allens towards the end of the year, 'lives that spirit of conscience, duty and fairness which has made the country great in the past, and if the severity of the struggle helps to revive it in the masses, whether rich or poor, which long times of indulgence have made less prepared for sacrifices than of old, there will be much spiritual gain in the end to balance in a way all the losses in lives & material wealth.'[48]

For his native land Stein feared a bleak future. Hungary was weak economically and had long been troubled by the 'nationalities' question: the divisions between the many different peoples who lived within her boundaries. Slovaks, Romanians, Germans, Slavs and Magyars all had their own, conflicting, aims and Stein told Publius that he feared the 'complete break-up of the historic State' in Hungary if the Austro-Hungarian Empire were defeated. The imperial attempt to solve the Slav problem by force in Serbia seemed to him an ominous warning. He also foresaw German 'meddling' in India – and perhaps in Afghanistan – through Islamic agency, and worried what that might imply for his hopes of reaching Bactria.

The fact that the Allens believed in the justice of the conflict comforted him. But there was little solace in the thought of what might have happened to his brother's family in Vienna. The children were both old enough to be drawn into the war: Thesa had recently gained her Ph.D. and Ernst had his twenty-third birthday that September. He had been excused military service twice prior to the war on the grounds of unfitness and had been due for his third and final examination in May. Stein had not heard the result, but he knew that military service for Ernst, who aspired to the life of a university professor and was prone to hypochondria, would be 'a sore trial' even in peacetime. Moreover, Jetty, or Harriet as Stein had begun to call her as he became increasingly Anglicized himself, would be inconsolable if her son were sent anywhere near the battlefields.

On the assumption that letters had no chance of reaching his sister-in-law if sent by the conventional route through Russia, Stein wrote via China and the United States. But letters from Harriet ceased in October and he had to pass many months in anxious ignorance of her welfare before news finally came from Vienna.

The division of loyalties that Stein might have been expected to feel, on finding his country of birth at war with his country of adoption, seems not to have troubled him. He had a detached view of Hungary, commenting on her economic and political difficulties in sad but dispassionate tones. His uncle and brother had brought him up to be a citizen of Europe rather than of the Magyar state, he had few friends there and had lost all the members of his family to whom he was closest. Budapest was a place that belonged to his distant past; and he had lived under the protection of the British Empire for so long that his reflexes had become, at least as far as public affairs were concerned, completely Anglicized.

His closest friends knew that well. But his natural reserve may have concealed it from others. Keltie, at the Royal Geographical Society, seems to have been one who wondered where Stein's sympathies lay, as he discreetly implied in a letter of mid-1915. Stein responded immediately:

> Well, they have always been and are now entirely on the side of England and the Empire with which I threw in my lot for better or for worse when renouncing my Hungarian citizenship more than 27 years ago. Ever since I have eaten the salt of British India and have felt proud of taking my humble share in the work of the Empire to which I was attracted by every sentiment even long before I came out first to India. Even if I had not enjoyed the privilege of living and working during by far the greatest portion of my adult life among people who, I believe, represent the best traditions of British character, I could not possibly fail to realize that England is now fighting not for its security alone but for the freedom of Europe.[49]

Reports of the war that reached him from friends and colleagues varied in outlook. Publius regarded it as a 'wicked attempt at aggression' by the Kaiser and was particularly distressed by the German destruction of Belgium, a country he and Helen had often visited in the course of their Erasmian researches. Both he and Fred Andrews wrote sympathetically of their unhappiness at finding themselves at war with Austria-Hungary, whom they felt was suffering for being 'the catspaw of the "Mad Dog of Europe"', as Andrews put it.

Stein's army friend Dunsterville, on the other hand, expressed an ebullience not unusual in military and other circles during the early days of the conflict. His remark that, regardless of the outcome, 'we shall all be the better for it',[50] contrasted sharply with Andrews' more perceptive report. 'I cannot tell you of the fearful carnage, and how the poor troops on both sides have been swept to death,' he told Stein in November 1914. 'The Austrians appear to have lost great numbers, and it looks as though every family in Europe will be in mourning.'[51]

It is not clear from Stein's letters how he felt at being so far from the scenes of strife. He told more than one friend that he thought it self-indulgent to be continuing with his expedition in such circumstances, and that he wished he were twenty years younger so that he could go and fight. But one senses that these were sentiments based more on guilt than gut feeling. He sent money to Helen Allen for local relief funds in Oxford; he waited anxiously for news from friends such as Gyula Halasz, the Hungarian translator of his books, whom he knew would be called up; and he followed the course of events as best he could through the outdated copies of *The Times* and *Punch* that reached him in the desert. But his primary interest remained his work, and the Allens' friend John Johnson was perhaps right when he remarked that Stein at that period was 'one of the few happy men in the world'.[52]

By early November 1914, Stein and his party had reached the Turfan depression after a testing two-month journey along the mountain ranges that cross the Gobi Desert from south-east to north-west. His leg had not yet recovered and he had been forced to spend part of the time in a litter. Nevertheless, he immediately set to work at a series of sites near Turfan, most of which had been examined and partially excavated by the Germans several years earlier. Since their visits, local treasure-hunters had emulated Bartus's crude methods and chipped away at remaining frescoes for saleable souvenirs, and Stein believed that removal was the only way of safeguarding what was left. In a gorge in the hills outside Turfan, he told Publius he had had to practise calm on seeing the destruction wrought by Bartus in the old Buddhist shrines that puncture the wall of the cliff there. Despite that destruction, however, he was able to carry away frescoes, some of which were eleven by sixteen feet in size.

While Shams Din was engaged in detaching the frescoes from their walls – work which took six weeks – Stein made a rapid visit to Urumchi, the capital of Sinkiang, north-west of Turfan. Here he could pay a call on his old friend Pan, who was now provincial treasurer, and consult the doctor at the Russian Consulate, who pronounced that his leg would make a full recovery from the accident.

Stein told Publius that, thanks to Pan's influence, the provincial governor's attitude towards him and his work was 'benign'; but it was to prove a short-lived benignity. In February 1915, Stein heard that orders from Urumchi demanded that he stop all archaeological work immediately. The order reached him a few days after he had packed up all his finds from the Turfan area into fifty camel-loads and had seen the convoy start for the two-month journey to Kashgar. The timing might have been a fortunate chance, but Stein believed that the Amban of Turfan had turned a blind eye to his activities until they were safely completed. He himself was about to plunge into the desert again, glad to be putting himself beyond the reach of the authorities. But the words which von Le Coq had written to him the previous year may well have rung in his ears: 'I fear that gradually the Chinese will interfere with the investigations sent out by more advanced nations', his fellow-archaeologist had warned, '& therefore each line of writing & each specimen of carving, moulding, etc. that you will bring away will be a piece rescued – may their number increase a thousandfold!'[53] However much the two men might be in competition over their 'spoils', they were both of one mind when it came to the fate of Chinese Turkestan's antiquities: the only safe place for them was the 'advanced' West.

Stein returned to the desert with relief. He had uncovered remarkably well-preserved tombs at Astana, near Turfan, where, by crawling through passages half-filled with drift sand, he had found all the items with which the dead had been buried including fancy pastries that had survived in the varied shapes (inspired by Indian motifs) in which they had originally been baked. But he thought the surroundings 'suburban' compared with his true desert sites. Examining minor remains as he went and sending the surveyors out on various missions, he made a gradual return to Kashgar, arriving at Chini Bagh on the last day of May 1915. There he stayed for five weeks (though without the company of a host, for the Macartneys had gone home on leave and their stand-ins, Colonel Sir Percy Sykes and his sister Ella, a travel writer, were hunting in the Pamirs.)[54]

Stein had been looking forward to his return journey to India. Having seen his antiques repacked into 182 heavy cases and dispatched, in the care of Lal Singh, over the Karakoram to Kashmir, he set out with Afrazgul on 6 July 1915. His plan was to travel down through Russian Turkestan, following the route the ancient silk traders would have used from China to the middle Oxus. The Government of India had agreed to arrange permission for this through the British Ambassador in Petrograd (St Petersburg) and its task had undoubtedly been eased by the fact that Russia was now Britain's ally. Where once he might have expected to meet suspicion and hostility, Stein received a hearty welcome. Assistance came from Russian officers at every Pamir post, and villagers along the route were forewarned and instructed to help with guides and transport.

The journey was made all the happier by the knowledge that contact with Harriet had been re-established, thanks to Thomas Arnold and a friend, Professor F. Vogel, in Leiden, Holland. Both had offered to act as 'post-boxes' for Stein and his sister-in-law. Harriet and her children were still together in Vienna; Ernst had not been called up and Thesa was working in a hospital.

Following the old Silk Route down the broad Alai valley on the northern rampart of the Pamirs, Stein then turned south across high, snowy mountains towards the Oxus. The serrated ice-peaks delighted and frustrated him at the same time, for survey work was not included in his travel permit. At the gorges of the Murghab River, he was forced to scramble along steep mountainsides and across great slides of rock debris caused by an earthquake in 1911 which had blocked the valley and created a seventeen-mile-long lake on what had once been a favourite grazing ground of the Kirghiz nomads. Without the hillmen who were with him, further progress would have been impossible. But their ability to built *rafiks*, or ledges, out of brushwood and stones enabled Stein and his baggage to cross treacherous scree slopes and precipices, and pass through the devastated area to the far older Yeshil-kol Lake.

His route led on to Lake Victoria, where the borders of Russia and Afghanistan meet in the Great Pamir and which Marco Polo believed to be the highest place in the world. It was at this point in the Venetian's journey that he had described the magnificent horned wild sheep which is named after him, *Ovis poli*, and which every Western explorer and hunter on the Pamirs at one time hoped to acquire as a trophy. Stein was no different in this respect, though it was Afrazgul who shot the specimen that he took back to Kashmir.

'Many points of the historical geography of Pamirs & the high valleys around them have become clear to me on this journey to a degree which no poring over maps & books could assure,' Stein wrote to Publius.[55] It was the sort of journey he loved best, where he could identify the places and routes described by early writers, and observe the different racial characteristics and languages or dialects of the tribes inhabiting the region. The first Iranian-speaking settlement of hill Tajiks, and the people of the remote Roshan valley, interested him in particular, since their alpine isolation seemed to have preserved the customs and culture of a much earlier age.

From Roshan and Russian Wakhan, adjacent to the Oxus, there were tantalizing glimpses of Afghan territory on the far side of the river. But he had to be content with no more than glimpses. On 22 October he reached Samarkand at the end of a journey from Kashgar of more than three months and 1,700 miles.[56] After a couple of days spent sight-seeing there and at Bokhara, he boarded the Transcaspian Railway to Ashkhabad on the Iranian border, and was in the British Consulate in Meshed, Iran, four days later.

The fact that war had begun since Stein planned this final stage of his journey through Iran did not make for ideal circumstances. Both Germany and Turkey had ambitions to use the country as a route to Afghanistan, from which they could threaten British India. But Stein was well-equipped with help and advice from his hosts in the British consulates. The occasional cryptic comment in his letters suggests that the trip from Meshed to Sistan was not without incident, passing as it did through country frequented at the time by scouts and spies. But he committed little to paper on the subject, either publicly or privately, beyond describing his escort as 'picturesque fellows provided with an abundance of modern weapons such as any Pathan might envy'.[57]

Sistan was an area that had interested him since his student days. His hope was to find proof of an Iranian-Hellenistic culture; and it was amply rewarded when, in early December, in well-known ruins on the hill of Koh-i-Khwaja, he made a thrilling discovery. Hidden behind later masonry were the remains of a Buddhist sanctuary, with a fresco which, he estimated, dated from Sassanian times (the third to seventh centuries AD), while another part of the building held wall-paintings that were probably older, and distinctly Hellenistic in style. Here was the explanation of the Persian Bodhisattva he had found painted on a panel at Dandan-Uiliq fifteen years earlier.

Despite the fact that they had been ravaged by white ants, Stein was able to remove the panels, determined to take to India this first tangible proof of the extension of Buddhist worship and artistic style into Iran proper, and of the Iranian link in a chain that stretched from the Mediterranean to China.

His resolve nearly caused a diplomatic incident in Tehran. News reached the Iranian Minister of Arts that he was 'digging for treasure' at Koh-i-Khwaja; and the local officials in Sistan duly received an order that anything found was to be sent to the capital. 'This fortunately could not be done', the British Consul in Sistan later reported in a telegram to the British Minister in Tehran, 'as the frescoes would doubtless have been destroyed in the unpacking. In their present condition they have no value.'[58] The British diplomats had seriously underestimated the effect Stein's visit might have, and were aware that any further digging would raise the issue of the monopoly concession which the French held on excavation in Iran.

Meanwhile, Stein, wily as ever where the machinations of officialdom were concerned, had already packed his finds on to camels and dispatched them to India. He fully recognized the nature of his behaviour: 'unabashed interloping', as he described it to a friend at the British Museum, Lionel Barnett.[59] A few weeks later, he followed the same route westward across Baluchistan to Quetta and onward to Delhi. It was late Feburary 1916 and he had been away for two years and eight months. His explorations had carried him nearly 11,000 miles across Central Asia, his finds were more numerous than ever and his reputation as an authority on the archaeology of the Silk Road was unchallenged. But the war cast long shadows, and in some ways he was as uncertain of the reception he would receive as he had been as an ambitious, inexperienced young academic thirty years earlier.

I I

On the Trail of Alexander the Great

———————◆———————

STEIN'S UNCERTAINTY HINGED on the origin of his name. This time it was not its Jewishness that threatened to attract unwelcome attention, as it might have in Austria-Hungary at times during the past thirty-odd years. The question in his mind concerned the reception that might be given, in a country at war with Germany, to a man whose name was obviously Germanic.

'I sometimes wonder what change in personal relations I must be prepared for on my hoped for return to England in the spring,' he had written to Publius late in 1915. 'It is impossible for me to advertise my feelings about the country to sundry & all, and I do not expect to escape unpleasant or even trying experiences.'[1] Thousands of enemy aliens had been interned in Britain, and German-owned shops had been looted. Stein evidently doubted that his British citizenship would shield him entirely. A letter from Andrews reporting that an artist in Kashmir had been treated badly by some residents because of her German origins, despite having been born a British subject, seemed to confirm his apprehensions.

Several friends in India tried to dissuade him from going to Europe at such a time. But he had made his plans long before, and the outbreak of war only intensified his desire to arrange a reunion with Harriet somewhere on neutral ground. Against the prospect of prejudice he would protect himself by seeking refuge with the Allens in Oxford.

It was all he could do. However strong his own views, he had always avoided confrontation and sought to maintain civil relations with others. He shrank from the idea of 'unpleasantness' – the nearest term he could bring himself to use to describe being branded as the enemy – and could hope to escape it only by attracting as little attention as possible. Though he presented a paper on his expedition to the Royal Geographical Society soon after arriving in England in mid-1916, his anxieties were evident in his reply to an invitation from Keltie to speak again the following year: 'I *earnestly* hope, I shall be excused from speaking at the Meeting,' he confided. 'I feel strongly that under present circumstances it would not be advisable for me to speak in public. Few in the audience would know more about me than my mere name, – and this is enough to counsel silence.'[2]

In India he felt more comfortable. Arriving in Delhi from Sistan at the close of his expedition in late February 1916, he stayed with Hailey, one of his old Lahore circle of friends who was now in charge of the creation of the new capital.[3] He saw the site of New Delhi with its architects, Edwin Lutyens and Herbert Baker; he visited the Viceroy. He spent a few days at Dehra Dun with the head of the Trigonometrical Survey; was a guest of the Governor of the Punjab, Sir Michael O'Dwyer, in Lahore; stayed with Marshall (now Sir John) at Taxila; and in Peshawar enjoyed a brief reunion with his old military friend Dunsterville, now a general.

Some of the most influential posts in the land were filled by men he had known for many years, and his journeys in India were now punctuated by social calls. The comparative sociability of his life sometimes surprised him. But he found security and reassurance in the long-standing friendship of these men and the knowledge that they were in charge at a time of such uncertainty.

Through the man he had known longest of all, Edward Maclagan (now Education Secretary), he volunteered his services to the Chief of General Staff in India for work in Iran. Since his immediate task was completed, he told Publius, he felt he owed it to the empire 'which has treated me so generously and to which I feel proud to belong'.[4] His offer was never taken up and it was Dunsterville, in charge of what became known as Dunsterforce, who went to north-west Iran and the Caucasus in 1918 to counter German and Turkish ambitions in Asia.[5]

Before sailing for England, Stein returned briefly to Kashmir. Apart from his desire to enjoy the valley again in spring, his favourite season, he was eager to see the Andrews and assure himself that they had settled happily at Srinagar. Delightedly, he reported to Publius that they seemed even more content than he had hoped, 'as if the long years in grimy London which separate their Lahore & Kashmir lives, had been obliterated'.[6] They had decided to build a new house in the compound of the Institute, but for the time being were living in a pleasant rented place and had made many friends.

Stein felt that Fred Andrews was making a good impression among both European and state officials. From long experience he knew all the drawbacks to work in India; but he was also convinced that this was the best opportunity his friend would ever get to convert his gifts and expertise into real professional achievement. The main threat to that prospect lay in the discouragement to which Andrews was prey, for it was discouragement that had prompted him to leave Lahore in 1898 and which had worn him down in Battersea. Stein could only hope that the charms of the mountain kingdom would help to disperse the irritations that were bound to come his way. Despite his faith in Kashmir's healing powers, however, he kept a watchful eye for signs of discontent, like an anxious parent fearing the recurrence of illness in a child. Events were soon to prove his caution only too well-founded.

He had an additional reason for hoping Andrews would settle in Kashmir. The collection of antiquities from his third expedition was to stay in India, having been funded solely by the Indian government, and he had won permission for most of it to remain temporarily in Srinagar while it was examined and catalogued by his friend.

This was doubly satisfactory. Not only did Andrews' work on previous collections in London make him, in Stein's opinion, the best person for the task, but Stein would not have to leave the valley in order to work on his latest finds. The Kashmir Darbar even agreed to spend an extra Rs3,000 on the building of an annexe at Andrews' new house to provide the necessary working space. Marshall had arranged for the frescoes to be housed separately at Lahore; everything would eventually be transported to a proposed museum at Delhi. In the meantime, Stein hoped to persuade Andrews' assistant at the British Museum, Miss Lorimer – nicknamed by them the Recording Angel – to continue in her role, at the Indian government's cost, by coming out to Kashmir.

Stein himself could not start work on the results of his third expedition until his labours on the second were complete. *Serindia* was only half finished and he was threatened with the division of the second collection before he had time to return to London to see it intact. The Indian authorities and the British Museum had reached a not altogether amicable agreement about the destination of each piece – each side believing the other to have been greedy – and the Government of India was now anxious to see its share safely returned to the East. No doubt helped by the danger of transporting it during wartime, Stein won a delay until he could reach London and finish his book. In April 1916 he set out again for the West with more than a year of work ahead of him and, equally important, the hope of a reunion with his sister-in-law.

England in wartime was a grimmer place than he had known. London was pock-marked by bomb damage and pitch dark after nightfall. The introduction of conscription coincided with his arrival, and most of his friends had sons, husbands or brothers at the Front. In Oxford, Helen Allen was devoting herself to the care of Belgian refugees, of whom there were more than 100,000 in the country. There had been changes in the Allens' domestic life too. When Stein left England in December 1911, his friends moved from Longwall Cottage to 23 Merton Street. This much larger house had been occupied by Helen's parents until their deaths in 1910 and 1911. Now Publius and Helen shared it with her sister Olga and his sister Maud – and, of course, Dash the Great.

The house (which stood on the site now occupied by the Eastgate Hotel), looked on to the Examination Schools, temporarily in use as a hospital. From the back there was a view of Magdalen Tower, gardens and the village of Iffley in the distance. Stein knew that view well from Publius's letters, in the same way that he knew so much about England. Through the couple's recent explorations of the Cotswolds he was introduced to the Plough Inn at Ford, near Stow-on-the-Wold, and occasionally spent a few days there when he needed to work. But for longer periods away from the British Museum, which he planned from September onwards in order to finish writing *Serindia*, an inn was not ideal. Shortly after taking a brief holiday in Cornwall and Devon with the Arnolds, he advertised for a 'retreat' in the West Country and in August 1916 made several excursions from Exeter in order to choose between those which had sounded suitable in replies.

He settled on the rectory at Ashreigney, a small village on the windswept uplands of North Devon above the Taw valley. In his initial enthusiasm he likened the Georgian wing of the building to Clanville, the Hampshire house where he had stayed so happily with the Andrews in 1903. But the similarities were, in fact, slight and his contentment was short-lived. The Bennetts, whose home it was, provided 'primitive' food which prompted a recurrence of Stein's old problem, dyspepsia. They combed Exeter and Barnstaple for a better cook but without success. Eventually, Stein left in search of a diet that would not disrupt what he called his 'internal economy'.

He turned to another house which he had already visited, and which was to become his English substitute for Mohand Marg: Middlecott, near Haytor on the southern slopes of Dartmoor. It stood alone amid small fields and narrow lanes, a little way below the crags of the tor itself and outside the village, then a remote and quiet place. Its owner, J. H. Lyon, was an architect whose designs included the chapel at Sydney Sussex College, Cambridge, as well as the lych-gate of his local church at Ilsington.

Lyon's policy was to let a few rooms to gentlemen in need of peace and seclusion, an arrangement which suited Stein perfectly. From his study there were splendid views, and there was no need to fraternize with other guests – though, in fact, he enjoyed the company of the two young men who were recovering there from the fighting in France. His work proceeded well, each day ending, as was his habit on Mohand Marg, with a walk of about two hours, which here took him across the moors and through surrounding hamlets and villages. And the cooking at Middlecott suited his digestive system.

Lyon himself was 'full of culture and humour' and Stein thought his garden one of the loveliest he had ever seen. He remained at Middlecott for the rest of his stay in England, venturing out occasionally on trips to London and a brief Christmas holiday with the Allens in Oxford: his first spent with them there. The only regular interruption he allowed to his reclusive habits were Sunday evening visits to Edymead in the nearby village of Bovey Tracey, the home of an old acquaintance from Lahore days, Alfreda Maynard, the American wife of Herbert John Maynard of the ICS. The Maynard home became what he described as a 'lit-up window' in his life at a time which was otherwise overshadowed by events in Europe.

Plans to meet Harriet developed slowly. Stein had begun enquiries soon after arriving in England, and had managed to arrange the necessary permissions for himself to travel to neutral Switzerland. But he was frustrated at being unable to do the same for his sister-in-law, since she seemed unwilling to summon up the requisite energy to organize matters for herself in Vienna. She was in mourning for her sister's elder son, Richard, who had been killed in action, and she received little help in practical affairs from her own self-centred son Ernst. Moreover, her performance as a correspondent did not match Stein's and he often had to beg her to communicate, if only on a postcard, simply to let him know she was still well.

In late June, she did write, but only to say that she felt unable to face the prospect of the journey alone across Austria to Switzerland. Stein's swift reply, urging her to persevere, reveals the thinking behind his own determined approach to problems. It was the hope of seeing her that had brought him to Europe 'in spite of difficulties & misgivings', he told her. He understood her reluctance, but implored her to consider the reasons for overcoming it:

> In the first place long experience in the course of my travels has shown me how often difficulties & obstacles in the way of one's programme are exaggerated by distance and the effect of novel conditions on one's imagination. I have always made it a point to counter-act the pessimistic disposition which by nature I share with you, by ascertaining the facts as accurately as possible beforehand and sticking to my plans unless the information should prove them quite impracticable. Could you not do the same and assure yourself whether a lady of your position & character would really be exposed to indignities such as you apprehend?[7]

Harriet agreed to keep trying. But on 17 August – the birthday of his brother which Stein never failed to mention each year in his letters to her – a telegram announced that she had failed to get a permit, and that the reunion must therefore be cancelled. Stein had already packed in anticipation of starting for Switzerland in the next day or two. The news, he wrote in his diary, came as a 'great blow from the blue'.[8]

Work on *Serindia* presented its own problems. The business of eliciting appendices from scholars in several different countries, which he had first tackled for *Ancient Khotan*, required patience and tact at the best of times. Though it was now nearly a decade since his return from the second expedition, much remained to be done. Pelliot had withdrawn his offer to catalogue the Chinese Tun-huang manuscripts in 1913, but two cases of material sent to him in 1910 had still not been returned, and he was now on military duty outside France. Another collaborator, Petrucci, died in 1917 before finishing his contribution and Hoernle died on Armistice Day.

Stein had not been pleased to hear in 1914 that Edward Denison Ross, the man who had succeeded him at the Calcutta Madrasah in 1901, had taken over the cataloguing of his collection at the British Museum on Andrews' departure for Kashmir. In letters to his friend at the Museum, Lionel Barnett, he made several rather snide remarks about Ross, referring to his 'meteoric flittings' and his ambition for 'some more conspicuous preferment'.[9] Ross remained for only a few months before being moved to the War Office, becoming (as Stein had expected) head of London University's new School of Oriental Studies in 1916.[10]

The sole thread of continuity on the Stein collection was provided by Miss Lorimer, who had worked at the Museum for several years and knew more about the organization of the material than anyone apart from Andrews.[11] In 1914 she had arranged antiquities from the second expedition to provide the opening exhibition in the main hall of the then new King Edward VII galleries.[12] Later, she too was tempted by a position at the School of Oriental Studies; but she decided to stay and to move out to Kashmir in 1919 to continue her connection with Stein's work. Stein had hoped she would arrive earlier, and thought she was dissuaded from travelling by fear of submarines and ill-health. Arnold put him right by pointing out that she would have been ready to leave sooner if Stein had not given her so much to do in London first.

The greatest blow, however, came in early 1918 with news of the death, at only 53, of Edouard Chavannes, the French Sinologist who had been Stein's advocate and colleague for many years. He had always been an enthusiastic, inspired and reliable collaborator whose expertise in early Chinese documents Stein admired enormously. 'Oriental research has suffered far more by his premature death', Stein wrote to Marshall, 'than it possibly could have by any half-dozen of workers like myself... nobody will ever replace Chavannes.'[13] For practical purposes, however, a replacement had to be found to work on the Chinese documents collected during Stein's third expedition, and it was Chavannes's successor at the Collège de France, Henri Maspero, who undertook that task.

———————◀————◀———————

The war was still raging when the time came for Stein to return to India. It was late September 1917: the third campaign at Ypres, otherwise known by the name of its last battleground, Passchendaele, was grinding towards its total of half a million casualties. America had entered the war and Russia was seeking a separate peace following the abdication of the Tsar in April.

Stein had suffered little personal inconvenience as a result of the conflict, apart from the cancellation of his trip to see Harriet. His work had proceeded as planned and there was nothing to prevent him travelling back to India, so long as he was undeterred by the threat of enemy submarine patrols in the Mediterranean. During a couple of bizarrely inappropriate days such as the conditions of war always provide, he even managed to go sightseeing in Avignon and Arles while waiting to embark at Marseilles. But the effects of the conflict were all around him and his chief wish was to retreat to Mohand Marg, where he could cut himself off from the horrors of the present and lose himself in study of the past.

He did not remain totally aloof from the war. He was doing his best to arrange for books to be sent to his Hungarian translator, Halász, who was a prisoner-of-war in Romania; and for tea and cigars to reach Harriet's nephew, Alexander, a captive in Siberia. He sympathized deeply with friends and acquaintances who had lost sons, husbands and brothers, regardless of whether they had fought with the Allies or the Central Powers. But he was afflicted by moments of despair and the fear of being unable to fend them off. By nature pessimistic, he believed he could keep such feelings at bay by determined action and a steady succession of plans and absorbing work. But in Europe his resilience had faltered. He felt too far from the deserts and mountains of Asia, and the reassurance they gave of timeless, unchanging strengths.

In Kashmir, his life now began a pattern more regular than anything he had known for years. He spent the summers on Mohand Marg with his band of servants and clerks, sometimes as many as twenty in number. (They continued to live under canvas, however, since the idea of building a hut on the Marg seems to have been abandoned.) The local people had a proprietorial interest in their 'sahib' and he tried to live up to their expectations, applying for an irrigation channel to be rc-opened for them, for example, and helping Hatim secure a piece of land. At the same time, he pressed for a land grant in the Punjab for Lal Singh and promotion for Afrazgul Khan: he was more aware than most of the contribution his surveyors and assistants had made to the success of his expeditions. He sent wild flowers regularly to Publius, Helen and other friends: some still lie between the pages of his letters where they were left by their recipients.

In October he would move camp (with the help of forty or fifty men) down to an old Mogul garden beside the Dal Lake, and stay there until the cold weather forced him into warmer accommodation. At first this was Dal View Cottage, his old winter haunt, which had become a cosier retreat since the installation of electric heating. Later, he lived nearby in Almond Cottage and, for a couple of seasons, in a villa farther away at Jyethir. He described their comforts rather self-consciously to Publius but evidently enjoyed filling them with books and with the carpets that were one of his few luxuries.

Fred Andrews had hoped that his old friend would stay at the Technical Institute's new official residence each winter. But the building was still in a chaotic state and Stein was not prepared to bear the inconveniences of living on a construction site as the Andrews did. He was dismayed to witness their growing obsession with the project and the continual frustration they suffered. Andrews was a perfectionist and a poor delegator: he made by hand no fewer than 30,000 red tiles for the roof of the house, rarely allowed himself more than half a day away from the Institute compound, and ignored his annual holiday entitlement.

As the years went by the couple seemed to become more and more enslaved by their home. Neither of them adjusted to the ways of Kashmiri workers, their building costs snowballed (though the Kashmir Darbar agreed to go on paying) and Alice Andrews grew so concerned about security that she rarely left the house. What had seemed like the opportunity of a lifetime had turned into what Stein privately, in letters to Publius, described as the 'baronial prison'. He tried several times to tempt his friend up to Mohand Marg for a few days' holiday (Alice Andrews was not the type to enjoy climbing and camping) but seldom succeeded – though it was gratifying to witness

Andrews' enjoyment when he did come. Describing the first such occasion (in August 1918) to Harriet, Stein remarked: 'Nature helps one so much, if one can only be with her, to bear up against cares and anxieties to which we humans are subject – and to which we give rise.'[14]

Whatever cares and anxieties Andrews left behind him when he climbed to Mohand Marg, he found that it still paid to be wary when sharing his friend's table. He knew that Stein was anxious to please him in culinary matters and so was equally keen to return the compliment by showing his satisfaction, especially when something was produced specially for him, such as the porridge that was served one morning. 'But there was a queer tang with it which at first puzzled me,' he recalled later.

> [Stein] detected something in my expression in spite of my care to hide it, and after breakfast showed me his store chest wherein the bag of meal had been packed. There were a few books and files and such relatively harmless things and, as protection against moth and other devouring insects, a lot of loose naphthalene balls! Kerosene I knew as a frequent flavouring element in camp food in India, but naphthalene was a novelty.[15]

Andrews also recorded, however, that Stein once gave him a traditional Hungarian dish he had prepared himself, which suggests his knowledge of food was a little less basic than others supposed. His diet was certainly simple, however, and was pared down further when, a few years later, he virtually gave up meat on the advice of a doctor, in order to combat the first signs of rheumatism in one arm. Otherwise, his physical fitness remained unimpaired. His maimed foot gave him only occasional minor discomfort and he was still able to make the climb to the Marg in the same time it had taken years earlier. Perhaps this was because he carried no excess weight. He was leaner than he had been when young, weighing only nine and a half stone in 1916.

According to the terms of his employment, he was due to retire at the age of 55, in other words, at the end of 1917. It was a date he had looked forward to during earlier periods of his life, when he had seen retirement as the only way of escaping frustration with the ways of Indian bureaucracy. Now that it was not difficult to arrange things to his own satisfaction, however, he preferred to stay on. Through Maclagan he obtained an extension of service on 'special duty' which, though only annual, was to be renewed until he had completed work on his third expedition.

His writing work seemed unending. He was busy with the text for the portfolio, *The Thousand Buddhas*, as a complement to the still-unfinished *Serindia*, and an atlas of Central Asian maps was to follow. At last, in mid-1918, he wrote the final words of *Serindia* on the Marg, lighting a massive bonfire to signal the news to the Andrews, over twenty miles away. Now could begin the lengthy task of assembling *Innermost Asia*, his scholarly report on his third journey. This was the only one of his Central Asian expeditions of which he wrote no popular account. While he did give a number of lectures, and his address to the Royal Geographical Society was long enough to fill a short book, he felt that this wide coverage of his activities excused him from what he regarded as the chore of producing something for the general public.

At the same time, he began to pay regular visits to Delhi. For some time there had been talk of the creation of an Ethnological Museum in the new capital and this was to be the ultimate destination of his third collection, once Andrews and Miss Lorimer had catalogued it in Srinagar. The frescoes, however, were soon transferred to Delhi, and Stein and Andrews moved there each cold-weather season to oversee the construction of a separate building where they were eventually mounted (and where they remained, while what became the National Museum of India was built alongside). For the first few years, Stein shared a bungalow with Andrews and his wife in Queens Way, near the Museum. Later they all stayed at the enormous new Western Court, built as a hostel for legislators.

Stein saw much more of the Haileys during these visits than he had for years and was inevitably drawn into a certain amount of socializing. He valued the opinions of the influential men he met and sympathized more and more strongly with their difficulties, as opposed to those of the India Office in Britain. When the Punjab erupted and the infamous 1919 Amritsar Massacre, in particular, attracted much criticism outside India, he viewed the crisis entirely from an Anglo-Indian position, defending the provincial governor, his friend Sir Michael O'Dwyer, and accusing critics at home of weakness and ignorance of conditions in the East.

His disgust at anti-imperial agitation in India, however, was mild compared with his mortification at post-war confusion in Europe.

Bolshevism seemed a 'contagion' and what he heard from Macartney, who stopped for a few days in Kashmir on his way home from a final assignment in Russian Turkestan, convinced him that it was 'plain mob rule spread simply for the spoliation of those who own something by demagogue robbers'.[16] The 'contagion' reached Hungary early in 1919 but its reign was brief and it was followed by something even worse. The terms of the Treaty of Trianon of June 1920 ripped the country apart, assigning the south to the new state of Yugoslavia, the north to Czechoslovakia and giving Transylvania, in the east, to Romania. Hungary was left with a third of her pre-war territory and population, and hundreds of thousands of Magyar refugees.

However detached Stein had been about his homeland in the past, Trianon made his blood boil. He could not refer to events in eastern Europe without appending scathing remarks about the supposed wisdom of the Allies, and Harriet's reports of raging inflation and starvation in Vienna made him increasingly bitter. His sister-in-law had never liked the city, and Stein himself called it 'doomed', sunk in 'ruin, disgrace & starvation'; but he railed against the crippling reparations demanded by the victors of the war. Having pinned his hopes at first on Woodrow Wilson's plans for peace, disillusion quickly followed and even prompted him into scornful responses to the Allens' more optimistic outlook. Though he regarded their attitude as saintly, and told them so, his letters of the early 1920s often sound angry; he was simultaneously admiring and dismissive of their unworldly views. His difficulty, he once commented to Andrews, was that he did not possess Publius's 'strength of faith to close my eyes to facts'.[17]

At the very end of 1919, Stein sailed again for Europe. Despite his reluctance to get a closer view of the 'body on the dissecting table', as he called the former Austro-Hungarian Empire, he was determined to see Harriet. They met on the newly redrawn Austro-Italian border on 25 January 1920. It was more than eight years since they had last been together. He thought his sister-in-law had aged (perhaps he had too, though that may not have occurred to him) but that she was otherwise still spirited. Wishing to bring her relief from the worries of the past six years, he took charge of their holiday, bearing all the costs himself and ushering her off to the shores of Lake Como for several weeks. Italy was inexpensive against the Indian rupee and even Switzerland offered cheaper living than England. He brought her a fur-lined cape from

Kashmir (dyed black since he knew she would not otherwise wear it), comforted her by recollecting their happy past before the 'great cataclysm' and, putting his own doubts to one side, encouraged her to think positively of the future.

She was still concerned about her children: less so for Thesa, who had begun to study medicine, than for Ernst. His desire for an academic career remained unfulfilled and he was no easier to live with than before. Stein offered to help support his nephew and niece until they found careers for themselves (though he felt it would do Ernst no harm to be forced to make an effort and earn some money for himself). To persuade Harriet to let him contribute, he invoked the memory of his brother in the pious accents he always used in that context: 'You know best what the sacrifices made by our dear dead during my youth meant for me and how sacred to me is the obligation they entailed.'[18] On hearing of Ernst's conversion to Catholicism, however, he could find little to say. The family was Protestant in culture and temperament and his nephew's renunciation of that inheritance (however recent) amazed him, wounded Harriet and certainly drew neither of them any nearer to Ernst.

Stein's 1920 visit to Europe was a distraction from revived plans for a tour in Afghanistan. This time, he felt, he was near to achieving his ambition. In February 1919, the Amir Habibullah was murdered and his third son, Amanullah, succeeded to the throne, almost immediately issuing aggressive statements and preparing his eastern frontiers for war. For a month, Afghan and Indian forces sparred while the British Indian authorities tried to assess the seriousness of the threat.

As soon as Stein heard of what he called the Amir's 'propitious folly', he fired off copies of his 1912 Bactrian proposal to Simla. He did not relish the thought of travelling in the wake of an invading army, as he had done in Buner in 1898, but he could no longer afford to insist upon ideal circumstances. He was approaching his sixtieth birthday; he had been waiting for four decades for an opportunity to follow in Alexander's footsteps to the banks of the Oxus and he was aware that health and fitness could desert him at any time. He asked for permission to use the opportunity presented by war to explore the Kabul, Pandshir and Ghorband valleys. If operations were to extend beyond the Hindu Kush, perhaps he would be able to go on to Bamian and Balkh. He was already on 'special duty', so no special arrangements concerning his employment need be made. He began to refresh his memory of the Pushtu language. Letters flew from Mohand Marg to all his eminent friends.

The Third Afghan War, however, was a brief affair. The British had no stomach for prolonged fighting after the events of the past few years and the Afghans were intimidated by their use of aircraft to bomb Kabul and Jalalabad. A ceasefire was declared on 3 June 1919 and negotiations began soon afterwards. For the sake of peace in India and the Muslim world, Stein was glad the fighting was over. Besides, he saw in the changing relationship between the two countries a chance for India to stake a claim to exploration beyond the Hindu Kush. And he saw himself, naturally, as the person who would represent her in that task.

Of all the friends who offered encouragement at this period, none was more supportive than Alfred Foucher, the French scholar whom Stein had first met when he visited north-west India with his aunt, Madame Michel, in 1896. Foucher had become an authority on the art of Gandhara in the intervening years. When Stein heard that he was anxious to escape the gloom of wartime Paris, he strongly recommended his friend to the Archaeological Survey of India. The two men – who were about the same age – met whenever possible in Paris; Stein admired his colleague's abilities and enjoyed his company. So he was delighted when, thanks in part to his own influence, the Government of India and the government of the Nizam of Hyderabad extended a joint invitation to Foucher, which he accepted.

He was to be paid Rs 10,000 to produce a descriptive account of the Ajanta frescoes in the Nizam's state, to help catalogue Gandharan sculptures at Taxila and Peshawar, and to contribute to a monograph on the Buddhist monuments of Sanchi, in Gwalior, which Marshall had been restoring for some years. In letters to friends in the months preceding Foucher's arrival, Stein referred enthusiastically to the forthcoming event and India's great good fortune in securing the services of so talented a scholar.

The two met again on Indian soil in January 1919 when they spent several days with Marshall at Sanchi. Stein was one of the few people to whom Foucher confided the reason for his abrupt departure from that site. He was going to Ceylon in order to welcome and marry his fiancée, a former student of his at the Sorbonne who was nearly thirty years his junior. Stein took an innocent delight in the shared secret (necessary, said Foucher, because of his aunt's disapproval of the match) and considered his friend's happiness well-deserved. He was to go on believing the best of Foucher's intentions until there could be no room for doubt, and events forced him to recognize the treachery of a friend.

Knowing of Stein's eagerness to exploit the Afghan crisis of mid-1919, Foucher offered to help by seeking the support of orientalists in France. At the time, Stein did not notice that his own name featured indistinctly in his friend's enthusiastic recommendations of the project to colleagues in Paris. Meanwhile, the moment for a British invasion passed; Stein spent 1920 in Europe, holidaying with Harriet and finishing writing tasks associated with the second expedition, and resumed his campaign for an expedition to northern Afghanistan only on his return to the East. Plans to see Foucher at Muttra and Agra in December 1920 had to be altered when Foucher suddenly seemed to evade the meeting, but Stein, busy now with the results of his third journey to Chinese Central Asia, gave the matter no more thought. He saw the Viceroy, Lord Reading, in Kashmir and found him ready to raise the matter of archaeology with the Afghans. Sir John Marshall promised to find the necessary funds for an expedition from his department's budget, hard pressed though it had been since the war.

But 1921 passed, 1922 dawned and still there was no definite progress. A new British minister arrived in Kabul, Major Francis Humphrys, the son-in-law of Stein's old frontier friend Sir Harold Deane. Through him Stein hoped for better news. At the same time, he heard that Foucher, who had left India for Iran in April 1921, had been invited to Kabul. 'That F. is specially going to Kabul in order to antici-pate my B. plans I do not believe,' he told Publius.[19] He doubted if his friend would welcome the physical hardship of such work, particularly since his wife was with him; besides which, the betrayal of his own plans by a friend was something he preferred not to contemplate. On the other hand, he knew that Foucher, for reasons that were unclear, wanted to stay away from France and *la tante terrible*, and that he had a highly placed friend in the French foreign ministry who was responsible for securing the invitation.

An Afghan mission had been in Europe recently and had invited various foreign scientific expeditions to the country – excluding, of course, the British. It was clear that the Amir's establishment of relations with other nations was a demonstration of his determination to do as he wished in foreign affairs, regardless of British India's claim to control his country's external affairs. But Stein continued to believe in diplomacy. He met Humphrys in Delhi and gave him a detailed proposal of his trip, emphasizing that it should be made clear to the Amir that he did not intend to claim any objects found, nor to remove them from Afghanistan. He knew he was suspected of wanting to hunt for 'treasure' and was happy to renounce finds (which he was certain, anyway, would not be the sort of 'treasure' his potential hosts would covet) for the sake of simply being able to explore the ground that Alexander's Greeks had once trodden.

The first outright refusal from the Amir came in early April 1922. Stein's application to visit Afghan Turkestan was dismissed because of the 'disturbed state' of that area. Humphrys promised to try again; but to no avail. Stein recognized the game the Afghans were playing. He preferred to regard Foucher as a pawn in that game rather than a leading player, and to attribute his 'driving power' to the ambition of his wife. But he could not deny that he felt sadly let down by the friend whose employment in India he had done so much to facilitate.

Foucher had apparently been given a warm welcome in Kabul and was planning to visit various sites. Soon he wrote to Stein. He did not want to seem ungrateful to the Archaeological Survey of India, he said; he admired Stein's work and did not expect the Afghans to refuse him access much longer. He claimed his hosts had forced the present arrangement 'down his throat'. Stein could not but react sceptically to such protestations – he called them 'prevarication and cant'. The French had used archaeological enterprise as a political instrument before, he pointed out to Publius, in Egypt, Syria and Iran, and they could do so again in Afghanistan. He suspected that they were bent on securing an archaeological monopoly (though he excluded his other colleagues in Paris from this ambition; they appeared embarrassed and apologetic).

While this was a dismal prospect, it seemed to him that it offered a gleam of hope, too. For surely the threat of such an exclusive arrangement would rouse the authorities in India and Britain, even if his own ambitions were not enough to make them fight? A visitor to Mohand Marg, the former United States Chargé d'Affaires in Tehran, Cornelius

Van Heinert Engert, encouraged him to think the issue important enough to attract international support for his line of argument. So he set about one last burst of lobbying.

Despite agitation on his behalf by friends in England, however, and protests to the Amir from Delhi and London, his efforts were in vain. In May 1923, France agreed a convention with Afghanistan whereby she gained a monopoly of all archaeological work in the country. Some newspaper reports claimed Foucher would invite Stein to collaborate with him; others, in France, accused Stein of intriguing against the French concession. Once more, a tantalizing opportunity had slipped through his fingers. His opinion of Foucher had also been irrevocably altered by letters from Madame Michel, who damned her nephew in one succinct phrase: *Foucher ment comme les autres respirent* ('Foucher lies as others breathe').[20]

Disappointed though he was, Stein was not a man to bear grudges. He hoped for Foucher's sake that he was given funds and opportunities, and took comfort in Engert's forecast that, one day, when the Afghans had tired of 'twisting the lion's tail', there might yet be an Anglo-American archaeological expedition into Afghanistan. To Publius he wrote: 'My hope of reaching Bactria made me take to Oriental studies, brought me to England & India, gave me my dearest friends & chances of fruitful work, and for all this I must be deeply grateful to Fate.'[21]

The prospect of further 'fruitful work', however, was what preoccupied him now. Unstable conditions in China cast doubt on the idea of a return to the Tarim Basin; and he feared he would not be retained much longer by the Archaeological Survey which, in any case, was critically short of funds. Awards and medals continued to arrive, but they were no substitute for the chance of exploration.[22] He spent the winter days of 1922–3 working on his third collection, and his evenings sorting books in order to give the most valuable to the Hungarian Academy of Sciences. His thoughts often turned to death and his dread of being desk-bound and immobilized by advancing age. On hearing that his beloved Dash the Great had been killed by a motor-bus in Oxford late in 1918, he had remarked to the Allens that he would like to leave the world equally swiftly, causing no one any inconvenience, but preferably as a victim of avalanche or Pathan knife rather than of 'annihilating "civilization"'.[23]

He missed his dogs. A year after Dash II's death in Oxford, Dash III, who had lived with the Andrews since 1916, was attacked and killed by other dogs in Srinagar, and Stein enquired in vain for a replacement. He had bought a fine horse called Kenrod in the winter of 1918 but had had to sell him before leaving for Europe; and it was not until the summer of 1921 that he found the puppy that became Dash the fourth.

He was losing other friends, too. His faithful secretary in Kashgar, Chiang, died in 1921,[24] and the Haileys' daughter Gemma, whom Stein regarded as the embodiment of the ideal daughter and sister, tragically succumbed to cholera in 1922. The Dunstervilles had retired to the Isle of Man, the Macartneys to Jersey, and the Andrews were homesick for England after six months' leave there in 1920–1. Even the fact that their house in Srinagar was at last complete, after seven years of work, could not detain them. All the contents which they had collected over those seven years were put up for sale within twelve months of their return from leave, along with the two-seater Ford which they had bought and seldom used, and they left India in 1923.

For several years afterwards, they made winter visits to Delhi so that the Baron could continue to work on the frescoes (an arrangement Stein had been anxious to secure, since he felt some responsibility for his friend's employment). But their companionship had gone from Kashmir: there was no one to light bonfires for, or to receive flowers sent twice a week from the Marg. Kashmir itself was changing, filling with ever larger numbers of visitors and motor-cars each summer, and India was a different place since the war. Stein warned Publius that young Oxford graduates seeking a career there would find 'their ardour damped & much of their vigour useless' unless they were genuinely interested in things Indian and prepared to adapt to Indian thought and method.[25] The prestige of work in the empire was much reduced and the atmosphere in India tense.

———————◄———

While Stein's own work prospects seemed to contract, his plans for travel expanded. He had recently developed an interest in the Middle East and Asia Minor which had been stimulated by the friendship of Sir George Lloyd, Governor of Bombay, and Engert, both of whom knew the region well. On his way to and from Europe, Stein had spent the Christmases of both 1919 and 1920 with the Lloyds (whom he had first encountered in Kashmir), and in their home had met Gertrude Bell, the amateur British archaeologist whose work – and 'pluck' – he admired. Since then, ideas of a trip to Europe via Egypt, Syria and Constantinople had begun to take shape: 'my first attempt at qualified "globe-trotting"', he called it in a letter to his British Museum friend, Barnett.[26] In February 1924, having seen his third collection safely packed in Srinagar for transport to Delhi, he sailed from Bombay for Port Said with Dash IV (though there they parted, Dash going on to quarantine in England).

With his customary attention to language, he had engaged a Yemeni in Delhi beforehand in an attempt to learn some Arabic. His preoccupation caused some alarm at first in the shared Stein/Andrews household, as Fred Andrews later described. Alice, having heard shouts and strange, gurgling sounds coming from Stein's room during the lesson, made some anxious enquiry when they met later at tea.

> [He] explained that he had been trying to pronounce some of the gutterals, and in his endeavour to understand how to produce the sounds he had made the Arab open his mouth to display the position of the tongue in making the particular noise. As the lesson progressed their earnestness increased, they spoke louder and louder until they were shouting at one another.[27]

Lessons continued, with different tutors, throughout Stein's tour of Arab countries. In Egypt he stayed in Cairo and Luxor, visited the tomb of Tutankhamun with reluctance because of its 'notoriety', and was enchanted by the scenery and ruins at Aswan. Armed with an introduction from the Indian Foreign Department to Harry St John Philby, British chief representative at the court of Trans-Jordania (and father of Kim), he crossed the desert from Amman and basked for three days in the glory of the 'dreamland site' of Petra, together with two friends from the Alpine Club.

At Jerusalem he saw a 'strange medley of newcomers from all corners of Eastern Europe', which prompted him to refer, in a letter to Publius, to 'that questionable scheme of a "National Home"'. His education had made him unsympathetic towards the idea of a destiny for European

Jews separate from the rest of Europe, but he also saw what some chose to ignore: 'Fresh problems & conflicts are sure to be brewing there for the future.'[28] He travelled on to Acre, Haifa, Damascus, Baalbek and Beirut, and there was greeted by Publius's cousin, the consul-general H. E. Satow. Aleppo and Antioch followed, and a dozen Roman or Byzantine sites where he dismissed his official guide and gendarmes, preferring to rely on an escort of armed villagers. After a few days in Constantinople, he boarded a train in early May for the sixty-hour journey to Budapest.

He had been hoping to pass unnoticed through his home city. But his arrival coincided with the Academy of Science's annual week of meetings and he was welcomed there as a national hero. His presence was particularly poignant since the future of oriental studies in Hungary seemed so bleak. The country was in the grip of a reactionary regime under Admiral Horthy. Jewish and liberal intellectuals were being ostracized, the chair of Indo-European linguistics had been suspended in 1920 because of the holder's involvement in the progressive movement, and the only kind of orientalism that was approved concerned the ancient roots and gods of the Magyar race, a highly imprecise science.

It is in this context that Stein's gifts to the Academy of books and money (the latter, 20,000 Hungarian crowns, given anonymously) should be seen. He also ensured that the last unreserved copy of his portfolio, *The Thousand Buddhas*, went to the recently opened Hopp Ferenc Museum, which housed the oriental collection of an old friend of his father.[29] Magyar chauvinism was not at all to his taste and such donations were the only way in which he felt able to express his support for a nobler academic spirit.

By this time he had also drawn up plans to leave money in his will for a trust fund that would support both British and Hungarian orientalists in their research, an idea he had been nursing for years. But his support was carefully directed. Whatever he might have thought privately, he seems to have been scrupulous in avoiding any connection with political viewpoints. A letter he wrote in 1925 to his fellow Hungarian explorer, Emil Torday, demonstrates just how anxious he was to distance himself from any suggestion of partiality, perhaps to the point of showing some meanness of spirit. Torday had asked Stein to help find support for the establishment of a Readership in Hungarian in one of England's universities. Stein wrote in reply:

You are aware of the deep interest I take in the past and present of Hungary, the country which I feel it a privilege to claim as the land of my birth, and to which I owe a great deal as regards the direction my life's work as a scholar has taken.

But as a faithful subject of the British empire, to which I am attached by far more than the formal adoption secured many years ago, and also in view of my official position [toward] the Indian Government which I am proud to serve, I consider myself obliged to avoid even the semblance of any public activity as regards political relations between the land of my birth and the country of my adoption. As a student who likes to view things of the present, too, in historical perspective, I feel, I can do no more towards mitigating the effects of the past ill-fated conflict than to keep to my chosen field of research and to justify the trust placed in me by those who have generously helped me to do my work all through my Indian career.[30]

———————◄►—◄———————

Stein did not return to the final stretch of his Indian career until the end of 1925. He spent part of the summer of 1924 'in purdah', as he liked to term his periods of seclusion, working on *Innermost Asia* at a house on Shere Common in Surrey, the home of some friends of the Andrews. The rest of the season he passed in the Tyrol with Harriet, who was happier now that Thesa had qualified as a doctor.

He had always longed to share holidays on the Continent with the Allens. But such meetings had always eluded them and this time, though achieved, amounted to only thirty-six hours in Basle. Disappointment, however, was amply outweighed by the delight of seeing his dearest friend's talents finally recognized in full. Late in 1924, the Fellows of Corpus Christi College in Oxford elected P.S. Allen to be their President. Stein had wanted a position such as this for him for years: every time Publius gained some lesser distinction, it was to future honour that Stein always looked in hope and expectation.[31] Now the honour had been bestowed; and Stein was in England to share the celebrations. The following summer, after the Allens had moved into the President's Lodgings, they insisted on Stein occupying spacious rooms on its first floor until his departure for India in November.

Merit had also been recognized in the other members of Stein's original band of Lahore friends. On retiring from the India Office, where he had looked after the educational needs of Indian students in England for eleven years, the Saint (Thomas Arnold) was knighted in 1921 – and duly raised to the status of Hierarch by his friends. In 1924 Andrews' work also received recognition in the form of an OBE. The only jarring note in the harmonious mood of Stein's last months in England was the death of Dash IV. Stein had had the little dog for only four years and berated himself for having brought him to England (as, on the death of the first Dash, he had berated himself for having left him in Kashmir).

While for Stein the 1920s were a period in which horizons seemed to be narrowing, the decade was one of major discoveries in other archaeological fields. The *Illustrated London News* ran one excited feature after another: the first spectacular finds at the tomb of Tutankhamun in 1922; the unveiling of a hitherto completely unknown ancient civilization in the Indus valley (announced publicly by Marshall in 1924); and Leonard Woolley's work at Ur in Iraq which uncovered exquisite treasures of lapis lazuli and gold.

Stein rarely mentioned the work of these fellow-archaeologists in private correspondence, unless he was actually visiting one of their sites, as in Egypt in 1924. In general his view of other people's work was generous. Though he disliked the enormous publicity surrounding Carter's work in Egypt, for example, he commented to Barnett that 'such a "find" properly recorded on the spot must prove very helpful to research & may stir some intelligent millionaires to subsidize work elsewhere'.[32] He had always considered Schliemann's circumstances ideal – an archaeologist with enough money of his own to be completely independent – but welcomed any indication that the British government or wealthy individuals might be showing interest in supporting exploration.

If he ever wondered why he did not have as great a public following as some other archaeologists, he did not articulate the question in letters. He was not the type to court or enjoy the attentions of the press; his chief priority had always been to be left alone to pursue his work as he wished. And he had been fortunate in this respect for, once finances had been granted him by the Indian government, there could be no practical monitoring of his progress in the great wastes of Chinese Turkestan – as he had demonstrated whenever threatened with interference by local officials there. But the geographical remoteness of his work, coupled with his diffidence, seems to have taken its toll on his renown. Though his finds were exhibited intermittently, though he was recognized as an intrepid explorer and considered by some who knew him to be one of the greatest of all, the significance of his archaeological discoveries seems not to have captured the public imagination.

No doubt if he had worked in the Mediterranean or the Middle East, where tourists were used to wandering and whose ancient culture they had all been taught as children, his name would have been on more lips. If he had had a flamboyant patron, or dug up gold, his fame would almost certainly have increased. And his reputation might have spread farther had he been as adept at writing for the general reader as Woolley proved to be; but the vast majority of his writing remained beyond the public ken in hefty scholarly tomes and specialist publications.

He himself was not troubled by such concerns. The chief preoccupations of his latter years were, first, finding work that was congenial and kept him active; and, second, the efficient management of his savings in order to be able to finance family members or other causes as he saw fit, and to provide for the foundation of an archaeological trust fund after his death.

Though he had started life in India entirely dependent on his salary, and seems to have inherited nothing more than 2,000 crowns left to him by his brother in 1902, he had been careful with money all his life and by the 1920s had accumulated respectable savings. Papers in the Bodleian Library's Stein archive show that he had securities to the value of £24,794 at the beginning of 1922, and this information came from only one of the several different banks he used in Britain, India and Switzerland. There were other sources of income, too, such as royalties from his books which, though rarely published in print runs of more than 750, always sold out. He still had his salary, about Rs 1,250 per month as it had been since he joined the Archaeological Survey, and the promise of a pension after retirement.

And there was work to be done, albeit on a far smaller scale than the expeditions he had been used to in the past. On returning to India in late 1925, he heard that the ruler of Swat was prepared to admit him to his kingdom and to provide an escort and guides for a journey to the Pir Sar spur above the Indus. This was the place Stein hoped to identify as Mount Aornos, which Alexander the Great had captured from a local army on his way to the Indus in 327 BC.

Stein had been following the trail to Aornos for many years now. In

1904 he had visited and ruled out Mount Mahaban in Buner. In late 1921, while awaiting news from Kabul, he had made a rapid tour of the Hazara border near the left bank of the Indus to view the Pir Sar spur which a friend had long ago suggested might solve the mystery. At last, in mid-1925, settled conditions on the right bank of the Indus seemed to offer the ideal opportunity and Stein submitted a proposal to Sir Norman Bolton, Chief Commissioner of the North-West Frontier Province. The wheels of border diplomacy rolled into action, Marshall provided Rs 2,000 and by early March 1926 Stein was on his way, by car, across the plains to the Malakand Pass.

Entering Swat in 1926 was a very different experience to his early visits there in the 1890s. Where there had been only forts, hastily built military roads and armed escorts at the Malakand, there were now whole settlements of bungalows, a new canal bursting from beneath the hills and the freedom of movement that had come with pacification of the area. These were the benefits of the British Raj, and Stein approved. But what dictated his benevolent mood was the realization that the expedition ahead promised to be more relaxed and more purely enjoyable than any of his others. There was no detailed schedule to follow, no complex accounts to calculate, no hiring and discharging of bands of workers and no long list of sites spread across thousands of miles to visit. There was simply an extended ramble through beautiful, unknown territory evoking a romantic past, with the prospect of Alexander's Aornos as the climax of the trip. It was a seductive vision and Stein was not disappointed. He described his visit as 'the happiest wandering that I ever enjoyed between the Pamirs and the Indian Ocean'.[33]

Swat was ruled at the time by Miangul Gul-shahzada, who had pacified the area in the tradition of his grandfather, the saintly Akhund of Swat. After years of clan warfare among the local Pathans, the benefits of peace were beginning to appear. But the valley still knew little of the prosperity it had enjoyed in the early centuries AD, when monks from distant China made special pilgrimages to its Buddhist monasteries and shrines. Nevertheless, Stein found its modern condition in many ways as interesting as its past. He met and immediately liked its ruler, and devoted many pages of his book on the expedition to an account of him, his kingdom and his plans for its improvement.

The two and a half months he spent in his host's territory united many delights. There was the exhilaration of knowing that he was the first European since Classical times to tread its paths; the constant reminders, in its remains, of the succession of Aryans, Buddhists, Hindus and Muslims who had lived, fought and worshipped there; the knowledge that his 'patron saint', Hiuen Tsiang, had looked on the same landscape thirteen centuries earlier. Best of all was the fact that he could follow the track of Alexander the Great not only through the pages of the chronicler Arrian but on the ground itself, searching for clues and pursuing leads in a topographical version of a detective hunt.

Inspecting the ruins of Buddhist monuments as he went, he travelled on foot through the valley, his own party of surveyor, handyman and orderly augmented only by local guides. Chief among these was an acquaintance from another mountain fiefdom, Shah Alam, who had been his guide in Darel and Tangir in 1913 but had been forced to flee to Swat after his uncle, Raja Pakhtun Wali, had been murdered in 1917. At Birkot Hill and Udegram Stein identified the sites of the ancient towns of Bazira and Ora, which Alexander sacked after reaching Swat from Bactria and Sogdiana in 327 BC. In the upper, alpine part of the valley he recorded specimens of the local Dard language which had survived the fifteenth-century Pathan conquest.[34] Then he crossed the Swat-Indus watershed eastward, on the trail he hoped would lead to the Rock of Aornos.

The historians left no precise topographical information about the site where Alexander defeated the 'barbarians' on his way to the Indus. Their mere description of a rock-bound fastness which the Indians, or Assakenoi as they were known, hoped would protect them from the Macedonians, would have deterred a less dogged sleuth from attempting an identification. But Stein was in his element. He filled seven chapters of his book with details of the puzzle that confronted him, recreating the scene as refugees from Bazira, Ora and elsewhere gathered on Aornos in a last attempt to escape the relentless advance of the invaders. Carefully he assembled fragments of information from different sources: the stones of ancient ruins, the topography of the mountains and the local people. Though they knew no tales of 'Sikandar' – the Alexander of Indian legend – they told him of the alpine plateau of Pir Sar, high above the Indus near Besham, and a peak beyond it that was higher still and which bore the name Una.

This, Stein was sure, was a phonetic derivative of the name the Greeks had reproduced as Aornos. He felt nearer to a solution to the

Alexandrian mystery than ever before. Through conifer and ilex forests carpeted with violets, across snow-filled gullies and along knife-edge crests he pushed on until one evening, in near darkness, he and his weary party scrambled up to the grazing grounds of Pir Sar. The final obstacle in their path was a narrow and precipitous ravine and it was this that persuaded Stein that he had finally achieved 'the fulfilment of a scholar's hope, long cherished and long delayed'.[35]

The chronicler Arrian had described how Alexander's advance had been checked by a gap between his forward position and the Rock of Aornos itself. He had instructed his men to fill it with a great earthwork so that they could cross without being at the mercy of the Indians high above. The narrowness of the gully at its base – it was only ten yards across – and the mass of fallen trees that had accumulated there irresistibly recalled that story and convinced Stein that this was indeed the place where the invaders had built their mound, stormed the Rock and terrified the natives with their ingenuity and daring.

From Aornos the defeated Indians had fled, leaving the way clear for their conqueror's advance across the Indus. And Stein, too, had to leave reluctantly, at the end of an absorbing and triumphant treasure-hunt. He returned through Buner to the capital of Swat, Saidu Sharif, and a final dose of the ruler's hospitality; and by the end of the following summer had written his book, *On Alexander's Track to the Indus*. An ascent of Swat's Mount Ilam detained him *en route* to Saidu, for he was interested in its ancient tradition of sanctity. But he appears never to have considered it a serious contender for identification as Aornos itself, as others have done since.[36]

Stein spent the rest of 1926 quietly in Kashmir. There were writing tasks to be completed (including a contribution to the seven hundredth anniversary Festschrift of his old school in Dresden) and administrative duties to be observed. Responsibility for his collection at the museum in Delhi left him still prey, after all these years, to 'the Boa Constrictor of Babudom'. In addition, Fred Andrews had unwittingly bequeathed a problem to solve in Srinagar. A combination of his reluctance to delegate and his ineptness with accounts at the Technical Institute had resulted in financial irregularities for which the state authorities were now threatening to hold his erstwhile clerk responsible. Since this was

Pandit Govind Kaul's son, Nilakanth Kaul, whom Stein had recommended to Andrews, Stein felt an obligation to help settle the matter.

In the passing of the days there was no canine companion to cheer him, since he could find no suitable fox-terrier. But there was solace in the friendship of Ernest Neve, one of the Srinagar mission doctors, and his wife, whom he had known for many years. Their assistant, a young doctor called Norman Macpherson, came with his own dog on a visit to the camp on Mohand Marg and Stein described him to Publius as 'a worthy guardian of the Marg when I am away – or when I am no more'.[37] He had also found a good friend in a major in the Survey of India at Dehra Dun, Kenneth Mason (later Professor of Geography at Oxford), regarding him and his family as replacements for friends no longer in India and enjoying their holiday visits to Kashmir.

The Allens tried to tempt their friend back to Oxford with the suggestion that he allow his name to be proposed for the vacant Sanskrit chair. But he deflected their well-meant approach. He had drifted away from Sanskrit studies, he told them, and would not be able to catch up with developments sufficiently to be worthy of the position. The work he had done since neglecting Sanskrit had been in fields 'appealing more to my tastes and also my abilities'.[38] Much as he enjoyed his sojourns in Oxford, he was determined to let neither the supposed limitations of old age nor the blandishments of even his closest friends lure him into the maw of dreaded 'civilization'.

It was one form of civilization, however, that came to his aid. Just when the prospect of further interesting field work seemed bleakest and when nearly all his writing was complete, the newly discovered ancient civilization of the Indus valley presented him with an opportunity. Not that he had any intention of working on the Indus sites themselves. They were the preserve of the Archaeological Survey of India, whose officers had been excavating at Harappa in the Punjab and at Mohenjodaro in Sind for some years.

In both places, evidence had been found of a prehistoric urban culture, hitherto completely unknown and dating from the third millennium BC, long before the arrival of the Aryans. These cities proved to have been extraordinarily sophisticated, laid out in grid plans and equipped with water supplies and drainage systems which would have been the envy of many Indians thousands of years later. They had huge granaries, plain and painted pottery, weapons of copper, bronze and stone, many domesticated animals and a population which, in part at least, could afford to clothe itself in wool and cotton, and adorn itself with gold, silver and precious jewels. In the comparison which was inevitably drawn between this Indus civilization and that of Sumeria, Stein glimpsed a field that he could call his own.

He had already noticed evidence of prehistoric settlement in the course of his travels, not only in Chinese Turkestan but also in Baluchistan and Sistan. Now that the Indus cities had come to light, there was work to be done in recording such sites and exploring the connection between two great cultures in the lands that lay between. Marshall agreed, but did not succeed in drawing Stein into direct collaboration with those already at work on what he called the 'Indo-Sumerian' antiquities. Threatened with the prospect of having to work up results alongside other members of the Archaeological Survey at Simla, Stein told Publius he would rather resign from the service.

As usual, he had things his way. His prehistoric explorations began early in 1927 with a four-month trip to Baluchistan, the region he had once traversed as an inspector of education and archaeological surveyor combined. This time he had both cars and horses at his disposal and the assistance of a member of the Survey of India called Brendish who, unusually, was a 'European'. This adjective was usually a code-word in India for someone of mixed or uncertain race (and therefore automatically socially inferior) though Stein described him to Publius as being 'of pure British breed and looks', as if he were a promising young horse. Brendish was 21 years old and a capable helper, and Stein was rather concerned that he should be earning only the normal Survey salary for non-officers of Rs130 per month. He was, however, reassured as to his standard of living when Brendish told him that he had recently received a motor-car as a gift from his grandmother.

When he returned to Kashmir in late April 1927, Stein brought not only plentiful evidence of prehistory in the borderlands, such as ceramic fragments and stone implements, but also a white Powinda puppy. This was a large, strong breed kept by the nomadic Powinda people: not at all in the Dash tradition, but useful as a guard on Mohand Marg, where a thief had recently made off with Stein's KCIE insignia. The name of Dash V, however, Stein finally bestowed on a young Airedale, perhaps in response to his friend Arnold's comments regarding the difficulty of finding another reincarnation. 'Is it not possible', the Hierarch had suggested gently, 'that the most recent avatar has not taken the form of a smooth-haired fox terrier, and that the auspicious signs must be looked for in a puppy of another form and colour, and that Dash is expectantly awaiting his master's recognition under some unfamiliar shape?'[39]

The joy of sharing life again with canine friends did not extend, however, to Stein's next tour. Shortly before his departure from Kashmir at the end of 1927 for southern Baluchistan, both dogs were bitten by a rabid mongrel. Both recovered, despite his fears, but not before he had to leave once more alone, feeling that Fate must be determined to deny him travelling companions.

On this second, four-month Baluchistan tour, Stein's sights were fixed on Kalat and the Makran coast. It was his first visit to a remote and little-known region. Southern Baluchistan is virtually waterless, a naked waste crumpled by successive mountain ranges, scored by the sweeping paths of flash floods and coloured only by layers of minerals and the bright pinpricks of isolated oases. Even today there are few paved roads; in the 1920s only one or two small, isolated outposts, far beyond the military centre of Quetta, represented British rule there. Stein had two Dodge trucks at his disposal, but could use them only intermittently in the eroded hills and deserts. At one point, he had to abandon them to a suddenly rising flood, taking to camels instead. Nevertheless, he managed to cover an area measuring roughly 280 by 250 miles in four and a half months, and to identify a number of prehistoric sites which seemed connected with others farther north. His finds were limited mainly to pottery shards but they provided hitherto unknown information about conditions in this part of the Indo-Iranian borderlands during what Stein referred to rather loosely as the 'Chalcolithic' period, having no real expertise in prehistory.

The freedom and clean air suited him. He thrived, too, on the knowledge that his great hero, Alexander, had seen this same coast in 325 BC on his return westward, when the region was known to the Greeks as Gedrosia. At Gwadar (one of two towns which belonged to the Sultans of Muscat from the eighteenth century until 1958), he imagined the Macedonian ordering the revictualling of his fleet. The climate was no kinder than it had been to the exhausted Greek armies – bitterly cold inland, hot and fly-blown by the sea – and other extreme contrasts characterized the forgotten coastline. Stein remarked that, while the ancient settlements he found were enclosed by stone walls, the twenti-eth-century population dwelt in huts built only of matting and hurdles.

People supported themselves by date-farming and fishing, much as they had done for centuries; but they used matches made in Japan or Europe, and protected themselves against raids from across the Iranian border with .303 rifles. The general, rather than the specific, interest of this tour was perhaps more important to Stein than on most previous expeditions: prehistory, after all, was not his first love, though he was glad of the chance of what was clearly pioneering survey work. He was fortunate, too, to see the old hill-town of Kalat, once the centre of a powerful khanate, before an earthquake seven years later, in 1935, reduced it and most of Quetta to ruins.

The logical extension of his work would have led him into Iran. But he was not optimistic that his interest would be welcomed, either by the Iranians or by the French who had enjoyed an archaeological monop-oly there since 1897. Besides, the sort of explorations they conducted did not appeal, as he remarked to Publius: 'To sit down at an old site and dig down for months or years deeper & deeper is really not quite in my line'.[40] He returned instead to Kashmir, driving one of the lorries himself for the last 300 miles to Quetta, only, he told Publius, because there was no likelihood of meeting anything coming in the opposite direction.

His homecoming in early May 1928 was happy enough. The dogs, once more in fine fettle, gave him a boisterous welcome. His multi-volumed *Innermost Asia*, about to be published, was already largely pre-sold. He had been freed at last of responsibility for his collection in Delhi. And he was trying to arrange a trip to the Indus Kohistan, that mysterious region north of Swat and below Tangir which no European had seen and which the old Chinese pilgrims had known as the fearful 'route of the hanging chains'.

But the arrangements failed.[41] With final retirement from forty-one years of service in British India looming at the end of November, Stein had few plans beyond spending the last six months of leave owed to him in Mesopotamia, Greece and Dalmatia. On the day of his official retire-ment, at the age of 66, he was on his way to Karachi to board a ship bound for Basra, along the same coast that part of Alexander's army had seen as it made its way back to Persia. But there were no Alexandrian pursuits ahead, no happy prowls through the mountains of the North-West Frontier arranged nor flexible arrangements made with the Archaeological Survey. Only the tenuous hope of one last grand project revolved in his mind, a faint possibility of an expedition which he had been nursing intermittently for the past three years, but which nobody encouraged him to believe would succeed. If realized, it would give him the chance to relive his earlier triumphs in Central Asia with a return to the deserts of Chinese Turkestan.

12

Chinese Débâcle

———————————

STEIN'S FIRST EXPEDITION to the sands of the Tarim Basin lay
nearly thirty years behind him. His first steps on Chinese soil had
been taken in the far-off days of June 1900; and he was well aware in the
late 1920s that success would be harder to attain than it had been then.
In 1900 China was still in the grip of the Manchu dynasty: an increasingly feeble grip but one, nevertheless, that had held its empire for more
than 250 years and wielded the sword that had restored imperial authority in Eastern Turkestan. The stable but distant influence it had exerted
in the New Dominion had enabled Stein to work uninterrupted
throughout his first two expeditions, and the revolution of 1911 had
caused him only minor difficulties during his third.

No simple formula had been found in China since then to fill the
vacuum left by an age-old legacy of dynastic rule. But if there was one
issue which the vulnerable Nationalists hoped would unite the people,
it was a hatred of foreign interference of all kinds. And among the influential scholars and intellectuals who knew something of the finds Stein
and his rivals had made in the past, feelings of resentment ran high.

It is not difficult to understand that resentment today. Modern visitors to the great museums of western Europe and North America no
doubt still expect to see antiquities from all over the world, but their
admiration and interest is shadowed now by a collective guilty conscience which their forbears certainly did not share. They know that the

objects were acquired often without reference to the peoples of the countries where they were found, by explorers, antiquaries and collectors complacent in their assumptions of cultural and intellectual superiority. When Greeks demand the return of the Elgin Marbles to their rightful home on the Athenian Acropolis, the British face a dilemma. Should their response be a claim to ownership based on more than a century of possession; the defence of Lord Elgin's action as a rescue mission; or acceptance of the principle implicit in the Greek demand and the return of most of the items in the British Museum to their countries of origin?

Stein, his competitors and many of his colleagues had no such qualms. However much they respected the antiquity of Chinese culture and the accumulated learning of generations of mandarins, they believed unequivocally that the best place for archaeological finds was in the museums of the West, where they could be recorded, studied and displayed. Indeed, it seemed natural to Stein that, once he had explained what he was trying to do, he would gain the support of men such as Governor Pan. For him it was axiomatic that, if he did not identify and excavate the sites of the Tarim Basin, the antiquarian evidence they contained would probably perish. Local treasure-hunters would destroy it in their search for gold; farmers would scatter it to the four winds while seeking rich soil for their crops; ardent Muslims would gouge out the faces of statues and painted figures.

All this had already been done in several of the places Stein visited. There were any number of examples of similar desecration in India too: the stones of Buddhist temples carted off to build roads in Kashmir, the 4,000-year-old bricks of ancient Harappa used as ballast for the Lahore-Multan railway. Besides, if Stein did not investigate the Silk Road sites, some other Western archaeologist would – as the Government of India had always recognized.

The idea that he should leave the sites alone, despite the risks, so that the Chinese themselves could examine them whenever they had the means or inclination to do so, undoubtedly would have seemed preposterous to him. One of his supporters, Sir James de Boulay, private secretary to the Viceroy, Lord Hardinge, expressed commonly held sentiments when he told Stein in 1915, after the first signs of obstruction in Sinkiang, that he would sympathize more with the Chinese if they showed any interest in their own relics. But 'as matters stand they are being removed solely in order to secure their perpetuation for the use of posterity, and I can conceive it possible that some future enlightened generation of Chinese, will offer you posthumous honors [*sic*] for having saved these rare treasures from annihilation'.[1]

One acquaintance, however, left a record of his disagreement with Stein on this matter. Arthur Waley worked on Stein's collection in the British Museum after 1913, wrote the catalogue of Buddhist paintings brought from the Tun-huang caves (published in 1931) and enjoyed a long career as a Chinese scholar. In his *Ballads and Stories from Tun-huang*, published in 1960, he raised the subject of Stein's and Pelliot's activities at the Caves of the Thousand Buddhas. He invited his British readers to imagine how they would feel if a Chinese archaeologist discovered a hoard of medieval manuscripts in a ruined English monastery and bribed its custodian in order to carry it off to Peking.

Waley knew Stein was aware that the Chinese were more interested in their own remote past than were, for example, the Bedouins.

> But I was never able to convince him that the Chinese scholars who in the eighteenth and nineteenth centuries wrote about the geography and antiquities of Central Asia were anything more than what he called 'arm-chair archaeologists'; though they had in fact, as Generals or administrators, spent far more time in Central Asia and travelled far more widely than Stein himself.[2]

Such minority views played no part in Stein's calculations. He knew the Chinese were not out in the desert digging up the cities of the Silk Road, and he knew that was where he wanted to be. So he set about trying to organize one last expedition to Central Asia: an expedition that would prove he was still every inch the explorer he had been and set the seal on his reputation as the first and greatest of Silk Road archaeologists. It was an ambition that was to tempt Fate too far, and culminate in a humiliating débâcle.

———————◆◄———————

Warlords, Communists and the Nationalists of Chiang Kai-shek's Kuomintang wrestled for control of China. But the instability of conditions there seemed less problematic to Stein than the question of where to find the necessary financial backing for his plans. Sir John Marshall's department was operating under stringent economies and Stein's battles to extract money from it for his early expeditions now seemed to belong, by comparison, to a halcyon era. There was one other possible source of support, however, the Boxer Indemnity Fund, and over the past three years he had been lobbying to win its backing for his proposal.

The Fund was the result of a decision in 1922 by the British government to remit the balance of the indemnity owed to it by China as a result of the Boxer Rising of 1900. Instead of being paid into a sinking fund, the money was to be devoted to 'objects beneficial to both countries'. Stein had no difficulty associating his own aims with such objects. Assuming his salary and those of two surveyors would be paid by the Government of India, he had applied to the Fund for a grant of £12,000 in March 1925, at the same time submitting a formal proposal for the expedition to the Foreign Office.

As usual, he had underpinned these applications with personal approaches to various people who could provide useful information or clear his path. The advice they offered made it plain that things were not as straightforward as they had been in the past. The Professor of Chinese at Oxford, W. E. Soothill, suggested that Stein might win Chinese approval by offering them first choice of his finds, since they were concerned about the 'wholesale exportation of their treasures', and by helping to establish a School of Chinese Archaeology.[3] Eric Teichman, Chinese Secretary to the British Minister in Peking, recommended that Stein visit China to explain his objectives, and that he carry out his work under Chinese government auspices rather than Indian ones since there was 'a growing (and very natural) feeling against the carting off of these things to foreign museums'.[4] Teichman felt he should drop the idea of bringing Indian surveyors, and that a sample of his previous collection sent to Peking would make a good impression.

Whatever Stein thought of such advice, he made sure that his responses were measured. His friend Sir Michael Sadler, Master of University College, Oxford, and originator of the idea to approach the Indemnity Fund, lobbied the Fund committee on his behalf, explaining that the expedition would be carried out 'in close conference with Chinese scholars, and would, I suggest, appeal to their sense of national dignity'.[5] Stein himself remarked to Soothill that he would very much like to spend six months getting to know the Chinese and their language, if only the means were assured for his ultimate aim. And he told Teichman that he entirely agreed with him 'that antiquities brought to light from Chinese soil ought to be preserved in China, provided that their safe preservation can be assured'.[6] What he planned privately at this stage is unclear; but in these glib assurances there is an echo of the smooth-tongued calculation of his Tun-huang methods.

Initially, there was little enough encouragement to believe his plans would get very far. The Indemnity Fund was not yet properly established; and Soothill, in Peking in 1926 as a member of the Fund delegation, wrote a disheartened letter:

> I put out more than one feeler to see if the plans you & I discussed could be dealt with at once, but soon discovered that my endeavours would be wasted. There is a spirit of grudging on the part of intelligent Chinese which depresses me. They seem to want archaeological research to be in their own hands. A spirit of xenophobia is nothing new to the Chinese. It is here still. How to overcome it is not clear . . . They hate a foreigner to do what they cannot do, & belittle his achievements.[7]

Frustrated but undeterred, Stein began to consider making a preliminary trip to the Far East at his own expense. The fact that other European explorers seemed to be succeeding in working in Sinkiang, despite the supposed difficulties, encouraged him to think the problems were not so great as they were portrayed. Two European geologists were in China in 1927: a Swede called Andersson who planned to extend his work into Sinkiang with the help of Sven Hedin, and a German, Dr Emil Trinkler, who called on Stein in Kashmir before starting northward.

Stein envied them the patronage which enabled them to get their expeditions off the ground. It seemed to highlight his own difficulties. He could not feel free to pursue his investigations in Central Asia because cases full of 'finds' were necessary to satisfy his backers' desire to see a return on their 'investment'. How he regretted, he told Publius, the fact that 'archaeology in recent years (thanks to Tutankhamen & the rest) has become too much associated with the idea of "treasures" such as appeal to prevalent financial instincts'.[8]

The distinction Stein made between 'treasures' and his own finds was a subtle one, developed, one senses, at least partly out of frustration. He had, after all, become known for the long and heavily laden camel trains that carried booty away from his desert sites. It took Fred Andrews and his colleagues at the British Museum years to clean, reassemble, mount and catalogue all the thousands of manuscripts, statues, and fragments of painted stucco and carved wood that constituted the 'treasure' of the Silk Road, and the haul from the Caves of the Thousand Buddhas had been spectacular in its quantity as well as its content. How else could an archaeologist justify his work, if not by displaying the evidence?

Stein's complaint implicitly contrasted his own finds with 'treasure' of the kind that captured the imagination of newspapers and their readers – such as the glories of Tutankhamun's tomb. Unlike many before him, he had come to archaeological exploration via an academic career and his approach remained scholarly, even though he infinitely preferred an active to a desk-bound life. The value of his finds, for him, lay in the information they could provide and the problems of history they could elucidate. That was why he was anxious always to see them properly recorded and published by reputable institutions for the benefit of scholars. Their failure to draw huge crowds never bothered him – in fact, it suited his temperament very well. He scorned the idea of pandering to a public desire for archaeology laced with romance, mystery and glamour.

If his only hope of working again in Sinkiang lay in leaving finds in China, he was prepared to compromise. He would not object in principle to an arrangement whereby the finds were examined and recorded in the West and returned to Peking later, so long as Peking could guarantee to house them safely (though this was a proviso in which he had little faith). The problem with such an agreement was that his previous backers, the Indian Archaeological Department and the British Museum, would not support an expedition whose finds they could not keep. No other source of financial support seemed available, until help suddenly appeared from an unexpected quarter.

Stein may have lived an isolated life for much of his time in the East but he knew a great many people. He lectured in various countries, belonged to a number of learned societies and was well-known among Anglo-Indians. The socializing was not always to his taste; nonetheless, he did a fair amount. It was on one such occasion in 1924, at a tea-party given at her London club by the travel writer Ella Sykes, that Stein met an American who was already one of his most ardent admirers. Carl Tilden Keller was ten years younger than Stein, a wealthy and well-connected businessman from Cambridge, Massachusetts, and a dedicated armchair traveller in Chinese Turkestan.

Out of that meeting grew a correspondence which lasted until the end of Stein's life. Keller initiated it and apologized more than once for taking such a liberty with the man he called 'the master that they all follow'.[9] But his letters, besides giving Stein an insight into American affairs, in fact proved immediately interesting. In what appears to be his first, written in November 1924, he mentioned a friend who had recently been to the Caves of the Thousand Buddhas. That friend was Langdon Warner, the only American to follow the archaeological trail which Stein and Pelliot had blazed, and the last Westerner to see the caves before Chinese action placed them beyond the reach of Western 'robbers'.

Warner first visited Tun-huang in early 1924 and returned there the following year. He was in his early forties, a fit and robust man who combined, like Stein, the activities of scholar and archaeologist. By training he was an art historian. But he had travelled with the explorer Raphael Pumpelly to Russian Central Asia, had met leading orientalists and inspected the major oriental collections of Europe, and had seen a good deal of China and Japan. By the time he set out on the road to Kansu he was a director of Harvard University's Fogg Art Museum. His companion, Horace Jayne, ran the Museum of Pennsylvania in Philadelphia. In December 1926, at Keller's suggestion, Warner wrote a long letter to Stein, describing his experiences in Kansu.

The Americans' first expedition to the western frontiers of China in 1924 was almost a disaster, with foul winter weather and sordid sleeping conditions dogging their steps all the way, and frostbitten feet forcing Jayne to retreat to Peking. When Warner reached the Tun-huang shrines, he found many of them horribly scarred by the scratches and scribbles of four hundred White Russian cavalrymen who had taken refuge there after being driven into China by a Bolshevik general. He had intended not to remove wall paintings, merely to examine them and acquire a few flakes for analysis back in the United States. But having seen the damage the Russians had done, he told Stein, he felt no compunction in removing a statue and three sections of T'ang-period fresco. 'I believe that neither you nor your patron saint, Hiuen Tsang [*sic*], would disapprove of my vandalism,' he wrote.[10]

He and Jayne's return visit, in 1925, was a fiasco. They took with them 'a full battery of cameras' and four assistants in order to supplement Pelliot's published descriptions and plates of the cave interiors. 'It was in my mind, in case the destruction was going on apace & our methods proved practicable, to try to preserve the paintings from one small chapel entire & to set it up in Peking for the benefit of all scholars reserving only typical fragments for Harvard,' he continued in his letter. But their arrival in the valley of the Thousand Buddhas coincided with news of the shooting of several Chinese students by a British policeman in Shanghai, and the reaction of the people in the oasis was so violently xenophobic that they had no choice but to beat a swift and disappointed retreat.

Warner heard that the magistrate who had approved his activities in the previous year had been expelled for having allowed him to carry off 'untold treasures'; that the magistrate's successor had met the same fate 'for failing to produce me dead or alive'; that he, Warner, had been blamed (in his absence) for a drought and partial famine that had afflicted the area; and that his flashlight photographs 'had gravely offended the Gods'. Wang, the old guardian of the caves, had been threatened with death, and stories had circulated describing the previous visits of Stein and Pelliot, as well as Warner, as 'huge bandit expeditions'.

Warner believed part of the blame for his troubles could be attributed to Dr Ch'ien from the National University of Peking, whom he had agreed to take with him despite suspecting that he was a spy. Since leaving the expedition abruptly on the pretext of having to visit an ailing grandmother, Warner recorded, Ch'ien had written 'a series of articles about his amazing adventures with the foreigners, attributing to my assistants the vilest motives'.

So Warner's activities had merely added to the grievances the Chinese had against foreign archaeologists. But it may well have been Warner who was responsible for suggesting to Stein a way round his own immediate problem, that of securing finance for his own plans. In early 1928 he wrote to invite Stein to contribute to a scholarly journal with which he and Jayne were connected. Perhaps to prove that American readers were worth reaching, he dangled an appetizing carrot before the older man's eyes. Stein's name was 'perhaps the only one known in connection with the subject [Asia] by many Americans', he declared. 'To help stir up an interest in our country will have untold results, as my countrymen are as you know quite as generous to foreign research as to our own. I believe that in lending us your aid you will find an unexpected and gratifying repercussion which may lead to important results.'[11]

Similar hints were dropped (whether coincidentally or not is unclear) by other American correspondents at about the same time, and Stein made tentative responses, explaining his situation. But he was wary. Soothill, who had just returned from a lecture tour in the United States, reported meeting a young man there called Owen Lattimore, who had travelled in western China and was busy raising money for a return trip by lecturing around the country. Stein dreaded the thought of having to do the same. Lectures in themselves he did not mind, but the idea of fund-raising by giving performances like a barrel-organ monkey was anathema to him. Neither did he receive any encouragement to think otherwise from his longest-standing correspondent in the States, the orientalist Charles Rockwell Lanman of Harvard University.

Lanman had studied under Roth at Tübingen a few years before Stein, and the two had been writing to each other since the 1890s, though they had yet to meet. When Lanman heard that Keller, whom he knew, had latched on to the idea of Stein coming to the States, he immediately scribbled a note of warning. Keller was 'a most amiable gentleman', he wrote. But he feared he was not the sort to understand 'how a man like you isnt working for popular applause or for money . . . What he thinks will be a great favor to you is probably what you wd surely think unwelcome if you could know how things go here . . . in the case of lionized strangers.'[12] Stein underlined the last two words.

But he could not afford to pass up such a chance. There was no sign of help from the Boxer Indemnity Fund, he was about to retire from the Indian Archaeological Department (as was his ally, Sir John Marshall) and he wanted to get back to Chinese Turkestan while his health lasted. So Keller proceeded with his plan to bring his hero to Harvard and soon an invitation arrived from the university's Lowell Institute to give a course of six lectures for a fee of $600 – nearly £3,000 in today's money. It was a novel proposal for Stein and one which, with his usual diffidence, he did not accept immediately. Instead, he contemplated sailing to America from England towards the end of 1929. In the meantime, he could leave India late in 1928 knowing that, though his service there was now at an end, another avenue had at last opened which might lead to one final expedition.

What he saw on his archaeological tour of the Middle East during the following weeks perhaps encouraged him to make plans. Arriving at Basra in early December 1928, he went straight to Ur and spent four days with Leonard Woolley and his wife. He inspected the ziggurat and the tombs and admired Woolley's 'practical improvisation & grasp of opportunities'.[13] From Ur he travelled to several other sites under German, French or American administration. At Mosul, on the border of Iraq and Syria, he seized the opportunity to view the ground from the air, something he had imagined in the far-off days of 1900–1 in the mountains of the Kun-lun. Courtesy of the 6th Squadron of the RAF, he cruised for more than a thousand miles in the cockpit of a Bristol fighter, gazing down at the Jabal Sinjar area, where the Roman border line once marched across the Mesopotamian desert. Group Captain C. Hilton Keith later recalled the experience: 'On one occasion', he wrote, 'I was terrified that I had lost him from the open cockpit behind me. I stood up at my controls and was just able to lean back to see him crouched on the floor, busy with a huge book of reference.'[14]

This experience of aerial survey was something Stein stored up and returned to later. For the time being, it merged with others which brought him in touch with the latest developments in archaeology. It was hardly likely after such a trip that he would easily abandon his plans to make one more expedition to the Central Asian desert which he thought of as his own.

At the end of March 1929, he sailed from the Middle East to Cyprus and Athens, where he haunted the Acropolis. Then it was on to Dubrovnik – or Ragusa as it was then known – in early April, in time for a long-anticipated reunion with the Hierarch. He found Arnold 'beaming in radiant rotundity' at the prospect of their two-week holiday together along the Dalmatian coast.[15] Stein was to relive that happy period many times in his memory, for it was the last he was to spend with his friend. Accompanied for part of the time by Olga and Maud Allen, he and Arnold then crossed the Adriatic to Italy, sailing into

Venice on a bright, clear morning across a glassy sea and watching the city rise in an array of glorious colours that dazzled them both.

While Arnold returned home on the Orient Express, Stein paid a visit to a friend and fellow-explorer, Filippo de Filippi, at his villa outside Florence. Then he, too, returned to England, via Budapest, Vienna and Paris as usual. By the time he arrived at the Allens' home in Oxford, his friends and admirers at Harvard had already written to say that they could raise funds to support his dream of another expedition to Central Asia.

Stein escaped extraordinarily lightly from the duties that other explorers in need of finance might have been expected to undertake. He had explained his hopes to only one or two people in the USA and had held out a begging bowl to no one. He had merely expressing the hope that they would be able to suggest ways in which he might find backers in America. No doubt he felt this was as it should be: he had always regarded himself simply as a scholar who wanted to be allowed to get on with what he did best. The implication behind this assumption, of course, was that he knew better than others what he should be enabled to do, and that it was not for them to judge but simply to pay up and stand back.

He had proved himself amply on his three previous expeditions to Chinese Turkestan, however. Perhaps his sponsors felt also that age exempted him from certain publicity-oriented activities which younger men might not have found offensive. Plainly, too, they regarded themselves as fortunate to have a man of such reputation undertaking an expedition in their name. Their institution was a young one compared with some in Europe, but it boasted the highest aims and aspirations which could only gain from association with the grand old man of Central Asia.

The lectures were fixed for the first half of December 1929 and Stein arrived in New York on the SS *Transylvania* (a name redolent of the unhappy recent past for any Hungarian) on the second day of the month. Snow fell gently as he caught his first glimpses of America: the streams of cars, the massive buildings, the 'Cyclopean' Grand Central Station. He gasped for air in the 'tropical' temperatures inside trains and buildings, struggled to stay awake at his first dinner and had hospitality heaped on him everywhere he went. In Cambridge, Massachusetts, he stayed first with his old and affectionate friend, Lanman, then with

Professor Paul Sachs, an associate director of the Fogg Art Museum, in a house hung with paintings by masters such as Cranach and Dürer.

At the Fogg he was welcomed by Warner and his fellow-director, Forbes (a grandson of Emerson), and made an Honorary Fellow for research in Asia. He gave the first of his series of lectures in the 1,200-seat hall of the Lowell Institute to a packed house, and went on to speak at the Boston Museum of Fine Arts and the Freer Art Gallery in Washington. Then, in mid-January 1930, he boarded ship for his return journey. By this time, the necessary funds of $100,000 (about £500,000 today)[16] for three years' work (and publication of the results) had been secured, despite the Wall Street Crash. Half came from a large endowment left to Harvard for research bearing on China and half from Harvard's own Yenching University Fund.

In view of the controversy that Stein's expedition was later to cause, it is important to note what he said at the time about the way in which the money was raised. Soon after reaching Massachusetts, he told Publius: 'With such an encouraging prospect on this side, my chief care and that a serious one remains. It is how to avoid the obstacles & entanglements which Chinese nationalist agitation is likely to raise unless things are managed very quietly & cautiously. Fortunately the need for discretion is recognized by my friends here and will be on the other side also.'[17] He had not tried to disguise from his American friends the difficulties he might face in China, having warned earlier, in a letter to Keller, that he was likely to encounter 'serious obstruction', though he hoped that his friendship with several long-serving mandarins in Sinkiang itself would help him once he reached the desert.

In that same letter, he remarked that the way to gain the necessary approval from the Chinese government would be to make concessions to 'Chinese amour propre' by avoiding any claim to archaeological finds. It would be better, he suggested, to trust to 'the generosity and traditional laissez faire of the Chinese when it comes to the disposal of "archaeological proceeds"'. The evasive wording of this suggestion was no doubt deliberate, for he continued to insist that proper examination and reproduction of all finds, and the publication of all surveys, were essential and could be done only in the West.[18]

His Harvard backers clearly recognized the possibility of failure from the outset. When Sachs informed Stein, early in January 1930, of the fact that the entire sponsorship sum had been raised, he wrote: 'If conditions in China make it obvious that your hoped-for results cannot be obtained, you are please to feel at liberty to change your plans and to direct your attention to the region of Persia (or elsewhere in Asia) and to use the fund, or part of it, in pursuing your investigations.'[19]

———————▶ ◀———————

Stein returned to England for the month of February 1930 before sailing again, this time for China. He had decided to make his preliminary trip to the Far East, as originally planned, before starting the expedition from Kashmir. Both he and his friends hoped that by arriving in Sinkiang via India, rather than by setting out from China proper, he would draw as little attention to himself as possible. But official approval from the lately established Chinese Nationalist government of Chiang Kai-shek was still necessary. Moreover, he was anxious to make use of any diplomatic representations which the British Minister in Nanking, the Kuomintang's new capital, could conduct on his behalf. For this reason he had stressed to Harvard the importance of making his expedition a joint American-British one and had persuaded Sir Frederic Kenyon, the Director of the British Museum, to promise him £1,000 a year over three years.

The journey to Nanking took the best part of two months. Stein travelled by train across North America, and sailed to Japan from Vancouver. He had been wanting to visit Japan in order to see its Buddhist art treasures, though he had heard several years earlier through a fellow-scholar that the collection brought from Chinese Central Asia by the Japanese monk Tachibana was apparently no longer there. (Part of it had been seen in Seoul, Korea, in 1916, but in 1922 Tachibana and his mentor, Count Otani, told Stein's informant that most of the manuscripts were in a library in Port Arthur, Manchuria.)[20] Stein was impressed with Japan. 'There is an amazing energy in modern achievements, roads, electric railways, etc., to be seen on all sides', he told Publius, 'and yet along with them humanity that has preserved its national heritage undiluted.'[21] He sailed on to Shanghai, and was in Nanking by 28 April.

If Stein made crucial mistakes at any time during preparations for his fourth Central Asian expedition, it was now, in Nanking. Up to this point, he had been concerned mainly with gathering information and finding financial support. He had received advice from people well qualified to give it, including some who dealt with the Chinese every day of their working lives. Nobody had underestimated the difficulties he faced – except himself. For, while he had acknowledged the antipathy of 'Young China' towards foreign archaeologists, he had continued to assume that, somehow, he would find a way round the objections. He had a touching faith in the influence of British officials in China, despite the fact that one of them, Teichman, had warned him that the Nanking government with which they dealt was 'feeble and unrepresentative'.[22] And he believed complacently in the power of his own friendship with the mandarins of Sinkiang. But his faith was not rewarded, though his stay in Nanking was superficially a resounding success.

On the evening of his very first day there, a decision was taken which sealed the fate of the expedition. Stein met 'in conclave' with his three chief British contacts, the Consul Sir Miles Lampson, Eric Teichman and Sir Frederick Whyte, who was an unpaid adviser to the Chinese government; and they agreed that submission of Stein's plans to the influential National Council of Cultural Associations was 'undesirable'. The Council, while it comprised and represented the sort of fellow-scholars who might have a legitimate interest in what Stein was planning, was known to be fiercely anti-foreign, and was sure to press for the imposition of a variety of conditions which Stein had already decided he could not accept.

He had heard that both an American, Roy Chapman Andrews (from the American Museum of Natural History), and the indefatigable Sven Hedin had submitted to such conditions in order to carry out their latest expeditions.[23] But he had already made it plain to Whyte that he would not work by sharing control with a 'Chinese leader', for example, or by taking along a party of Chinese students. It was hardly surprising that he should feel this way about unknown companions. Besides being sceptical about most scholars' aptitude for camp life in the desert, he had always avoided working with anyone other than assistants and servants under his orders; but the Chinese were not to know that.

Perhaps Lampson and his colleagues were wrong to advise Stein in this way. But they probably did so because they knew that avoidance of the issue was his only hope. Given Stein's attitude, there would be no pleasing the cultural associations. But if he and his plans could be got past the relevant officials of the Nanking government, what he did later in far-off Sinkiang might possibly escape the attention of the people likely to object. As Lampson was to write in a communication with the Indian Foreign Secretary, if Stein was planning to go into the interior for three years, the problem of what was to happen to his finds 'was not a very pressing one'.[24]

Thus decided, Lampson and Teichman approached the Chinese Foreign Minister the following day armed to the teeth with diplomatic explanations and assurances of their best intentions. Stein differed from other explorers, Lampson assured the Minister, Dr Wang. He 'merely worked on his finds for the purpose of his study in tracing ancient lines of contact between China and the West'. The items that attracted his interest were only the contents of 'ancient waste-paper baskets and other rubbish dumps' and his work was 'of interest to the whole of mankind and future generations'.[25] Two days later, Stein was taken to meet Dr Wang who, he noted in his diary, was 'strongly built, with steady eyes; speaks ext. English, but listens still better . . .'.[26]

He launched into the story which he had always found so useful when dealing with mandarins elsewhere: that of Hiuen Tsiang and the close connection between topography and historical research. Dr Wang replied that the Chinese government recognized his good work and would give him every facility – though, as Teichman noted drily in the official minutes of the meeting, he had to take advantage of 'a momentary pause in Sir A. Stein's disquisition' to say so.

Together with a meeting with Hu Han-min, said to be the most important man in the government after Chiang Kai-shek himself, this was the sum of Stein's official dealings with the Chinese. The permission and the passport he sought were granted without difficulty, and without discussion of the thorniest question of all, the destination of any finds. Lampson had deliberately avoided it and Stein had not raised it, though both knew that Stein expected removal to the West at least for the period of examination and record. Despite this obliqueness, and the condescending assumption that the highly educated Dr Wang would not consider 'ancient rubbish dumps' of any historical interest, Lampson told Stein a few days later that the essential point in dealing with the Chinese was to remember their regard for 'straightness & fair dealing; resentment of patronizing air; old regard for scholarship & mental effort'.[27]

Stein spent a total of only three weeks in China. It was a very much shorter visit than he had originally claimed to be planning; but he was delighted to have got off so lightly. From the fairly detailed diary he kept throughout his time there, it is clear that, though he met a number of people, he avoided anyone who would challenge his aims. He dined with the American Minister, whom he already knew from New York, and met at his table the Minister of Education. He contacted one of the few American members of staff at Nanking University, a Professor Bates, in order to organize a few lessons in Mandarin for himself; he exchanged visits with a Harvard graduate, H. H. Chang, and his Chicago-educated wife; and he told Publius that, having made a few acquaintances among 'Young China', he had begun 'to feel a little more hopeful about its future'.[28]

But he chose to ignore an appeal from one or two Westerners connected with Yenching University, to which he briefly alluded in his diary, to refer to the 'Peking Council' – perhaps the same that his British advisers warned him to avoid. Indeed, on Lampson's advice he did not visit Peking at all. On 13 May he sailed from Shanghai for Calcutta, via Singapore and Rangoon, and was back in Kashmir by early June.

Though he seemed so far to have avoided compromise in China, Stein made an uncharacteristic concession in the matter of his expedition party. His American friends had invited him to take his pick of assistants from among the talented young men of Harvard. He had cloaked his dislike of the idea in a cautious response, telling Keller that he could consider such an addition 'only after very careful testing of personal and scientific qualifications'.[29] Indeed, he had already revealed to Soothill just how careful he would be, after Soothill suggested in 1928 that the young man he had met in America, Owen Lattimore, would make a suitable travelling companion. The making of such a choice, Stein wrote in reply, was 'almost as serious an affair – as marriage'.[30] And yet, in the end, he agreed, under what was almost certainly pressure from the Americans, to travel with an assistant. Bramlette, a young geologist from Yale University, had been chosen and approved by Dr Sachs, and Stein himself had met him in Boston before travelling to Vancouver and China.

Having bowed to the wishes of his sponsors on this matter, Stein clearly intended to make sure he got maximum use out of his new assistant. Shortly after their first meeting he wrote to Bramlette with instructions on preparing for the expedition. It was late March and he expected the young man to arrive in Kashmir not later than mid-August, having run various errands for him during a week in London *en route*. Bramlette should read *Sand-Buried Ruins of Khotan* and *Desert Cathay* as well as the parts of all the detailed reports relating to geographical observations. He should also read Stein's Royal Geographical Society paper, 'Innermost Asia', for brief information on the archaeology of the region which would suffice for the time being. He should organize for himself three or four days' training on the Marconi Wireless Time Signal Receiver which he was to collect in London, and get some practice in developing photographic negatives, since their equipment would include glass plates, cut films and pack films. Before leaving the States he should acquire practical experience at the Fogg Art Museum in applying the chemical method of removing wall paintings (which Warner had used at Tun-huang) and bring the necessary materials with him; and he should learn some colloquial Hindustani. 'No exact grammatical knowledge is needed,' Stein told him, 'but capacity for giving simple orders.'[31] No doubt Bramlette was relieved to hear, amidst all these instructions, that he would not be expected to read the indigenous writing as well.

There were no Chinese assistants on the expedition and Stein felt justified in this omission. He had made clear to the Nanking authorities his intention of taking two – a topographer and a 'literatus' such as Chiang had been in 1906–8 – but he had received no official help in trying to find them. Besides, shortly before leaving Nanking, he had heard (via India) that they might not be admitted into Sinkiang by the 'chairman', or governor, of that province. It is not clear why the Governor of Sinkiang would have wanted to exclude them. He had been in office only two years, having taken over after the assassination of Governor Yang, whom he had served as second-in-command. But he was less talented and less respected than his predecessor and perhaps regarded the prospect of a European explorer with two Nanking assistants prowling round his province as a threat to his authority.

Stein had been happy to abandon his search as soon as he heard the news, since he had initiated it mainly in order to please the Chinese government. But he realized he had made an error in mentioning the matter to his Nanking acquaintance, H. H. Chang. 'Chang wants to know from whom this advice,' he had noted in his diary on 9 May.

'Obliged to keep reply indefinite . . . Had better omitted this piece of news.'[32] That was a verdict which one or two British and American officials in China came to share, applied generally to Stein's affairs. They felt he had talked about his plans not too little but too much, making himself a hostage to rumour and misrepresentation.

Stein's small expedition party set out from Kashmir on 11 August 1930. To outside eyes, it might have seemed a happy restaging of scenes first enacted thirty years earlier. But there were several inauspicious circumstances attached to its start, among them the fact that Stein was going to Chinese Turkestan by a route he already knew – the route by which he had travelled north to the desert for the very first time in 1900. Repetition of a journey was something he had always managed to avoid before, and only disturbed conditions on the Frontier forced it on him this time. He had with him two surveyors, his favourite, Afrazgul Khan, and a younger man, Fateh Muhammad; but before reaching Hunza, the latter fell ill with pneumonia and had to turn back. Moreover, the ebullient Dash V, the biggest and most affectionate of all the Dashes, accompanied his master only as far as Kashgar, where he suddenly sickened inexplicably and died.

But by far the gravest blow hit Stein while he was still finalizing his plans from Mohand Marg. A letter from Andrews arrived, near the end of which he wrote, in a strangely brief and emotionless paragraph buried among his concluding remarks, that Sir Thomas Arnold, one of Stein's most cherished friends, was dead. Stein was devastated, not only by the news but also by the way in which it had arrived, seemingly almost as an afterthought, with no details of how or when the Hierarch had died. He sent to Publius a telegram whose necessarily brief message could only hint at his distress: 'Cast in deepest grief. Convey profound sympathy poor Hierarchess.'[33]

Arnold had suffered a heart attack and died at his home in Gloucester Walk, Kensington, on 9 June. Doctors had warned him before of the threat posed to his health by over-exertion, and also by the strong coffee of which he was so fond. He had told Stein of these warnings on their Dalmatian holiday in 1929. But he was an enthusiast for life and loved his work. In early 1930 he had gone to Cairo University as visiting professor for a few months, and had been back only a couple of weeks when his heart failed. Quite why the news took two and a half weeks to reach Stein is unclear, but it would have had the same effect on him, however it had arrived. He regarded the loss of this friend as the greatest he had experienced since the death of his brother. The Allens in Oxford heard two days after the event and Publius wrote immediately to Stein with intuitive sympathy:

> What a joyful friend he has been! As gay as a child, and yet how wise and firm in the affairs of life and how masterly in his knowledge of the things he studied . . . We grieve to think that this blow will reach you when probably you are alone: with no one who knew and loved him to talk to about him, and tell the happy days . . . What a delightful band it has been that gathered round their General in Mayo Lodge! What a store of memories, of outings together and holidays, and days of parting and days of meeting again. So this is the first break, our sweet Saint whom we all love so; the maker of gaiety and happiness, with his fine laugh and his incurable youth. Bless him.[34]

With such thoughts in mind, Stein took the familiar road out of Kashmir, across the mountains to the Indus valley and up to Gilgit. And that was as far as he got before word of trouble caught up with him. News came from Kashgar that the Governor of Sinkiang, under instruction from Nanking, had ordered him to be denied entry into China. This was a bad start. He had been relying on being able to slip in quietly by the back door, and the British authorities had hoped that the Sinkiang Governor would be amenable, since he was being supplied from India with valuable arms and ammunition.

Stein moved up to the Hunza valley in order to make use of his time by studying 'old world conditions' there, while he waited to hear whether anything could be done to reverse the order. His faith in British powers of persuasion was rewarded: a couple of weeks later he heard that the way was clear. The journey proceeded without incident and the party reached Kashgar on 8 October 1930.

But the game of cat and mouse had begun and Stein, in his heart of hearts, no doubt knew it. However strong his old resolve and his scorn for difficulties, he had heard enough about changed conditions to recognize that he would need a great deal of luck (or a miracle, as Langdon Warner frankly put it) to carry off this fourth expedition. Moreover, his closest friends would have been able to detect a change in his approach. In the old days, it was all or nothing. He would contemplate nothing less than complete success in his plans, because there was no worthwhile alternative. Failure in Chinese Turkestan would have condemned him to a life on the Frontier circuit of the Archaeological Survey of India. This time, an alternative was assured by the existence of his grant from Harvard, which enabled him to finance work wherever it could be feasibly undertaken. He had already spent years uncovering the secrets of the Silk Road in Central Asia. He was nearly 70 years old. He was not prepared to battle indefinitely with unbending opponents in China when opportunities awaited him elsewhere.

In one way, at least, his burden was eased soon after arriving in Kashgar, when Bramlette decided to leave. Stein had initially reported to Publius that the young American was proving 'a keen worker & a pleasant quiet companion'.[35] But the journey from Kashmir had revealed other aspects of his assistant's character with which he had less sympathy. Bramlette had been feeling the cold, especially in his feet, and had suffered intestinal trouble since Gilgit. If he found night temperatures in Kashgar uncomfortable at just below freezing, Stein held out little hope for him in the desert. Attributing such weaknesses to years of work in the tropics (Bramlette had worked in Ecuador and Venezuela), Stein pointed out that illness would impede the work ahead. He therefore concurred (no doubt a little too readily) with Bramlette's disappointed conclusion that he should retrace his steps while the passes to India were still open. There would be less to interest him in the desert, in any case, Stein explained to Publius, and, since his company was 'at no time exactly stimulating' and latterly rather depressing, 'it will be easier for me to be once more by myself'.[36]

Ease, however, was something he was never to associate with this expedition. Though he and the new British Consul, Captain (later Sir) George Sherriff, had an amicable meeting with the chief dignitaries of Kashgar (including the son of his old friend Pan), he had to wait while they negotiated with Urumchi over his start. When he did set off at last on 11 November, he was obliged to take a Chinese with him who, he felt certain, was there for no other purpose than to spy on him and prevent him from working. He was closely watched in Khotan; and at Domoko, one of his old sites, he received a message from Sherriff that the Sinkiang chairman had prohibited him from doing any digging. On reaching Keriya he was laid up with bronchitis and at Niya, his favourite ruins, the twelve labourers he had brought with him were frightened away by a hostile emissary sent by the Keriya Amban.

His original plan had been to skirt the Taklamakan by this southern route, before going into the Lop Desert and then to the Kuruk-tagh Mountains. While at Kashgar he had resisted the Sinkiang Governor's suggestion that he visit Urumchi to discuss his work, since the long journey to the capital would have ruled out the completion of his winter programme. But now the request was made again and, having had a taste of the obstruction that could so easily disrupt his schedule, he decided to submit himself to official scrutiny after all. Having visited Lop, he would head north for Urumchi and hope that, in the meantime, the influence of Lampson in Nanking would be enough to untangle the knotted line of communications stretching between the Chinese capital and the New Dominion.

It was a vain hope. Lampson had a shrewd idea of what was going on, but he was powerless to influence events. He had judged, weeks before Stein even set out, that Dr Wang, the Chinese Foreign Minister, however well-meaning, would be unable to withstand the demands of the influential cultural societies. Once they heard about Stein's plans and began their lobbying, Wang would be forced to go back on the promises he had made in person during his meeting with Stein.

In view of the stories about Stein that reached Wang's ears, it is not surprising that this is what happened. At the beginning of 1931, various newspapers in China published what they alleged was a report on Stein's meeting with his Harvard sponsors. Whether or not Wang believed the report, its publication made it hard for him to resist the scholars' demand that Stein's work be prohibited. The tone of his reproaches to the British in Nanking, as recorded in their official minutes, suggests that he was genuinely offended and upset. But it is possible that he was simply taking advantage of an opportunity to solve his own difficulties. He could certainly justify withdrawing his support from Stein – and thus satisfy the scholars – by appearing to believe the report, since it presented a picture of Western cultural imperialism that was offensive indeed.

Issued by the Kuo Wen news agency, the attack claimed to quote remarks which Stein had allegedly made the previous year at a meeting of the board of trustees of the Harvard Yenching Institute:

I only know Old China and do not pay the least attention to the slogans and catch-words of Young China. The Kuomintang is most disreputable and should not be heeded by foreigners . . . Moreover, Sinkiang is not Chinese territory, and there is no central government in China. Sinkiang is not fully civilised. I think I can do with Sinkiang officials today what I used to do with those of the old regime. If you can give me some additional money with which to bribe them, I can have everything my own way in Sinkiang.[37]

No one familiar with Stein's letters would accept this as a direct quotation, no matter how cleverly it twists his opinions for maximum effect. The style is not his, and certainly does not accord with the quiet, cautious approach he had considered so necessary in America. As he wrote later to Publius, when he heard of the allegations against him: 'I never had an occasion there [at Harvard] to appeal for funds or to deliver an "address" on my plan. As you know, all this was spared to me by the quiet effort of my friends from the Fogg Art Museum.'[38] Whoever wrote the report had, perhaps, a way with caricature; but he had not perfected the art of imitation.

As a piece of xenophobic propaganda in China, however, the report had a devastating effect. Dr Wang and his deputy told British representatives in Nanking that they felt they had been fooled and tricked. Their indignation was reinforced by exaggerated reports of Stein's finances, their distrust of his surveying activities, and what they then learnt of his own published descriptions of the methods he had used to remove valuable relics from Chinese temples and graves.

His passport still held good, Dr Wang graciously pointed out, for the purposes he had originally described, of completing his life's work by tracing the ancient highways between China and the West. But it was now essential that he provide a signed, detailed breakdown of the work he proposed to do and the timetable he planned to follow.

In an attempt to salvage something from the situation, Lampson offered assurances that Stein would remove nothing from Sinkiang without Chinese consent; but it was far too late for such gestures. The offer had been held in reserve, having seemed unnecessary (Lampson claimed) at the time of the original agreement with Wang. Now it was useless. From various remarks made in the official correspondence in the archives of the British Museum, it is clear that several British and American diplomats in China felt Stein had brought difficulties on himself: whether by writing so openly about his exploits in earlier books, by not being more explicit at the outset about the question of finds, or by failing to contact the cultural societies. Lampson himself believed there was still a chance that Stein could complete his expedition if he made the effort to go to Urumchi and persuade the Governor there of his best intentions.

But Stein had had enough. He had little faith in the beneficial effects of a journey to the provincial capital, and even less in any attempt to appease his opponents in Peking. He had almost reached Charchan by late February when he received yet another message from Captain Sherriff about the cancellation of his passport, and the news pushed him into a final decision. He would abandon all his plans and head back to Kashgar, via Charkhlik and Korla. Once there he would apply for permission to spend the summer in the T'ien-shan. If it was refused, he would return to Kashmir without further delay.

It was a sadly ignoble end to a successful career in Central Asia. But failure seems not to have had the profound effect on Stein which it would almost certainly have had in former years. Though this final expedition had been nobody's idea but his own, and he had planned it with his usual care, he treated it with emotional detachment – a detachment which, perhaps, contributed in some way to its empty conclusion.

Within a few weeks of having cancelled his programme, he was writing to the Indian Foreign Secretary to enlist his help in securing permission for an archaeological survey in Iran. To Publius he admitted that his 2,000-mile circumambulation of the desert felt like nothing so much as a farewell tour. Together with old retainers including his camelman, Hassan Akhun, he enjoyed the opportunity of seeing for the last time many friends, such as Badruddin Khan in Khotan, and 'familiar scenes full of happy memories'.[39] He was by this time a famous figure among the people of the Tarim Basin. Peter Fleming, who travelled through the area five years later, frequently heard him spoken of 'with respect and admiration', and C.P. Skrine, British Consul in Kashgar from 1922 till 1924, wrote that 'all antiquities other than gold brought in by the "Taklamanchis" or treasure-seekers of the Takla Makan are regarded as his property and to be kept for him'.[40]

He returned to Kashgar with few results. His Pathans had surreptitiously collected some ancient documents from one part of the Niya site, and Afrazgul Khan had made longitude observations with the wireless apparatus at dead of night in order to avoid the attentions of Chang, the 'sneaky' Chinese who had accompanied the party. At the

British Consulate, Sherriff helped Stein photograph the documents so that the originals could remain until the question of their ultimate destination was settled (which it was when the authorities in Kashgar insisted on retaining them on behalf of the scholars in Peking). Then, having had no reply to his request for permission to visit the T'ien-shan, Stein took his leave of Chini Bagh for the last time, turned his back on the shifting sands of the Tarim Basin and headed for home across the Pamir Mountains.

———————◆◆—————

Initially, Stein's inclination was to seek to publicize his version of events in Sinkiang. Perhaps public self-justification and righteous indignation helped soothe a pride hurt by bitter defeat at the hands of cultural organizations which he considered 'specious'. Publius had already written to *The Times* in defence of his friend;[41] but Stein told Helen Allen he was disappointed by the way in which the papers at home had dwelt on his difficulties, in contrast to the scant attention they had given his earlier, more successful expeditions. To counteract this, he sent *The Times* his own account which it published on its leader page on 16 July 1931.[42] He also hoped Professor Vogel in Leiden would help put his explanation of events before the forthcoming International Congress of Orientalists there, so that the Congress could express an opinion which might have 'some useful effect' on scholars in China and bring them to 'a more discriminating frame of mind.'[43]

When he suggested to Lampson that a copy of his account be presented to his Chinese opponents, however, the response was discouraging. Lampson sympathized with Stein and regretted the unfortunate course events had taken. 'It is always the same story with the Chinese,' he wrote; 'when they think they have a grievance, they rush immediately to extremes, spoil by their outrageous behaviour whatever cause they may have had (and there is usually something to be said on their side to begin with), and thus put themselves utterly in the wrong . . .'. But he felt that no purpose would be served by further publicity for Stein's case. 'Times have changed, and in this and other respects the Chinese are nowadays masters in their own house.'[44]

Ultimately, Stein chose to forget his fourth expedition to Chinese Turkestan. Later in life he seldom referred to it, and it was not mentioned by his obituarists. Perhaps he simply felt it to be unimportant because it produced no results, and because he quickly moved on to other projects. But one cannot help suspecting that its disappearance from the record of his work indicates a conscious desire on his part to eradicate an unpleasant, if not humiliating memory from his mind. He was not used to failure and had always prided himself on overcoming obstacles. But on this occasion he had badly misjudged the nature of those obstacles, and his errors had been mercilessly exposed.

While he was still in Chinese Central Asia, an eloquent plea had been issued to Stein's sponsors. In the name of the National Commission for the Preservation of Antiquities, nineteen Chinese academics – professors and lecturers, heads of colleges and directors of research institutes – invited Harvard, the Archaeological Survey of India and the British Museum to consider 'whether in the interest of science and international good feeling they should continue their support promised to Sir Aurel Stein'. They claimed that Stein had used his interest in Hiuen Tsiang to conceal the fact that he intended to take archaeological objects from Sinkiang and had thus obtained his passport dishonourably; that the wholesale removal of documents from the hidden library of Tun-huang was little short of 'commercial vandalism'; and they pointed out that other countries had enacted laws prohibiting unauthorized excavations and the export of archaeological treasures. The Chinese government had promulgated just such a law in June 1930, they said, and they believed they had 'the sympathy of all true students of scientific archaeology all over the world' in opposing any attempt by Stein or other foreigners to excavate under false pretences and smuggle historical objects out of the country.[45]

Hindsight is a facile gift. The National Commission for the Preservation of Antiquities itself made use of it in referring to the days of 1907, when there was nothing to stop Stein removing items from the Caves of the Thousand Buddhas and several reasons for him to believe that they would eventually be dispersed and lost if he did not do so. Exercising the same faculty today, it is easier than it was for Stein's Western friends and colleagues to see matters from the point of view of the scholars of China: people whose country had been exploited shamelessly by Europeans for decades, and who were finding a sense of modern nationhood at least partly in their desire to claim their inheritance.

13

In Search of Another Dead Desert

IN JUNE 1932 at a meeting in London, the speaker, Stein's old friend Sir Edward Maclagan, used an Iranian anecdote to explain Stein's approach to his work. The story concerned a young officer in the army of the eighteenth-century Iranian ruler, Nadir Shah, who, hearing his king qualify his praise of a certain sword by the observation that it was too short, gave the word of command: 'One pace to the front'. That, observed Maclagan, had been the motto of Stein's life. Whatever difficulties he had encountered, he had relied on his own resources, taken 'one pace to the front' and conquered all setbacks.

At no time had such a motto been more relevant to Stein's circumstances than in the aftermath of his fourth expedition to Chinese Turkestan. Of the admiring orientalists who gathered at 74 Grosvenor Street, London, that day in 1932 to see Stein presented with the Royal Asiatic Society's gold medal, perhaps only Maclagan knew Stein well enough to sense that there was more to his friend's sustained activity, as he approached his seventieth birthday, than simply the desire to complete his work successfully. It was true, certainly, that he felt there were tasks as yet uncompleted. But whether those tasks existed as reminders of things long intended, or whether he had created them precisely in order to give himself further goals, was a question left unanswered by the laudatory addresses at the Society's presentation.

Stein had no desire to share the fate of Maclagan and others like him, who had come home to an English retirement after a career in India. His only real ties were to his work, his summer camp and the peripatetic life that had obliged the Society to seek him in Kashmir, Baluchistan and Iran before their enquiries finally tracked him down in Istanbul. More work must be found, therefore. And, having quit Chinese Central Asia for good, it was to Iran that Stein turned to find it.

The possibility of conducting what he liked to call 'archaeological reconnaissances' in Iran had occurred to him years earlier, and especially since his tours of Indian Baluchistan and the Makran in the late 1920s. To cross the border westward would be the logical extension of his search for prehistoric sites linking the culture of the Indus valley with that of Sumeria. It would also revive his own past when, as a student in Tübingen, he had studied the Avesta, the ancient sacred book of the Iranian Zoroastrian faith. But Iran had been the archaeological preserve of the French since 1897, when the French government secured exclusive rights to dig there so that Jacques de Morgan could excavate the now famous site of Susa, in Khuzistan. Stein felt the monopoly had not served Iran particularly well, since it had resulted in extensive research at a handful of places at the expense of all else. The positive aspect of this, however, was that there was plenty of scope for the sort of pioneering survey he enjoyed.

By the time he went to Boston in late 1929, the French monopoly had lapsed and his sponsors happily agreed that, if his Chinese project proved unsuccessful, they would support whatever work he cared to do in Iran. It was the promise of this new field that insulated him from the dismay he might otherwise have felt in Sinkiang during 1930–1. When Chinese objections to his presence seemed insuperable, he could write his application to visit Iran, and return to India in the knowledge that new doors were opening even as older ones slammed shut.

The wholehearted support of his American friends encouraged him to plan for more than one project. For some years he had been contemplating a short tour in the Punjab in order to tackle an Alexandrian mystery of the type he so relished. The question of exactly where Alexander the Great had crossed the Jhelum River – or Hydaspes as the Greeks had known it – had been much discussed already. Scholars had pored over the historians' accounts in the isolation of their studies, and classically educated men in the service of the Indian government had pondered the matter on the banks of the river itself. There was a particular fascination in the fact that it had been the penultimate feat of the conqueror before he abandoned his relentless drive eastward. Once across the Jhelum, Alexander had defeated Poros, king of the region beyond, in a great battle, and had planned to lead his army on across the River Beas (or Hyphasis). But his own troops, depressed and exhausted by the endless succession of conquests and advances over difficult terrain, had forced him to turn for home.

Stein, familiar with all the theories concerning the exact location of the river crossing and subsequent battle, but dissatisfied with them, was eager to search for clues on the ground before starting for Iran. On his return to Kashmir from Kashgar in July 1931, he set about organizing the necessary permissions for both places. From Iran he would be allowed to remove his finds in order to have them studied and recorded, on the understanding that they would then be divided equally between the Iranian authorities and his sponsors. In India, however, legislation meant that it was now as difficult as it was in Chinese Turkestan for a privately funded archaeologist to excavate or remove antiquities – a similarity which, if Stein noticed, he did not remark upon. An amendment to the Ancient Monuments Preservation Act of India which would create more flexibility had been delayed and was unlikely to be passed in time to be of use to him.

Resigning himself to these limitations, he left Srinagar at the end of October, equipped with baggage and kit for the Punjab, for Iran and for the visit to Europe which he planned for the following summer. But more notable than this long-range itinerary was the fact that he had chosen to be accompanied by an assistant. Neither an Indian employee nor an American pressed on him by his sponsors, this was a young man Stein knew by repute and whose background perhaps reminded him of his own youth.

The assistant was Károly Fábri, a 31-year-old Hungarian orientalist from Budapest, who had studied under Sylvain Lévi in Paris and had been working for some time with Stein's colleague, Vogel, at the Kern Institute in Leiden. He came from a well-off Jewish family whose fortune had evaporated after the war, and had worked hard to gain qualifications in Indology in the face of obstruction from the Hungarian regime. He was enthusiastic, hard-working and talented – and he was one of Stein's greatest admirers.

It was not unusual for Stein to be in contact with Hungarians interested in India and the East. One or two had visited him on the Marg, including Ervin Baktay, a writer who became known in India and his home country for his work on Kőrösi Csoma. But Fábri's eagerness seems to have struck a particular chord. The Harvard grant meant Stein was free to offer him paid employment in the East, a chance for which he had long been hoping and which would enable him to look for a permanent post. He joined Stein at Lahore in early November and immediately made a favourable impression. Stein told Publius that he was 'thoroughly businesslike, an indefatigable worker and in addition very modest & genuinely attached. There is some risk of his spoiling me by his solicitude for my comfort & ease.'[1]

There was also the company of a new Dash, the sixth in line and 'a very promising reincarnation of Dash the Great'.[2] This fox-terrier had no pedigree, which Stein took as an encouraging indication of hardiness (the Airedale, Dash V, had been better bred, but had had what he considered an over-sensitive constitution). Dash VI was ten months old, robust and chirpy, and Stein was pleased to find that both his new companions, canine and human, seemed equal to all that the sometimes harsh conditions of camp life demanded of them.

The few weeks spent in the Salt Range of the Punjab and beside the Jhelum River were a gentle introduction to that life. Fábri enjoyed them for the first insights they gave him into Indian ways, and Stein was glad to have returned to the site of his early archaeological investigations. This time, on the trail of the Macedonians, he measured distances and compared geographical features with those described by the historians Arrian and Curtius, stalking the ground and assessing the evidence as if performing his own, topographical variation on the theme popularized by Conan Doyle.

Believing Alexander to have used the same route through the Salt Range as was mentioned later by Muslim chroniclers, via the Nandana Pass, Stein argued that he would therefore have reached the Jhelum at a point near the modern village of Haranpur. From there, it was the same distance to the town of Jalalpur as the Alexandrian historians gave for the ride along the river in search of a crossing place. Jalalpur occupied a position on the riverbank which fitted their descriptions, and the level ground on the far bank was extensive enough to accommodate a battle such as Poros waged and lost.

Having proved to his own satisfaction that this was the point of the crossing, Stein took his investigation one step farther. It was at Jalalpur, where coins had been found dating from the periods of Greek Bactrian and Indo-Scythian rule in the north-west (in other words, immediately before and after the beginning of the Christian era), that he believed Alexander had founded his city of Boukephela, named after his famous horse which had died there. The conclusions he drew from this short tour in the Punjab still carry weight today though, as with other Alexandrian questions, there may never be a definitive interpretation of the evidence.

The appeal of the Salt Range extended to its people, too. Most of the able-bodied men had seen service in France, Mesopotamia or Iran during the war and retained a loyalty to 'sahibs' which contrasted, reassuringly for Stein, with the extremist agitation of nationalists else-where in the country. Nothing the members of the Indian Congress Party said could persuade him that India would be better off without the British Raj, and the view he enjoyed from the hills seemed aptly to justify his opinion. Across the distant plains he could see mile upon mile of fields where semi-desert conditions had prevailed before the canal-building and settlement work, now several decades old, of men such as his old friend Malcolm Hailey.

The fact that Hailey was now Governor of the United Provinces, and a delegate at the Round Table Conference on the future of India, was a gleam of light in a world he saw darkening around him. Violence was increasing, and the communal conflicts which seemed irrevocably linked with talk of independence had recently spread to Srinagar, where Hindu families had lived peaceably with Muslims for as long as Stein had known the state. He believed them to be the work of out-siders from the Frontier, where blood feuds and periodic uprisings against imperial rule were a way of life among the Pathans. But he had little faith in the ability of the new ruler of Kashmir, Hari Singh, to show the necessary leadership. In letters to Publius he described the Maharaja as more interested in spending money on lakeside boule-vards, Rolls-Royces and visits to Europe than on providing flood relief schemes which would ease the distress of his people.[3] It was a depress-ing situation. And for Stein, as usual, the antidote lay in contemplation of the past.

The work Stein carried out in Iran spanned four years and thousands of miles. Beginning on what was then the Indo-Iranian border (now the border between Iran and Pakistan), he travelled initially through Iranian Baluchistan in 1932 and along the Persian Gulf during the winter and spring of 1932–3. In late 1933 he returned for a journey through eastern Fars, the ancient Persis; and in 1935–6 he explored the western part of the same province before moving into Khuzistan, Luristan and north-ward into Iranian Kurdistan.

As in Chinese Turkestan, the scene of his earlier exploits, the aim was not detailed excavation but rapid examination of the ground, with limited trial digging in order to establish key facts. The French had made Susa and Persepolis famous through their intensive studies over many years, and to compete with such work would have been too costly, even if Stein had wanted to attempt it. But he had never been attracted by the prospect of long months spent on a single site, and four expeditions in the Taklamakan Desert had only reinforced his preference for small-scale, highly mobile and meagrely staffed archaeological exploration.

Iranian prehistory was a suitable target for such methods. Little was known about it, and Stein himself felt that his best contribution to the subject would be in the form of 'archaeological reconnaissances' which, literally, scratched the surface, providing a record of sites which future generations of archaeologists could investigate more fully. It was modest, unglamorous but pioneering work; the sort that many archae-ologists might hesitate to undertake at all, let alone begin so late in life. There were no quick pay-offs in the form of rewarding finds, as there had been in the Taklamakan Desert. Stein achieved as much as he did simply by plodding across the countryside.

He did not find all the sites that are known today, nor could he date what he found with any great accuracy. But he covered the ground with his usual efficiency, and produced detailed maps with the help of his surveyor, Muhammad Ayub Khan, who accompanied him on each of his Iranian journeys by courtesy of the Survey of India. Almost all the archaeological work done in Iran since then has followed up Stein's initial reports.

The surveying which had aroused the suspicions of the Chinese in Sinkiang did not escape the notice of the Iranians either. Though initial difficulties were quickly settled, his activities were always open to mis-interpretation. Political tensions over the status of the Anglo-Persian

Oil Company may well have influenced the authorities in their decision to refuse him permission to complete parts of the itineraries he planned.

Generally, however, he found arrangements far easier to make than in modern China. Negotiation for the necessary permissions was conducted through the Foreign Office, the British Minister in Tehran and the various consulates in which he stayed during his journeys, and the Iranians dealt with his roving habits by insisting that he was accompanied by an armed escort as well as, on the last two expeditions, an inspector of antiquities. Stein enjoyed the company of both inspectors but, unsurprisingly, thought the escorts a needless precaution. He discovered that they had their uses, however, when their commanding officers were able, by their influence in the areas visited, to recruit labourers or procure information about local sites.

Iran in the 1930s was a fast-developing country. It had played an undignified role during the First World War as reluctant host to Russian, British and German soldiers, diplomats and spies. But it had begun to assert its independence under the leadership of Reza Khan, an army officer who had hurtled to prominence in the confused aftermath of the war and been crowned Shah in 1926. His aim was a strong, independent country, freed from foreign interference but organized on Western lines by means of social and economic reforms and industrialization. With the onset of the Depression in the 1930s, however, these changes took the form of growing centralization. To Stein, travelling through remote areas of the country, state control manifested itself chiefly in the form of military surveillance, and in delays while any request that deviated from or added to his original proposals was considered in Tehran. He also noticed the difficulties imposed by social reorganization on the nomadic tribes, who could not easily adjust to enforced settlement in a single place.

With his usual interest in ethnic matters, he included such observations in his written accounts of his Iranian journeys, together with references to tribal unrest where it arose, and the 'independent' chieftains who helped him along the way. His scholarly enthusiasm for noting such details seems to have dimmed his appreciation of their political implications. In April 1934 the British Minister in Tehran, Sir Reginald Hoare, having seen the earliest of Stein's reports, felt constrained to write with a word of advice. It would be better, he suggested, not to forward any reprints of the article in question, in the Royal Geographical Society's *Geographical Journal*, to any Iranian officials, or even to André Godard, the French Director of the Iranian Archaeological Service. Most of what Stein had written was unexceptionable, he assured him. But the references to tribal chiefs and unrest were 'just the sort of things which the Persian Government didn't want you to see or hear about. Moreover, it might do some of the chiefs who helped you no good to be mentioned.' Of course, it was possible that people in Iran might see the article anyway, but it was best not to draw attention to it if Stein wished to continue working in the country.[4]

Stein's first season of work began in early January 1932, when he crossed the border from India near the port of Gwadar with his small party, consisting of Fábri, Muhammad Ayub Khan and two Kashmiris who acted as cook and clerk. Within two days he was excavating his first site, clearing sixty-odd cairns in an ancient burial ground and dating them to the centuries immediately before and after the beginning of the Christian era – like others he had identified earlier in Baluchistan and the Makran. Nearby lay the remains of a fort containing ceramic ware from Sassanian or early Muslim times; a later period than he was primarily concerned with, but which stimulated his interest throughout his time in the country.

In this way he travelled through the inhospitable landscape of south-east Iran, from Bampur north-west to Kerman, digging far enough into old mounds to find items such as pottery or ceramic shards, stone implements, bronze objects, alabaster cups and funerary deposits. They showed similarities both with his finds across the border and with discoveries made, for example, at Susa in the west of Iran, confirming his expectation that the same civilization had extended across the region at about the close of the fourth millennium BC.

At the same time, thoughts of Alexander's journey through the region were a pleasant distraction. And when the day's tasks were done he could avail himself of Fábri's ability to take dictation in four languages directly on to a typewriter, which relieved him of much of the desk work he found so dreary. His young assistant provided genial company of a kind Stein had not previously known. Years later, Fábri described how they sometimes sat together in the evenings, in front of their tents, reading the poems of the nineteenth-century Hungarian poet János Arany.[5]

This unusual period in Stein's life proved short-lived, however. In March 1932, Paul Sachs wrote from America to say that, as a result of the severe economic depression, he felt it best not to call on the third and final instalment of funds. He left the ultimate decision to Stein, and emphasized that the sponsors had so far paid up without complaint. But it was clear that, since many of them had recently incurred heavy financial losses, he did not want to ask them to honour their pledges.

Stein's response was immediate and without any sign of umbrage (though some of his friends were indignant on his behalf when they heard what had happened). He agreed entirely with Sachs, observing that, in any case, careful use of the money already granted to him would enable him to return for a second expedition without the need to ask for more.[6] The only economy he would be obliged to make would be to do without an assistant. Fábri was due to spend the summer of 1932 working at the British Museum with Fred Andrews on the material collected so far in Iran, and would then return to Leiden. Stein consoled himself with the thought that this would suit his young friend well, since he missed his English wife.

With his own return to Iran planned for the autumn, he set out for a summer in England. *En route* to the port of Bushire, he made a brief detour to Persepolis to meet Professor Herzfeld, the archaeologist in charge, who had been a good friend of Thomas Arnold. Another break in the journey at Istanbul was a deliberate pilgrimage to the place where the Hierarch had spent a week on the way home from Egypt, just before his fatal heart attack. Stein received a warm welcome from more of Arnold's friends, scholars of various nationalities working in the city, and lingered among the paintings in the Old Seraglio which he knew his friend had loved.

If Stein hoped that England would offer an escape from the oppressive political climate of India, he would find it only by immersing himself in the cloistered world of Oxford academia, for there was little solace beyond. The economic slump which had already engulfed his American sponsors was wreaking havoc in the British Isles too. He had followed events from afar and had been heartened by the result of the general election in October 1931, when the Conservative-dominated 'National Government' took over from a limping Labour Party. But there was little room in his heart for sympathy with the grievances of the working classes. In a letter to Publius he expressed the view that the British were too interested in high wages, reduced output, heavy meals and 'vicarious exercise' (by which he meant spectator sports such as football) for their own good, and that they would be better off making do with simpler standards of living, as did the French.[7] Indeed, he regarded universal franchise as a 'millstone' round the neck of democracy.[8]

Worries over national issues were completely overshadowed, however, by the ill-health which afflicted Publius that same summer. Allen had been showing signs of strain for several years, and his duties had become heavier since he had agreed to be chairman of the committee overseeing the construction of the new Bodleian Library building. In June he caught a chill that exacerbated what was probably an existing prostate condition, and no fewer than three operations followed in the space of a few weeks before the problem was thought to be solved.

It proved a false hope. Despite holidays by the sea in East Devon, he continued to succumb to new infections just when full recovery seemed at hand. During a visit to old haunts such as Tübingen and Dresden, and to Harriet and her ailing sister Justine, Stein wrote more frequently than ever to Helen, willing the recovery of his friend. But it was a pitiful image, of Publius dogged by disease, that he was forced to carry away with him when he set off again for Iran in September 1932 on his second expedition.

In contrast to his journeys back to India, the trip to Iran could be done entirely overland, and almost entirely by train. Having called at Vienna and Budapest, Stein travelled through Serbia, Bulgaria and Thrace to Istanbul, changing there to the Taurus Express which carried him down to Aleppo and Baghdad. From the Iraqi capital it was a relatively short motor ride across the border to Tehran, where he met the Ministers of Foreign Affairs, Education and War, as well as the Chief of Staff. And from there, using Reza Shah's newly built roads, he travelled to Isfahan where he met Godard, the Director of Antiquities, for the first time.

Beyond lay Kerman, where Ayub Khan had spent the summer (with Dash) surveying nearby ground in anticipation of Stein's return. Ali Bat, the Kashmiri cook, and a new clerk (who for reasons of caste also had his own cook) had made their way there after a steamer journey from

Karachi to Bandar Abbas. Stein had conveyed details of their travel arrangements to them through a long-serving clerk in Srinagar, Pandit Ram Chand Bali. Included in those details were instructions as to what Ali Bat was to bring in the way of supplies for the forthcoming expedition through the poor, parched country of the Persian Gulf.

Stein's official escort for this second Iranian tour, which started early in November 1932, was one-fifth the size of the eighty-strong party provided for the first, and he hoped for an uneventful journey through the south. But his aims were partially obstructed, first by an unhelpful officer in charge of the escort who prevented any survey work or excavations until Stein managed to have him replaced, and then by government fears of unrest which banned him from the hill country of Laristan. There was no sign along 600 miles of the Gulf coast of any prehistoric remains, lending weight to the argument which Stein seems to have supported, that trade between this region and the Indus civilization was unlikely to have existed. But he found fragments of Chinese porcelain, stoneware and copper coins that testified to contact in medieval times between the Gulf and the Far East, and he enjoyed the massive, silent remains of Siraf, a great maritime centre in the early Muslim period.

Apart from a brief climb into the cool, green, narcissi-clad hills behind Siraf, he was forced to keep to the coast, dodging looters and walking part of the time in order to spare the puny donkeys. Transport became increasingly difficult to secure in this famine-ravaged region, where no rain had fallen for two years. So in mid-January he struck on the idea of taking to the sea in order to reach Daiyir, forty miles beyond Tahiri, where camels might be found.

The only vessel available was an old, battered, 45-foot local boat which Stein's men viewed with trepidation. But he loaded them in and they set sail in good conditions, passing Tahiri by nightfall. Before long, however, the wind veered from south round to north and increased to gale force. The leaky little boat pitched violently, sending all but Stein into paroxysms of sea-sickness. With difficulty its navigators reefed the sail and aimed for the shore, two men bailing all the while with old kerosene cans. When day broke, it revealed a village which Stein and his party had passed, on land, more than a month earlier. The storm had driven them farther back down the coast than the point from which they had started.

It was typical of Stein that he should regard this episode with detached, academic interest. Recalling the voyage of Nearchus, Alexander's admiral, from the Indus to the Gulf, he wrote: 'The misery endured by my people and escort on this short cruise [a characteristically inadequate choice of noun] provided in a way a useful antiquarian experience; for it let me realize better than I might have done otherwise how Nearchos' [*sic*] men may have felt in their crowded small ships when making their way along a coast so exposed to strong and rapidly changing winds as that of the Persian Gulf.'[9]

A more down-to-earth view came from Kenneth Mason, who was now (thanks in part to Stein's recommendations) Professor of Geography at Oxford and a trustee of his will in place of Arnold. Mason remarked to a colleague: 'I wish . . . that he wouldn't go doing the Nearchus trick in an Arab dhow in the Persian Gulf. I don't want to have to settle his estate for many years yet: and I call it an unfriendly act at the age of 70 to tempt providence.'[10]

Stein prided himself on the sort of careful planning that avoided the tempting of providence. So perhaps he chose to report his sea journey in such detached terms in order to understate what he recognized privately as a particularly ill-judged risk. In any case, he saw no need to make his age a consideration. Having reached Bushire on 20 February and learned that the government had banned him temporarily from further travel, and having decided to return to Kashmir for the summer, his chief concern was for the health not of himself but of Publius. But, going first to Swat, in order to follow up his work of 1926, he fell from his horse and cracked his collar-bone. He told the Allens this news only on 13 May after he had reached Srinagar, had had his shoulder X-rayed and could truthfully say that all was well. He preferred not to announce accidents except when necessary (and not to mention them at all to his sister-in-law). He reported this fall now, he told the Allens, only because he was prompted by their 'very just remark about the need of being told the plain facts'.[11]

The plain facts about Publius's health were ominous. Two bouts of 'flu weakened him early in the year, and these were followed by a lengthy fever. In the increasingly brief spells of recovery between these relapses, he followed college affairs and studied Erasmus, in the hope that he would be able to complete his work on the proofs of the eighth volume of letters and begin the next. But it was evident that his health was failing, despite the 'undaunted courage and strength of soul' which Stein so admired both in him and in Helen.[12]

Stein himself was distressed at being so far from them and so help-less in the face of such a crisis. For all his powers of overcoming set-backs, there was nothing he could do now for his dearest friend but wait impotently for news. On hearing that members of the college had given blood so that Publius could undergo a transfusion, he wrote that he would willingly give 'all that my blood sustains' in order to restore him to health. He himself had lived long enough, he told Publius, and his departure would make little impact. 'The tragedy is that in the fight with illness life cannot save life as it might in battle.'[13]

Publius never read the letter. He died, five days after it was written, on 16 June 1933 in the President's Lodgings at Corpus, shortly before his sixty-fourth birthday. The cable announcing his death reached Stein on Mohand Marg four days later.

At the same time as Stein received the news he had been dreading, Publius's funeral took place in the small chapel of Corpus, while Merton, next door, held a service simultaneously. That evening, Fred Andrews sat down in his home on Sydenham Hill in south-east London to write to the only other surviving member of the original band of friends who had once shared Mayo Lodge. 'I went to the Chapel and attended the Service,' he told Stein. 'I saw Madam [Helen] but could not speak to her. She was brave, as you know she would be. Her brother, Ernest, was supporting her and Hailey was also with them. I send you the printed copy of the proceedings and service which I took from a vacant place beside me in the Chapel where I felt you were in spirit.

'Forgive me if I do not write more now. I do not know what to write. I cannot yet bring myself to realize that he is gone out of our lives.'[14]

The loss of Publius created a permanent, aching void in Stein's life. He had relied on him, as a faithful correspondent, a supportive friend and a totally dependable provider of refuge. The influence and example of Publius had suffused his life in more ways than could be counted. And the memory of him was with Stein constantly. In everything he did and in every letter he wrote to Helen there was an awareness of Publius's spirit which created, like the compass point in Donne's poem, a 'fixed foot' to which Stein remained attached wherever he went.[15]

Publius had returned his friend's love, perhaps in equal measure. Using, like Donne, a metaphor to describe their bonds of friendship, he had written to Stein, after the latter's departure for India in 1920:

> And now the chain begins to lengthen again, and you go off to Heaven knows what . . . 'And surely never lighted on this orb, which he scarcely seemed to touch, a more delightful vision.' In 1922 I look forward to walking down again into the garden behind you and to seeing that light step and erect bearing which makes the quotation above so appropriate. But whether it be 1922 or 3 or even 4, the chain that binds us all together is so well and truly forged that no distance of time, space or anything else, can break or strain it: whereat we rejoice exceedingly.[16]

Stein's dedication to the memory of his friend found expression in his devotion to Helen Allen. Devotion in itself was not new, for he had often declared it. His letters to Publius, he would tell them, were meant for them both. The very fact that they were a couple, living 'in happiest unison of thought, feeling and labour',[17] had always been important to him, representing an utterly secure foundation on which he could rest his need for family contact. Nevertheless, it was to Publius rather than Helen that he had addressed his private thoughts during more than thirty years. Apart from the fact that the two men had first met when Publius was still a bachelor, Stein could never have developed a close friendship with an unrelated woman, such as he enjoyed with Helen, other than through another man.

Now Publius was dead; but his death made a continuing link with his widow essential. Without the sustained friendship of Helen, Stein would lose not only his greatest friend but also the living connection with all his memories, which he needed almost as much as he needed bodily sustenance. And Helen Allen recognized this. Almost immediately, she wrote promising that the weekly letter from Oxford would continue to be sent, just as before. She addressed him in a variety of affectionate forms, sometimes calling him Aurel, but more often 'Dear Huzoor' or 'My dear Sahib'. And in the closing greetings of those letters, she sent not only her own, but also Publius's love, as if she was relaying messages sent directly from beyond the grave.[18]

Stein acknowledged her loyalty with gratitude, and his own letters to the Allen household left Mohand Marg with their customary regularity. But they were not the same. Though they gradually reverted to a more familiar form, with interest in news from 'home' followed by a report of his own activities and plans, for a long time he filled them with expressions of concern for her welfare and pious tributes to her and to Publius's memory. He was to spend the last ten years of his life in close contact with Helen Allen, either through letters or in person, and the intimacy of their friendship was always infused with and qualified by the reverence with which he had learned in childhood to regard the few women he knew well.

Despite Harvard's withdrawal of support from Stein's work in Iran, there was more he wished to do there. His savings had grown in the past couple of years; so he felt able to fund a third journey from his own pocket. Renewed permission to travel was necessary, however, and localized unrest in tribal areas was making the Iranian government hesitant about granting it. While he waited, Stein worked on the results of his first two tours there, and on the lecture he was due to give the following year at the Royal Anthropological Institute in London, to mark their award to him of the prestigious Huxley Medal.

He picked flowers on the Marg and sent them to Helen for Publius's memorial stone on the altar steps of Corpus Chapel, beneath which his ashes lay. And he busied himself with arrangements for the disposal of his belongings after his own death in an effort, he said, to ease the duties of his executors (of whom Helen Allen was now one, in place of her husband). He sent thirty carpets home, for storage or use by friends, catalogued those of his books intended for the Hungarian Academy which had not been dispatched in 1924, and arranged for books normally kept with the Allens to be housed temporarily by Mason at the Geographical Institute in Oxford, while Helen made arrangements for her move from Corpus.

Late in Publius's life, the Allens had decided to give their fondness for weekends in the Cotswolds a firm footing by taking the lease on a house there. The property they chose, Barton House, stood on the Corpus estate at Temple Guiting, in the same valley as the hamlet of Ford, where they had often stayed and to which they had introduced Stein. Publius did not live to enjoy the new arrangement, but his widow decided to keep the house, partly in memory of his delight at having secured it. Stein heartily concurred with this decision. He sent flower seeds to be planted in the garden, and ordered a copy of the relevant Ordnance Survey map in order to be able to visualize the area and to follow Helen's walks there with her sister Olga, with whom she now lived. In response to her hope that he would regard it as his home when in England, he persuaded her to accept £80 per annum towards its rent, on the basis that this was the sum of the annuity he had already arranged for her to receive after his death.

In November, he returned to Iran with his surveyor, Muhammad Ayub Khan. The British Consulate at Bushire had housed much of his equipment since his last trip: shovels, pick-axes, hoes, buckets, tent pegs, kettles, pans, lanterns and kitchen stores all could be collected there. There was also pleasant news awaiting him. The British School in Iraq had offered to support his third tour up to a maximum of £500, which he accepted gladly. His plan was to travel in the province of Fars, the original region of Persia, home of the Achaemenid dynasty which ruled from the sixth century BC until the coming of Alexander. The Iranian government had granted him permission and Godard had arranged for him to be accompanied by a young Inspector of Antiquities, Mirza Azizullah Khan Kazimi. One of the British diplomats in Tehran explained that, though Kazimi did not have the advantage, in dealing with petty officials, of belonging to a notable family, he had proved himself a good assistant to other archaeologists and was the only man suitably 'active' for Stein's needs.[19]

Fars had received little archaeological attention beyond the Achaemenid sites of Pasargadae and Persepolis, and Stein was able to log a number of prehistoric sites yielding remains similar to those found both in Iranian Baluchistan and much farther west. But he also came across many reminders of the Sassanians, whose dominance lasted from the third century AD until the coming of Islam and included some forty rulers. Massive buildings whose stones were set in hard mortar, and whose great domes had survived successive centuries practically unscathed, still reared out of the arid and otherwise empty landscape. In the 'town of Ij' at the foot of the Tudej range, he wandered among ruins that had lain empty and desolate since the Mongol invasions of the thirteenth century. He photographed two colossal rock-wall relief sculptures commemorating the victory of the Sassanian Shapur I over the Roman Emperor Valerian, and concluded his journey with a return to the area of Pasargadae and Persepolis, riding through the defile of Bulaki along a gallery built into the cliff walls by the Achaemenids to carry their kings between the two royal seats.

The work was full of interest, but not in the same category as his expeditions to Chinese Central Asia. Writing to Helen in March 1934, he told her: 'Please do not think of my present travelling as "heroic" in any way. Compared with the Taklamakan and the Kun-lun travel both in these valleys & across the mountains seems very "tame" work.'[20]

————◆—◀——

Europe was tamer still; but a combination of duty and the ties of friendship and family called him there again in the summer of 1934. The Huxley Memorial Lecture which he gave at University College, London, on the last day of July – 'The Indo-Iranian Borderlands, their Prehistory in the Light of Geography and of recent Explorations' – was only one of several official engagements. When he could escape from the capital he stayed with Helen in her new house in Oxford, 22 Manor Place, which she had had built on land owned by Merton College. It was designed by T. Harold Hughes, the architect who had extended the President's Lodgings at Corpus at the beginning of Publius's term of office, and it had hot and cold water on tap, with a suite specially designed to provide Stein with his own bedroom and study.

The house at Temple Guiting, however, saw more of him. It had all the qualities he demanded of a 'retreat' where he could work on his books and papers, though it took him some time to get used to being there without Helen and Olga. (Helen had already resumed her trips to the Continent in search of Erasmian documents in order to complete her husband's *magnum opus*.) His affection for the English countryside and the place-names of its villages had its roots in the early days of the century, when he had stayed with Fred and Alice Andrews at Clanville. He was a member of the National Trust, and had once confessed to Helen that an article she had sent him from the magazine *Country Life* had interested him rather less than the house advertisements on the reverse of the cutting. The advantages of a rural way of life over an urban one seemed clear to him, and the rapid development of cities during his lifetime only confirmed him in this view. When he visited Budapest now, he stayed in a hotel on St Margaret's Island, a parkland refuge in the Danube just upstream from the centre, in order to escape the noise and crowds of metropolitan life.

No visit to Europe passed without time spent in the city of his birth. He was always welcomed, his presence and the award to him of medals and other honours always reported in the press. He was not exaggerating when he remarked to Helen, regarding the gold medal presented to him by the (British) Society of Antiquaries in 1935, that it was being treated 'as a matter of national satisfaction, in a small way, of course'.[21] For a nation which had not recovered from the humiliation of the Great War and its aftermath, the achievements of her most illustrious sons were a welcome and important antidote.

The attentions of the press seemed to Stein a dubious form of flattery. He was touched by interest from institutions which reminded him of his youth, such as the Ludovica; but it was only personal connections that brought him back to Hungary. Many friends and relatives had died but others, such as a cousin, Rosa, and an old acquaintance, the geographer and politician Count Pál Teleki, remained. One of his closest contacts was Gyula Halász, the writer and journalist who translated his books and whose precarious working life had become something of a concern for Stein. He had introduced Halász's daughters to the Allens in the difficult years after the war, had become a godfather to one of his grandchildren and was always pleased when the translation of a book or report on an expedition resulted in royalties for his friend.

During the summer of 1934, however, Stein spent more time in Vienna than elsewhere in continental Europe. Harriet, now in her eightieth year, was mourning the loss of her sister, Justine. Fortunately, however, her sadness was balanced by affection for her new son-in-law, Gustav Steiner. He was 35 and therefore much younger than his wife. Like her he was a doctor, specializing in neurology, and he had made a great impression on his elderly mother-in-law with what Stein described as his 'fine character and unfailingly tender devotion'.[22] The contrast with her own son was implicit in the remark. Ernst, however, had at least succeeded in his academic aspirations and had acquired a devoted wife. Having begun his career in Berlin, he had been working for some time in Brussels but was about to leave, with his wife Jeanne, for a year in Washington as an exchange professor at the Catholic University there.

In the early autumn, Harriet was troubled with a recurrence of old renal problems and developed a fever. Her condition varied over the next few days and Stein watched anxiously for signs of improvement. On 2 October, having been reassured that there were grounds for hope, he left for Budapest where he was due to give a lecture at the Academy on the 11th. He could receive frequent reports of her health by telephone and planned to return as soon as possible. But on the 11th, arriving back at his hotel on St Margaret's Island from his lecture, he received a call from Thesa. Harriet had died, thirty-two years, short of a day, after her husband.

The affairs of his sister-in-law kept Stein in Vienna until the end of the month. The funeral service, at the central cemetery, was conducted by the Pastor of the Reformed Church, who had been a classmate of the younger Ernst; but Harriet's ashes were taken to the old Protestant cemetery on the other side of Vienna, to lie with those of her long-dead husband. Stein stayed on afterwards to oversee the division of her belongings, mainly in order to prevent any later dispute between her offspring, who were barely on speaking terms.

Sifting through his brother's old books, and the boxes of letters which Harriet had stowed away over the years, Stein was cast back into the long-vanished life of his family. As he had always tried to do during her lifetime, he dwelt only on Harriet's best qualities. She had, he told Helen, 'such a wonderful faculty for letting her thoughts ever surround and shelter those dear to her. And her letters never failed to convey this loving care to me however great the distances separating us and however different the life and surroundings.'[23]

In the circumstances, the hospitality of the Allen household seemed more important than ever. On the evening of Harriet's death, Stein wrote to Helen that, were it not for her friendship and the memories of her husband, he would feel 'very lonely indeed'. That November, unlike so many others, he passed his birthday in the company of the woman who knew better than anyone the need in this solitary man for the comfortable certainties of 'home'. He told her sister, Olga, afterwards that he would cherish 'as long as life lasts the recollection of the brightest festa which ever fell to my share'.[24]

One other friend played an increasingly major role at this time. This was Filippo de Filippi, an Italian climber and surgeon who first met Stein through the Alpine Club in the early years of the century. He had led a major expedition to the Karakoram in 1913–14, under the auspices of the Indian government, and the two men's shared interest in Central Asia had kept them in touch ever since. De Filippi was, as an obituarist later described him, 'a good Italian, but cosmopolitan in the best sense of the word'.[25] He and Stein had much in common: a fastidiousness in domestic order – however different their domestic environments – intellectual tolerance and a refusal to become involved in politics, and stature. The description of de Filippi which the historian G.M. Trevelyan left might well, one senses, have been written of Stein: 'As often happens with men of small stature and great physical and mental energy, he gave a sense of compressed force that was a true interpretation of his mind and character.'[26]

De Filippi had lost his beloved English wife in 1911 and now shared his villa, La Capponcina at Settignano, outside Florence, with his brother's widow and her two daughters. To Stein, bereft of his closest male friend and with more time on his hands than for many years, the de Filippi household was a delightful haven, with its interest in the East, its hospitality and the high spirits and optimism of youth with which his host's nieces infused its atmosphere. The girls seem to have conformed to the same mental picture of the ideal daughter which had made him so admire Gemma Hailey and mourn her loss.

It was to La Capponcina that he went, early in 1935, as a prelude to a holiday in southern Italy. This was a tour he had been anticipating for years, and he was not disappointed. The treasures of the Museo Nazionale at Naples enraptured him, and he paid several visits to Pompeii, sitting among the ruins to eat his packed lunch and pondering the differences and similarities between his present surroundings and those at his 'own' dead cities of Miran and Niya.

In Sicily, with its reminders of his uncle Sigismond's exploits in support of Garibaldi, he explored all the sites; but it was not historic sites alone that made an impression. The cleanliness and the peace that had descended on the streets brought from him unstinted praise. 'How glad one must feel for being able to view all these treasures of Italy's great past in art & culture at a time when fine modern buildings, beneficent innovations and public order attest the great awakening of the nation,' he wrote to Helen.[27]

His sympathies lay naturally with the authoritarian rule of Mussolini that resulted in such public evidence of discipline and order. It was by such signs that he felt paternalistic British influence abroad manifested itself, too, and without which he believed India would be immeasurably poorer. The crisis which Mussolini precipitated by invading Abyssinia seemed to him an irritating distraction. He thought that 'barbarous' country would probably benefit from a taste of the same sort of medicine that India had received from Britain; but that her welfare was unimportant compared with the looming threat of German ambition in Europe. The priority, in his opinion, was to extricate the Italians from quarrels in the Mediterranean in order to have them as allies in a potentially far more damaging conflict.

German ambition had again raised its head since Hitler came to power and Stein was no doubt already aware that, this time, it was ominously tinged with anti-Semitism. So it was a disappointment when, travelling through Germany in May 1935, he was greeted by so many of the superficial signs he had come to associate with regimes he admired. 'It seems so hard to realize', he wrote, almost wistfully, to Helen, 'that a country where all looks so spick & span, even at industrial centres, can by its very spirit of discipline endanger the future of Western civilization.'[28]

———————◆◂———————

The trip through Germany took him back to India to prepare for his fourth and final expedition in Iran, funded from his own pocket. In England he had almost finalized arrangements for the printing and publishing (by Macmillan) of his book on the first two Iranian journeys, and had dedicated it to the memory of Publius.[29] Andrews had taken charge of the division of antiquities between the Iranian government, Harvard and the British Museum, and Sachs was due to arrive from Harvard that summer (*en route* to a visiting professorship in Paris) to sanction his decisions.

Stein was not the only archaeologist in Iran during the 1930s. But no one emulated the long-distance reconnaissance tour which he had made his own. It was a method which might have suited other visitors who wanted to travel through Iran for different reasons. The British travel writer Freya Stark, for example, had announced in the journal of the Royal Asiatic Society that she wanted to accompany any archaeologist going to Luristan. This was one of the areas on Stein's itinerary for his fourth expedition. He admired Stark's writing and sympathized with her aim but, as he commented to Helen, 'in my unsociable way could scarcely comply with it!'[30]

Instead he travelled with his retinue of undemanding male followers: the surveyor Muhammad Ayub Khan, Dash, a couple of servants and a small Iranian escort. A new inspector of antiquities also accompanied him, Mirza Bahman Khan Karimi, a plump, jovial and willing young man who took an enthusiastic interest in photography and received Stein's gift of a camera, at the end of the expedition, with huge delight.

The route for this final tour began in Shiraz in the province of Fars. From there, Stein travelled roughly in a north-westerly direction so that, by the following summer, he had reached the shore of Lake Urumia in Kurdistan. His transport mules were less expensive than on previous occasions, since no Iranian seemed to use them if there was a motor-ized alternative. Stein eschewed such modern methods, except where long stretches of road helped him cross areas in which he had no inter-est. In total during this tour he covered 2,400 miles, either on horseback or on foot.

When he left Shiraz in November 1935, its British Consulate garden was bright with the russet and yellow colours of chinar trees and chrysan-themums. But soon he was back in the familiar bitter cold of winter uplands, enjoying the marching, he told Helen, for the opportunity it gave him to dwell on happy times in the past, spent with friends or on fruitful work. There was another aspect to his enjoyment, which he had experienced once before when in Swat. How good it was, he wrote, 'to carry on my reconnaissances without owing an account to government, learned body or other patrons for the results or the cost involved'.[31]

Free to linger wherever he chose, Stein indulged his interest in the different layers of history that presented themselves along his route, including the Biblical and the Alexandrian. He examined and photo-graphed the massive ruins of Sassanian bridges, rock-cut tombs and carvings dating from various periods, and the ruined town of Deh-dasht, built during the reign of the Safavi dynasty in the sixteenth and seventeenth centuries AD, whose ghostly streets and houses unnerved his men. His curiosity about the region was intensified by the fact that, despite a 1918 revision of a quarter-inch map by the Survey of India, it remained largely unsurveyed.

In some places, he only updated, by his photography, the record of things first 'discovered' years earlier by explorer-antiquarians such as Sir Henry Rawlinson and Sir Henry Layard. In others he found previously unknown prehistoric remains. And at Malamir he was shown remark-able marble and bronze sculptures which had only recently been unearthed accidently by villagers. His descriptions and photographs of all these things fill his book on the year-long fourth Iranian journey, *Old*

Routes of Western Iran, which Macmillan published in 1940, making it a valuable record of an area which is again, today, as inaccessible to the non-specialist visitor as it was when Stein was there.

Despite the antiquarian nature of his tour, Stein was impressed by the aggressive, industrial modernity of the Anglo-Iranian Oil Company (as the Anglo-Persian Oil Company became in 1935), whose hospitality he enjoyed in early 1936 at Maidan-i-Naftur. 'It has been a novel & delightful experience to see the manifestations of a well-planned and ordered modern enterprise asserting itself in a forlorn corner of a barren land,' he told Helen,[32] though he was less enthusiastic about the adoption of Western ways by the Iranians themselves. From the oilfields he made a brief diversion to Susa, where excavations were now directed by de Morgan's successor, de Mecquenem; and from there moved on into Luristan. He spent the summer of 1936 in Iranian Kurdistan, where the Turki-speaking, melon-growing district near Lake Urumia reminded him of the oases of Chinese Turkestan.

By October he was back at the British Consulate in Kermanshah, awaiting permission to visit the area bordering Iraq. But refusal came instead and, though he planned an alternative itinerary, he was forced to abandon it shortly after reaching Behistun to see the famous inscriptions deciphered by Rawlinson. This time it was not the state that interfered with his aims but his old enemy, dyspepsia. The attack was so violent that his first letter to Helen afterwards was written in an uncharacteristically shaky hand.

The expedition was over. Travelling down the Karun River in an oil company steamer in late November 1936, he surrendered himself to a thorough medical examination at the refinery colony at Abadan. Then, leaving Dash with a sympathetic company employee and his camp kit at Basra, he travelled by train and ship to Italy, to the haven of the de Filippi home.

Ironically enough, the ill-health and surgery that followed were not caused by the indigestion which had troubled Stein periodically throughout his adult life. There was little any doctor could do, other than offer advice on dietary habits, to relieve that problem. He could not gloss over the fact that, this time, dyspepsia had attacked him under the outdoor conditions which he liked to think offered protection from illness (he shared de Filippi's view that 'houses are poisonous').[33] But he had something more serious to consider than the upsetting of a favourite theory. He had been suffering from a prostate condition for several years now, and had decided that an operation to remove the offending gland could be postponed no longer. Confirming this view with de Filippi in early 1937, he travelled, via Budapest, to Vienna where a bed awaited him at a private sanitorium on the outskirts of the city.

Stein wanted as little fuss as possible. His decision to have the operation in Vienna was dictated partly by regard for the surgeons there, but partly also by the fact that he had practically no acquaintances in the city. On the way to Austria he was irritated by the way in which journalists in Budapest reported a fall he had in the lobby of his hotel which laid him up for a couple of days. He wanted to avoid all possibility of such a thing happening over the impending operation.

He waited until the last moment to inform Helen, though she had already guessed by then. Only when the operation had to be delayed by a few weeks and he was confined to bed did he confess that he had already sought advice on several earlier occasions. A minor operation in the summer of 1932, while staying with Harriet and her sister at a sanitorium in Innsbruck, he had reported at the time in dismissive terms. But another the following year, and the subsequent evidence that it, too, had failed, he had kept to himself.

The Vienna urologist performed the operation on 14 April 1937. Stein received the devoted attentions of his niece and her husband throughout his time at the sanitorium, and showed no sign of disquiet in his letters to Helen. But prostate trouble was not so easily rectified in the 1930s as it is now. There were no antibiotics to protect the patient, and the state of Stein's kidneys had made the surgeon cautious about the timing of the operation. The evening before it took place, Stein wrote to Helen on the subject of his will, closing with valedictory expressions of his love for her and Publius. He was 74 years old and more threatened here, in the unlikely setting of Vienna, than he had ever felt during all his journeys.

Any apprehensions he might privately have acknowledged, however, proved groundless. The operation was a success and with characteristic robustness he rallied immediately. Soon his plans for new work, which had already occupied him throughout his Iranian tours, were uppermost in his mind again.

14

'Ready to Return to Duty'

———————◆◆◆———————

AS STEIN APPROACHED his seventy-fifth birthday, his hopes lay
in a venture which would extend his skills into a pioneering field
of archaeology. In the deserts of Iraq and Jordan were the remains of
an ancient defensive road system, similar to the wall he had traced so
successfully in Chinese Central Asia (he referred to both by the Latin
term, *limes*). This system marked the fringes of a different power, the
Roman Empire. But its purpose was fundamentally the same as that of
the old Chinese fortifications: to protect a distant frontier from enemy
invasion.

Attracted by the prospect of work which, in another context, he had
found so satisfying years earlier, Stein recognized also that the course
of these *limes* could be followed most effectively from the air – and in a
region where the British Royal Air Force maintained a substantial presence. He had day-dreamed about the usefulness of aerial surveys in the
mountains of the Kun-lun years before the first aeroplane flew east of
Suez. His tours in the Middle East since 'retirement' had simply whetted
his appetite for flight as a means to research. While he worked in Iran
in 1935–6, therefore, he applied himself intermittently to the task of
gaining the necessary permission for such work.

Aerial photography was not a new idea. The first such pictures had
been taken from a balloon above Paris in the mid-nineteenth century. But
it was the development of the aeroplane that expanded its possibilities.

Whereas the archaeologist H. S. Wellcome had used cameras mounted on box kites to photograph his sites in the Sudan during the early years of the century, aerial activity during the First World War demonstrated how much more usefully such surveys could be undertaken from the cockpit of a small aeroplane. The view from above revealed archaeological details that often escaped even the trained eye on the ground.

In Britain this method was developed initially by O.G.S. Crawford of the Ordnance Survey. At the same time in the Middle East, Père Antoine Poidebard of the University of Beirut began his survey of the Roman *limes* in the Syrian desert, work which extended over seven years between 1925 and 1932 and which was recorded in his book, *La Trace de Rome dans le Désert de Syrie*. Aerial reconnaissance was ideal in this region of vast barren tracts, where scarcity of water made travel difficult and where the remains of roads, watch-posts, wells and signal stations might lie just beneath the loess-like soil and yet be invisible at ground level. Stein's idea was to extend Poidebard's survey into what was effectively British-run territory, thus providing a complete view of Rome's eastern defences which practical difficulties had prevented earlier scholars from achieving.

However conservative in other matters, Stein was generally enthusiastic about scientific advances, and the idea of flight had always appealed. Years earlier, in 1913, he had referred glumly to the design of a new ocean liner in a letter to Publius and commented (with poignant lack of foresight into the future of air travel): 'It will be much finer to fly across the Atlantic in an aeroplane & feel clear of condensed humanity, packed above & between decks.'[1] He had introduced his aged sister-in-law, Harriet, to flight on a journey to Berlin from Vienna; and, knowing of Poidebard's work, had been keen to use his methods in the Punjab during the search for Alexander's route across the Jhelum. Aeroplanes had been in use in India for some years by then – Stein's friend Kenneth Mason had been up in the first to arrive there (a Sommer bi-plane) in 1910[2] – but none was available for Stein's purpose in 1931. Four years later, in the Middle East, he returned to the idea.

The minor campaign which this involved stirred memories of the strategy he had had to develop in the organization of his early Chinese expeditions. Both Iraq and Trans-Jordan, having become British protectorates immediately after the Great War, had been established as new kingdoms in 1921. But both were run by the British 'advisers' who stood behind their Hashemite thrones. So the way ahead, through the tortuous 'colonial' territory of carefully cultivated contacts, diplomatic approaches to the highly placed and the influential, and the gradual accumulation of information, had at least the virtue of being familiar. The seeds of Stein's plan had implanted themselves in his mind in 1924 at Petra, when he met three RAF officers conducting an aerial survey of that site. But it was a large step from the idea to its implementation, and he had yet to receive commitments from anyone who mattered.

His ability to get his own way, however, was unaffected by increasing years. Hinks, the man who had succeeded Stein's old ally John Scott Keltie as secretary to the Royal Geographical Society, had referred to Stein ten years earlier as having the 'characteristics of a begger [sic]'. In 1935 he commented, in an internal memo regarding the way Stein had ensured that the cost of some map-drawing had come out of the Society's coffers rather than his own: 'As usual I found that in spite of the best efforts I had been defeated by Stein.'[3] Among those who were used to dealing with him on matters of business, Stein's reputation as the most demanding of correspondents was almost legendary.

In November 1935, Sir Frederic Kenyon, now Secretary of the British Academy and President of the Society of Antiquaries, provided Stein with a statement of support from both bodies for his proposed survey in Trans-Jordanian territory. Using tactics which Stein had employed to advantage many years earlier, the statement appealed to competitive instincts, stressing the desirability of matching the support Poidebard had received in Syria from the French Air Force and the Académie des Inscriptions et Belles Lettres. A map of the Roman Empire was currently in production by the Ordnance Survey, it pointed out, and it would be 'very unfortunate' if the area least well represented was the eastern frontier for which Britain was responsible.

When, in April 1936, Stein submitted his formal application to Lieutenant-General Sir Arthur Wauchope, High Commissioner and Commander-in-Chief of Palestine and Trans-Jordania, he was careful to supplement his requests for financial and practical help with the remark: 'I need scarcely point out that the results of the proposed survey would prove of distinct use for other purposes also.'[4] If such a hint could sway the authorities in his favour, he would not scruple to drop it.

It was from Iraq, however, that a positive response came. While the

Colonial Office, to which Wauchope had forwarded his request, replied that it was 'not a very propitious time'[5] to approach the Jordanian government, Stein's contacts across the border were much more encouraging. The RAF there signalled their readiness to help, and C. J. Edmonds, adviser in the Iraqi Ministry of the Interior, volunteered what proved to be the single most useful piece of advice. The country's own survey department had no one available who could assist Stein, so he suggested enlisting the help of the Iraq Petroleum Company (IPC), in whose concession area the *limes* lay. The company had 'unlimited resources' in transport and must have good surveyors, he suggested; moreover, it was known to spend substantial amounts on 'entertaining, assisting travellers and the like'.[6] Its chairman in London, Sir John Cadman, was the man to see.

Stein, in England for much of the second half of 1937 following his prostate operation that April, invited Cadman to one of his lectures. Addressed to the Royal Central Asian and Asiatic Societies in London, its subject was his reconnaissances in Iran and he was careful to pay full tribute in it to the help he had received from the Anglo-Iranian Oil Company, of which Cadman was also chairman and which was a share-holder in the IPC. Though Cadman himself did not attend, an employee came as his representative, and soon afterwards Cadman invited Stein to lunch.

Stein made sure that a copy of his official proposal reached his host before he did, and the result was an affable meeting at which the chair-man immediately offered his support. The scale of Stein's needs (amounting to the assistance of a surveyor and the provision of trans-port with drivers), which had apparently been insurmountable to officialdom, proved no obstacle to the mighty oil company.[7] Permission to work in Iraq arrived a short time later from the country's Ministry of Foreign Affairs and by the end of the year, Stein was on his way east-ward to begin yet another new project. Like his work in Iran, it consti-tuted a pioneering survey which has not been repeated, and which provides what is still the only information on some sites.

As usual, his habit of preparing the ground as carefully as possible yielded fruit. With his trip to Iraq already arranged, he heard shortly before leaving England that his prospects in Trans-Jordan, too, sud-denly looked brighter. With Kenyon, he had met the Colonial Secretary, W. G. A. Ormsby-Gore, in London and the two men's calculated appeal to Ormsby-Gore's known interest in the arts 'evidently did more than 2½ years' correspondence with that high official'.[8] An invitation came almost immediately from Sir Arthur Wauchope, offering to hold a conference in Jerusalem to discuss Stein's requests in the presence of two others: the officer commanding the RAF in Trans-Jordan and Major John Bagot Glubb of the Arab Legion (Glubb Pasha of Anglo-Arab fame). The conference took place in January 1938, so by the time Stein began work in Iraq he knew he would be able to extend his research into Trans-Jordan in the following year.

He had already calculated that the entire project would take two years. There was only a limited period, during late spring and early summer, when conditions in the desert were favourable; so all reconnaissance flights, ground survey work and aerial photography had to be crammed into that season. The results could be written up later in Kashmir or Oxford. He prepared himself by spending several weeks, early in 1938, in a secluded hotel in the hills behind Beirut, studying Arabic ('a sadly elaborate language')[9] and meeting Père Poidebard in order to benefit from his generously offered knowledge and experience.[10]

It was 8 March when he took his place for the first time in Pilot Officer Hunt's Vincent aeroplane for the initial reconnaissance flight from Mosul. Standing up from his seat in the middle cockpit in order to see properly, protected only by a thick flying suit and goggles as he was borne at 100 m.p.h. into the blast, he was able to look down on ground between the Tigris and the Euphrates where the Roman/Parthian border once lay. On his instructions, Leading Aircraftsman Pascoe photographed two sites; and the first flight came to a successful conclusion. The following day, Stein moved out to his base camp near the small town of Balad Sinjar, the Roman Singara, the only definitely known site on the *limes*.

From then until mid-May, his days were spent either in Hunt's aeroplane or in the desert, surveying the Roman *castella*, or fortified posts, he had identified from the air. Linking his survey in the north with Poidebard's in Syria, Stein traced a series of *castella* forming an outer line of defence in the desert east of Balad Sinjar, through which the main line ran. The desert also contained many prehistoric mounds, and in the Sinjar range of hills he found Roman posts defending the saddles between the hills from possible Parthian invasions. Out in the grassy plains, he had the help of the chief of the Bedouin Shammar tribe which grazed its animals there in winter and spring. Sometimes work was interrupted by heavy rain which immobilized his borrowed saloon car and 30-cwt. truck. At one point he found the way blocked by a long chain of salt marshes stretching south to the Euphrates, which the Romans had incorporated into their line of defence, just as the Chinese had done far away in the Lop Desert. The work absorbed him, casting him back into the long-dead past and distracting him from the turmoil spreading throughout every other region he had known.

At times it was as if he were marooned on his own small island of tranquillity, while storms gathered over every land mass. In Chinese Turkestan, Soviet influence had reached such levels that absorption into the USSR appeared almost inevitable to many observers; and China proper had been invaded by the Japanese from their bridgehead in Manchuria. Stein was unsurprised by the former development. He kept abreast of affairs in his old stamping-ground and corresponded with Pan's son, who was in Nanking when it was bombed by the invaders. But he seems to have resigned himself, after his abortive fourth expedition there, to the fact that he would never see the Taklamakan Desert again.

About India's fate he was less phlegmatic; and his pessimism about its future was intensified by the fact that most of the senior ICS men he knew had retired. Hailey was one of the few still working, but he had been enlisted into the service of East Africa. The tensions that gripped Europe, however, loomed larger than those in any other part of the world, and the gravity of their implications was forced upon him through the experience of his own niece, Thesa, and her husband in Vienna.

In March 1938, Hitler invaded Austria and began the process of converting the country into a province of Germany. Stein remarked to Helen Allen that the change was inevitable, given the collapse of the Hapsburgs and the inability of the people, through lack of training, to govern themselves. He was disturbed by the Nazis' unscrupulous methods, but at the same time seems to have believed they would have little effect on ordinary Austrians, even those of Jewish descent. Helen, ever alert to the circumstances of others, suggested that Thesa and

Gustav take a holiday with her in Oxford; but Stein felt such a move might antagonize those on whom Gustav relied for work. Instead, he took comfort from the fact that his niece's husband had always maintained a 'wise reserve' with regard to the different Austrian regimes under which he had lived.

How far Stein himself really believed in the power of 'reserve' to withstand the anti-Semitism of the Nazi regime it is difficult to know. His education and instincts told him that a Jewish ancestry should make no difference to an individual's status in life. He never referred to his own Semitic background, nor that of anyone else, and gave no hint that he personally had ever encountered racial prejudice. One might assume, therefore, that the issue was genuinely utterly irrelevant to him. But in his reaction to Thesa and Gustav's predicament, there is something that suggests otherwise: a half-conscious, desperate desire to go on believing nothing was wrong despite misgivings; or even a wish to conceal his Jewish origins. Perhaps it was easier to attribute their difficulties to their own anxieties rather than to face the sinister reality of the Nazi crusade against the Jews. For that crusade now threatened to sweep away the cultural foundations on which his brother and uncle had raised him, and to demolish his belief in a unity of purpose among right-minded people, regardless of their roots.

In June 1938, Stein heard that Gustav and Thesa had made up their minds to leave Vienna and to qualify for medical work in Britain, the Dominions or the United States. He told Helen Allen that their decision had been influenced by Thesa's 'lively temperament', which was his way of criticizing her for being nervous. He would have admired them more had they gritted their teeth and announced they were staying. But he would not allow himself to say so. Instead, he asked Helen's brother, Louis, for help in securing the necessary permits, and immediately set about arranging an income for them from his savings. At Helen's gentle insistence, he gratefully agreed that they should regard Manor Place as their first English home – provided she recouped her costs from the account of his to which she and Publius had always had access.

His niece and her husband arrived in Oxford in late August. In the few months during which Stein had been forced to contemplate the unpleasant reality of their predicament in Austria, he had gradually grown to appreciate the dangers, and greeted the news of their escape with relief. Perhaps the blatant nature of Nazi discrimination against

Jews made it easier for him to acknowledge the facts. Austrian soil had 'long been prepared for racialism in excelsis', he commented to Helen in a moment of openness.[11] But still, in almost every letter he wrote to her, he repeated one request: to keep the matter to herself. Next to his desire to help his closest relatives, his most urgent wish seems to have been to prevent the affair being discussed beyond the small circle of those directly involved.

Britain's position in an increasingly war-threatened Europe caused him fewer problems. He admired Chamberlain's 'courage and judgment' and approved his policy of negotiation as a way of gaining time in which to increase the country's strength 'before the storm breaks'.[12] He sent in his 'founder's subscription' to the Army and Home Defence League immediately on reading its appeal in *The Weekly Times*, and blamed 'the limited intellectual horizon of the millions' for any lack of preparation.[13]

But the plight of Czechoslovakia, as the Germans closed in on three sides, elicited no sympathy. To Stein, the very existence of that country was an insult to Hungarian sensibilities and a constant reminder of the humiliations of Trianon. He viewed the prospect of her liquidation not simply with equanimity but with the hope that this would ensure peace, and his hope was qualified only by fear of how France, her ally, would feel obliged to respond.

By the summer of 1938, he was writing these remarks from Kashmir. He had returned there in May, collecting Dash VI at Basra and sailing back to Karachi with the entire first-class promenade deck of the ship to himself. Srinagar, by contrast, was crowded, not only with British but also with a growing number of Indian visitors including ladies out of purdah who, he noted with distaste, were 'not always too graceful'.[14] He retreated to Mohand Marg to write up his fourth Iranian journey. The 3,000-foot climb from his usual intermediate camp took three hours, a little longer than usual. 'I mention this merely to assure you that I do not altogether pretend to ignore my years where physical exertion is involved,' he told Helen.[15]

It was the deaths of old friends, however, rather than his own physical condition, that raised his conciousness of advancing years. Many familiar names crop up in his letters during the 1930s only to be registered regretfully as having passed away: Sylvain Lévi, Soothill and Harcourt Butler were among them. Dunsterville wrote of the death of his old schoolmate Kipling,[16] and Hailey's wife, whom Stein had always liked, died in 1939. But the loss that hurt most was that of de Filippi, who succumbed in 1938 to the angina that had nagged at him for several years.

'I feel the loss of such a friend deeply,' Stein wrote to Helen, 'not merely because we had so many close interests in common. The encouragement he always most generously gave me was a great asset in my life for the last thirty years. It pains me deeply that he like Publius and our Saint, years younger than myself, should have departed from me.'[17]

Publius had been buried beneath the chapel altar of his beloved Corpus Christi College; de Filippi's body was interred in the family vault in Turin. There was no such building or historic resting place awaiting Stein's demise. Any bond he might have felt with Budapest, as the burial ground of his parents, had long ago weakened, and his affection for Oxford sprang from, and was secondary to, the far greater love of friends who lived there. Mountains and deserts were the only places where he felt truly in his element and, of those, Mohand Marg was his spiritual home. For years he had referred to a craggy outcrop above the Marg as his 'tomb' and in a letter to Helen had recently expanded on his hope that he would be buried there.

'It has only struck me of late', he had written in a letter of 1936, 'how easy it would be for my devoted friend Dr. Macpherson, of the C.M.S. Hospital, to carry out an idea often merely played with, if my humble remains got a chance of being cremated when life here below ends. But, of course, in my wandering life it will not be quite easy to arrange this! Far more important is my wish that the end when it comes, should find me in a place where it would not mean trouble to my dearest of friends.'[18]

What Stein thought might lie in store for him after death he never described. His education and experience had given him an insight into several religions. He had studied the earliest prayers of the Aryans; he knew the epics of the Hindu faith. He had an unrivalled familiarity with the iconography of Buddhism as it carried its message eastward to China; and he had learnt much of Islam from Thomas Arnold. His inheritance was Jewish. His uncle and brother – the first a Jew, the second a baptized Christian – had encouraged him to have faith in the twin gods of the Enlightenment, reason and humanity. But he had also been taught as a schoolboy by members of the Hungarian Catholic and Lutheran churches, and he had developed an affection for the Church of England through the example of his godly friend Publius. In the circumstances, it is not surprising that he seems to have eschewed the dogma of organized religion and drawn what he needed from a private faith.

He certainly had a fondness for Buddhist concepts such as reincarnation and the earning of merit, references to which frequently crop up in his letters. Whether this was because of his familiarity with them through study, or because they struck some particular chord, is hard to say. However important they may have been to him, he had no wish to share them with the growing number of people in the West who were attracted to Buddhism in the early decades of the twentieth century. Having glanced at Alexandra David-Neel's 1931 book on Tibet, he remarked, with some disdain, that she knew 'how to write & to play up to a certain morbid taste' but that he had no time for the modern 'craze' for 'mystics & magic'.[19]

By nature he must have seemed to some who knew him a natural member of an Anglican congregation. He was reserved, undemonstrative, someone who had been drawn to Britain since early manhood by her traditions and history. And the Church of England apparently did offer him something, for there were times, in the periods when snow kept him from the Marg, when he attended its services in Srinagar, usually in the company of his mission doctor friends, the Neves.

This church-going, which appears to feature only in the latter part of his life, seems more than anything else to have been an affirmation of belonging. In his early winters in Kashmir, Stein had been an outsider, poring over his work in isolation, witnessing the cosy family life of English residents only as he passed by their windows on chilly, solitary walks. But by the 1930s his fidelity to the kingdom had made him one of its best-known figures and given him a comfortable familiarity with its people and places. He did not need or want to be treated as a famous person; but he did find deep satisfaction in being accepted unquestioningly as a member of the British community.

This aspect of Stein's character found expression in various ways throughout his life. Part of the attraction of the friends he found in

Lahore was the vicarious experience they provided for him of what it was to be English. Through them he absorbed their attitudes towards their education, their lives as undergraduates at Oxbridge colleges, their fondness for tradition, their sense of honour, their enjoyment of country cycling holidays and old buildings, their garden parties and social graces. He envied them the strength of their identity: he knew he could never be as they were, but their companionship satisfied at least in part his own feeling of affinity with their inheritance. The strength of that affinity was revealed in many chance remarks, such as one in a letter written to Publius shortly after arrival in the United States in 1929: 'What gives me particular pleasure is the attention shown to me as a British scholar. You will understand what I mean. It makes one feel so much more at home in this outlier of Old England which "New England" really is.'[20] Four years later, in a letter to a colleague, he commented that the offer of a grant from the British School in Iraq for his third Iranian journey was made all the more acceptable by the fact that 'it comes from a British source'.[21]

In everything that has been written about Stein, the enduring image of him is of a solitary man, living in camp on a Kashmir mountain or on pioneering expeditions in the wilds of Asia. No evidence has ever been found to contradict the impression that he shared this life with no one save his servants, his surveyors and the occasional guest. But, many years after his death, a claim was made that such evidence did indeed exist, and that it proved Stein had formed an amorous relationship with a woman in Kashmir.

The claim came from a respectable pandit family, the Balis of Srinagar, one of whom had served Stein for many years as clerk and factotum. It was Ram Chand Bali who met Stein on his return from the failed Chinese expedition of 1931 and he whom Stein, when away from Kashmir, entrusted with orders and arrangements concerning his Iranian tours. Ram Chand's letters kept Stein informed not only of his own affairs but also of conditions in Kashmir such as food shortages or the communal disturbances of the 1930s.

The pandit worked as a temporary clerk in the Archaeology Department of the Government of India for ten years, before becoming a supervisor in the state stationery depot in Srinagar. It was while he held this latter post that Stein arranged for him to spend part of each year as his assistant. In 1929, Stein secured for him an honorarium from the Archaeology Department of Rs 200 in recognition of his services since the mid-1920s: Ram Chand was a devoted servant and Stein always appreciated such loyalty among his men. He may not have out-lived Stein himself, for the latter was already referring to him as 'old' in 1930. The impression one gets of Ram Chand sits oddly beside the story his descendants later had to tell.

In 1970, the state archive department in Kashmir was carrying out a survey and collection of papers owned by private individuals for preservation in their Srinagar repository. The man responsible for the collection, Pandit B. K. Challoo, visited the Bali family and returned to his superior, the Director of Archives, with surprising news. The Balis claimed that they had in their possession letters written by Stein and Ram Chand's younger sister to each other; that the two had been in love for many years but had become resigned to the fact that a formal mar-riage was impossible for religious and social reasons; and that their inti-macy continued until Stein's death. The Director instructed Challoo to buy the papers; but the deal was never concluded because the Balis demanded too high a price.

Both Pandit B. K. Challoo and his director, Fida M. Hassnain, are adamant that this love affair had occurred. Hassnain claims to have seen some of the letters and that they 'clearly depicted that Stein had devel-oped intimacy and affection for this lady and it was a life long love bondage'. Challoo, more reticently, says he saw no written confirmation of the relationship and that it must have been conducted in the utmost secrecy, since the Bali family were strictly orthodox and would not have tolerated it had they known.

Is it possible that Stein could have kept such a secret? However soli-tary and enigmatic he may have seemed to Europeans used to the conventions of family life, his isolation was only relative. He may have passed weeks or months without the company of his own kind, but it is highly unlikely that he was ever totally alone. On Mohand Marg it was normal for him to be surrounded by as many as twenty servants or staff of one sort or another; and during winters spent in Kashmir there were always at least two or three looking after him in the houses he rented. It is hard to believe that they would have been unaware of clandestine assignations with a lover, or that news of such assignations would not have spread, particularly when the lover in question was the sister of a pious pandit.

Besides such practical considerations, there is the question of whether such an affair conforms with all else that is known of Stein. As far as it is possible to tell, he was not a secretive man, though he was certainly reticent and discreet. He appears to have had no serious attachments with the opposite sex. A Hungarian writer once suggested that Sir Harold Deane's daughter had been fond of him, but when Stein himself saw the reference, he is said to have scribbled a question-mark in the margin. He responded far more positively to a remark made by his friend and colleague, the philologist Sir George Grierson, who wrote on one occasion that he wished Stein, like himself, could have found a wife. 'But what then would have become of Central Asia! You chose her for a bride, with the blessing of your Patron Saint, Hsuen Tsiang; and you are a confirmed monogamist.'[22] Stein called Grierson's conceit 'happy and delightfully true'.[23]

If an attachment such as Hassnain and Challoo describe did indeed exist, Stein must have used all his powers of efficiency to erase any record of it, for there is no suggestion of it in his papers or his will. Nor is there any reference to it, or, in any context, to Ram Chand's sister, in his letters to the Allens. The absence of evidence does not in itself disprove its existence. But a more prosaic and less revelatory interpretation of the relationship seems more likely. A number of other background details in the story, as told by the Balis and repeated by Fida Hassnain, are inaccurate, lending more force to the suspicion that the 'love bondage' might owe something to imagination as well as to memory.

It may well be true that Stein first met Ram Chand's sister in 1899, when she was only 14 but already 'a beautiful maiden'. Perhaps, after Stein's death, she did arrange for her own body to be cremated on Mohand Marg in memory of him, as the story claims. But perhaps, too, the deep admiration or love that she felt for him was reciprocated only by an affectionate regard which, after both had passed away, gradually and imperceptibly developed into something more in the collective memory of the Bali family.[24]

One more season of work on the Middle Eastern *limes* lay ahead of Stein. He returned there, with Dash, in October 1938 to find that his request for the services of the same surveyor, pilot and wireless crew had been met and he could begin immediately on his survey east of the River Tigris. From there he planned to move westward, then up the Euphrates to the Syrian border, and into the desert south-west towards Trans-Jordan. By the beginning of 1939 he had reached Amman.

Up to this point, he had been able to pursue his own objectives with few reminders that the people and organizations on whom he was dependent might have anything else on their minds besides satisfying his needs. But in Trans-Jordan he was brought face to face with their preoccupations. The dreadful probability of another war in Europe confronted them all. The fact that Stein could not borrow the same aeroplane and pilot from the RAF in Iraq to continue work across the border was rather less remarkable than that there were any aircraft at all available for his use. He tried using the one offered, a Wellesley, but its faster speed (170 m.p.h. as opposed to the Vincent's 100 m.p.h.) made detailed observation impossible.

Still, he pushed on with the survey at ground level, for he knew that the unstable conditions, as well as his age, meant he could not rely on being able to return for a third season. Despite the bleak outlook, he enjoyed the work. In the nine months which he devoted (in two separate periods) to the Middle Eastern *limes*, he traced their course from the middle Tigris to the Gulf of Aqaba, across thousands of miles of desert. The book that resulted from this work remained in manuscript form until long after his death. He himself expected his report to be published after the war by the Society of Antiquaries, but his executors decided initially that the relevant papers were not sufficiently well-ordered to allow for publication. It was not until 1985 that Stein's report appeared in print, accompanied by a few of the six hundred aerial photographs which by then were scattered amongst the archives of the Institute of Archaeology, the British Museum and the Bodleian Library.

Having seen the plain in Iraq where Alexander finally defeated the Persian Emperor Darius at the Battle of Arbela, in Trans-Jordan Stein could trace a road opened by the Roman Emperor Trajan from Aqaba towards Syria. The milometer in his borrowed Chevrolet car could not fault the Roman milestones encountered along the route. In the south-east he travelled for some time alongside the mangled remains of the Hejjaz railway, where Lawrence's Arab partisans had fought the Turks in 1917–18. And when he reached Petra he was able to enjoy the glory of its ruins in total solitude, for in the month following Hitler's invasion of Czechoslovakia there were no Cook's tours there to disturb the silence. Soon afterwards, he saw Dash off on the journey back to Kashmir and himself turned once more for Europe, for fleeting visits to Paris and Louvain and the bright, welcoming light of Oxford.

The ostensible reason for this return to Britain was to see his book on his fourth Iranian journey, *Old Routes of Western Iran*, through the press. But the threat of war may have increased his desire to be with Helen Allen again. She had spent the winter of 1937–8 in South Africa with her sister Olga, visiting a nephew and compiling a collection of her husband's letters (many of which were supplied by Stein). During the following winter she and Olga, whose health was fragile, retired to the South of France and had hoped to enjoy a reunion there with Stein. But the imminence of war sent them home early. By the time Stein reached them in Oxford, Hitler had demonstrated the emptiness of his promises to Chamberlain, Britain had declared its support of Poland and Olga was preparing blackout blinds for Barton House and Manor Place. The euphoria of the Prime Minister's message of 'peace in our time', which Helen had reported the previous year, had evaporated.

Gustav and Thesa had moved into a flat in the High Street and Gustav had already been given some research work, thanks to Helen's many connections. Stein worried about the fact that his niece's husband missed Vienna and disliked being dependent on others; but the couple's problems were minor compared with those they had left behind. While Stein's allowance of £40 a month paid for the spacious flat, Gustav's family in Vienna had already fallen victim to Nazi persecution. On first reading reports of such persecution, Stein had decided they were exaggerated. Now he heard that Gustav's parents had been turned out of their flat and imprisoned for a time, that one of his sisters had been obliged to move three times in as many weeks, and that the husband of another sister had been taken away to Dachau.

In Hungary, too, things were not turning out as he had hoped. His old friend Count Teleki had become Prime Minister and was trying to persuade Hitler to support Hungarian claims to land lost under the Treaty of Trianon. Stein told Helen in late 1938 that he was 'naturally much cheered' by the prospect of those claims being satisfied.[25] He did not dwell on the equivocal and morally dubious nature of such a relationship; but he knew Teleki was balancing on a tightrope which Hitler might cut at any time. Hope soon turned to apprehension and concern for the responsibility his friend had shouldered; and his fears were tragically to be proved justified.

Amid such ominous portents of war, Stein received an invitation from the India Office to fill in a card for the National Service Central Register, specially issued to retired members of the Indian and Burma Services who were physically fit, under 60 years of age and prepared to return to service in the East. His response was enthusiastic. 'I felt truly grateful for having the chance of asserting my readiness & physical fitness for this,' he told Helen. 'I thought it but right to point out that my topographical experience and my familiarity with much of the ground might be utilized with advantage on the N. W. Frontier and beyond. If the occasion were to arise I trust, the entry about my age might benevolently be overlooked!'[26]

He returned the form to the Under-Secretary of State for India, enclosing an accompanying letter which explained:

In connexion with the above it may not be out of place to mention that under the conditions of university military service prevailing at the time in the country of my birth, I received systematic military instruction for one year in the Hungarian Military Academy, Budapest, and at its close qualified in 1886 for a commission as a Lieutenant in the Reserve.

The topographical training received in that Academy proved very useful to me afterwards. On gaining my first employment in India I resigned that commission along with my Hungarian citizenship in 1888. Together with the practical experience gained in the course of my protracted exploratory travels in Central Asia, Baluchistan, Persia, etc., this early training may help to support the suggestion indicated under the last heading of the card as regards fitness for some specific work . . .[27]

Under the heading in the form, 'Particular Aptitude', he had written 'Topographical and kindred surveys' and added: 'Ready to return to duty . . .'.

Britain declared war on Germany on 3 September 1939. At Barton the local farmer was gathering in his harvest; in London, where Stein stayed with Fred Andrews in the middle of the month, the unfamiliar darkness of night filled the unlit streets. By November, his work was done and nothing could prevent him from returning to India, as he had returned on a previous occasion during the Great War. Indeed, it probably strengthened his resolve to go. Helen told him how she admired 'the apparent ease with which you fit into a household of other people, when you return from the freedom of camp-life'.[28] But he had no desire to endure idle captivity in the civilized West when he might be on active duty in Asia, as he hoped, or at least on the Marg, instead. On 9 November, Helen and her brother Louis travelled with him to Victoria Station, to watch him leave on the Folkestone train. They never saw him again.

15

'Death in Some Far-off Country'

━━━━━━━◆━━━━━━━

INDIA IN LATE 1939 offered many contrasts to the country Stein had first seen more than fifty years earlier. The assurance of British rule had faded in that half-century. Strident demands for independence dominated political life, and the imperial era, with all its certainties, was visibly drawing to a close. But in his private life there were many consolations which helped to preserve for him the India to which he was attached. He could still visit friends whose values represented the old order, stay in a summer camp that remained unchanged and rely upon the services of many faithful retainers.

In some ways his life was far more privileged than before. Age and reputation guaranteed him a respectful audience whenever he needed help with a pet project, and rulers of native states enthusiastically offered their hospitality. He was a well-known figure of the Frontier, and a frequent guest at the Governor's house in Peshawar. His old pupil, Raja Daya Kishan Kaul, arranged transport for him from Rawalpindi to his bungalow in Kashmir. Friends and acquaintances asked to bring their sons up to Mohand Marg for an introduction. Such were the rewards of old age which, though he himself gave little thought to his status, helped to make his life comfortable and reinforce the sense that this part of the world was really one where he could feel at home.

Frequently now he let his mind dwell on his early life there, and every visit to old haunts recalled times long past. The fondly remembered landmarks of Lahore seemed forlorn and Kashmir, swiftly becoming a haven for wartime refugees from the Middle East, overcrowded and noisy. But such changes did not have the depressive effect on him which they might have exerted set against the backdrop of Europe. None of the political events in India so far had prevented him from carrying out his work, and his last years there were to be as full as they had ever been, albeit with less ambitious projects. Tours and writing tasks succeeded one another smoothly and easily; sponsors offered unsolicited grants. Stein organized and enjoyed his work from 1939 onwards in an apparently tranquil mood which acknowledged that it might end at any moment, and that each achievement was a bonus.

In one way he was helped by political changes on the Frontier. The region was volatile at the best of times and a potential combustion point when Britain was at war and vulnerable. So when Stein's old friend, the Wali of Swat, extended the tentacles of his rule into the Indus Kohistan, the British had cause to be thankful. The Wali was not only a friend of the Raj, he was also a strong and progressive ruler whose control of a wild and remote part of the Frontier would spread peace and extend knowledge of an area so far utterly unknown to Europeans. For Stein, the development offered an opportunity he had been poised to exploit ever since, in 1900, he had first stood on the mountains above the Indus *en route* from Kashmir to Gilgit and gazed downstream at the distant, tantalizing peaks of the Kohistan. 'From this height', he had written then, 'the Indus Valley, in its barrenness of rock and sand, could be seen descending far away towards Chilas and Darel. The day will come when this natural route to the Indian plains will be open again as it was in old times.'[1]

The stretch of the Indus from the great bend, beyond Chilas and Darel, where the river turns south, to the point at which it runs beneath Pir Sar at Besham, was known to the early Chinese pilgrims as 'the route of the hanging chains'. There, where the mountains plunge so steeply to the river that no snow lies on them even when it blankets lesser slopes, they had to make their way as best they could. Time and again they crossed the river by means of ropes or chains, edging their way along cliff-faces on fragile *rafiks* built out from the rock on branches and stones.

Stein was 77 at the end of 1939. He had no way of knowing whether communications had improved in the Kohistan during the centuries since the pilgrims made their journeys. But he would not give up the chance to realize a long-cherished ambition simply because of a factor – that of age – which hitherto he had always successfully ignored.

The omens – to adopt one of his favourite expressions – at first seemed auspicious. The Surveyor-General of India offered not just one man but a small party to accompany him on the trip, explaining that he was 'specially interested' in the area. Muhammad Ayub Khan, Stein's well-tried and trusted surveyor, was keen to return from retirement to join the expedition. Early in 1940 Stein moved to the archaeological bungalow at Taxila in order to be close at hand should the Wali give immediate permission. But word came instead that the tour must be delayed.

Bad weather and the poor condition of paths were ostensibly the reasons, but Stein suspected political difficulties too. He postponed his plan with reluctance. But compensation for the disappointment soon volunteered itself. His friend Sir George Cunningham, Governor of the North-West Frontier Province, offered him a spare seat on a flight to Gilgit; so it was from the air that he enjoyed his first view of the hidden valleys of the Indus Kohistan.

The journey took place on 15 February. It was only four years since an aeroplane had flown for the first time in winter along the same route.[2] On that occasion, the aeroplane had been an Avro; Stein flew in a Valencia, in the company of two nurses and an intelligence officer, all *en route* to new appointments at Gilgit. The aeroplane reached the Indus valley just below the Pir Sar plateau, flying at about 12,000 feet, and followed the course of the river closely as it wound its way northward between the mountains. Despite adopting, as usual, his pedestrian 'personal narrative' style in order to describe the experience to Helen Allen, Stein found himself almost lost for words at the scale of the view below. The scenery was 'inexpressively grand', he wrote (revealing the capacity for occasional lapses in English vocabulary to which he was still prone); the glacier-clad peak of Nanga Parbat seemed 'overwhelming' at such close quarters.

Not the least overwhelming aspect of the trip was that it lasted about three hours, in bizarre contrast to the two weeks Stein had needed in the past to cover the more direct route between Srinagar and Gilgit. Though he was a far more sophisticated air traveller than most people of the period, and familiar with aerial views as archaeological tools, he was awe-struck by the sight of the Indus gorges and the close-ranked, towering mountains that enclosed them. He strained to identify signs of communication and small patches of cultivation at the mouths of side valleys, which might indicate a route he could later follow on foot. But this flight confirmed what he had been quietly pleased to be told three weeks earlier by aerial survey officers of the Survey of India: that their work, where the deep-sunk Indus gorges were concerned, was no match for a ground survey such as the one he planned.

While he waited in Kashmir for better news from the Wali, Stein worked on the report of his Middle Eastern *limes* survey. Simultaneously he was also negotiating for the publication of another work which he had long wished to see in print. This was a portfolio of the wall-paintings he had brought back from the Taklamakan and which Fred Andrews had painstakingly recreated in the display cases of New Delhi's Museum of Central Asian Antiquities. Nothing had been done with photographs of the paintings taken fourteen years earlier and the frescoes were beginning to show signs of deterioration in the Delhi climate, so that publication of a record was now urgent. An acquaintance in the government did some discreet lobbying on his behalf, and the Member of Council for Education, Sir Jagdish Prasad, favoured the plan. So at last Stein heard, later in 1940, that the portfolio would be published at government expense. Even so, he was destined never to see the finished book, for it appeared only years later, after the end of the war, under Andrews' editorship.

It was in return for this interest shown by officialdom that Stein allowed himself, albeit reluctantly, to be drawn into a controversy then agitating members of the Archaeological Survey. He had had little to do with the Survey since retiring from its service in 1929. Privately sponsored work had preoccupied him and he had been happy to put behind him the experience of bureaucratic shackles. His relations with the men who had succeeded Sir John Marshall as Director-General had been cordial but distant. In addition, he was as reluctant as ever to become involved in political issues of any kind. But his sense of decency dictated a positive response when he was approached for advice by Sir Jagdish Prasad.

The subject on the Member for Education's mind was the Woolley Report of February 1939. This had been commissioned by the Viceroy,

Lord Linlithgow, to examine the state of archaeology in the sub-continent and propose improvements. Sir Leonard Woolley had spent three months in India in 1938 and his conclusions had shocked and upset the predominantly Indian department. Invited to comment on exploration and the agencies best qualified to undertake it, methods of selecting and training officers, and any other points he thought fit to raise, he had written a report which, though constructive, was frank in its criticism of the decay that had spread throughout the Survey since Marshall's departure in 1929.

Stein seems to have been asked to comment on the report in the hope that his long association with India and the Survey would make him more sympathetic to the department's difficulties. And he proba-bly did offer some solace, for he told Sir Jagdish that he felt many of the shortcomings noted by Woolley could be explained and excused by 'the traditional outlook inherent to Indian culture' – in other words, the lack of an historical tradition. To the Director-General of the Survey, Kashirath Narayan Dikshit, he wrote: 'You are certainly right in believ-ing that there is much in Sir L. Woolley's comments reflecting inade-quate knowledge of the special conditions which confront archaeological work in India and differ greatly from those to be met with in Europe or the Near East directly influenced by it.'[3]

But he also made it clear that he knew from personal experience of Woolley's fine qualities. And he took the opportunity to make his own suggestions, based mainly on opinions he had long held. Lasting improvement would come not solely from Woolley's proposal to bring in a European adviser, but from continuity of direction and selection for appointments by an advisory body of scholars such as that used by the Ecole d'Extrême Orient in Hanoi (an institution he had always admired). Moreover, he felt that Woolley's recommendations for staff training had ignored a point dear to his own heart: the need for Indian archaeologists to have a thorough grounding in Sanskrit, Buddhist and other texts.

No archaeologist of the Classical world would be expected to work in the field without an appropriate academic training, he pointed out, and for work in India a BA from an Indian university with Sanskrit as the classical language was not enough. Indians, whether Hindu or Muslim, should study at post-graduate level with competent academ-ics either in India or the West. For this reason, scholars from Europe and America should be encouraged to take up posts in Indian institutions.

Woolley's emphasis on the importance of reconnaissance surveys and of the study of pottery naturally attracted his approval, describing as it did the sort of work to which he had devoted himself since the late 1920s. And he backed up the report's advocacy of 'outside help' in excavations. Properly qualified institutions should be welcomed, he told Sir Jagdish (no doubt with his own attempts to excavate in the Punjab on behalf of Harvard in mind). The ultimate destination of finds was less important than their record, publication and accessibility, and the light they threw on India's past. Carefully blunting any implied criticism of Dikshit and his staff, he made an oblique remark about Marshall's success in overcoming many of the difficulties that were still seen, even now, to be hampering progress.

It is idle but interesting to speculate on what might have happened had the author of the report been Stein rather than Woolley. Stein was a man of strong views; but at the same time he disliked controversy. Moreover, his sedate, prolix style of writing took the edge off any criticism and obscured the radicalism of his own ideas for reform. Privately he considered Woolley's report 'rather outspoken'.[4] In this view he was, perhaps, closer than he knew to that of the babus whom he reviled, and less helpful to Indian archaeology than Woolley with his fearless objectivity.

There were no immediate reforms as a result of the Woolley Report. It was withdrawn by a timid Indian administration, so that its negative effects were fully felt without the mitigating encouragement which positive changes might have brought. The Survey, already demoralized by the financial stringency of the 1930s and by its inheritance from Marshall – who had not excelled at training others to replace him – defended itself as best it could and struggled on. Only in 1943, in anticipation of Dikshit's retirement, was the government bold enough to offer the directorship to Mortimer Wheeler, whom Woolley had originally privately recommended.

When Stein left England during the period of the 'phoney war' in late 1939, he had hoped, by returning to India, to find some more positive way of living through the conflict than by being trapped in the West. His offer to 'return to duty' on the Frontier was not taken up. War, at this stage, seemed much farther away from the subcontinent than it had in 1914–18. There were no immediate threats to India's borders, though nearly 200,000 Indians had volunteered to fight for the imperial cause despite Congress's policy of non-cooperation. His life seemed little affected by events in Europe until, in 1940, news of his nephew Ernst's misfortunes filled him with the sense of impotence which he had hoped to evade.

Ernst and his German-Jewish wife Jeanne had been living in Louvain since their return from Washington in 1936. Ernst had achieved academic respectability with the post of Professor of Byzantine History and Literature, had had his work published and was in the course of writing another book when war broke out. Financially, however, he seems still to have been dependent on an allowance from his uncle to supplement his Louvain salary. This Stein paid willingly in memory of his own brother, who had taught him the merits of saving so long ago. But it is clear from muted comments in his letters to Helen Allen and to Jeanne that he found it difficult to admire much in his nephew's character. Ernst seemed to him a self-centred hypochondriac whose chief redeeming feature was the fact that he had a strong-minded wife. 'He has been a source of cares ever since his boyhood,' he once told Helen, 'and in the absence of other qualities his capacity for learned research, etc., has afforded little compensation for them.'[5]

Stein's anxiety on behalf of his relatives in Belgium grew from the start of the war. As he commented to Helen, recalling a map he had known at school, more blood had been spilt in the Low Countries than anywhere else in the history of European conflict. His fears were confirmed in May 1940 when the Germans marched into Belgium. He heard nothing from Ernst. All he knew was that his nephew had not obtained Belgian naturalization and that, while working in Berlin in the early 1930s, he had expressed anti-Nazi views 'rather freely'. Like his uncle, Ernst and his sister had been baptized into the Christian Church and Ernst had since converted to Catholicism. But it seems that Jeanne had made no attempt to lose her Jewish identity – though this, of course, was not a subject mentioned by Stein.

At last, in mid-June, he received a letter from Jeanne, written from Montpellier in southern France. She and Ernst had fled Louvain two days after the invasion of 10 May. The part of the city where they lived, close to the railway and a strategic bridge, had been one of the first to be bombed and they had been forced to leave taking only what they could carry. They had walked to Brussels and had managed to get visas there for France, where they were now staying as paying guests with one of Ernst's fellow scholars. A few weeks earlier, Ernst had sent copies of the ten completed chapters of his book to his friend, but all his other work was lost.

In this and other letters of the same period, Jeanne implored Stein to help find Ernst employment in America. Stein rather grumpily dwelt on the thought, easy to entertain in hindsight, that they had been foolish to return to Europe from Washington. But he said little to Jeanne in this vein, promising instead to do what he could. He wrote to Carl Keller, his old admirer in Boston, and Keller immediately dispatched letters of his own to contacts at Harvard and Yale. But American universities were under siege from refugee academics who had already arrived on their doorsteps, and there was no hope of placing Ernst from a distance. Nor, for the time being, did there seem any means by which Stein's allowance to his nephew could reach him in Montpellier, and several pathetic, beseeching letters arrived at Mohand Marg predicting imminent destitution (though Ernst seems to have left the task of writing such letters entirely to his wife).

Despite his reservations about his nephew, Stein was upset by his predicament and preoccupied by his own inability to help. Ernst might exaggerate his difficulties as a matter of course but, this time, his circumstances clearly were grave. Indeed, Stein told Helen, when he first heard of the invasion of Belgium, he felt that Ernst's health was so weak that 'undue strain may easily precipitate the end'.[6] He had already had one heart attack, just before leaving America. Stein consulted his financial adviser, Helen's elderly brother Louis, on the possibility of getting money out of England and into Vichy France. He instructed his bank to increase the original monthly allowance of £18 to £25. But the money remained in Britain and Stein could do nothing more than advise Jeanne to borrow from her friends in France, on the understanding that he would settle their debts after the war.

In the meantime, he couched his letters to her in a somewhat tendentious style.

I wish the time may yet come when you both could look back on these experiences with gratitude to a kindly dispensation which allowed you to pass through such a grievous trial safely and without lasting injury to your health . . . You know best that E. has always felt more concerned about his ailments, even when small, than was justified or good for himself. But, of course, he must not be allowed to fall into the opposite error and in any way neglect care, especially against overwork. In you, dear Jeanne, full trust can be put.[7]

After their arrival in Montpellier, Stein heard nothing directly from his nephew and wife for nearly three years. Eventually, in March 1943, a letter arrived from Berne in Switzerland. Jeanne and Ernst had moved from Montpellier to Marseilles and then to Grenoble, where they obtained false identification cards under the name of Sernet (still preserved in papers kept by Jeanne's relatives). From Grenoble they had managed to escape across the border to Switzerland in late 1942. However, they were still in dire straits. In a telegram sent two months later, Jeanne described their condition as 'near starvation'.

It was impossible to send money from England, but Stein still had an account in Lausanne, the remnant of funds he had placed there for Harriet in 1920. In response to yet another telegram, this time from Ernst, he wrote explaining that a modest allowance per month from this source was the best he could offer, and that the support he had given both to Ernst and to his sister in England already exceeded the amount of his own monthly pension. He was living off the income from his savings, and did not want to break into his capital for fear of jeopardizing the provisions of his will – which, he pointed out, 'will benefit you both also when I am no more'.

Then, having drawn attention to the fact that Ernst's telegram was 'rather expensively worded', he told his nephew that he had never concealed his belief that 'every able-bodied man, when grown up and trained for whatever profession, learned or otherwise, must in the first place be prepared to earn his livelihood'. Unfortunately, this had been possible in Ernst's case only at intervals; but he hoped that he would now 'endeavour by whatever means are available in your new milieu to earn something by teaching, clerical or any other work'. And he advised him not to allow his health to be '*unnecessarily*' affected by imaginary apprehensions such as had caused so much care and anxiety to your poor mother. What is much wanted nowadays is firm courage.'[8]

Events in distant Europe formed a hazy backdrop to Stein's correspondence with Helen Allen. His letters were the usual mixture of concern for her health and work, and reports of his own activities, with the added element of a sprinkling of names that charted the war as it spread farther and farther across the globe. Finland, Norway and Denmark, the Low Countries, Italy's entry into the war, the fall of France, Greek resistance, Albania and Libya: countries and peoples whose fates he could consider only in terms of their place in the battle against Fascism, which he remained confident Britain would win. News was filtered through the Indian newspapers – whose understandable preoccupation with internal politics irritated him – or arrived months out of date in letters from friends.

It was those friends whose individual fortunes moved him most. In the spring of 1940 he heard that Helen's 'ideal sister', Olga, had died; Publius's sister Maud, who had been very ill for some time, followed her less than a year later. In July 1940 Gustav was interned, first in Devon, then in Cheshire and Liverpool. Stein was dismayed. He had offered to help pay for Thesa and Gusti (as Gustav was known in the family) to move to America when the threat of internment first loomed but they had decided to stay and continue their (mostly voluntary) work in Oxford. He would not openly criticize the British government for its decision; but he kept a newspaper cutting bearing a letter from the historian, G. M. Trevelyan, on the unfairness of treating friendly refugees as potential enemy aliens. Gusti was luckier than some: one or two of Helen's university friends pressed quietly for his release and he was home again in September. He and Thesa moved to North Oxford, to become lodgers in the home of the daughter of John Masefield, the Poet Laureate.

Stein had hoped, ever since his niece and her husband arrived in England before the war, that they would put down roots there and give up any thought of returning to Vienna. He believed it would be years before racist 'venom' was eradicated from Austria and would have liked to see them espouse Britishness as he had done. But he could not help admiring Gusti's dislike of the dependent life of the refugee and his determination to resume his career as soon as possible.

'As to our prospects,' Gusti wrote to him in 1940 (in English), 'they are nil to put it bluntly, as long as there is a single British doctor out of job and our chief [Professor Cairns at the Nuffield Hospital] said that there are still several thousands. I quite understand the position, these things are only natural under the present circumstances, but the day will come where we shall be not refugees, but decent citizens again with an even chance for work.'[9]

Stein's links with Hungary became increasingly tenuous. In 1942 he heard of the death of his elderly cousin Rosa, with whom he had often stayed in the past in her house on the slopes of the Buda hills. But news of the demise of his old friend Count Teleki was far more shocking. Stein had watched with growing apprehension as the Prime Minister tried to steer a course between national self-interest and outright alliance with the Axis powers; but he was unprepared for the tragic outcome. Hungary, having avoided being drawn into active support of Germany at first, had established a bond of friendship with Yugoslavia under the regency of Prince Paul. Teleki hoped by such means to limit German dominance in the region; but in 1941 Serbs overthrew the regent and German soldiers crossed Hungarian territory to invade Yugoslavia, supported by Hungarian forces acting without their Prime Minister's permission. Teleki's strategy had failed. He committed suicide.[10]

This was not the only friend of Stein's to meet a violent death. Many of those who had reached high office in India were potential targets for extremist attacks but Sir Michael O'Dwyer, comfortably retired in London, might well have expected to be low down an assassin's list. It was more than twenty years since he had been in charge of the Punjab on the fateful day of the Amritsar Massacre. The officer commanding the soldiers who fired on the crowd, General Dyer, was long dead and the event had been superseded by other milestones in the nationalists' trek towards independence. But at least one veteran of Jallianwalla Bagh had waited patiently for the chance to exact retribution. One day in 1940, at the end of a meeting at Caxton Hall, he lobbed a home-made bomb towards the assembled Anglo-Indian worthies. Several were wounded, and O'Dwyer died immediately.

Such events naturally shocked Stein. But it was the less dramatic, steady erosion of his circle of friends that made the most impact. His American correspondent of fifty years, Lanman; his old philologist colleague Sir George Grierson; the politician and statesman Lord Lloyd whom he had first met in Bombay; all were dead before the summer of 1941. Oppressed by such losses, Stein told Helen he would gladly face the threat of torpedoes in order to see her again – if it were not for the fact that he still had work to do.

In the autumn of 1940 he relived his first years in Kashmir. Travelling back to places which, in some cases, he had not seen for half a century, he took a series of photographs for a new edition of the *Rajatarangini* which the Prime Minister of the state was keen to fund. Then, on 14 December, he set out with his small party (including his usual bearer Alia and cook Alibat) for the princely states of western Rajasthan (known then as Rajputana). His aim there was to trace the dried-up course of the Gaggar River, which Hindu tradition identified as the 'lost' Sarasvati of the Rig-Veda and later texts. He had Muhammad Ayub Khan to help him, thanks to an unsolicited grant from the Archaeological Survey which paid the surveyor's salary.

Travelling (mostly by car) through Bikaner, Jodhpur and Jaisalmer as the guest of their rulers, he spent January and February 1941 investigating the prehistoric sites that lay adjacent to the river-bed, regretting that aerial surveys were impossible but enjoying the 'tame' desert, the carved stone architecture of the cities and the lavish hospitality of the princes. These men impressed him with their respect for tradition, their paternalistic concern for their states and, not least, their 'perfect English manners' – a well-nigh ideal combination of qualities in Stein's book. His five-day camel journey from Jaisalmer to the last state in his tour, Bahawalpur, lay across what, in just over six years, was to become the new frontier between Pakistan and India. From Bahawalpur he travelled to Dera Ismail Khan and by mid-March 1941 was back on familiar ground as a guest of the Cunninghams at Peshawar's Government House.

Despite – or perhaps because of – his age, he remained addicted to activity. In late March, thanks to Cunningham, he was able to move freely around the Khyber Pass, which was closed to visitors and was one of the few places along the Frontier which he had not yet seen. He had never tried to visit it before, believing he ought to see it only while *en route* to Afghanistan itself in pursuit of his oldest goal. But now that the chance presented itself, and his goal seemed as unattainable as ever, he relaxed his self-imposed conditions.

At the same time, he heard from the Wali of Swat that conditions in the Indus Kohistan were now more favourable for his visit. So by the autumn of 1941 he could at last prepare for the sort of expedition that pleased him most, a foray into unknown territory. He had had a fruitful summer on the Marg, writing up his Rajasthan trip with the help of Muhammad Ayub Khan, who regularly accompanied him on his evening walks. But preparations for the departure were blighted by the loss of Dash VI, now 11 years old, who disappeared during one of those walks and whose body was found the following morning in a ravine, where he had plainly been ambushed by a leopard. Stein's men buried the dog's remains, wrapped in his felt rug, in a grave below the camp. Stein mourned the loss of the faithful creature who had followed him across Iran and Iraq, and whom he considered 'a worthy successor' to his favourite, Dash the Great.

The three-month journey in Kohistan began from Peshawar on 26 October, a month short of Stein's seventy-ninth birthday. Before leaving Kashmir, with characteristic regard for order and efficiency, he wrote a letter to John Johnson at the Oxford University Press. In it he gave the names of his trustees (Mason, Helen and her brother Louis) and detailed the whereabouts of all his as yet unpublished work: notes for the new edition of the *Rajatarangini* and material for his *limes* report. As he had clearly indicated in his will long ago, he intended his affairs to cause minimum inconvenience, even in the event of his death 'in some far-off country'.

Thanks to the Surveyor-General's interest in the impending trip, the services of Muhammad Ayub Khan and a photographer, Abdul Khai, were provided, and Stein took along Alia and Alibat. Once he reached Swat and the farthest point of the road leading towards Kohistan, many more men were necessary to carry loads over the difficult paths that lay ahead. The fact that Stein wrote nothing to Helen for more than a fortnight gives an indication of how demanding were the conditions that he faced.

From Swat, the route to the valley of the Kandia River, which joins the Indus at the northern end of the 'route of the hanging chains', lay eastward across the 15,000-foot Bisau Pass. Part of the path had been built specially as a mule-track for Stein's party, but riding over it was too uncomfortable in places to be worthwhile. After taking anthropometrical measurements of the Dard-speaking Kohistanis in a small village, Stein began the ascent to the pass over boulder-strewn slopes.

The only ground sufficiently level to accommodate a camp on the way up was exposed on a high ridge, and the wind was icy.

On the far side of the pass, the descent led first through the wet snow of late afternoon, on through dusk and darkness down a snow-filled gully. Only a small torch illuminated the blackness of the night, directed on to the path by the leading guide so that Stein, and the two men who supported him, could see the way ahead and avoid the steep ravine that lay alongside. They did not reach their next camp until one in the morning and there was little enough comfort to be had there, for it lay at 10,000 feet and was bitterly cold.

After the exertions of that crossing, the party stayed for a week at a large village in the Kandia valley. Alia had been carried down on a stretcher, and Stein himself took to his tent for several days in order to dissuade a cold from turning into bronchial trouble. The indefatigable Muhammad Ayub Khan meanwhile was out surveying the valley – a place so wild and remote that, even today, visitors to Kohistan are strongly advised not to go there alone. However, Stein described the local people as cheery and 'tame', and was more impressed by their extreme poverty and their fleetness of foot than by any signs of hostility. Money in the form of cash was only just beginning to be known; and paths had only very recently been improved as a result of the Wali's influence. Even so they were still mere ladders and galleries, unfit for laden animals.

In the valley of the Indus itself, they were scarcely better. This was the place where the early fifth-century Chinese pilgrim, Fa-hsien, described how a man's eyes became unsteady when he looked at the towering walls of rock that lined the boiling waters of the river. The monk had had to traverse those walls by means of ladders and paths cut into the rock. Stein's experience was made slightly easier by the work done in the previous three years under the eye of the Wali's governor. But his route lay along the same cliff-faces a thousand feet above the river-bed, and involved constant climbs to breaks in the cliffs and descents again almost to the banks of the Indus. Seven or eight miles a day at most could be accomplished on such terrain, though occasionally the party were forced to cover greater distances because of the scarcity of ground level enough to accommodate a tent. Nevertheless, Stein considered the paths marginally easier than the treacherous *rafiks* he had used in Hunza and Roshan.

What conditions had been like before the Wali's improvements he could gauge by looking across at those on the far side of the river. 'Only strong aggression could have made people take to such mountains,' he mused in a letter to Helen.[11] To Keller he confessed, on seeing part of the old, unimproved route below him one day, 'I felt heartily glad not to have been obliged to follow it.'[12] The experience of seeing and surveying this wild country – which he left in late January 1942 – only increased his admiration for the ruler of Swat who could exert such a positive influence on the farthest-flung corners of his wild kingdom, despite being unable to read or write.[13]

<hr>

While Stein roved round the Frontier, war consumed the West. Almost all Europe was in the thrall of Germany and, in late 1941, the Japanese attack on Pearl Harbor and Hitler's declaration of war on the United States extended turmoil across the globe. In India the following year, the Congress Party's 'Quit India' campaign erupted into violence after the arrest of Gandhi and other leaders. And the plight of Ernst and Jeanne meant that Stein could never forget the events of the war, even if he had wanted to. But inner strengths bolstered him. Early in 1943 he commented to Helen: 'The experience in my life of disappointments having often proved to turn to advantage has provided me with an optimistic kind of resilience.'[14] It was an appropriate time to voice such sentiments, only a few weeks before an invitation arrived which was to offer him, at the age of 80, the opportunity for which he had waited all his adult life.

Since returning from the Indus Kohistan in early 1942, he had already turned another disappointment to advantage, and been on a further excursion into the Indian desert in Bahawalpur. Following his survey of the 'route of the hanging chains', he had hoped to complete his exploration of that secret stretch of the Indus by visiting the left bank later in 1942. But a minor fakir was at large in the Indus valley that summer, encouraging unrest by advocating *jihad*, and no satisfactory arrangement could be concluded regarding Stein's tour.

It was still possible, however, for him to make something of his plans. Guided by the most helpful of the local tribesmen, he trekked through the Thor Mountains down to the scorching Indus valley at Chilas, where discoveries of rock-carvings had recently been made. It was the time of year when even the local people avoided the town. The great barren, sandy bowl in which the town lies was ablaze with heat. Stein spent many uncomfortable hours trying to photograph the Sanskrit graffiti, inscribed on rocks near the river. But he survived the experience in rude health and returned to Kashmir by following in reverse the route he had used years earlier in 1913 to reach Darel and Tangir.

By early December 1942 he was off again, back to Bahawalpur to complete his survey of the Gaggar River down to the Indus. The state government made him a small grant and loaned him a car, and he stayed with the (British) Prime Minister in congenial surroundings that reminded him of his Lahore days. In the New Year, he travelled down to Karachi to visit the Governor of Sind province, Sir Hugh Dow, before moving on to the small state of Las Bela to trace Alexander the Great's route towards ancient Gedrosia across still unsurveyed ground. Not until the end of March 1943 did he return to Peshawar in order to be present at a reception for the Viceroy. And it was there, on the last day of the month, that a telegram arrived for him from Afghanistan.

The message came from Cornelius Van Heinert Engert, who had encouraged Stein not to abandon hope of reaching Balkh back in 1922, and who was now the US Minister in Kabul. He invited Stein to pay him a visit and mentioned that the Afghan Foreign Minister would also be pleased to welcome such a visitor. This was news of the sort that would have sent Stein's spirits soaring twenty years earlier. Yet his response now was measured. He admitted to Helen that the telegram was 'distinctly encouraging', and he sought Sir George Cunningham's advice immediately. But after so many raised hopes and bitter disappointments over the years, his expectations were muted. It was not the first time since Foucher's triumph in Afghanistan that he had been invited to visit and view the archaeological work being done there. But he had no interest in going simply as a 'globetrotter'. If that was all that was on offer now, he preferred to stay in India, where he had things to do.

However, he made contingency plans – not simply because it was possible that something really might come of the invitation, but also because experience told him that the Indian government would want details in writing of what he proposed doing there. For the benefit of the Foreign Department he described how, without interfering with French work, he would want to visit sites in Bactria and the Helmand valley, and to follow ancient routes to Kabul from the east and north.

Much as he admired Stein, Engert was probably disappointed when he heard of this reaction to his invitation. His chief aim had been simply to get Stein to Kabul. Once that had been achieved and good relations established with various people in authority, he believed the Afghan Foreign Ministry could be persuaded to let its visitor do some work without the need for inter-governmental negotiations. He understood Stein's desire not to waste time, he wrote, 'and to that end a formal assurance that you would be permitted to see and do certain definite things would of course be necessary. Only I fear lest a formal inquiry or request put your trip on an entirely different footing.'[15]

Stein clearly felt that, whether the visit was arranged informally or through official channels, its outcome was too uncertain for it to interrupt the work he already had planned for the summer. He decided to finish his report on Las Bela and try again to complete his survey of the Indus Kohistan before going to Kabul in the autumn. Even the persuasive letter which Engert wrote in mid-May did not elicit a definite date for his visit:

> I think I should tell you that since writing to you last I happened to see the Afghan Foreign Minister, Ali Mohamed Khan, on some business and, without my having mentioned your name, he said: 'By the way, isn't Sir Aurel Stein coming to Kabul?' When I explained that you were, much to your regret, unable to come now but might come later in the year, he said literally: 'I am very sorry to hear that, *especially as His Majesty – when I told him Sir Aurel was planning to come – instructed me to do everything possible for this distinguished visitor of whose fine work His Majesty had heard so much.*'[16]

By August, Stein had still had no luck in reaching the eastern part of the Indus Kohistan. So at last he contacted Engert to tell him of his intention to reach Kabul by mid-October. By then he had given the Indian government an outline of his plans together with a request for staff (a trained surveyor and a photographic assistant), a breakdown of costs for a year-long expedition and an application for a grant. It was satisfying, he remarked to Helen, to be able to write such a document on the same square yard of earth on Mohand Marg where, forty-five years earlier, he had written the proposal for his first expedition to Chinese Turkestan.

Somewhere in the interval between that first expedition and the one he hoped for now, however, Stein seems to have lost the knack of treading sufficiently delicately among the sensibilities of foreign powers and their representatives. Perhaps the loss dated from his visit to Nanking in 1931. Or perhaps it was simply that old age had eroded his awareness. While the Indian government readily agreed to provide him with assistants and money, the British Minister in Afghanistan advised him to leave his staff behind for the time being. Stein was threatening to arrive in Kabul fully equipped for an expedition before any of his hosts had had the chance to be introduced.

Stein paid little attention to the fact that he was now, at the start of what he hoped would be another major expedition, in his eighty-first year. He made sure all his papers were in order; but he had been taking this precaution before long trips for some years now. Intermittently over the past two or three years he had been suffering from his old complaint, dyspepsia, as well as from a urinary infection on which he had sought Gusti's advice. But these problems concerned him no more than the sight of a photograph accompanying one of his articles in 1940, which he complained to Helen made him look 'wrinkled and old'. He had certainly not stopped commenting pityingly on the deleterious effect which the ageing process seemed to have on others: Nilakanth Kaul, looking 'sadly aged' at 55, had been one of the latest objects of his sympathy.

One indication of his faith in his own stamina was his acquisition, in August 1943, of yet another Dash, the seventh in the series. Early the previous year he had told Helen, 'at my age I may as well tread my path alone while in Asia'.[17] But, encouraged by her, he gradually ceased to dwell on Dash VI's death as the sad conclusion to a history of canine companionship, and began to enquire after a replacement. This duly arrived in the shape of a ten-month-old fox-terrier which, with its sister, had been given to his friend Macpherson by the mother of one of Macpherson's patients. So it was in the traditional way, with a couple of servants in attendance and a dog at his heels, that Stein – the 'old Odysseus', as Hailey had once called him[18] – came down from Mohand Marg in late September to prepare for yet another expedition, a couple of months before his eighty-first birthday.

He spent his last few days in Kashmir with the Neves at Srinagar. The night before leaving, faintness suddenly overcame him and he had to be revived with a whisky. Neve wrote later that he and his wife 'felt it a bad omen for a start on a journey which, later, would be strenuous'.

However, on the following day Stein went down to Peshawar as planned, to stay at Government House. From there he wrote to Helen, telling her of his immediate plans and regretting the fact that he had heard nothing from Thesa, his niece, since the beginning of the year. There was no valedictory message such as he had written before undergoing his operation in Vienna six years earlier. After all, he anticipated only a lorry ride of two or three days, followed by a period in Kabul in which something, or nothing, might be achieved.

It was 19 October 1943 when Stein saw Kabul for the first time. He rode into the city in transport supplied by Engert and went directly to the US Legation, where he was to stay during his visit. The following day, he and Engert visited the British Minister, Squires, and later called on the Afghan Minister for Foreign Affairs. Stein was full of enthusiasm at the thought of spending the winter in the Helmand valley, and the possibility (though he had been warned it was a very faint one) of reaching Bactria when the weather improved the following spring.

Three days later, he caught a cold, supposedly from studying in the notoriously icy museum. He cancelled a couple of appointments and tried to shake it off. But instead, he rapidly became ill. The following evening his heart began to weaken and he had a stroke. Was he then able to recall some of the comments he had made in the past about his hopes for the time when death came, his desire to end his life 'in the saddle' rather than gradually, drearily, cooped up in some European 'prison'? Perhaps he thought of Dash VI and Helen's consoling remarks regarding the little dog's end. 'But you are right when you refer to a swift close of a happy life being much to be desired,' he had replied to her then. 'I share fully that feeling for myself. If only it were possible to assure that happiness to the end.'[19]

Death did not deny him his wish. He lay only two days longer in his bed at the American Legation, never fully conscious. He had known, even before the stroke, that he might not recover and had spoken calmly to Engert about his desire for an Anglican funeral. Whether he wished he was back on Mohand Marg, or whether he was content to die in a place he had hoped all his life to visit, we shall never know, and nor did his friends, since he left no instructions. Macpherson, to whom he had entrusted his affairs, went to Kabul for the funeral and, with Engert and Squires, was among the pall-bearers.

The first that one of the oldest friends of all, Fred Andrews, knew of what had happened was when he opened his copy of *The Times* on the morning of 28 October, two days after Stein's death, to find a photograph of that familiar face in the obituary column.

'It seemed incredible that Stein the indomitable, so full of energy and eagerness, the close friend of more than fifty years, could be really gone,' he wrote later. 'As I lifted my eyes from the fateful words I noticed, lying before me on my table, a little packet recently received from Mohand Marg, on which Stein had written: "A few flowers picked on the climb to my tomb".'[20]

Epilogue

F AME BESTOWS ITS blessings – and its curses – haphazardly.
Among explorers and archaeologists, Amundsen is remembered
for conquering the South Pole, Scott for dying there. Carter is a household name as a result of unearthing the tomb of Tutankhamun; but
Stein and the treasures he found along the old Silk Road have occupied
a less prominent place than all these in the collective memory since his
death more than fifty years ago.

Anyone who read his obituaries at the time might be surprised at this
fate. The *Sunday Express* declared that his name 'will live in history with
that of Marco Polo as one of the great explorers of Central Asia', and
The Times described his second expedition in Chinese Turkestan as 'geo-
graphically and archaeologically . . . one of the first importance'. Those
who knew something of geographical research regarded his work in
that area alone as sufficient to earn him lasting fame.

Lasting fame, however, comes to few explorers and probably even
fewer archaeologists. The simplest way for Stein to achieve it would
have been by dying prematurely, ideally in harrowing or mysterious circumstances, somewhere in the desert. The remoteness of Central Asia
might then have become a factor in promoting interest in him, rather
than hampering it, as seems to have been the case. For all the romantic
appeal of the Silk Road, the region of western China which it traverses
attracts scant attention, even from academics.

In the early part of this century, Stein's work there perhaps seemed more relevant and comprehensible than it has done in the decades since his death. Interest in India and the East was still widespread among the educated classes, at least some of whom had worked there and had amateur antiquarian interests. The entire region of Central Asia retained a political significance as a result of the late nineteenth-century 'Great Game' contested there by the British and Russian empires.

Even given this background, Stein still had to struggle to win support for his expeditions, and he often remarked that finance would have been easier to arrange had he been exploring the Biblical or Classical past. Despite its great historical significance, the route by which the Buddhist culture of north-west India reached China was never likely to make a startling impact on the European, and particularly the British public – unless, that is, it yielded glorious booty. Had he unearthed a hoard of gold – jewellery, perhaps, or coins, or funerary objects – he and his desert sites might well have been precipitated into the public eye.

Desire for renown, however, was not a motivating factor. Stein disliked publicity for its own sake; but he also feared anything that might compromise his research. He relished his time in the Chinese desert precisely because of its obscurity. However remarkable his transformation into a man of action, he remained a scholar in his approach to his work. Most of his books were aimed at other scholars, he lectured to learned societies and he found writing for the general public a bore. He was reserved in company, quiet and unassuming in his style of life, and even in death contrived to avoid the public gaze, expiring in a remote place at a time when attention was firmly focused elsewhere.

Most of those who knew him well died long ago. Gustav Steiner, his niece's husband, died most recently, in 1983 at the age of 84. He and Thesa remained in Oxford until after the end of the war, but eventually returned to Vienna, as they had wished. Stein's nephew, Ernst, lived little longer than his uncle. It seems there was, after all, some basis for his fears for his own health. No doubt suffering from the stress of escape to Switzerland and perilous finances, he had another heart attack and died in Fribourg in February 1945. His wife, Jeanne, moved to England in the 1950s to be near members of her family who had fled there before the war, and died in North London in 1980.

Of Stein's oldest friends, Maclagan, Hailey, Dunsterville, Oldham, Andrews and Helen Allen outlived him. Fred Andrews remained in his home above the woods on Sydenham Hill, enjoying his collection of Asian handicrafts and continuing to attend meetings of the Royal Society of Arts in London until the end, which came in 1957. Helen Allen lived on in her house in Manor Place, Oxford, until her death in 1952, maintaining her links with Corpus Christi by giving tea parties for new undergraduates (at least some of whom had little idea why they were there). She earned several honorary doctorates for her contribution to Publius's *Letters of Erasmus*, and their joint achievement remains an authoritative work.

Oldham was Stein's chosen obituarist and the research he undertook for the obituary which was published, as Stein knew it would be, in the *Proceedings of the British Academy* (in 1943) elicited many tributes to his subject. Most were written in the quavering hands of men (they were, with the solitary exception of Helen, all men) whose careers in India or Indology were long past. They could not always provide precise details; but Oldham asked Fred Andrews a long list of questions, and answers came back to them all. Helen Allen replied on the reverse side of a piece of notepaper from her home on which Stein's firm, clear hand had started to write '22 Mohand M'.

Mohand Marg itself lies within the military zone in hapless Kashmir. Fate was kind to Stein when it allowed him to die without seeing the torment and tragedy of Partition in 1947; but how much worse, how utterly insufferable it would have been for him to witness the disintegration of his beloved Kashmir and the stationing of troops in the vicinity of his private 'kingdom'. A memorial stone, inscribed in both English and Urdu, was erected after his death on the site of his summer camp – perhaps by Macpherson or the Neves – and some years ago was said to be in need of repair. Its current condition is not known.

In the wild places that Stein loved there has been comfortingly little change. It is satisfying to know that the Taklamakan Desert is still sufficiently remote and intimidating to attract an expedition, which made the first successful west-east crossing – a journey of 700 miles – in 1993.[1] Travellers may now reach Chinese Turkestan from Pakistan in relative comfort along the Karakoram Highway; but the mountain country to either side of that remarkable road remains wild and inaccessible.

The chief cities of the Taklamakan oases, however, are beginning to defy a prediction Stein once made that they would not see streams of tourists for many years to come.² To cater for their visitors, the Kashgar authorities recently built a six-storey hotel in the compound of the old British Consulate. A few yards away from the rear wall of the hotel, the house built in 1913 by the Macartneys still stands, repainted and well maintained, and still enjoying an uninterrupted view across the oasis to the distant mountains.

Many of the items which Stein resurrected from the desert arrived in the West only to be buried yet again. Of the large Stein Collection at the British Museum, only a fraction is displayed in the renovated oriental gallery named after its new benefactor, Joseph E. Hotung. In 1914, when this gallery first opened as part of the Edward VII wing, Stein's finds provided the inaugural exhibition and easily filled all the cases. Since then, however, most have been stored in the basements where they were first unpacked, and the only way to appreciate their range was – and remains – to look through the museum's card index which contains their photographs.

It would be fatuous to suggest that the whole oriental gallery be given over to Stein now. When a single room – albeit a vast one – must represent all the museum's antiquities from the Far East and Southern Asia, the collection of one archaeologist will inevitably be illustrated by only a fraction of the total. Nevertheless, it seems something of a lost opportunity to give so little prominence to the Silk Road, and to the man who was largely responsible for discovering its lost civilization, when it has such romantic appeal (not least among the museum's many Japanese visitors).

In the National Museum in Delhi, Stein's finds from Chinese Turkestan receive more attention. There are two large rooms full of wooden writing tablets, painted silk banners and small objects from the desert sites. Other parts of Stein's booty found separate homes. The manuscripts are divided between the India Office Library and the British Library, including forgeries by Islam Akhun who would surely be delighted and amazed to know how his work has been preserved. The Victoria and Albert Museum holds some textiles; and there are Sanskrit manuscripts in the Indian Institute in Oxford, now part of the Bodleian Library. The banners and paintings from the Caves of the Thousand Buddhas are in the British Museum: they are too delicate to be on permanent display but were exhibited there in 1990. The Silk Road artefacts collected by archaeologists of other nationalities can be seen in museums scattered across the globe: the Hermitage in St Petersburg; the Museum of Indian Art in Berlin; the Guimet in Paris; the Tokyo National Museum; the Fogg Art Gallery in Cambridge, Massachusetts; and Stockholm's Ethnographical Museum.[3]

The Tun-huang caves themselves look out upon a very different scene from that which greeted Stein when he first rode into the valley one morning in 1907. What was then a remote spot, animated only once a year by cavalcades of local pilgrims, has become the site of a prestigious academy and the destination of countless tourist groups from all over the world. No Chinese art student's education is complete without a visit, and the effect of so many thousands of people inhaling and exhaling in the once dry atmosphere of the grottoes so threatens their wall paintings that they may soon be closed to the public.

Research into the manuscripts and paintings of the hidden library continues, and is now infused by a spirit of co-operation between the countries involved. A series of volumes is being published which will reproduce in facsimile all the non-Buddhist texts in the various collections – in Britain, France, Japan and China – so that students may have access to them, wherever they study. This amicable arrangement does not necessarily neutralize Chinese feelings about Stein. In the preface to the Chinese edition of Peter Hopkirk's *Foreign Devils on the Silk Road*, Duan Wenjie wrote of the history of 'robbing and plundering' recorded in the book, referred to Stein and others as 'robbers' and 'thieves', and expressed the hope that all Tun-huang relics would one day be returned to the caves.

This is a sentiment familiar to anyone who has followed the debate about the Elgin Marbles, which Greece would like to see sent back to Athens. It is an idea with ready appeal and one which, perhaps, the British are less qualified than others to judge, since their own antiquarian treasures have generally remained in their possession. But arguments such as that used by Stein's colleague at the British Museum, Arthur Waley, seem to miss the point.

Waley asked how an Englishman might feel if a foreign archaeologist bribed the custodian of an old, English monastery to hand over medieval manuscripts, offering this as a direct comparison with Stein's behaviour at Tun-huang. But the differences are clear. Anyone hoping to smuggle such manuscripts out of Britain would know they were removing them from a country able and eager to conserve them, and with laws governing the ownership and removal of such objects. When Stein first went to Chinese Turkestan, there were no such laws in operation, he found no evidence of interest from the Chinese in investigating the sites and, most importantly, many signs that antiquities would be harmed, if not destroyed, if left to the predations of local treasure-seekers and iconoclasts.

This does not explain away his cavalier behaviour in 1931, when he deliberately tried to evade the proscriptions of the Chinese scholars who, he knew, were trying to establish a legal framework for archaeological work in their country. But that was three decades on from his first foray into the desert when, no matter how unlikely it may sound now to his critics, concern for historical research was his overriding concern.

Waley's point of view was an unusual one for its time, which we may choose to describe as 'enlightened' now because it happens to accord with our modern opinions. But one lone voice is insufficient reason to dismiss the behaviour of the vast majority of people who thought and acted in the manner of their times. The use of hindsight to judge a person's actions in the past all too often indicates a lack of imagination and, more worryingly, a wish to deny the reality of that past. It seems glib to condemn a man for acting in a way entirely consistent with the period in which he lived and the Western world in which he was raised.

Where archaeological 'booty' is concerned, it also disregards the care and study which the objects often received in their new homes. This is unlikely to have been their fate had they remained *in situ*, prey to a variety of destructive forces while waiting for Chinese scholars to arrive many years later.

Stein's hopes for future work in the areas that had interested him lay with British and Hungarian researchers. The Stein-Arnold Fund which was established after his death, according to the terms of his will, awards a maximum of three modest money grants each year to such applicants, preferably those engaged in exploration. The awards are made by the British Academy and have supported work in Iran, Pakistan and Sinkiang.

In the one country Stein longed to see, archaeological excavation since his death has proved the accuracy of his expectations. At the French-run site of Ai Khanum, on the banks of the Oxus in northern Afghanistan, a Greek Bactrian city has been discovered which vividly demonstrates the strength of Greek culture there, as well as its adaptation to local conditions.

It will not be there, however, that Stein is reincarnated. If his semi-serious belief in the return of the soul were to provide him with another life, he would not be found at work in a field already occupied by others. He thrived only where he knew he was the first to cut a path: the first archaeologist in the Taklamakan Desert and the first to conduct a survey of prehistoric Iran; the first European to enter the Indus Kohistan; the first historian to claim the mountain of Una as Alexander's Aornos.

Bactria belongs to other archaeologists now. But Stein's grave lies in the shady surroundings of Kabul's Christian cemetery – miraculously unharmed by the battles all around – as proof that only death denied him the chance he had been wanting all his life. 'He enlarged the bounds of knowledge,' says its inscription. More important than this tribute, however, are the final words on the tablet. For someone who felt himself so often an outsider, who was so touched by marks of friendship, a memorial that describes him as 'A man greatly beloved' is surely the best tribute of all.

Chronology

26 Nov. 1862	Marc Aurel Stein born in Tüköry utca, Budapest
1871–3	Piarist gymnasium, Budapest
1873–7	Lutheran Kreuzschule, Dresden
1877–9	Lutheran gymnasium, Budapest
1879–80	Studies Sanskrit and comparative philology at university in Vienna
1880–1	Moves to University of Leipzig
1881–4	Studies Indology and Old Persian at University of Tübingen
1884–5	In England to study oriental collections
1885–6	Military service at the Ludovica Academy, Budapest
1886–7	Further study in England
Oct. 1887	Stein's mother dies
Nov. 1887	Stein leaves Europe for India
May 1888	Stein's father dies
1888–99	Registrar of Punjab University and Principal of Oriental College, Lahore
Nov. 1891	Stein's uncle, Ignaz Hirschler, dies
1899–1900	Principal of Calcutta Madrasah
1900	*Kalhana's Rajatarangini, a Chronicle of the Kings of Kasmir*, published
May 1900–May 1901	First expedition to Chinese Turkestan: travels

	north from Kashmir via Gilgit, the Hunza valley and Tashkurgan. Explores desert sites in vicinity of Khotan, including Dandan-Uiliq, Niya, Endere and Yotkan; surveys headwaters of Khotan River in Kun-lun Mountains, connecting area with Indian Trigonometrical Survey. Returns to Europe across Russia.
Summer 1901	In Europe to unpack his collection in the British Museum and visit family
Nov. 1901–Dec. 1903	Inspector of Schools in the Punjab
May 1902–Dec. 1903	In England to work on collection and visit invalid brother Ernst
June 1902	First attempt to work in Afghanistan
Oct. 1902	Ernst Stein dies
1903	*Sand-Buried Ruins of Khotan* published (popular account of first expedition)
1904–10	Inspector-General of Education, and Superintendent of Archaeology, in North-West Frontier Province and Baluchistan
Sept. 1904	Becomes a British subject
Oct. 1905	Goes to Kashmir to prepare for second expedition
Apr. 1906–Oct. 1908	Second expedition to Chinese Turkestan: travels north via Chitral and Wakhan corridor of Afghanistan. Revisits old sites and digs at new ones, including Lou-lan, Miran, the 'Chinese *limes*' and Ming-oi. Arrives in Tun-huang in March 1907 and obtains thousands of manuscripts and paintings from the Caves of the Thousand Buddhas. Crosses Taklamakan Desert from north to south, early 1908. Surveys in Nanshan Mountains and traces Khotan River to its source. Suffers frostbite in feet and has toes of left foot amputated, Oct. 1908. Returns to Kashmir via Ladakh
1907	*Ancient Khotan* published (detailed report of first expedition)
Jan. 1909–Dec. 1911	In Europe, on leave and to work on new collection at British Museum. Lectures in several countries, stays in Italy and then at Merton College, Oxford

1910–17	Superintendent of Archaeology in the North-West Frontier Province and Honorary Curator of Peshawar Museum
1912	Second attempt to work in Afghanistan
1912	*Ruins of Desert Cathay* published (popular account of second expedition)
June 1912	Made KCIE
July 1913– Feb. 1916	Third expedition to Chinese Turkestan: travels north via Darel and Tangir. Revisits old sites, traces ancient route across Lop Desert and digs at Khara-khoto in Gobi Desert, and at several sites in vicinity of Turfan including Astana. Extracts more manuscripts from Caves of the Thousand Buddhas. Injures leg in riding accident. Returns to India via Russian Turkestan and Iran, uncovering Buddhist remains at site in Sistan, south-east Iran
Apr. 1916–Sept. 1917	In England to write detailed report of second expedition. Lives mainly in Devon
1917	Official retirement. Obtains extension of service on 'special duty' to work on books, collection from third expedition and other projects. Divides time between Kashmir and Delhi
Dec. 1919–Dec. 1920	In Europe, to write and see sister-in-law
1919–22	Third attempt to work in Afghanistan; foiled by Foucher
1921	*Serindia* published (detailed report of second expedition)
Feb. 1924–Nov. 1925	First visit to Middle East; continues to Europe. Writes at house in Surrey; holidays with sister-in-law in Austria
1926	Tour of Swat and identification of Mount Una as Alexander's Aornos
1927–8	Two explorations in Baluchistan, to seek links between prehistoric civilizations of Indus valley and Sumeria
1928	*Innermost Asia* published (detailed report of third expedition)
Nov. 1928	Final retirement from service in India
	Second visit to Middle East; continues to Europe
1929	*On Alexander's Track to the Indus* published

Dec. 1929–Jan. 1930	Visits America from England
Mar.–May 1930	Visits China from England
June 1930	Returns to Kashmir
	Stein's old friend Sir Thomas Arnold dies
Aug. 1930–June 1931	Fourth expedition to Chinese Turkestan: travels north via Gilgit and Hunza. Chinese prevent excavations and Stein abandons work, returning to Kashmir
Oct. 1931	Short tour in Punjab in search of Alexandrian evidence on banks of Jhelum River
1932	First Iranian expedition, in Iranian Baluchistan
Summer 1932	In Europe
1932–3	Second Iranian expedition, along Persian Gulf
1933	*On Ancient Central Asian Tracks* published
Summer 1933	In Kashmir
16 June 1933	Stein's closest friend, P. S. Allen, dies
1933–4	Third Iranian expedition, through eastern Fars
May 1934–May 1935	In Europe, including holiday in southern Italy
11 Oct. 1934	Stein's sister-in-law dies
1935–6	Fourth Iranian expedition, from western Fars to Iranian Kurdistan
Apr. 1937	Undergoes prostate operation. Remains in Europe
1937	*Archaeological Reconnaissances in Northwest India and Southeast Iran* published
Jan. 1938	Travels to Middle East
Mar.–May 1938	Aerial survey of Middle Eastern *limes* in northern Iraq
Summer 1938	In Kashmir
Oct. 1938–May 1939	Aerial survey of Middle Eastern *limes* extended from Iraq into Trans-Jordan
June–Nov. 1939	In England
Nov. 1939	Returns to India
1940	*Old Routes of Western Iran* published
Dec. 1940–Mar. 1941	Archaeological tour in Rajasthan
Oct. 1941–Feb. 1942	Explores 'route of the hanging chains' in Indus Kohistan
1942–3	Short tours in Bahawalpur, Chilas and Las Bela
19 Oct. 1943	Stein sees Kabul, Afghanistan, for the first time
26 Oct. 1943	Stein dies at the US Legation, Kabul

Notes

For the sake of brevity, the following abbreviations are used within the notes:

AS	Aurel Stein	HMA	Helen Mary Allen
BL	British Library	IOL	India Office Library
BM	British Museum Central	PSA	Percy Stafford Allen
	Archives	RAS	Royal Asiatic Society
Bod	Bodleian Library, Department	RGS	Royal Geographical
	of Western Manuscripts		Society Archives
FHA	Fred Henry Andrews	TWA	Thomas Walker Arnold

Chapter 1: A Singular Inheritance

1. The building was destroyed during the Second World War, but a large commemorative plaque now marks the place where it stood.
2. Theresa Steiner (née Stein) to C.E.A.W. Oldham, 5 Apr. 1944, IOL MSSEur D1167/11.
3. The Indologist, Ervin Baktay. He recalled his visit in the Hungarian periodical *Élet és Tudomány*, 1962.
4. '. . . historical remains which I loved to visit as a boy, now, alas, improved away by modern "progress"'. 'In Memoriam Theodore Duka', by Sir Aurel Stein, written for the Hungarian Academy of Sciences and privately published in English, Oxford, 1914.
5. 'In Memoriam Theodore Duka'.
6. Bequeathed by Sir Aurel Stein, together with other family papers, to the Hungarian Academy of Sciences in 1921. Because of the inaccessibility of

these letters (see Acknowledgements), the author consulted Vilma Boros, *The Youth of Aurel Stein – the correspondence of Ignaz Hirschler and Ernst Stein about Aurel Stein, 1866–1891*, published in Magyar and German, with an English summary, by the Hungarian Academy of Sciences, 1970.

7. *Journal of the Royal Asiatic Society*, 1895.
8. Duka, *The Life and Works of Alexander Csoma de Koros*, 1885.
9. Ernst Stein to Ignaz Hirschler, 9 Feb. 1885, quoted in Boros.
10. *Ancient Khotan*, 1907, and *Innermost Asia*, 1928.

Chapter 2: First Taste of the British Raj

1. The term 'Anglo-Indian' was adopted officially in 1900 for those of mixed race, but before and after that date was commonly used to describe the British in India, as it is here.
2. Once he left home, Aurel's given name was used only by members of his family and, much later, by one or two very close friends. To everyone else he was Stein, in the custom of the day. People who did not know him addressed him by his full name and he always tried to correct this, for he himself never used the first part, Marc.
3. AS to PSA, 2 Mar. 1924, Bod MS Stein 19.
4. The legislators were also aware that a taste for Western goods might well arise from a Western-style education. Michael Edwardes wrote, in *High Noon of Empire*, 1965: 'As an exercise in social engineering based firmly upon ideological thinking, its only real parallel is the re-education and "thought control" policy of communist China today.'
5. Sir William Rattigan (1842–1904), the son of an illiterate private in the Indian Army, may have been the model for Rudyard Kipling's character Kim (see Angus Wilson, *The Strange Ride of Rudyard Kipling*, 1977). His grandson was the playwright Terence Rattigan.
6. Ernst Stein to Ignaz Hirschler, 30 Jan. 1888, quoted in Boros.
7. The name Kashmir is used here as if it referred solely to the valley in which Srinagar lies. But the state of Jammu and Kashmir, ruled by the Singh dynasty from 1846 until shortly after Partition, encompassed Gilgit and Hunza in the north, Leh in the east and Jammu in the south.
8. AS to Ignaz Hirschler, 14 May 1889, Bod, MS Stein 117.
9. Georg Bühler to AS, 14 Nov. 1890, Bod MS Stein 392.
10. Translated by Stanislas Julien, 1858.
11. Quoted by AS in his 'Memoir on the Ancient Geography of Kasmir', in *Kalhana's Rajatarangini, a Chronicle of the Kings of Kasmir*, Vol. II, 1900.
12. Rudyard Kipling, *Kim*, illustrated by J. Lockwood Kipling, 1901. Kipling's Tibetan lama asks the curator of the museum if he knows of any translations of Hiuen Tsiang's travel record and is shown Julien's book.

13. AS to Ernst Stein, 27 May 1890, Bod MS Stein 118.
14. Bod MS Stein 277.
15. Major-General L.C. Dunsterville, *Stalky's Reminiscences*, 1928. De Justh's sensibilities had been offended when, after he had played the piano at an evening gathering, someone suggested he give a rendition of a popular music-hall song.

Chapter 3: Ambition Finds a Way

1. Andrew Dalgliesh, a trader who travelled frequently between Leh and Kashgar, was murdered near the Karakoram Pass in 1888.
2. The expedition to Chinese Turkestan and Tibet, in 1891–4, of Jules Dutreuil de Rhins, a former naval officer, was financed by the French Government and the Academy of Inscriptions and Letters. His travelling companion, Fernand Grenard, brought his papers back to France after his murder.
3. 'The Jews were blamed for being rich and poor, clever and stupid: for trying to become like the rest of the population or for remaining different from it . . . At the turn of the century political anti-Semitism existed wherever the Jews and the Gentiles came into contact.' Z.E.B. Zeman, *Twilight of the Hapsburgs*, 1971.
4. Quotation of John Johnson by HMA in her typescript of 'Letters of P. S. Allen' (1939), Bod MS Stein 35.
5. All quotations of HMA on her visit to Lahore are from letters to her mother, Bod MS Allen 174.
6. Sir Edward Denison Ross, *Both Ends of the Candle*, 1943.
7. FHA, 'Sir Aurel Stein: the Man', in *Indian Art and Letters*, Vol. XVIII, No. 2 (1944). Arnold received the designation 'Saint', as PSA explained to HMA, 'partly because of his saintly disposition, partly as the translator of the Little Flowers of St Francis' (15 June 1899, Bod MS Allen 167). The elevation from Saint to Hierarch seems to have been a spontaneous response to his knighthood in 1921.
8. FHA, 'Sir Aurel Stein: The Man'.
9. Winston Churchill, who described the expedition in *My Early Life* (1930), reflected that, had the General been able to tell the opposing Pathan tribes the story of how his seventeenth-century ancestor, Colonel Blood, tried to steal the Crown Jewels, they would have been so sympathetic that there would have been no need for the invasion.
10. Dunsterville, *Stalky's Reminiscences*.
11. He also had a sense of humour. Once, when Governor of the Punjab, he walked out into the rain, alone with his dog, and, incognito, joined a passing peaceful protest to see how the police dealt with it. He was

delighted to read later in the police report that the procession had been joined by 'a disreputable European with a dog'. See P. Woodruff, *The Men Who Ruled India,* 1954.

12. Quotations from Hoernle's letters are from Bod MSS Stein 278, 289 and 290.
13. All quotations from AS's pocket diaries are from Bod MSS Stein 233–58.
14. Ross, *Both Ends of the Candle.*
15. AS to HMA, 13 Sept. 1899, Bod MS Stein 1.
16. Bod MSS Stein 233–58.
17. Bod MS Stein 290.
18. AS to FHA, 31 Dec. 1898, Bod MS Stein 36.

Chapter 4: Birth of a Great Adventure
1. The term 'Silk Road' or 'Route' has been in use only since the nineteenth century.
2. The circus-owner Carl Hagenbeck arranged for a number of Prejevalsky's horses to be brought to Europe where they were popular performers and exhibits.
3. The Anglo-Russian Pamir Boundary Commission of 1895 defined the two countries' spheres of influence in the region and established what is now known as the Wakhan corridor as Afghan territory within the British sphere.
4. Macartney to AS, 22 Mar. 1899, Bod MS Stein 289.
5. Office of the British Minister in Peking to Stein, Bod MS Stein 289.
6. The term 'the Great Game' was popularized by Kipling in his 1901 novel, *Kim,* but is believed to have been used first by Lieutenant Arthur Conolly, *c.* 1830, when he was travelling in Russia, Persia and Afghanistan: see Peter Hopkirk, *The Great Game,* 1990.
7. AS, *Sand-Buried Ruins of Khotan,* 1903.
8. Ibid.
9. Ibid.
10. Bod MS Stein 290.
11. AS, *Sand-Buried Ruins of Khotan.*
12. Ibid.

Chapter 5: Lost Cities of the Silk Road
1. Lady Macartney, *An English Lady in Chinese Turkestan,* 1931.
2. Ibid. Though Catherine was her first name, Macartney's wife signed herself by her second, Theodora, in letters to AS.
3. Ibid.

4. AS, *Sand-Buried Ruins of Khotan*.
5. Macartney, quoted in C. P. Skrine and P. Nightingale, *Macartney at Kashgar*, 1973.
6. Bod MS Stein 234.
7. AS, *Sand-Buried Ruins of Khotan*.
8. Bod MS Stein 234.
9. Ibid.
10. AS, *Sand-Buried Ruins of Khotan*.
11. AS to PSA, 4 Nov. 1900, Bod MS Stein 1.
12. Sven Hedin, *My Life as an Explorer*, 1925.
13. Ibid.
14. AS to PSA, 8 Mar. 1901, Bod MS Stein 1.
15. Bod MS Stein 290.

Chapter 6: A Fight for Freedom

1. *Journal of the Asiatic Society of Bengal*, 1899 and 1901. Hoernle had thought the books were set formulae for repetition, probably Buddhist prayers. 'It would seem', he had written in Part One, 'that there existed somewhere in the Takla Makan a kind of library, or store of books, the locality of which seems to have been discovered by native treasure seekers, being perhaps an ancient monastery . . . The mystery of the scripts – so many, and so intricately arranged – is, no doubt, a difficulty. But to solve it by the hypothesis of forgery is only to substitute one riddle, and a harder one, for another. How can Islam Akhun and his comparatively illiterate confederates be credited with the no mean ingenuity necessary for excogitating them?'
2. AS to PSA, 30 Aug. 1901, Bod MS Stein 1.
3. The decision to create the NWFP greatly upset the Lieutenant-Governor of the Punjab, Sir Mackworth Young, whose departure AS witnessed while on a brief visit to Lahore, on 5 March 1902. AS wrote in his diary: 'To station at 12.20 to see Sir M Young & Lady Y off. A sorry parting. Both near to breakdown.' Bod MS Stein 235.
4. AS to PSA, 1 Dec. 1901, Bod MS Stein 1.
5. Bod MS Stein 235.
6. AS to PSA, 10 May 1902, Bod MS Stein 1.
7. Bod MS Stein 235.
8. 20 Dec. 1901 (to W. F. Watson), reproduced in H. M. Allen (ed.), *Letters of P. S. Allen*, 1939.
9. Lockwood Kipling to AS, 15 Aug. 1903, Bod MS Stein 90.
10. TWA to AS, 19 Aug. 1903, Bod MS Stein 64.
11. FHA, 'Sir Aurel Stein: the Man'.

12. Bod MS Stein 337.
13. Bod MS Stein 293.
14. 28 Mar. 1904, ibid.
15. AS to PSA, 11 June 1904, Bod MS Stein 1.
16. Younghusband to AS, 25 Apr. 1904, Bod MS Stein 274.
17. AS to PSA, 15 Mar. 1905, Bod MS Stein 2.
18. AS to Pipon, 8 Sept. 1904, MS Stein 293.
19. AS to PSA, 17 Sept. 1904, Bod MS Stein 1.
20. AS's proposal, dated 14 Sept. 1904, BM.
21. Maclagan to AS, 20 Jan. 1905, Bod MS Stein 295.
22. Sir Mortimer Wheeler, *Still Digging*, 1955.
23. John Marshall to AS, 16 June 1905, Bod MS Stein 355.
24. AS to Marshall, 24 June 1905, ibid.
25. TWA to AS, 5 Oct. 1905, Bod MS Stein 64.
26. 25 Jan. 1906, Bod MS Stein 236.
27. Macartney to AS, 10 Nov. and 29 Dec. 1905, Bod MS Stein 296.
28. AS to PSA, 30 Mar. 1906, Bod MS Stein 3.

Chapter 7: Race to the Desert

1. 'Personal Narrative', Bod MS Stein 261.
2. Ibid.
3. Ibid.
4. Ibid.
5. In correspondence with the Survey of India, he listed the instruments he would need: 2 hypsometrical apparatus each with 3 boiling-point thermometers, 2 mapping instrument cases, 1 drawing instrument case, 2 mountain mercurial barometers, 3 plane-tables with stands and magnetic needles, 3 aneroids, 2 clinometers, 1 Abney's pocket level, 2 Chesterman's metallic tapes (100 feet each), 4 standard thermometers, 4 pocket compasses, 2 pedometers and 2 half chronometer watches. RGS.
6. FHA, 'Sir Aurel Stein: the Man'.
7. AS, *Ruins of Desert Cathay*, 1912.
8. AS to PSA, 3 Feb. 1906, Bod MS Stein 3.
9. AS to PSA, 3 Mar. 1906, ibid.
10. AS to Macartney, 6 Feb. 1906, Bod MS Stein 297.
11. AS to FHA, 28 Mar. 1905, Bod MS Stein 36.
12. Macartney, secret report to Government of India, 19 Oct. 1905, Bod MS Stein 296.
13. AS to PSA, 20 Jan. 1906, Bod MS Stein 3.
14. AS to the Amir of Afghanistan, 23 May 1906, Bod MS Stein 298.
15. AS to Andrews, 10 June 1906, Bod MS Stein 36.

16. Macartney to AS, 7 May 1904, Bod MS Stein 96.
17. AS to PSA, 25 June 1906, Bod MS Stein 3.
18. AS, *Ruins of Desert Cathay*.
19. AS to PSA, 14 Sept. 1906, Bod MS Stein 3.
20. Deane to AS, 3 Sept. 1906, Bod MS Stein 72.
21. AS to PSA, 19 Nov. 1906, Bod MS Stein 3.
22. William Foster to John Scott Keltie, 22 Nov. 1906, RGS.
23. AS to PSA, 19 Nov. 1906, Bod MS Stein 3.
24. AS to PSA, 10 Oct. 1906, ibid.
25. AS to Keltie, 10 Oct. 1906, RGS.
26. AS, *Ruins of Desert Cathay*.

Chapter 8: Treasures of the 'Black Hole'

1. *The Book of Ser Marco Polo*, trans. and ed. Sir Henry Yule (third edition, 1903).
2. This information is courtesy of Peter Hopkirk.
3. AS, *Ruins of Desert Cathay*.
4. AS to PSA, 17 Dec. 1906, Bod MS Stein 3.
5. AS returned Hedin's tape-measure at an informal dinner at the RGS in February 1909. Hedin gave it to the RGS, where it remains in their collection.
6. AS, *On Ancient Central Asian Tracks*, 1933.
7. AS to PSA, 2 Feb. 1907, Bod MS Stein 4.
8. FHA later distinguished between tempera paintings and frescoes, and placed all the wall-paintings brought by AS from Chinese Turkestan to Delhi in the former category. On the basis that the distinction is a technical one, I have used the term 'fresco' throughout as one that is generally, if inaccurately, understood. See FHA, *Catalogue of Wall Paintings from Ancient Shrines in Central Asia and Sistan*, Delhi, 1933.
9. AS, *Ruins of Desert Cathay*.
10. Quoted by AS in *Ruins of Desert Cathay*.
11. AS, *Ruins of Desert Cathay*.
12. Ibid.
13. Ibid.
14. AS to PSA, 26 Apr. 1907, Bod MS Stein 4.
15. AS, *Ruins of Desert Cathay*.
16. Ibid.
17. AS to Keltie, 18 June 1907, RGS.
18. AS to FHA, 15 June 1907, Bod MS Stein 36.
19. AS to PSA, 9 June 1907, Bod MS Stein 4.

Chapter 9: A Hero's Welcome

1. AS told Keltie, 8 July 1908, during the packing of antiquities for the journey to India: 'There are times when I might feel tempted to envy those who can devote themselves to purely geographical work & carry back their results conveniently compressed in maps, notebooks & photos.' RGS.
2. AS to PSA, 16 Aug. 1907, Bod MS Stein 4.
3. AS to PSA, 9 June 1907, ibid.
4. AS to FHA, 17 May 1907, Bod MS Stein 36.
5. Hedin had reached Tibet in 1906. He was away for almost exactly the same length of time as AS, returning to Europe in January 1909. Keltie told AS, 23 May 1907: 'I had a long letter from Sven Hedin the other day. He has been careering all over Tibet, and as usual is very full of the fact that he has done some hundreds of sheets of maps and some thousands of pages of notes.' RGS. For an account of Hedin's stormy relationship with the RGS see Charles Allen, *A Mountain in Tibet*, 1982.
6. Manichaeism was founded by Manes in Persia during the third century AD and spread throughout Central Asia, and even into eastern Europe, despite being considered heretical by other faiths.
7. AS to PSA, 2 Dec. 1907, Bod MS Stein 4.
8. AS to PSA, 10 Dec. 1907, ibid.
9. FHA, 'Sir Aurel Stein: the Man'.
10. AS, *Ruins of Desert Cathay*.
11. When AS later lectured on his expedition at the RGS, Macartney, who was in the audience, revealed that AS had dropped a camp chair somewhere on the way from Shahyar into the desert. The Amban of Shahyar had recovered it and sent it to Macartney, who sent it on to AS. AS replied that the chair was now with him in Oxford. *The Geographical Journal*, Vol. XXXIV, Sept. 1909.
12. The old man had travelled to Mecca via Samarkand and Istanbul, and returned via Bombay, Kashmir and the Karakoram Mountains.
13. AS, *Ruins of Desert Cathay*.
14. AS to PSA, 16 Oct. 1908, Bod MS Stein 5.
15. AS to PSA, 16 Nov. 1908, ibid.
16. The cutting, dated 6 March 1912, is among letters to AS from F. H. Brown, Bod MS Stein 66.
17. Colonel (later Sir Sidney) Burrard wrote to Stein after his visit: 'It is a great relief to deal with real geographical work after the rough sketches of Sven Hedin, which I cannot help thinking are given far more weight in the world than is their due.' 8 Dec. 1908; enclosed by AS in a letter to PSA, Bod MS Stein 5.

18. Bod MS Stein 237.
19. Bod MS Stein 279.
20. AS to PSA, 30 May 1908, Bod MS Stein 5.
21. PSA told AS (24 Dec. 1908) that Cannan, PSA's editor at the Oxford University Press, had been delighted by the discovery and had called to a colleague: "'Stein riding in a dhooly [litter] across the Karakoram discovered a new letter of Erasmus: that's what it is to be an archaeologist.'" Ed. HMA, *Letters of P. S. Allen.*
22. AS to PSA, 26 Oct. 1908, Bod MS Stein 5.
23. One of the assistants who worked with FHA on AS's collection was Leonard Woolley, later to win fame as the archaeologist who unearthed the treasures of Ur in Iraq.
24. AS to FHA, 24 Apr. 1909, Bod MS Stein 37.
25. AS to Keltie, 26 June 1910, RGS.
26. AS to PSA, 2 Dec. 1907, Bod MS Stein 4.
27. AS to PSA, 16 Aug. 1908, Bod MS Stein 5.
28. 4 Sept. 1909, Bod MS Stein 237.
29. Macmillan to Keltie, 21 Feb. 1912, RGS.
30. FHA, 'Sir Aurel Stein: the Man'.
31. The Archduke Franz Ferdinand and his wife lunched at the hotel on 13 October, and Stein admired their appearance and bearing.
32. MS Stein 237.
33. FHA, 'Sir Aurel Stein: the Man'.
34. Dunlop-Smith to AS, 10 July 1909, Bod MS Stein 279.
35. Stein noted Maclagan's advice in his diary, without comment.
36. AS to Hailey, 22 Feb. 1910, Bod MS Stein 279.
37. AS to PSA, 5 Oct. 1909, Bod MS Stein 6.
38. Marshall to AS, 21 Mar. 1910, Bod MS Stein 279.
39. AS to PSA, 16 Oct. 1908, Bod MS Stein 5.
40. AS to PSA, 30 Nov. 1909, Bod MS Stein 6.
41. His own disappointments never made him churlish about the success of others. On hearing of the £20,000 awarded to Shackleton for his expedition to the South Pole, he told Publius he thought it was a well-deserved piece of generosity. 'The whole enterprise was a great moral success if I may say so, for the nation which just now in competition with scientific achievements abroad is in need of some stimulus. After all, if the rulers still cling to time-honoured principles about "private enterprise", etc., it is something to have at least a tardy contribution towards the costs when success has come. On the whole an encouraging precedent.' 26 Aug. 1909, Bod MS Stein 6.
42. Lionel Giles, *Six Centuries at Tun-huang*, 1944.
43. Bod MS Stein 261.

Chapter 10: Escape from Civilization

1. AS to PSA, 24 Apr. 1912, Bod MS Stein 8.
2. AS to PSA, 29 Jan. 1912, ibid.
3. McMahon to AS, 9 May 1912, Bod MS Stein 338.
4. AS to PSA, 3 Jan. 1912, Bod MS Stein 8.
5. AS to PSA, 12 Mar. 1908, Bod MS Stein 5.
6. The artist Sir William Rothenstein, who made a portrait of AS in 1920, recalled that AS had told him how he deplored the decadence of Indian craftsmanship and the lack of interest in Indian culture among English officials (*Since Fifty*, 1939).
7. AS to PSA, 31 May 1912, Bod MS Stein 8.
8. AS to PSA, 17 June 1912, ibid.
9. PSA to AS, Bod MS Stein 12. Years later (20 September 1922), PSA told AS that an American friend who had heard of Dash II's fine qualities preached a sermon to children on the text of 'Don't Whine', and illustrated it with the story of 'the dog who only whined once'. *Letters of P. S. Allen.*
10. AS to PSA, 3 Nov. 1905, Bod MS Stein 2.
11. AS to PSA, 1 Sept. 1912, Bod MS Stein 9.
12. AS to PSA, 13 May 1912, Bod MS Stein 8.
13. McMahon to AS, 3 Sept. 1912, Bod MS Stein 338.
14. AS to Keltie, 20 Oct. 1912, RGS.
15. AS to PSA, 9 Sept. 1912, Bod MS Stein 9.
16. Skrine and Nightingale, *Macartney in Kashgar.*
17. Macartney to AS, 14 Oct. 1912, Bod MS Stein 9.
18. AS to PSA, 12 Nov. 1912, ibid.
19. Enclosed with letter from AS to PSA, 9 Sept. 1912, ibid.
20. Bod MS Stein 300.
21. AS to PSA, 30 Dec. 1912, Bod MS Stein 9.
22. AS to PSA, 14 Oct. 1912, ibid.
23. AS to FHA, 8 June 1913, quoted by FHA in 'Sir Aurel Stein: the Man'.
24. AS to PSA, 21 Apr. 1913, Bod MS Stein 10.
25. The surveyors were late leaving Dehra Dun for Kashmir because of the necessity of applying for permission through the Viceroy in Council to the Secretary of State for India. AS wrote of this process to PSA: 'If this document should be dug up 2000 years hence a future historian might well wonder how India could be governed on such lines.' 14 July 1913, Bod MS Stein 10.
26. AS to PSA, 28 July 1913, ibid.
27. On hearing the news from the Antarctic, Stein wrote to Publius: 'Scott's tragic fate has deeply moved me. In 1909 when I met him a few times at

the RGS I felt greatly attracted by his classic modesty & evident single-minded strength of character ... He has left the nation more than any scientific achievement can be worth, a great example how to face the worst of hardships and death with the calm courage of the great past.' He also wondered why Scott did not use dogs on his expedition. 'Dogs which can thrive on each other, seem an ideal solution of "transport & supplies" problems on such ground, whatever sentiment may suggest. Amundsen's "good fortune" has its explanation in his canine allies.' 10 Mar. 1913, Bod MS Stein 10.

28. AS to PSA, 21 July 1913, ibid.

29. 4 June 1913, Bod MS Stein 300.

30. On hearing of Macartney's KCIE, Stein told Publius that 'it was a special joy to see labours carried on for so long & beyond all public ken recognized as they deserved. Nobody now of influence in India has ever met him face to face which makes this recognition all the more valuable'. 7 Jan. 1913, Bod MS Stein 10.

31. Theodora Macartney shared this view. Of the officials who arrived at her New Year's Dinner at the start of 1915, she wrote: 'It was more pathetic than comical to see men who would have been imposing and dignified in their beautiful silks and amber beads making themselves look like scarecrows.' Macartney, *An English Lady in Chinese Turkestan.*

32. AS to PSA, 30 Sept. 1913, Bod MS Stein 10.

33. AS, 'A Third Journey of Exploration in Central Asia, 1913–16', *The Geographical Journal*, Vol. XLVIII, Aug. 1916.

34. AS to PSA, 30 Sept. 1913, Bod MS Stein 10.

35. AS, 'A Third Journey'.

36. AS to PSA, 1 Nov. 1913, Bod MS Stein 10.

37. AS, 'A Third Journey'.

38. Hedin, *My Life as an Explorer.*

39. AS to PSA, 8 Dec. 1913, Bod MS Stein 10.

40. Lectures given at the Lowell Institute, Boston, and published as *On Ancient Central Asian Tracks*, 1933.

41. AS to PSA, 30 Dec. 1913, Bod MS Stein 10. Boreas was the Greek god of the north wind.

42. AS to PSA, 7 Mar. 1914, Bod MS Stein 11.

43. AS to PSA, 27 Mar. 1914, ibid.

44. AS to Andrews, 23 Apr. 1914, Bod MS Stein 42.

45. Some of Koslov's finds were displayed in London in the Royal Academy's 1992 exhibition of the art of Tibet.

46. AS to PSA, 14 Aug. 1914, Bod MS Stein 11.

47. Lord Roberts of Kandahar, a famous soldier of Empire, became

President of the National Service League in 1905 in order to promote compulsory military service as a means of improving home defence.

48. AS to PSA, 12 Nov. 1914, Bod MS Stein 11.
49. AS to Keltie, 11 July 1915, RGS. Keltie, in reply, told him, 'I need not say how gratified we all are to have a loyal backing from a man like yourself.'
50. Dunsterville to AS, 23 Dec. 1914, Bod MS Stein 13.
51. FHA to AS, 11 Nov. 1914, ibid.
52. Quoted by PSA to AS, 4 Sept. 1914, Bod MS Stein 12.
53. Von Le Coq to AS, 23 Jan. 1914, Bod MS Stein 11.
54. The Macartneys' 1915 journey home from Kashgar took them across Russia to Petrograd (St Petersburg), through Finland, Sweden and Norway, and across the North Sea to Newcastle. The boat that delivered them safely to England was torpedoed on its return voyage. Theodora Macartney never saw Kashgar again. By the time her husband's leave was over, women were forbidden to travel and he returned alone to complete the final three years of his service. Stein, in the meantime, met Sykes and his sister by calling at their Pamir camp *en route* to Russian Turkestan.
55. AS to PSA, 23 Aug. 1915, Bod MS Stein 13.
56. In Samarkand Stein saw many Austrian POWs. He told Publius: 'Their officers walk the streets freely and have good reason to be grateful for being interned in such a favoured place.' 22 Oct. 1915, Bod MS Stein 13.
57. AS to PSA, 26 Nov. 1916, ibid.
58. Telegram dated 9 Jan. 1916, Bod MS Stein 304.
59. AS to Lionel Barnett, 16 Nov. 1919, BL, OR.13114.

Chapter 11: On the Trail of Alexander the Great

1. AS to PSA, 12 Dec. 1915, Bod MS Stein 13.
2. AS to Keltie, 3 Mar. 1917. Stein told Publius he was grateful for recognition by the Académie des Sciences in Paris 'at a time when my name & origin might have been thought to stand in the way of such recognition in most places of the "Western Regions".' 22 Dec. 1917, Bod MS Stein 15.
3. The decision to move the seat of government from Calcutta to New Delhi was taken in 1912.
4. AS to PSA, 29 Mar. 1916, Bod MS Stein 14.
5. See *The Adventures of Dunsterforce*, 1920, which Dunsterville wrote with Stein's encouragement.
6. AS to PSA, 21 Mar. 1916, Bod MS Stein 14.
7. AS to Harriet, 3 July 1916, BA.
8. AS diary, 17 Aug. 1916, Bod MS Stein 241.
9. AS to Barnett, Dec. 1918, BL, OR.13114.
10. Denison Ross wrote in his autobiography, *Both Ends of the Candle*, that he

went to the British Museum with the desire to devote his life to the Chinese and Uighur documents in the Stein collection, but that war work diverted him from the task.

11. Miss Lorimer has been something of an enigma for many years but, at the time of writing, is due to receive attention in a paper by Helen Wang of the British Museum's Department of Coins and Medals.

12. Renovated and reopened in 1992 as the Hotung Gallery of Oriental Antiquities.

13. AS to Marshall, 26 Apr. 1918, Bod MS Stein 308.

14. AS to Harriet, 24 Aug. 1918, BA.

15. FHA, 'Sir Aurel Stein: the Man'.

16. AS to PSA, 20 Nov. 1918, Bod MS Stein 15.

17. AS to FHA, 5 Dec. 1916, Bod MS Stein 43.

18. AS to Harriet, 21 May 1919, BA.

19. AS to PSA, 19 Jan. 1922, Bod MS Stein 18.

20. Quoted by AS in letter to PSA, 15 Oct. 1922, ibid.

21. AS to PSA, 21 May 1923, ibid.

22. Among the awards and medals was the distinction of being made a 'Correspondent de l'Institut' of the Académie des Inscriptions et Lettres in Paris, a high honour which Stein particularly appreciated in the circumstances. 'It has never been made an object of exchange in scholarly courtesies, & that helps to remove an embarrassing thought which in view of F.'s Kabul activities you will guess,' he remarked to PSA. 1 Jan. 1923, ibid.

23. AS to PSA, 12 Dec. 1918, Bod MS Stein 15. HMA told AS: 'We had often felt that you had given us in the loan of Dash, one of the best happinesses of home.' Bod MS Allen 205.

24. On hearing of Chiang's death, AS sent Rs 300 to the British Consul in Kashgar as his contribution to the costs of transporting the body back to Chiang's home in Hunan. The Government of India provided Rs 600 in recognition of his services to the Consulate.

25. AS to PSA, 20 Mar. 1921, Bod MS Stein 17.

26. AS to Barnett, 7 Feb. 1924, BL, OR.13114.

27. FHA, 'Sir Aurel Stein: the Man'.

28. AS to PSA, 4 Apr. 1924, Bod MS Stein 19.

29. Ferenc Hopp was an optician, co-owner of Calderoni & Co in Budapest which made optical and other instruments. From him Stein had bought photographic equipment and an aneroid barometer in the 1890s. (This information comes from an article by Dr Mária Ferenczy in the 1993 Yearbook of the Budapest Museum of Applied Arts and its Ferenc Hopp Museum of Eastern Asiatic Arts.)

30. AS to Emil Torday, 21 Mar. 1925. Torday replied that he was as fond of Britain 'as any naturally British subject can be though I never acquired British nationality. I have never found that my devotion to Hungary clashed with the affection I have for the land where I have made my home and where my wife and child were born.' Bod MS Stein 109. He also pointed out that a readership in Czech and Romanian had already been established in England.

31. AS told the Allens that they were ideal for the position because they combined 'ardour for the advance of research with the love of tradition'. 20 July 1924, Bod MS Stein 19.

32. AS to Barnett, 1 Apr. 1923, BL, OR.13114.

33. AS, *On Alexander's Track to the Indus*, 1929.

34. To contribute to Sir George Grierson's *Linguistic Survey of India*. In a letter of 15 July 1923, AS told Grierson he felt 'truly proud' of having served 'as a sort of phonograph' in collecting specimens of another Frontier dialect, Tirahi. Bod MS Stein 81.

35. AS, *On Alexander's Track to the Indus*.

36. The debate continues as to whether Mount Ilam is Alexander's Aornos.

37. AS to PSA, 5 Aug. 1928, Bod MS Stein 20.

38. AS to PSA, 6 Dec. 1926, Bod MS Stein 19.

39. TWA to AS, 30 Aug. 1926, Bod MS Stein 64.

40. AS to PSA, 18 Apr. 1927, Bod MS Stein 20.

41. The Indus Kohistan was nominally under the control of the State of Kashmir. The authorities withheld permission because Stein proposed to be guided by Shah Alam, his old guide from Tangir and Darel, and they feared that Shah Alam would cross the border into Tangir and create trouble in support of his claim, on behalf of the late Pakhtun Wali's sons, to dominion there.

Chapter 12: Chinese Débâcle

1. Du Boulay to AS, 21 June 1915, Bod MS Stein 13.
2. Arthur Waley, *Ballads and Stories from Tun-huang*, 1960.
3. Soothill to AS, 20 Mar. 1925, Bod MS Stein 313.
4. Teichman to AS, 27 Mar. 1925, ibid.
5. Sadler to Lord Buxton, 28 May 1925, ibid.
6. AS to Teichman, 31 July 1925, ibid.
7. Soothill to AS, 21 June 1926, ibid.
8. AS to PSA, 27 May 1927, Bod MS Stein 20.
9. Keller to AS, 28 Nov. 1924, Bod MS Stein 89.
10. Warner to AS, 26 Dec. 1926, Bod MS Stein 111.
11. Warner to AS, 7 Feb. 1928, ibid.

12. Lanman to AS, 24 July 1928, Bod MS Stein 90.
13. AS to FHA, 14 Dec. 1928, Bod MS Stein 52.
14. Letter to *The Times*, 30 Oct. 1943, from Group Captain C. Hilton Keith.
15. AS to PSA, 11 Apr. 1929, Bod MS Stein 21.
16. Of which AS's salary was to take $460 per month, or about £90, roughly the same as he had been paid by the Archaeological Survey.
17. AS to PSA, 13 Dec. 1929, Bod MS Stein 21.
18. AS to Keller, 18 July 1929, BM.
19. Sachs to AS, 4 Jan. 1930, ibid.
20. See Peter Hopkirk, *Foreign Devils on the Silk Road*, 1980, for details of the dispersal of Otani's collection and its current whereabouts.
21. AS to PSA, 10 Apr. 1930, Bod MS Stein 21.
22. Teichman to AS, 27 July 1925, Bod MS Stein 313.
23. Sven Hedin returned to China in 1927 to map an air route from Berlin to Shanghai for Lufthansa. The expedition turned into a purely Sino-Swedish one at Chinese insistence in 1928, encountered opposition from the Governor of Sinkiang and was disrupted by the Muslim uprising in that province during the early 1930s.
24. Lampson to the Indian Foreign Secretary, 12 June 1930, BM.
25. Official minutes, 29 Apr. 1930, BM.
26. AS 'field diary', 1 May 1930, Bod MS Stein 224.
27. AS 'field diary', 4 May 1930, ibid.
28. AS to PSA, 5 May 1930, Bod MS Stein 21.
29. AS to Keller, 18 July 1929, BM.
30. AS to Soothill, 29 July 1928, Bod MS Stein 213.
31. AS to Bramlette, 22 Mar. 1930, Bod MS Stein 52.
32. AS diary, 9 May 1930, Bod MS Stein 224. The information had come from the Acting British Consul in Kashgar.
33. AS to PSA, 26 June 1930, Bod MS Stein 21.
34. PSA to AS, 11 June 1930, *Letters of P. S. Allen*.
35. AS to PSA, 4 Aug. 1930, Bod MS Stein 21.
36. AS to PSA, 5 Nov. 1930, ibid.
37. Dated 27 Dec. 1930, BM.
38. AS to PSA, 10 Apr. 1931, Bod MS Stein 22.
39. AS to PSA, 22 Feb. 1931, Bod MS Stein 22.
40. Peter Fleming, *News from Tartary*, 1936, and C. P. Skrine, *Chinese Central Asia*, 1926. Skrine heard many stories about Stein, some of which had been transformed into the stuff of legend, as in the following, where the tragic fate of the sapper Ram Singh (rather than the surveyor Ram Singh) became intertwined with the superstitions of those who feared Stein's tampering with old places. 'It is related', Skrine wrote, 'that a domed tomb

was discovered by Stein completely buried in sand, only one small aperture giving access. This was too small for Stein himself to enter, so he called for volunteers, but none of his local men dared to go in. Finally the Indian surveyor, Ram Singh, stepped (literally) into the breach. He squeezed himself in and when he came out again some time later he was blind!'

41. 'Apart from the question of discretion, which would deter anyone with such a project in view from making enemies, he is far too considerate for the feelings of others to use language which obviously could not fail to annoy even the least sensitive.' From PSA's letter to *The Times*, 3 Jan. 1931.

42. F. H. Brown, sub-editor at the paper, wrote to AS on 17 July 1931, saying he felt it 'so important to give it the earliest and most conspicuous publicity that I took the unusual step of disturbing the Editor at dinner to propose that your narrative should take the place of the special article of the day arranged for the leader page. The Editor accepted the suggestion, and as you will see from the cuttings enclosed you were given the place of honour.' Bod MS Stein 314.

43. AS to Vogel, 23 July 1931, ibid.

44. Lampson to AS, 19 July 1931, BM.

45. BM. I am grateful to Professor Whitfield's student at SOAS, Zhang Hongxing, for identifying the members of the commission.

Chapter 13: In Search of Another Dead Desert

1. AS to PSA, 17 Nov. 1931, Bod MS Stein 22.

2. AS to PSA, 11 July 1931, ibid.

3. The prime minister of Kashmir at the time, however, was a former pupil of Stein's in Lahore, Raja Hari Kishan Kaul, whose father had helped Stein find the *Rajatarangini* manuscript forty years earlier.

4. Hoare to AS, 24 Apr. 1934, Bod MS Stein 320.

5. Fábri, in a talk given in 1963 in Budapest and reported in *Élet és Irodalom*, No. 41, 1963.

6. The Stein Asiatic Exploration Fund statement in July 1932 showed that the first and second instalments, plus interest, totalled $78,195.58, and that total expenditure so far amounted to $42,478.90. It appears that, at Sachs' request, Stein later returned the unspent balance. Bod. MSS Stein 317 and 24.

7. AS to PSA, 20 Sept. 1931, Bod MS Stein 22.

8. AS to PSA, 27 Sept. 1931, ibid.

9. 'Archaeological Reconnaissances in Southern Persia', *The Geographical Journal*, Vol. LXXXIII, No. 2, Feb. 1934.

10. Mason to Hinks, 1 Dec. 1933, RGS.

11. AS to PSA, 13 May 1933, Bod MS Stein 24.

12. AS to PSA, 5 Apr. 1933, ibid.

13. AS to PSA, 11 June 1933, ibid.

14. FHA to AS, 20 June 1933, Bod MS Stein 54.

15. John Donne (1572?–1631), 'A Valediction: forbidding Mourning'.

16. PSA to AS, 8 Dec. 1920, *Letters of P. S. Allen*.

17. AS to HMA, 8 Jan. 1934, Bod MS Stein 25.

18. In late November 1939, HMA told AS that his friendship, which 'rejoiced Publius & me since its beginning over 40 years ago, still encourages me & helps me to be more worthy both of him & of his friends'. 12 Nov. 1939, Bod MS Allen 212.

19. L. Baggallay, first secretary to the British Minister in Tehran, to AS, 7 Oct. 1933, Bod MS Stein 319.

20. AS to HMA, 3 Mar. 1934, Bod MS Stein 25.

21. AS to HMA, 10 May 1935, Bod MS Stein 26.

22. AS to HMA, 23 Oct. 1934, Bod MS Stein 25.

23. AS to HMA, ibid.

24. AS to Olga Allen, 28 Nov. 1934, Bod MS Stein 25.

25. *The Geographical Journal*, 1938.

26. *The Times*, 4 Oct. 1938.

27. AS to HMA, 12 Feb. 1935, Bod MS Stein 26.

28. AS to HMA, 5 May 1935, ibid.

29. AS, *Archaeological Reconnaissances in Northwest India and Southeast Iran*, 1935.

30. AS to HMA, 25 Aug. 1935, Bod MS Stein 26.

31. AS to HMA, 2 Feb. 1936, Bod MS Stein 27.

32. AS to HMA, 9 Feb. 1936, ibid.

33. De Filippi to AS, 13 Mar. 1931, Bod MS Stein 22.

Chapter 14: 'Ready to Return to Duty'

1. AS to PSA, 7 July 1913, Bod MS Stein 10.

2. Mason later wrote (in *The Geographical Journal*, Jan. 1936) that this was the first aeroplane to carry authorized air-mails in India or, he thought, in the world, in January 1911.

3. Hinks to William Foster, 31 Oct. 1924, & Hinks's memo, 3 July 1935, RGS.

4. AS to Wauchope, 27 Apr. 1936, Bod MS Stein 328.

5. Colonial Office to AS, 3 Sept. 1936, Bod MS Stein 27.

6. Edmonds to AS, 9 Nov. 1937, Bod MS Stein 328.

7. AS told HMA: 'It all reminded me of the efficient way in which the East India Company could manage to help scientific enterprise in the good old days of Empire expansion.' 5 Dec. 1937, Bod MS Stein 28.

8. AS to HMA, 10 Jan. 1938, Bod MS Stein 29.
9. AS to PSA, 22 Dec. 1928, Bod MS Stein 20.
10. There was mutual admiration between the two men. Père Poidebard told AS that when they first met in the early 1930s, AS was one of the first to give him confidence in his methods; and that his review of his book (in *The Geographical Journal*, Jan. 1936) 'a fait le point avec toute votre haute autorité'. 12 Mar. 1938, Bod MS Stein 329.
11. AS to HMA, 25 Aug. 1938, Bod MS Stein 29.
12. AS to HMA, 4 Apr. 1938, ibid.
13. AS to HMA, 27 Apr. 1938, Bod MS Stein 29.
14. AS to HMA, 27 May 1938, ibid.
15. AS to HMA, 4 June 1938, ibid.
16. Dunsterville commented on Kipling in a letter to Stein: 'his task was completed long ago & his message will remain . . . '. His work would survive 'as a picture in bold colours of the Empire point-of-view of the period he lived in – it is a true picture and he preached an uplifting gospel. He was not a Jingo!' 8 Mar. 1936, Bod MS Stein 27.
17. AS to HMA, 9 Oct. 1938, Bod MS Stein 29.
18. AS to HMA, 14 Feb. 1936, Bod MS Stein 27.
19. AS to HMA, 9 July 1938, Bod MS Stein 29. Alexandra David-Neel's book was entitled *With Magicians and Mystics in Tibet.*
20. AS to PSA, 13 Dec. 1929, Bod MS Stein 21.
21. AS to Hinks, 29 Dec. 1933, RGS.
22. Grierson to AS, 10 July 1928, Bod MS Stein 82.
23. AS to Grierson, 19 Aug. 1928, ibid.
24. The last member of the Bali family is said to have died in Delhi in 1992. I am indebted to Peter Hopkirk for alerting me to the existence of the Bali family's claims, which he heard in Kashmir in the early 1980s.
25. AS to HMA, 21 Nov. 1938, Bod MS Stein 29.
26. AS to HMA, 10 Apr. 1939, Bod MS Stein 30.
27. AS to Under-Secretary of State, India Office, 9 Apr. 1939, Bod MS Stein 271.
28. HMA to AS, 12 Nov. 1939, Bod MS Allen 212.

Chapter 15: 'Death in Some Far-off Country'
1. AS, *Ancient Khotan.*
2. This took place on 16 Jan. 1936 and was described by Eric Teichman in *Journey to Turkestan*, 1937.
3. AS to Dikshit, 2 Feb. 1940, Bod MS Stein 359.
4. AS to HMA, 30 Dec. 1939, Bod MS Stein 30.

5. AS to HMA, 5 June 1943, Bod MS Stein 34.

6. AS to HMA, 5 June 1940, Bod MS Stein 31.

7. AS to Jeanne, 18 June 1940, Bod MS Stein 116.

8. AS to Ernst, 29 May 1943, ibid.

9. Gustav Steiner to AS, 24 Apr. 1940, ibid.

10. AS wrote to HMA of Teleki: 'He was a true friend, greatly respected by me for his high aims, his straightness as a man and his clear judgment as a geographer. Nothing but a strong sense of duty could induce him to take an active part in politics . . . He was fully conscious of having to face enemies on all frontiers & little hope of effective help from afar. The grave danger from Germany weighed heavily on him at all times.' 6 Apr. 1941, Bod MS Stein 32.

11. AS to HMA, 15 Dec. 1941, Bod MS Stein 32.

12. AS to Keller, 30 Dec. 1941, ibid.

13. The Wali of Swat handed over to his son in 1949, and Swat was absorbed into Pakistan in 1969.

14. AS to HMA, 11 Mar. 1943, Bod MS Stein 34.

15. Engert to AS, 10 Apr. 1943, Bod MS Stein 340.

16. Engert to AS, 13 May 1943, ibid.

17. AS to HMA, 17 Jan. 1942, Bod MS Stein 33.

18. Hailey to AS, 2 Sept. 1916, Bod MS Stein 82.

19. AS to HMA, 17 Mar. 1942, Bod MS Stein 33.

20. FHA, 'Sir Aurel Stein: the Man'.

Epilogue

1. The British Taklamakan Desert Crossing, in aid of the Leonora Children's Cancer Fund, took place in late 1993.

2. 'The time seems still distant when Khotan will see its annual stream of tourists'. AS, *Sand-Buried Ruins of Khotan*.

3. For more information on the whereabouts of Silk Road collections, see Peter Hopkirk, *Foreign Devils on the Silk Road*.

Select Bibliography

A LL WORKS WERE published in London except where otherwise indicated. For the sake of brevity, articles from newspapers and journals are not included here, but are listed where relevant in the notes.

Adamec, L., *Afghanistan, 1900–1923*, Berkeley, Cal., 1967

Allen, Charles, *Plain Tales from the Raj*, André Deutsch, 1975

——*Raj – A Scrapbook of British India, 1877–1947*, André Deutsch, 1978

——*A Mountain in Tibet*, André Deutsch, 1982

Allen, H. M. (ed.), *Letters of P. S. Allen*, OUP, Oxford, 1939

Along the Ancient Silk Routes – Central Asian Art from the West Berlin State Museums, Metropolitan Museum of Art, New York, 1982

Andrews, Fred H., *Catalogue of Wall-Paintings From Ancient Shrines in Central Asia and Sistan, recovered by Sir Aurel Stein*, Delhi, 1933

——*Descriptive Catalogue of Antiquities recovered by Sir Aurel Stein*, Delhi, 1935

——*Wall Paintings from Ancient Shrines in Central Asia recorded by Aurel Stein*, OUP, Oxford, 1948

Bacon, Edward (ed.), *The Great Archaeologists*, Secker & Warburg, 1976

Bailey, H.W., *The Culture of the Sakas in Ancient Iranian Khotan*, Columbia University/Caravan Books, New York, 1982

Bamberg, J.H., *The History of the British Petroleum Company, Vol. 2: The Anglo-Iranian Years, 1928–54*, CUP, Cambridge, 1994

Bayly, C. A. (ed.), *The Raj – India and the British, 1600–1947*, National Portrait Gallery Publications, 1990

Bechert, Heinz, and Gombrich, Richard, *The World of Buddhism*, Thames & Hudson, 1984

Bence-Jones, Mark, *The Viceroys of India*, Constable, 1982

Bethlenfalvy, Géza, *India in Hungarian Learning and Literature*, New Delhi, 1980

Blood, General Sir Bindon, *Four Score Years and Ten*, Bell, 1933

Boros, Vilma, *The Youth of Aurel Stein, 1866–1891*, Hungarian Academy of Sciences, 1970

Boulnois, L. (trans. D. Chamberlain), *The Silk Road*, Allen & Unwin, 1966

The Cambridge History of Iran, CUP, Cambridge, 1968–91

Churchill, W. S., *My Early Life*, Butterworth, 1930

Cumming, Sir John (ed.), *Revealing India's Past*, The India Society, 1939

Czigany, Lorant, *Oxford History of Hungarian Literature*, Clarendon Press, Oxford, 1984

Dabbs, J. A., *History of the Discovery and Exploration of Chinese Turkestan*, Mouton & Co, The Hague, 1963

Daniel, Glyn, *A Short History of Archaeology*, Thames & Hudson, 1981

Deasy, Capt. H. H. P., *In Tibet and Chinese Turkestan*, T. Fisher Unwin, 1901

Dewey, Clive, *Anglo-Indian Attitudes*, The Hambledon Press, 1993

Dilks, David, *Curzon in India*, Hart-Davis, 1969

Dunsterville, Lionel, *Stalky's Reminiscences*, 1928

Duprée, Louis, *Afghanistan*, Princeton University Press, Princeton, 1973

Edwardes, Michael, *High Noon of Empire*, Eyre & Spottiswoode, 1965

——*British India*, Sidgwick & Jackson, 1967

Errington, Elizabeth, and Cribb, Joe, *The Crossroads of Asia*, The Ancient India and Iran Trust, 1992

Fagan, Brian, *The Rape of the Nile*, 1977

Fairley, Jean, *The Lion River – the Indus*, Allen Lane, 1975

Fleming, Peter, *News from Tartary*, Jonathan Cape, 1936

Giles, Lionel, *Six Centuries at Tun-huang*, The China Society, 1944

Gregory, Shelagh, and Kennedy, David (eds.), *Sir Aurel Stein's Limes Report*, BAR International Series 272, 1985

Hedin, Sven, *My Life as an Explorer*, Cassell, 1925

Hoernle, Rudolf, *et al.* (eds.), *Manuscript Remains of Buddhist Literature found in Eastern Turkestan*, Clarendon Press, Oxford, 1916

Holt, Frank L., *Alexander the Great and Bactria*, E. J. Brill, 1988

Hopkirk, Peter, *Foreign Devils on the Silk Road*, John Murray, 1980

——*The Great Game*, John Murray, 1990

Kipling, Rudyard, *Kim*, 1901

——*Something of Myself*, Macmillan, 1937

Le Coq, Albert von, *Buried Treasures of Chinese Turkestan*, Allen & Unwin, 1928

Select Bibliography

Lukacs, John, *Budapest 1900*, Weidenfeld & Nicolson, 1989

Lyons, Islay, and Ingholt, Harald, *Gandharan Art in Pakistan*, Pantheon Books, 1957

Macartney, Lady, *An English Lady in Chinese Turkestan*, Ernest Benn, 1931

Mirsky, Jeanette, *Sir Aurel Stein – archaeological explorer*, University of Chicago Press, Chicago, 1977

Moorhouse, Geoffrey, *India Britannica*, Harvill Press, 1983

Morris, James, *Pax Britannica*, Faber & Faber, 1978

Orel, Harold (ed.), *Kipling: Interviews and Recollections*, Macmillan, 1983

Polo, Marco, *The Book of Ser Marco Polo*, translated and edited by Sir Henry Yule, 3rd edition, John Murray, 1903

Ross, E. Denison, *The Persians*, Clarendon Press, Oxford, 1931

——*Both Ends of the Candle*, 1943

Roy, Sourindranath, *The Story of Indian Archaeology, 1784–1947*, Archaeological Survey of India, Delhi, 1961

Shaw, Isobel, *Pakistan Handbook*, John Murray, 1990

Skrine, C. P., and Nightingale, Pamela, *Macartney at Kashgar: New Light on British, Chinese and Russian Activities in Sinkiang, 1890–1918*, Methuen, 1973

Shipton, Diana, *The Antique Land*, Hodder & Stoughton, 1950

Stein, Marc Aurel, *Kalhana's Rajatarangini, a Chronicle of the Kings of Kasmir*, 1900

——*Preliminary Report of a Journey of Archaeological and Topographical Exploration in Chinese Turkestan*, Eyre & Spottiswoode, 1901

——*Sand-Buried Ruins of Khotan*, Fisher & Unwin, 1903

——*Ancient Khotan*, Clarendon Press, Oxford, 1907

——*Ruins of Desert Cathay*, Macmillan, 1912

——*Serindia*, Clarendon Press, Oxford, 1921

——*Hatim's Tales: Kashmiri Stories and Songs*, editor with G. A. Grierson, John Murray, 1923

——*Innermost Asia*, Clarendon Press, Oxford, 1928

——*On Alexander's Track to the Indus*, Macmillan, 1929

——*On Ancient Central Asian Tracks*, Macmillan, 1933

——*Archaeological Reconnaissances in Northwest India and Southeast Iran*, Macmillan, 1937

——*Old Routes of Western Iran*, Macmillan, 1940

Szörényi, Làszló (ed.), *Ázsia halott szivében*, Helikon Kiado, 1986

Teichman, Sir Eric, *Journey to Turkestan*, Hodder & Stoughton, 1937

Toynbee, A. J., *Between Oxus and Jumna*, OUP, Oxford, 1961

Waley, Arthur, *A Catalogue of Paintings recovered from Tun-huang by Sir Aurel Stein*, 1931

——*The Real Tripitaka*, Allen & Unwin, 1952

——*Ballads and Stories from Tun-Huang*, Allen & Unwin, 1960

Warner, Langdon, *The Long Old Road to China*, Doubleday, Page & Co, New York, 1926.

Wheeler, Sir Mortimer, *Still Digging*, Michael Joseph, 1955

——*Flames Over Persepolis*, Reynal, New York, 1968

Whitfield, Roderick, *The Art of Central Asia: The Stein Collection in the British Museum*, Kodansha International Ltd. in co-operation with the Trustees of the British Museum, London & Tokyo, 1982

Whitfield, Roderick, and Farrer, Anne, *Caves of the Thousand Buddhas*, British Museum Publications, 1990

Wilson, Angus, *The Strange Ride of Rudyard Kipling*, Secker & Warburg, 1977

Woodruff, Philip, *The Men Who Ruled India*, Jonathan Cape, 1954

Woolley, Sir Leonard, *Spadework*, Lutterworth Press, London, 1953

Younghusband, Francis, *Kashmir*, Adam & Charles Black, 1909

Zeman, Z.A.B., *Twilight of the Hapsburgs*, BPC/Library of the Twentieth Century, 1971

Index

For convenience, individuals are listed under their last name, except in the case of rulers and those with Chinese names.